THE WAY TO GOD

AS TAUGHT BY SRI RAMAKRISHNA

SWAMI LOKESWARANANDA

THE RAMAKRISHNA MISSION INSTITUTE OF CULTURE
GOL PARK, KOLKATA 700 029

Published by
The Secretary
The Ramakrishna Mission Institute of Culture
Kolkata-700 029, India

First Published in March 1992
First Western Edition, September 1992
Revised Fifth Print : June 2018

ISBN 81-85843-49-X

Price : Rs.290

Printed In India
Computer typeset at the Ramakrishna Mission Institute of Culture
Photo-offset at Trio Process
P-128 C. I. T. Road, Entally
Kolkata - 700 014

To Swami Madhavananda

Publisher's Note

Śrī Śrī Rāmakṛṣṇa Kathāmṛta, the Bengali book by Mahendranath Gupta, who called himself 'Sri Ma' ('M.' in English translation), is a very accurate and trustworthy account of the conversations of the Great Soul of the nineteenth century, Sri Ramakrishna. Swami Lokeswarananda, a senior monk of the Ramakrishna Order and Secretary of the Ramakrishna Mission Institute of Culture in Calcutta, has for many years been giving weekly discourses on this book. Some of the recorded discourses were edited, revised, and published in 1985 under the title *Tava Kathāmṛtam*.

This was translated into English and published in 1992 under the title, *The Way to God As Taught by Sri Ramakrishna*. The present volume is a revised translation of *Tava Kathāmṛtam* bearing the same title as the earlier edition.

The bold portions of the text are quotations from *The Gospel of Sri Ramakrishna*, a translation of the *Śrī Śrī Rāmakṛṣṇa Kathāmṛta* by Swami Nikhilananda of the Ramakrishna-Vivekananda Centre, New York, which brought out the book in 1942. Page numbers of the quotations are given in parentheses after each quotation.

March 1997

Acknowledgements

We would like to express our gratitude to Swami Adiswarananda of the Ramakrishna Vivekananda Society of New York for his permission to reprint quotations from *The Gospel of Sri Ramakrishna*.

We would also like to express our appreciation to Ms Susan Walters for translating the *Tava Kathāmṛtam* into English, and for editing the Indian edition, to Mrs Dipti Basu for her expert assistance in that translation, and to Ms Cecile Guenther for many valuable suggestions in the editing.

Our appreciation also to Ms Abhaya Das Gupta, former Librarian at the Ramakrishna Mission Institute of Culture, for her help with references in the original edition of the book, and to the staff of our Publication Department for their dedicated labour.

CONTENTS

Introduction
Sri Ramakrishna

Sri Ramakrishna was born Gadadhar Chattopadhyaya in 1836 in the village of Kamarpukur, approximately sixty miles from Calcutta. His father, Khudiram, was poor but commanded respect from all classes of people because of his character. Chandra Devi, Sri Ramakrishna's mother, was a simple woman who loved to feed people. No visitor could leave without eating whatever food she had to give, though this sometimes meant she had nothing left for herself. In spite of poverty, the family was a happy one.

From his very boyhood, Sri Ramakrishna had an independent mind. He did not like school; he said that at school you learn how to earn money, but nothing about God. He preferred to roam the fields outside the village, alone or with other boys. They loved to sing together, and now and then they would stage little dramas using themes from the ancient Indian epics and Purāṇas.

A versatile artist, he had a degree of mastery in every form of art—singing, dancing, painting, and so on. He was very sensitive to nature. Once the sight of a line of white cranes against dark monsoon clouds sent him into ecstasy. Thinking deeply of God, he would also experience ecstasy. At first his relatives thought his unusual behaviour at these times was due to hysteria, but later they realized that it was a manifestation of deep religious experiences.

Even when he was a mere boy, his opinions were as profound as those of a wise old man. He played his share of boyish pranks, but he never erred when the choice had to be made between right and wrong. He was the pet of the village but also an object of awe. An old scholarly man privately worshipped Ramakrishna as an *avatāra*.

After Sri Ramakrishna's father died, the whole family looked to him to start earning something to mitigate their financial hardship. So Sri Ramakrishna at the age of seventeen came to Calcutta. His eldest brother, Ramkumar, who ran a Sanskrit school there and also worshipped deities at different places, had sent for him. He wanted Sri Ramakrishna to study Sanskrit with him and assist him in worshipping deities. The object of both was to earn money—an object repugnant to Sri Ramakrishna. He flatly refused to study Sanskrit seriously. He said the only thing he was interested in was God-realization. Ramkumar did not argue with him, for he knew arguing would serve no purpose. Sri Ramakrishna was one who would not budge an inch from his position. Although in the next three years, Sri Ramakrishna did help his brother occasionally by performing worship in private homes, he spent most of his time wandering around the neighbourhood where he would sing devotional songs in temples and visit some homes where he was much sought after because of his songs and funny stories.

In 1855, Rani Rashmani, a rich widow of Calcutta, founded a temple complex at Dakshineswar in the suburbs of Calcutta with Mother Kālī as the chief deity. She appointed Ramkumar as priest at Mother Kālī's temple. After much persuasion, Sri Ramakrishna agreed to help with dressing the deity. Hriday, his nephew, assisted him in this work.

On Ramkumar's retirement in 1856, Sri Ramakrishna took over as priest. As he worshipped Mother Kālī, he began to question what Kālī was—a piece of stone or Divinity in that form. If she was divine, could she not give some hint that she was pleased with his worship? He begged Mother Kālī to let him know who or what she was. He would say, 'Mother, I am your child just as the seers of the past were. You revealed your true nature to them, why should you not do the same to me? Are you neglecting me because I am ignorant? Can a mother love one child more than another?' As the days passed, his yearning for God increased. He could not sleep at night, and sometimes he could not even eat. As the sun set, he would cry out, 'Mother, yet another day has passed and I have not seen you!' He would roll on the ground crying, 'Mother!' He rubbed his face on rough ground till it bled. Some bystanders thought he had lost his mother, others thought he had gone mad. Fortunately Hriday looked after him or he would have died. It was becoming increasingly difficult for him to do the formal worship for he would burst into tears when he approached the Mother; he gave every sign that he was not in his senses.

His condition was reported to the authorities. Rani Rashmani, accompanied by her son-in-law Mathur Babu, paid a surprise visit to see what the truth was. They were moved to see so much love of God in any person in this age. They were convinced that he was no ordinary man, and gave instructions to the temple employees that Sri Ramakrishna was to be treated with the greatest respect.

As the days passed, Sri Ramakrishna's impatience for a vision of Kālī increased. Instead of performing the worship, he would cry, 'Mother, how long will you make me suffer? Are you heartless?' One day as he was crying like this, his eyes fell on the sword hanging on the wall. Seizing it he said, 'Mother, look, I'm going to kill myself! Life no longer has any meaning to me!' As he was about to cut his throat he saw a dazzling light emanating from the body of the Mother, filling the room. Sri Ramakrishna found himself in an ocean of light and fell down, unconscious of the outer world. After that, Mother Kālī was always alive, a real mother, and the relation between them was like that of an indulgent mother and a petulant child. Sri Ramakrishna, like a small child, could not bear to let Mother go out of sight for even a moment. And he demanded *Her* presence all the time. Mother and son talked, teased each other, laughed and played together. To others it seemed to be nonsense. It was clear that Ramakrishna could no longer perform any formal puja. He was, therefore, relieved of his duties as priest.

But Mother Kālī continued to possess him; he forgot his surroundings, he forgot even his physical needs. He would not eat or sleep, although Hriday would force a little food down his throat from time to time—otherwise he would have died of starvation. He was a mere skeleton now. Yet, most of the time he was in ecstasy, *samādhi*.

Soon word spread that he had gone mad. When his mother came to know of this, she sent word that he should be sent back home immediately. Under his mother's care, Sri Ramakrishna slowly improved. At least there was no sign of insanity in him. On the advice of her neighbours, Sri Ramakrishna's mother arranged for his marriage, which move, surprisingly, Sri Ramakrishna welcomed. Still more surprising, he suggested the girl who was to be his bride and indicated where she could be found. She turned out to be five year old Saradamani of the neighbouring village of Jayrambati. Sri Ramakrishna was then twenty-four.

Sri Ramakrishna returned to Dakshineswar soon after his marriage. With Mother Kālī's consent, he now started practising different branches of Hinduism, one after another. For each branch, a guru arrived just as he was about to start. In the shortest possible time, he reached the goal that each branch had in view. Hinduism's most difficult path is non-dualism. Few ever attempt it, or succeed if they do attempt it.

Sri Ramakrishna, however, mastered within three days what his teacher Totapuri, on his own admission, had taken forty years to accomplish. Once Sri Ramakrishna had reached the goal in a particular system, he seemed to know more about it than his teacher. The roles between teacher and student were often then reversed.

Sri Ramakrishna next turned to other religions, both major and minor. Whatever religion he chose to practise, qualified teachers were on hand to teach. The mystic experiences Sri Ramakrishna had through the practice of those religions convinced him that religions were like paths leading to the same goal. Religions differed in details, but their goal was one and the same. You might like your own religion better than another, but you have no right to think that your religion is the best or the only true religion. Holiness is not the monopoly of any particular religion; every religion has produced great saints and sages.

According to Sri Ramakrishna, it is a waste of time to argue about God and religion; this only shows your ignorance. When bees settle on a flower, they no longer buzz; they are quiet and happy. People love to talk, though they don't know what they are talking about because they have had no direct experience. Religion is love of God. 'Love God sincerely and intensely. Weep for Him; He will then reveal Himself to you'—this was the burden of his message. He favoured no particular creed or dogma; no particular ritual or practice; he rejected none either. Even things seemingly bizarre were acceptable to him provided they were prompted by a genuine love of God.

He used to say, 'When flowers are in blossom, bees start coming on their own.' This is what happened in the life of Sri Ramakrishna. Soon word spread that there was a remarkable man at Dakshineswar who seemed to *live* with God. The ecstasy and *samādhi* he had were also a much-talked-about subject. Curiously, a Christian missionary, serving as principal in a big college in Calcutta, was the first on record to have talked about these ecstasies. Next to be struck by Sri Ramakrishna's unusual spiritual character was Keshab Chandra Sen who was highly Westernized and head of a powerful religious community. He wrote about Sri Ramakrishna in his journals quoting his wonderful teachings. One by one, leading figures among Calcutta's intelligentsia came to see Sri Ramakrishna and were impressed.

Finally a band of extraordinary young men came. Sri Ramakrishna received them as if he were waiting for them. He was in fact anxious to have some followers who could not only understand his message, but also mould their lives after his ideals. First and foremost, he taught his wife Sarada Devi, who joined him when she was in her late teens. Sri Ramakrishna was awed by her spiritual potential and trained her so that she could take his place when he was gone. Among the young men he trained was Naren, who as Swami Vivekananda later became a world teacher, true to Sri Ramakrishna's prediction. He initiated some of these young men into monastic life shortly before his passing in August, 1886. Later these young men, with the blessings of Sarada Devi, were to form, with Vivekananda as their leader, the nucleus of the future Ramakrishna Order.

Mahendranath Gupta (M.), a popular teacher, started coming to Sri Ramakrishna about the time those young men arrived. He had been greatly disturbed by some happenings in his family and had been contemplating suicide. But Sri Ramakrishna's personality and his words so fascinated him that he found a meaning and purpose in life and became altogether a new man. He was in the habit of maintaining a diary, and his acquaintance with Sri Ramakrishna was such a momentous event that he naturally entered in the diary everything that happened during his many visits to him. These entries were for his own use. He never intended to make them public.

But under pressure from many quarters, he expanded and explained some of the diary notes and tentatively sent them to different journals. They at once became popular and there was a demand for more such material. Finally M. published, one by one, five volumes in Bengali, entitled *Śrī Śrī Rāmakṛṣṇa Kathāmṛta*. These volumes were later translated into English by Swami Nikhilananda and published in one volume under the title *The Gospel of Sri Ramakrishna*. The book has been translated into many other languages and is now a source of inspiration to people all over the world.

I

M. and *The Gospel of Sri Ramakrishna*

Tava kathāmṛtaṁ taptajīvanaṁ
Kavibhirīḍitaṁ kalmaṣāpahaṁ
Śravaṇamaṅgalaṁ śrīmadātataṁ
Bhuvi gṛṇanti ye bhūridā janāḥ

The nectar of Thy words is the life
for those who are scorched by the world;
Words which have been uttered
by the Knowers of Truth,
Which wipe out sins,
the very hearing of which is beneficial,
Which are beautiful,
pleasing to the ear, pleasing to the heart,
Which are inexhaustible.
Those who recount them on earth
are the Givers of Plenty.

This verse, addressed to Śrī Kṛṣṇa in the *Śrīmad Bhāgavatam*, was used by M. to address Sri Ramakrishna at the beginning of his Bengali book, *Śrī Śrī Rāmakṛṣṇa Kathāmṛta*. For just as we find Śrī Kṛṣṇa's words in the *Bhagavad Gītā*, the words of Sri Ramakrishna are found in the *Kathāmṛta*.

M. is the pseudonym of Mahendranath Gupta. It was he who meticulously recorded, just as he heard them, the captivating words that came from the lips of Sri Ramakrishna. These recorded words were to form the basis for the *Kathāmṛta* which was later translated into English and published as *The Gospel of Sri Ramakrishna*.

M. recorded only what he heard from Sri Ramakrishna himself and the discussions Sri Ramakrishna had with others. M. has written, 'The main book contains only the direct evidence which I have seen with my own eyes and heard with my own ears.'[1] It contains no hearsay.

Śrī Śrī Rāmakṛṣṇa Kathāmṛta came out in five volumes over a period of thirty years, from 1902 to 1932. M. had just completed checking the proofs of the fifth and last volume the day before he died. It is thought that he had enough material to write five or six more volumes, but these, of course, never came into being.

Before discussing the Gospel, we must say something about M. Two persons are always present in the Gospel: one is Sri Ramakrishna and the other is M. M., however, always makes Sri Ramakrishna the centre of the scene and he himself remains the eager listener and observer. Besides his well-known pseudonym 'M.', he also calls himself Master, Mani, Mohinimohan, and a devotee in the Gospel. But in Ramakrishna circles, he is known as Master Mahashay because he was a respected teacher.

He had been a brilliant student while at school, winning various prizes and medals. When he began his teaching career, he quickly acquired a reputation as an excellent teacher, and was especially noted for his lectures on Shakespeare. Although reserved, M. was loved and respected by his students. Swami Virajananda was a student at Ripon College when M. taught there and later described him: 'Bearded, a black caftan over a white dhoti and a finger always on his lips as if to say, "Don't talk," M. walked down the road looking straight ahead. One could easily sense that M. dwelt on a lofty spiritual plane. It was not surprising that his students held him in awe. He was well-read in *Caitanya Caritāmṛta* [the biography of Śrī Caitanya], and the Bible. He had read the Bible meticulously, and often quoted from it.'

It was by chance that M. first met the Master. We find this account in the Gospel: **M., being at leisure on Sundays, had gone with his friend Sidhu to visit several gardens at Baranagore. As they were walking in Prasanna Bannerji's garden, Sidhu said: 'There is a charming place on the bank of the Ganges where a *Paramahaṁsa* lives. Would you like to go there?'** (p.77)

M. went with Sidhu to the Dakshineswar temple and the two went directly to Sri Ramakrishna's room. From outside the room M. could see Sri Ramakrishna sitting on a cot speaking on spiritual matters while people sat silently on the floor, drinking in his sweet words. This was M.'s first glimpse of the Master. **It was as if he were standing where all the holy places met and as if Śukadeva himself were speaking the word of God, or as if Śrī Caitanya were singing the name and glories of the Lord in Purī with Rāmānanda, Swarūp, and the other devotees.**

M. could hear Sri Ramakrishna say: **When, hearing the name of Hari or Rāma once, you shed tears and your hair stands on end, then you may know for certain that you do not have to perform such devotions as the *Sandhyā* any more.** (p.77)

In speechless wonder, M. listened to the words of the Master. He thought to himself: **'What a beautiful place! What a charming man! How beautiful his words are! I have no wish to move from this spot.' After a few minutes he thought: 'Let me see the place first; then I'll come back here and sit down.'**

M. and Sidhu walked around the temple grounds. It was evening and *ārati* was beginning. The gong, bell, drum and cymbals were being played: the sweet music floated in from the southern boundary of the garden. It was spring; the moon had just risen. The whole place was very beautiful. M. and Sidhu visited the twelve Śiva temples, the Rādhākānta temple, and the temple of Bhavatāriṇī [Kālī]. And as M. watched the services before the images, his heart was filled with joy. (p.78) Sidhu told M. that the temples had been built by Rani Rashmani.

M. and Sidhu continued their conversation as they returned to Sri Ramakrishna's room. **When they reached Sri Ramakrishna's door again, they found it shut and Brinde, the maid, standing outside. M., who had been trained in English manners, would not enter a room without permission.** (p.78) He wondered what he should do.

At last he asked Brinde if the holy man was in his room and she said that he was.

M.: 'How long has he lived here?'

Brinde : 'Oh, he has been here a long time.'

M.: 'Does he read many books?'

Brinde: 'Books? Oh, dear no! They're all on his tongue.'

M. was astonished. If Sri Ramakrishna had not read books, what kind of holy man was he?

M.: 'Perhaps it is time for his evening worship. May we go into the room? Will you tell him we are anxious to see him?'

Brinde: 'Go right in, children. Go in and sit down.'

Entering the room, they found Sri Ramakrishna alone, seated on the wooden couch. Incense had just been burnt and all the doors were shut. As he entered, M. with folded hands saluted the Master. (p.78)

This unforgettable moment can be called the birth of *The Gospel of Sri Ramakrishna*.

Sri Ramakrishna asked M. to be seated and then began to ask him questions: 'Where do you live? What do you do? Why did you come to Baranagore?' M. noticed that although the Master was speaking, his mind seemed to be elsewhere. He later learned that this mood was called *bhāva,* ecstasy; sometimes Sri Ramakrishna would completely lose consciousness of the outer world when in that state. On this day there was no special conversation. After a few words, M. made *praṇāms* to the Master and was ready to leave. As he was leaving, Sri Ramakrishna said to him, 'Come again'.

On his way home, M. began to wonder: 'Who is this serene-looking man who is drawing me back to him? Is it possible for a man to be great without being a scholar? How wonderful it is! I would like to see him again. He himself said, "Come again". I shall go tomorrow or the day after.' (p.78)

M. did not know it at the time, but he had been close to the Master in a previous birth. Later the Master was to tell him: 'I have seen you with the companions of Śrī Caitanya. Hearing you read the *Caitanya-Bhāgavata*, I recognized you.' Sri Ramakrishna was Caitanya himself in his incarnation as Lord Caitanya. After a long time the Lord had come again, bringing with him his companions.

M. was one of them.

M.'s second visit to Sri Ramakrishna was on a morning when the Master was being shaved. As the shaving continued, he chatted with M. awhile then asked:

'Are you married?'

M.: 'Yes, sir.'

Sri Ramakrishna (with a shudder): 'Oh, Ramlal! Alas, he is married!'

Like one guilty of a terrible offence, M. sat motionless, his eyes fixed on the ground. He thought, 'Is it such a wicked thing to get married?'

Sri Ramakrishna: 'Have you any children?'

M.: 'Yes, sir, I have children.'

Sri Ramakrishna: 'Ah me! He even has children!' (p.79)

The Master seemed sad to hear that M. was married and even had children. What could M. do? He didn't know what to say. As an outstanding teacher, he was used to scolding his students, but he did not expect to be scolded himself. **His pride had received a blow.** (p.79)

After some time the Master's mood softened and he said to M. kindly: **You see, you have certain good signs. I know them by looking at a person's forehead, his eyes, and so on. Tell me, now, what kind of person is your wife?** (p.79) M. invited more trouble by answering, 'Good, but ignorant,' and received yet another scolding: 'Your wife is ignorant, and you are a man of knowledge, are you?'

M. was totally stunned. He had always assumed that, being a highly educated teacher, he could be called a man of knowledge. **He had yet to learn the distinction between knowledge and ignorance. Up to this time his conception had been that one got knowledge from books and schools. Later on he gave up this false conception. He was taught that to know God is knowledge, and not to know Him, ignorance. When Sri Ramakrishna exclaimed, 'And you are a man of knowledge!' M.'s ego was again badly shocked.** (p.80)

The Master continued his questioning: **'Do you believe in God with form, or without form?'** Because M. was a member of the Brāhmo Samāj which accepted only the formless deity, he replied, **'I like to think of God as formless.'** At this Sri Ramakrishna said, 'Very well, if your faith is in the formless, stay with that. But always remember that God with form and God without form are both true.' M. was perplexed. God with form and God without form—could both be true at the same time? **He had never learnt this from his books. Thus his ego received a third blow.**

Yet it was not completely crushed. M. tried to argue once more, **'Suppose one believes in God with form. Certainly He is not the clay image!'** Sri Ramakrishna interrupted him, **'But why clay? It is an image of Spirit.'** M. replied, 'Then should not those who worship the clay image be taught that what they are doing is mistaken?' The Master became very irritated and sharply retorted, **'That's the one hobby of you Calcutta people—giving lectures and bringing others to the light!'** (p.80)

At this time there was a surfeit of lectures in Calcutta. The members of the Brāhmo Samāj gave lectures on Brāhmoism; Christian missionaries gave lectures on Christianity; Hindus gave lectures on Hinduism—everyone felt compelled to say something about God. But Sri Ramakrishna was different. He said that you yourself must realize God before you start to speak about Him, otherwise your words will be in vain.

The Master continued: **Nobody ever stops to consider how to get the light himself. Who are you to teach others? He who is the Lord of the Universe will teach everyone. He alone teaches us, who has created this universe; who has made the sun and moon, men and beasts, and all other beings. . . . The Lord has done so many things—will He not show people the way to worship Him? If they need teaching, then He will be the teacher. He is our inner guide.**

Suppose there is an error in worshipping the clay image; doesn't God know that through it He alone is

being invoked? He will be pleased with that very worship. Why should you get a headache over it? You had better try for knowledge and devotion yourself. (p.80)

These words were new to M., yet he understood that they were absolutely true. His ego was now completely crushed. And never again did he argue with Sri Ramakrishna. **This was M.'s first argument with the Master, and happily his last!** (p.81)

M.'s surrender was now complete. All the way home he could think of nothing but Sri Ramakrishna. At the earliest opportunity, he again returned to Dakshineswar. As M.'s school happened to be closed for two consecutive days, he was free to go to Dakshineswar on a Sunday and Monday.

These were M.'s third and fourth visits to the Master. As soon as M. entered his room, Sri Ramakrishna jokingly said, 'Oh, look, look! he has come again!' Then he said: 'Once a man gave a peacock some opium. From then on, every day at the same time, the peacock came for another dose. You are like that peacock.'

Marx call religion the 'opium of the people'. In a sense, genuine religion is an opiate. It is intoxicating; if we but once taste the bliss of God, we can't give it up. We want to hear about God constantly and we hurry to places where there is talk about Him. The Master himself was like opium. If you saw him even once and listened to his words, there was no escape; you had to come back again. M. was in this condition. **Even at home he had been unable to banish the thought of Sri Ramakrishna for a moment. His mind was constantly at Dakshineswar and he had counted the minutes until he could go again.** (p.90)

From his boyhood, M. had the habit of keeping a diary. After meeting Sri Ramakrishna, M. recorded the Master's conversations in his diary. At that time he did not imagine that he would later publish a book from those diary entries; he wrote only for his own benefit.

As Śrī Caitanya had his Murāri Gupta* to write his biography, Sri Ramakrishna had his Mahendranath Gupta, M. M. had been chosen for that task, although he was not aware of it. Once one of the Master's young disciples (Swami Shivananda in later years) began to record Sri Ramakrishna's conversations. When the Master found out about it he told him that he didn't have to do that. Perhaps he wanted to suggest that the task had been reserved for someone else—M.

This seems to have been the reason that the Master often made a point of turning to M. in order to explain the meaning of some difficult subject under discussion. He was making sure that M. had listened attentively and understood the points he was making. From this we can infer that right from the beginning, Sri Ramakrishna had chosen M. to be the instrument to spread his message over the world.

M. never let anyone know that he was writing about Sri Ramakrishna. He wrote in secret, and reflected on what he had written secretly and alone. Especially after the passing away of the Master, M. would pour over his notes whenever he had any free time. Sri Ramakrishna was no longer there. So, M. would now depend on these notes to feel his presence. Swami Virajananda later recalled: 'They [the students] would notice that whenever he had no classes, their teacher [M.], a reserved man with a commanding personality, would retire to the roof, and there sit and read something with rapt attention.'

Those who observed M.'s behaviour were naturally curious about the contents of his notebook. When they

---

* Murāri Gupta was a contemporary of Śrī Caitanya and wrote his biography, *Śrī Kṛṣṇa-Caitanya Caritāmṛta.*

came to know that it concerned Sri Ramakrishna, they urged him to publish it. With some reluctance, M. expanded portions of his notes and sent them to several journals. The readers response was enthusiastic, and they clamoured for more material.

One day M. read a portion of his diary notes to Sri Sarada Devi, the Holy Mother. She was very pleased and said, 'It is as if I am hearing Thakur's* own words.' M. felt blessed and used her words at the beginning of the Bengali *Gospel*.

Holy Mother wrote M. from Jayrambati:

> Dear child, whatever you have heard from Him is nothing but the truth. You need not feel any diffidence about it. At one time He had left those words in your custody. And it is He who is now bringing them to the light of day according to the needs of the times. Know it for certain that unless those words are brought out, man will not have his consciousness awakened. All the words of His that you have with you—every one of them is true. One day when you read them out to me I felt as if it was He speaking.

There can be no better endorsement of the *Gospel's* authenticity than this.

Swami Ishanananda, one of Mother's attendants, recalled:

> 'In the evening, we would read the *Gospel* to Mother. As she heard it she would say, "Oh, it is as if the Master himself is speaking in our very presence. One's hair stands on end!" Once Mother remarked, "How intelligent people are these days—they have taken Thakur's picture. And M.—is he an ordinary person? He has managed to record everything Thakur said. Similarly, take the case of his picture. Is there another *Avatāra*

* *Thakur*, literally *God*, is the familiar name for Sri Ramakrishna.

whose picture is available? Or another *Avatāra* whose conversations are so meticulously recorded?'"[2]

On another occasion Mother said, 'M. has published in the *Gospel* much of what the Master taught.'

One version of the *Gospel* appeared in 1897, and was written in English. Part of it first came out in the magazine *Brahmavādin*; other sections then subsequently appeared in *Prabuddha Bhārata* and other magazines. It was concurrently brought out, part by part, in book form from Madras. The title given to the book was *The Gospel of Sri Ramakrishna (according to M., a son of the Lord and disciple), or the Ideal Man for India and the World*. This book referred to Sri Ramakrishna as *Bhagavān*, or *Lord*—the first time such epithets were used in print.

The *Gospel* was, however, first published in Bengali, though not in its present form. On 7 February, 1889, eight years before the publication of the English *Gospel*, Swami Vivekananda wrote to M., apparently in regard to a Bengali version:

> Thanks a hundred thousand times, Master! You have hit Ramakrishna in the right point. Few, alas, few understand him! My heart leaps with joy—and it is a wonder that I do not go mad when I find anybody thoroughly launched into the midst of the doctrine which is to shower peace on earth hereafter.[3]

While the *Gospel* may have first come out in the Bengali language, it was the English version of the *Gospel* which elicited the first real public response. Those who read it felt they had never before read anything so wonderful. When Swami Vivekananda returned from the West and was travelling in Northern India, he read the first section of the English version and immediately wrote to M.:

> Many thanks for your publication. Only, I am afraid it will not pay its way in a pamphlet form. . . . Never mind, pay or no pay—let it see the blaze of daylight. You will have many blessings on you and many more curses—but that is always the way of the world! This is the time.[4]

As Swamiji* noted, M. was publishing his material when the time was ripe for its appearance. When the second portion of the *Gospel* came out, Swamiji was even more profuse in his praise:

> It is indeed wonderful. The move is quite original, and never was the life of a great Teacher brought before the public untarnished by the writer's mind, as you are presenting this one. The language also is beyond all praise, so fresh, so pointed and withal so plain and easy.
>
> I cannot express in adequate terms how I have enjoyed the leaflets. . . . Our teacher and Lord was so original, and each one of us will have to be original or nothing. I now understand why none of us attempted his life before. It has been reserved for you, this great work. He is with you evidently. . . . P.S.—The Socratic dialogues are Plato all over; you are entirely hidden.[5]

Although M.'s English version was the first to attract public praise, he was urged to return to his original Bengali. People felt that this book should not be published in English alone, but in Sri Ramakrishna's mother-tongue. This prompted M. to write the *Gospel* in Bengali. It was first published in Bengali periodicals such as *Tattvamañjarī*, *Udbodhan*, and other journals. Later those articles were compiled to form the first part of the book, *Śrī*

**Swamiji* is the widely accepted name for Swami Vivekananda.

Śrī Rāmakṛṣṇa Kathāmṛta which was published by Udbodhan Press in 1902. M's Bengali pseudonym was 'Śrī Ma'. Coming out on Sri Ramakrishna's birthday, the book was dedicated to Holy Mother with these words:

> Mother, today is the grand birthday celebration of Thakur. Deign to accept this offering of ours on this joyful day. This *Śrī Śrī Rāmakṛṣṇa Kathāmṛta* is our new holy offering. Eagerly waiting for your blessings,
>
> —Your unworthy children, with salutations at your feet.

After the Bengali edition of the *Gospel* had been published in five volumes, Swami Nikhilananda translated it into English and published it in 1942 in New York. The foreword, written by the renowned author Aldous Huxley, describes the *Gospel* as 'a book unique...in the literature of hagiography'. Indeed, there is no biography like it in any country or language.

Huxley remarked that this was the first time that the words of an Incarnation of God, or any great soul, had been recorded with such meticulous detail. Romain Rolland also recognized the uniqueness of the conversations in the *Gospel*. He said: 'Their exactitude is almost stenographic'. M. was like a stenographer who writes down exactly what is dictated, not omitting or adding any words. The *Gospel* gives us the words of Sri Ramakrishna straight from his own mouth.

Indian scholars had much earlier recognized the great significance of the *Gospel*. Nagendranath Ghosh, a highly reputed scholar, wrote in the 29 May, 1902 *Indian Nation*:

> *Rāmakṛṣṇa Kathāmṛta*, by M., Part I, is a work of singular value and interest. . . . He has done a kind of work which no Bengalee had ever done before, which, so far as we are

aware, no native of India had ever done. . . . Its value is immense. We say nothing of the sayings themselves, for the character of the teacher and the teaching is well-known. They take us straight to the truth, and not through any metaphysical maze.

Their style is Biblical in its simplicity. What a treasure would it have been to the world if all the sayings of Śrī Kṛṣṇa, Buddha, Jesus, Mahomet, Nānak and Caitanya could have been thus preserved!

Another intellectual, Nagendranath Gupta, also wrote about the *Gospel*:

The *Gospel* of Ramakrishna Paramahaṁsa is a record taken at first hand. The words were taken down as they came fresh from the lips of the Master. His spoken words are available to all almost just as he uttered them.

As we have seen, Swamiji came to much the same conclusion, suggesting that M. was more faithful in reporting his Master's words than was Plato who placed his own ideas in the mouth of his great teacher, Socrates. It is difficult to find the real Socrates. In contrast, Swamiji told M., 'You are entirely hidden.' M. had so little egotism that he generally remains hidden in the *Gospel*, and all attention is focused on Sri Ramakrishna. We seldom notice M.'s presence.

Even so, M.'s narrative ability can be found throughout the *Gospel*. His style is simple and natural, and his manner of describing the Master is intimate. We feel that Sri Ramakrishna is actually present, coming and going before our eyes. When the Master goes into the state of *samādhi*, we see how he behaves, the setting, the circumstances, the devotees who are surrounding him. We watch him as he sings a song and dances with his disciples. He strolls around the temple grounds; then he is on his way to the pine-grove. Next we find him travelling along the streets of Calcutta in a horse-drawn carriage, or attending a performance at the theatre.

Authentic and expressive as M.'s accounts of Sri Ramakrishna are, the charm in the *Gospel* is not intentionally created. The sweetness in the *Gospel* comes from the person of Sri Ramakrishna and his entrancing words.

Of course M. could not tell everything about the Master. One reason for this is that M. did not see Sri Ramakrishna every day, and was therefore unable to hear all that he said. There is also another reason: when Sri Ramakrishna spoke to his future monastic disciples, he would speak of renunciation. He would not speak of this to others because their path was different. He used to say that all cannot digest the same food. He told his monastic disciples many things which M. could not know. Both Swami Premananda and Swami Shivananda have remarked that many of Sri Ramakrishna's teachings are not found in the *Gospel*.

Because of this, we should also read Swami Saradananda's comprehensive biography of the Master, *Sri Ramakrishna The Great Master*, reminiscences written by other monastic disciples of Sri Ramakrishna, and especially the works of Swami Vivekananda. The words of Sri Ramakrishna are the scripture; the words of Swamiji are the *bhāsya*, the commentary. If we study the *Gospel* along with the works of Swamiji and *Sri Ramakrishna The Great Master*, we will get a true picture of Sri Ramakrishna.

No one should assume from this that we are in any sense minimizing the importance of the *Gospel*. Swami Vijnanananda once told M., 'After inquiring, I have discovered that 80% or more of our monks have embraced the life of renunciation by reading the *Gospel*, and through contact with you.' Many monks and lay devotees have learned Bengali just to be able to read the *Gospel* in the original.

After the first volume of the five-volume *Śrī Śrī Ramakṛṣṇa Kathāmṛta* was published, seventeen more editions came out, and the seventeenth was reprinted twenty-four times. The second volume went through eleven editions with twenty-two reprints of the last edition, and the third volume had nine editions with eighteen reprints of the ninth edition. The fourth volume had seventeen editions, and the seventeenth was reprinted twenty-four times. The fifth volume had six editions, and the sixth edition was reprinted seventeen times.

The *Kathāmṛta* is popular even now, as shown by what happened when the original publishers, Kathamrita Bhavan, announced that their copyright of the book would expire in December 1982. Within a few days, small, medium and large publishing houses began printing the *Kathāmṛta*. On the first of January 1983, six publishing companies brought out various versions of the *Kathāmṛta*; within a few days, at least ten more companies also published the book. Yet the books from all these publishers—adding up to several hundred thousand books—were all sold out within a few days. Even with this competition, the *Kathāmṛta* published by Kathamrita Bhavan continued to sell well.

As a result of the tremendous competition, the price of the book was greatly reduced, so that it was read by more and more people. Some publishers priced the book at fifteen rupees, others at twenty and twenty-five rupees. One publisher even gave away the book free of charge if the buyer presented a 'life membership card' which cost only eighteen rupees! In one Calcutta neighbourhood there was such a rush to buy the book that the police had to be called in.

Booksellers in India stated that such enthusiasm for a religious book was unprecedented. Articles in newspapers carried such captions as, 'The *Kathāmṛta* Sales Explosion'. An article in Cochin's *The Week* bore the title, 'Ramakrishna Outsells Marx'. Translations into other languages, both Indian and foreign, also received a warm response.

The principal reason for the *Gospel*'s popularity is Sri Ramakrishna's liberal message. The Master did not teach any narrow religious doctrine, and he did not give undue prominence to any particular religious sect. Sri Ramakrishna emphasized the fact that all religions are true: '*Yata Mat Tata Path*'—'As many religions, so many paths to God' is one of his most fundamental teachings. Men and women of every religion are charmed by the *Gospel* because they find in it the essence of their own religion.

Sri Ramakrishna spoke in different ways to different people. He would speak in one way to young students, and in another way to Christian missionaries, and in still another way to Brāhmo householders. We find every spiritual path in the *Gospel*; the paths of Knowledge, Devotion and Work are discussed at length. Dualism and non-dualism, God with form and God without form are there, along with Yoga and Tantra and various kinds of popular religion. Holy Mother said that Sri Ramakrishna taught everything from the most primitive forms of religion to the heights of Advaita Vedānta.

The *Gospel* explains deep spiritual truths in a simple and appealing manner. By the light of his own spiritual experience, Sri Ramakrishna was able to make what is difficult to understand, clear and easily comprehensible. Before Sri Ramakrishna, it would have been inconceivable to speak of abstruse subjects in such simple language. To give an example: 'Break open the jack-fruit after smearing your hands with oil' is the Master's illustration of non-attachment. 'Oil' represents non-attachment: if you put oil on your hands, the sticky milk of the jack-fruit cannot stick to them. Similarly, if you possess the spirit of non-attachment, you will not get entangled in the world.

He tells us how we should live in the world using another example. 'When the mother turtle wanders about on the shore, she keeps her mind on the river bank where her eggs are hidden under sand.' In the same way, keep your mind on God while doing your worldly duties.

The *Kaṭha Upaniṣad* says, 'By His light, everything is revealed'—because God exists, everything exists. Sri Ramakrishna illustrates this by saying, Do you know how it is? After one, you write a zero, making ten; add another zero and you have *one hundred*, another zero and it becomes *one thousand*. As you increase the zeros, the number becomes larger. But if you erase the one, all the zeros—no matter how many—are worthless. In the same way, if God exists, everything exists; without Him there is nothing.

Thus, through Sri Ramakrishna's simple illustrations, the meaning of the scriptures becomes clear to us. The poet

Kālidāsa's similes may be extraordinary, but the Master's similes are more original, more apt, and cover a wider field. This has been discussed at great length by Achintya Kumar Sengupta, a leading literary critic of the present time. It is true that all religious teachers use similes and parables, but we cannot find another who uses them like Sri Ramakrishna. His supply seems inexhaustible.

It should also be noted that everything Sri Ramakrishna says can be found in the śāstras, the Hindu scriptures. Every one of the Master's teachings has its basis in the Upaniṣads, the *Bhagavad-Gītā*, the *Śrīmad Bhāgavatam* or the *Caitanya Caritāmṛta*—the most important Hindu scriptures. Many of the stories from Hindu mythology are also included in the *Gospel*. The *Gospel* is like a jar which contains the essence of all scriptures.

When I was a student in Calcutta, and even after I joined the Order, I used to visit M. on the upper floor of the Morton Institution where he could usually be found. When we were seated, he would ask, 'What is the date today? What day is it?' After we answered him he would begin: 'On a day like this the Master once said to us. . . ,' and so on, repeating the Master's words. He did not talk for the sake of teaching us—he seemed to be reminiscing for himself, speaking from the depths of meditation. If we listened, good; if not, he did not mind. He would go on speaking out of the joy of reminiscing. We noticed his great narrative and descriptive ability, already familiar to us from reading the *Gospel*. He would say only a few suggestive words, and at once a picture would appear—a living picture before our very eyes.

M. was an extraordinary man. Those who saw him understood that he was utterly unique. Paul Brunton, in his book *In Search of Secret India* recalls meeting M.: 'A venerable patriarch has stepped from the pages of the Bible, and a figure from Mosaic times has turned to flesh.' M. was a genuine Ṛṣi, a sage, and a man completely saturated with Sri Ramakrishna.

In the verse to Śrī Kṛṣṇa from the *Bhāgavatam* which is addressed to Sri Ramakrishna in the *Kathāmṛta*, and which begins this chapter, we find the words of God described as *amrta*. *Amrta* means both 'nectar' and 'immortality'. Those words are like nectar—a healing balm to those scorched by the world's miseries. They soothe our hearts and bring us peace. They also give us immortality, taking us beyond death, and birth as well. We are liberated by listening to these words and moulding our lives by them.

Sin, caused by ignorance, the darkest state of the mind, is 'wiped out' by the Lord's words, so the truly wise glorify those words.

Who are the *Givers of Plenty*? Not those who give the most material wealth, but those who proclaim the words of God and sing His glory.

A Bengali song about Sri Ramakrishna says that from *Gomukhī** the Gaṅgā of compassion has been carried into the heart of Bengal. Hindu mythology tells of King Bhagīratha, who by the power of his austerities, brought the Gaṅgā down to earth and conducted that river to the sea. Sri Ramakrishna is that Gaṅgā of compassion, and M.

---

* *Gomukhī* is a cave in the Himalayas shaped like the head of a cow. The Gaṅgā emerges from this cave.

is Bhagīratha, bringing the Lord's compassion to every door. Even today, M. continues that work by means of the *Gospel.*

Another Indian myth tells the story of the gods who obtained the nectar of immortality by churning the ocean. By churning the ocean of the scriptures, Sri Ramakrishna produced the nectar of immortality. And M. through the *Gospel*, has placed that jar of nectar in our hands.

M. was by nature very shy. He tried to remain hidden in the *Gospel*, but effacing himself, he has become immortal. As long as Sri Ramakrishna is in our hearts, as long as we need his words, M. will be with us.

References

1. *The Life of M. and the Sri Sri Ramakrishna Kathāmṛta*, Dharm Pal Gupta, Sri Ma Trust, Chandigarh, 1988, p.241
2. *Māyer Kathā*, 2nd Part (8th Edition), Udbodhan, Calcutta, p.87
3. *The Complete Works of Swami Vivekananda*, Vol.VI (5th Edition), Advaita Ashrama, Calcutta, 1981, p.204. Hereafter, C.W.
4. *Ibid.*, pp.412-13
5. *Ibid.*, Vol.V, p.140

II

No One Can Limit Him

Sri Ramakrishna said: **The magician performs his magic. He produces a mango-tree which even bears mangoes. But this is all sleight-of-hand. The magician alone is real.** (p.297) An Englishman once told of a magician he had seen in India. He said: 'I have seen with my own eyes what an Indian magician can do. First he brought out a mango seed. Then he planted it in the ground and watered it. A tree immediately started to grow, and it soon grew to maturity. Then fruit appeared and ripened. It was plucked from the tree and given to everyone to eat. Everyone tasted it. It was a real mango. But it was not long before the tree disappeared. It was no longer visible.' The person who did all these tricks alone was real. The magic was not real; only the magician was real. In the same way, **Brahman alone is real; the world is illusory.** (p.297)

In the Vedānta scriptures we find the simile of magic in many places.* Śrī Śaṅkarācārya said: 'The magician is real; the magic is unreal. In the same way Brahman is real; the world is unreal.' The phenomenal world is like magic—colourful, unpredictable, something happening all the time. But who performs all this magic? There is certainly a magician. And who is that magician? Brahman, ordinarily called 'God' (Īśvara). The *Mahānirvāṇa-Tantra*[1] says, *Māyayā kalpitaṁ jagat*—'The visible world is a projection of *māyā*.' In an instant it changes.

---

* For example, Śaṅkara's Commentaries on the *Brahmasūtra* (1.1.17;2.1.9) and the *Gauḍapādakārikā* (1.16-7). Also, his *Hymn to Dakṣiṇāmūrti*, 1-2

Today it is; tomorrow it is not—like a dream. I dream so many things. I dream I am flying through the air, going to foreign countries. Suddenly the dream breaks and I find myself lying on my bed. The world is like that dream—illusory because it is not permanent. When I dream, it never occurs to me that my dream experiences are not real. Our experience of the world is like that.

Sri Ramakrishna used to tell a story about a farmer who followed the path of Knowledge. One day his son suddenly died. His wife was crying—everyone was crying, but the farmer was silent. His wife complained to him, 'Have you no feelings? Our only son has died, and you have not shed one tear!' Then the farmer said: 'Why don't I cry? Last night I dreamed I was a king with eight sons and was very happy. Suddenly I woke up. Now I wonder who I should cry for—those eight sons, or this one son.' That one son was as illusory to him as the eight sons in his dream. Thakur said, **The farmer was a *jñānī*; therefore he realized that the waking state is as unreal as the dream state. There is only one eternal Substance, and that is the Ātman.** (p.652)

The Ātman is Brahman, which is *Sat-cit-ānanda*—Existence-Conscious-Bliss Absolute.

Sat is Existence Absolute, Eternal Reality. It exists in all three divisions of time—past, present and future. Because It exists, everything exists. We all feel that 'I am'. In all of us is this little existence, but it is only because of That Existence, Brahman, that we exist. Right now I am in this house, but I am not always here, so my present state of existence is not lasting. I certainly exist, but I exist conditionally, depending on something outside myself. What we regard as our existence is not lasting; it is not Absolute. But behin d our existence is Brahman. It is inherent in everything. The Upaniṣads say: 'Fire gives heat, because Brahman exists. The sun shines because Brahman exists.'[2] Without Brahman there is nothing.

Cit is Knowledge or Consciousness Absolute. There are many things in the world, animate and inanimate, and in all of them Consciousness is manifested. (It is less manifest in inanimate objects and not so apparent there.) *Tasya bhāsā sarvamidaṁ vibhāti*—'By His light everything is revealed.'[3] Because of that Consciousness, we are able to understand things; we are aware of happiness and misery. But that knowledge is not perfect knowledge. It is dependent on many things, such as outer objects and our sense-organs. I see a flower; I 'know' the flower. This is knowledge, but it is dependent on two things—the eye and the flower. If I am blind, then even though there is a flower, the eyes are not able to see it. Again, if there is no flower, I can't see it. All our ordinary knowledge is like that. It is conditional, dependent on our sense-organs and other things, and it is not lasting—so it is not Absolute. But underlying this knowledge is *cit*— Knowledge Absolute.

Ananda is Bliss Absolute, Perfect Joy. Brahman is the source of all the bliss in the world. *Raso bai saḥ*—'He is of the nature of sweetness.'[4] The sage Bhṛgu, in meditation, discovered the nature of Brahman. What did he find it to be?

> ***Ānando brahmeti vyajānāt***
> ***Ānandāddhyeva khalvimāni bhūtāni jāyante***
> ***Ānandena jātāni jīvanti***
> ***Ānandaṁ prayantyabhisaṁviśantīti—***

> **Brahman is of the nature of Bliss;**
> **From Bliss everything is created;**
> **Everything subsists in Bliss;**
> **When dissolution comes, all will be merged in Bliss.**[5]

All happiness in the world comes from Brahman, but worldly happiness is temporary and conditioned. For example, I eat a *rasagollā*. As long as I am eating it, I am happy. Still, this happiness does not last. After a little while my pleasure is gone, because it was limited to a particular time and to a particular object—the *rasagollā*. Such is all worldly happiness; it is limited to something or other. It is not 'Bliss Absolute' because it is not lasting and it is conditional. Yet all bliss comes from one source, Brahman.

Indeed, because Brahman exists, everything exists. The world is always changing. How can we understand that it is always changing? To understand movement, we need something stationary alongside it. For instance, how do I know whether or not the train is moving? Because the ground is firm and the track and platform are stationary, I can see that the train is moving. In the same way, behind this changeful world is something which never changes. We call it Brahman, Ātman, God or various other names. He is the very substratum of this world. Because He is, everything exists.

Sri Ramakrishna tells the story about the father who sent his two sons to a teacher to study the scriptures. When they returned home, he asked them to tell him about Brahman. One son quoted many verses from the scriptures—This is Brahman, that is Its nature, etc. The other boy only hung his head and remained silent, The father said to him, 'You have understood rightly.'

We cannot define Brahman. Brahman is infinite, unlimited. How can we express the unlimited through words? When we ascribe any attribute to Brahman, we limit It. But why only Brahman? How can we express in words any deep emotion—happiness or sorrow? Speech is always superficial; it cannot express anything profound. It is impossible to describe

Brahman. Speech is partial, incomplete. Brahman is beyond speech and mind.

Yato vāco nivartante aprāpya manasā saha—'Whence all words together with the mind turn away, unable to reach It.'[6] We are not able, or will not ever be able, to say anything about It fully.

Because of this, Sri Ramakrishna used to say that everything in the world has become defiled (passed through the mouth, i.e., spoken of), but Brahman has never been defiled: **The Vedas, *Purāṇas*, Tantras, the six systems of philosophy—have been defiled, like food that has been touched by the tongue, for they have been read or uttered by the tongue. Only one thing has not been defiled in this way, and that is Brahman. No one has ever been able to say what Brahman is.** (p.102) Sri Ramakrishna told this simile to Vidyasagar who was amazed and said, 'Today I have heard something new from you.'

A verse in one of the Tantras supports Sri Ramakrishna's words:

Ucchiṣṭaṁ sarvaśāstrāṇi sarvavidyā mukhe mukhe
Nocchiṣṭaṁ brahmaṇo jñānamavyaktaṁ cetanāmayam

'Defiled are all scriptures, all that we learn through the mouth;
Brahman is undefiled, unrevealed, Consciousness beyond expression.'[7]

The nature of Brahman cannot be expressed in words. Even a knower of Brahman is unable to express it. He becomes mute. Sri Ramakrishna said, **A boat, once reaching the 'black waters' of the ocean, cannot come back.** (p.268) In ancient times, most of the boats which went to the ocean never returned, and the men who did return could not give a proper description of the ocean. In the same way, a knower of

Brahman cannot express what he has experienced. If a mute person eats something, he is unable to describe the taste. A knower of Brahman is in that same condition. His words come to a stop and his reasoning ceases. He is unable to say anything about Brahman because he knows that whatever he says will be inadequate. He knows that he cannot express in words what he has felt, what he has perceived, so he remains silent.

Sri Ramakrishna has given other illustrations of this. For instance, if you immerse an empty jug in water, it makes a gurgling sound as the water fills it— *bhak bhak*, but when the jug is full, there is no more sound. Similarly, when Knowledge of Brahman is attained, there is silence. Another example: When guests are invited to a celebration, there is much talking and noise before the meal is served. Then when people start eating, there is less talk. And when all stomachs are filled and the last item, curd, is served, there is only the sound of *sup sup* as people eat the curd. After that everyone sleeps and there is no sound at all. In the same way, there is much reasoning and discussion of the scriptures until one attains knowledge of Brahman. Then all reasoning and talking come to a stop.

Sri Ramakrishna says that the many words about Brahman in the scriptures are like the words of a man who has returned from seeing the ocean. What can he say? 'O how vast it is! What waves! What billows!'—nothing more. Much of what is said about Brahman in the scriptures is similar to 'What waves! What billows!' Brahman, or Īśvara, cannot be defined. Books and teachers give hints—that's all.

A few verses from the Upanisads give hints, such as :

Viśvasyaikaṁ pariveṣṭitāram—'He pervades the universe.'[8]

Īśā vāsyamidaṁ sarvam—'All this—whatever exists in this changing universe—is covered by the Lord.'[9]

Sarvataḥ pāṇipādantat sarvato'kṣiśiromukhaṁ sarvataḥ śrutimalloke sarvamāvṛtya tiṣṭati—'His hands and feet are everywhere; His eyes, heads and faces are everywhere; His ears are everywhere; He exists compassing all.'[10]

A song in the Gospel says, **On every side—on land below, in sky above, beneath the seas: In every region of this earth—men seek Him tirelessly. And as they seek Him ever ask: Where is His limit, where His end?** (p.887)

He is within, He is without—immanent and transcendent. He is inseparably connected with everything in this world—He is immanent. But he is more than this world. He exists outside this world—He is transcendent. He is 'indivisible'—not divided into parts; 'actionless'—He does not do any work; 'perfect'—flawless, immaculate; 'stainless'—there is no impurity in Him, nor the faintest trace of *māyā* or ignorance. He is without qualities, without form—unattached. Please note that these attributes are negative. There is no way of describing Him. You can only say *neti, neti* —'not this, not this'. He is the basis of all attributes but has none Himself.

To speak of Brahman, you must use your mind, your organ of speech, etc. But the mind, which is by nature limited, cannot conceive of the limitless Brahman, so how can it find words to express it?

Yenedaṁ sarvaṁ vijānāti taṁ kena vijānīyād vijñātāramare kena vijānīyāt—'Through what should one know That owing to which all this is known—through what my dear, should one know the Knower?'[11]

You think that you know yourself, but what this you is, you can't say, because you can only know what is separate or different from yourself. But your own nature is Brahman, your real Self. You can't know It as something 'to be known' like any object of the world. Ordinarily, in order to know, two things are needed: the knower and the thing to be known. When both the knower and the thing to be known are present, there is 'knowledge'. But in the Knowledge of Brahman, the knower, the thing to be known, and knowledge itself are one and the same. Therefore I can't say, 'I have known Brahman.' Because of this, the *Kena Upaniṣad* says: *Yasyāmataṁ tasya mataṁ mataṁ yasya na veda saḥ*— 'He who says "I don't know", knows It; he who says "I know", does not know It.'[12]

Whoever says, 'I do not know Brahman', knows rightly, because he understands his own nature is Brahman. But if someone says, 'I know Brahman', it is an admission that he is different from Brahman, so it is like saying, 'I do not know Brahman.' It cannot be known as an object. In reality, it is very difficult to say anything about Brahman or the Knowledge of Brahman. Those who are ignorant speak about It, but the real *jñānīs*, the sages, will never do so. They will never claim to have said the last word about Brahman.

Here we must keep in mind one thing—the difference between 'Brahman' and 'Īśvara'. We commonly use these two words interchangeably; they are related to one and the same Reality, but there is a difference between them. Sri Ramakrishna discussed this point when speaking to Hazra: **Why do you address the Pure Ātman as Īśvara? The Pure Ātman is inactive and is the Witness of the three states.** (pp.654-55) The Pure Ātman means Brahman. He is actionless, qualityless, formless, independent—the witness, the observer. He does nothing, but is the witness of the three states—waking, dreaming, and deep sleep.

In the waking state we face two worlds—the outer, gross world (which we see with our eyes, hear with our ears, touch with our hands, etc.), and the inner, subtle world (I am thinking, I am deliberating, I am making plans). The outer world and the inner world are different. In the dream state, the outer, material world does not exist; there is only the inner, subtle world. In the state of deep sleep, when there are no dreams, neither the gross nor the subtle world exists. But Brahman is beyond these three states. **It is the witness of the three states of waking, dreaming, and deep sleep.** (p.651)

Sri Ramakrishna gives the illustration of light from a lamp. In the light of a lamp one person can read the *Bhāgavatam*, and another person can forge a document. The lamp does not become virtuous by the reading of the *Bhāgavatam*, and it does not incur sin by the forging of the document. These belong to the reader and the forger. The lamp is indifferent, the observer. It is the same with Brahman. In this world there are many things—good and evil, happiness and misery—but Brahman is aloof and impartial. **Brahman is beyond knowledge and ignorance, virtue and vice, merit and demerit, cleanliness and uncleanliness.** (p.900)

Brahman is in everything, but Brahman Itself is unaffected. Sri Ramakrishna gives another example : **It [Brahman] is like a magnet lying at a great distance from the needle. The needle moves but the magnet lies motionless, inactive.** (p.655) This is Brahman.

And what about Īśvara? Īśvara is one step below Brahman. Īśvara is Brahman united with *māyā*, Brahman with attributes. The *Vedānta Sāra* says, Īśvara is Ignorance associated with Pure Consciousness; as it has the *sāttvika* quality, it cannot delude Īśvara.[13] Sri Ramakrishna says, **When I think of the acts of creation, preservation and destruction, I call the Pure Ātman 'Īśvara'.** (p.655) In other words, if the world appears real to you, you cannot reject the creator. He is Īśvara. But Īśvara is not inactive like Brahman. Īśvara creates, preserves and destroys. He punishes the wicked, listens to our prayers, and has unlimited power, He is the receptacle of all auspicious qualities.

Now the question arises : Is Īśvara (God) with form or without form? If God is all-pervading, how can He be confined to a form? Swami Dayananda, the founder of the Ārya Samāj, upheld the concept of the formless deity, but as a boy he believed in God with form. When he was young he once fasted on *Śivarātri* day and then kept a vigil that night in a Śiva Temple. He was alone. Suddenly, in the middle of the night, he saw a mouse crawling on the Śiva *liṅgam* and eating the offered food. Śiva was certainly not in this stone image, he thought, or the mouse could not have taken His food. Because of that incident he became a worshipper of God without form.

But Sri Ramakrishna said that both the formless deity and the deity with form are real. Brahman is without form, but for devotees he assumes a form. **He is formless, and again He has forms. For the *bhakta*, He assumes forms. But He is formless for the *Jñānī*, that is, for him who looks on the world as a mere dream.**(p.148) A Bengali song says, 'Mother, you are the Saviour. You are everywhere, in everything. You are with form and again without form.'

Once Sri Ramakrishna told the story about a sannyasi who went to Puri to see Lord Jagannātha. When he was standing before the image, a question arose in his mind, 'Is God with form or without form?' He wanted to see if his staff would touch the body of Lord Jagannātha. Moving it from right to left, he noticed that it did not touch the body. So he understood that the Lord was formless. After that he moved his staff from left to right and it touched the image, meaning that Lord Jagannātha is *with* form. **Then he realized that God has form and, again, is formless.**(p.858)

Swami Vivekananda has discussed this matter at great length. When he was in the West, many people asked him if he worshipped idols. Swamiji replied, 'Yes, I do. You also worship idols, but you do not admit it. We do. You have so much reverence for the cross. Is that not idol worship? Why do you revere it so highly? Because it reminds you of Jesus Christ. It is a symbol. In the same way, all images are symbols of God. No one really worships the idol; they worship God in the image.'

When Swamiji was travelling in India, the Maharaja of Alwar once asked him about this. Swamiji was staying at the home of the Maharaja's dewan and when the Maharaja heard about Swamiji, he came himself to the dewan's house to meet him. After talking about various things, the Maharaja said, 'Look, Swamiji, many people worship images, but I do not believe in it.' At first Swamiji did not say a word, but after some time he asked someone to hand him the picture of the Raja which was hanging on the wall. It was given to him, and holding the picture in his hand Swamiji said, 'Now will someone come and spit on this picture?' Those present were aghast. 'What audacity! Asking us to spit on Maharaja's picture!' Swamiji said, 'Why, what is wrong in that? It is only a picture. It is only paper. Is Maharaja really in it?' Everyone remained silent. Then Swamiji said : 'Maharaja is able to understand that this picture is not just paper. You are not in it, yet again you are in it. This paper reminds us of you. It is a symbol of you. We dishonour you when we dishonour your picture. In the same way, the idol is a symbol of God. We do not worship wood or clay or stone. We worship the Supreme

Self, God. We are not able to grasp Him with our minds, so we imagine Him in a form.'

One of the *Purāṇas* says, *Bhaktānurodhāt sākāro nirākāro niraṅkuśaḥ*—'He who is formless and unattached, assumes a form because of the prayer of the devotee.'[14] He has taken on a form to fulfil the heart's desire of His devotee. Sri Ramakrishna says: **God reveals Himself to seekers in various forms and aspects. He reveals Himself in the form which His devotee loves most.** (p.150) And a verse from one of the Tantras reads : *Sādhakānāṁ hitārthāya brahmaṇo rūpakalpanā*—'For the welfare of the spiritual aspirant, the form is attributed to Brahman.'[15] He who is the most vast becomes small for His devotee. He who is limitless becomes limited for fulfilling the desires of His devotee.

Sri Ramakrishna says, **Do you know how it is? Brahman, Existence-Knowledge-Bliss Absolute, is like a shoreless ocean. In the ocean visible blocks of ice are formed here and there by intense cold. Similarly, under the cooling influence, so to speak, of the *bhakti* of Its worshippers, the Infinite transforms Itself into the finite and appears before the worshipper as God with form. That is to say, God reveals Himself to His *bhaktas* as an embodied Person. Again, as, on the rising of the sun, the ice in the ocean melts away, so, on the awakening of *jñāna*, the embodied God melts back into the infinite and formless Brahman.** (p.859)

In the Bible it is said, 'God made man in His own image.' But it is also true, as Swami Vivekananda says, that 'Man makes God in his own image.' When we worship God, we offer Him sweets and fruits, we sing songs to Him—everything to make Him happy. We do all these things because we ourselves like them. We think that perhaps He enjoys what we enjoy. Swamiji said that if a mud-buffalo thinks of God, he will think that God is also a buffalo, and that He is in a mud-heaven. Sometimes this buffalo-God rolls in the mud, and sometimes He eats grass. Indeed, we see God through our own spectacles.

Yā yasyā'bhimatā puṁsaḥ sā hi tasyaiva devatā—'A person *sees* God according to his own way of thinking, from his own point of view.'[16] We are like the blind men who wanted to know about an elephant. One held its trunk and thought the elephant was like a rope. Another man grabbed its leg and said it was like a pillar. Grasping its ear, another said the elephant was like a winnowing fan. This is how we see God, each in our own way. With our limited minds and intellects we try to understand Him, but our understanding is far from perfect. What we say about Him is only a fraction of the Truth. We imagine God according to the capacity of our minds. The image has meaning for us depending on how good and sensitive our minds are.

Several years ago I visited Aliporeduar. Some people there suggested that we visit a little city called 'Funt-so-lim', on the border of Bhutan. It is a beautiful place. On a mountain there is a big cave-temple, a Buddhist.Temple, which we decided to visit. As we entered, we were surprised to see an unusual image of Buddha. He had a snub-nose, a strong jaw and very high cheek-bones. His appearance was like that of a Bhutanese. A Bhutanese artist had made the image so it was like that. 'Man makes God in his own image.'

We heard from one of the monks of our Order that in his travels he had once visited a village in Kerala where he saw Sri Ramakrishna being worshipped in a fisherman's house. The people were illiterate. What food did they offer Sri Ramakrishna? Dried fish, which Sri Ramakrishna had never eaten. They liked it so they offered it to him. The monk asked them, 'Who are you worshipping?' And they said, 'Sri Ramakrishna.' When he asked them, 'Do you know where he is from?' They said, 'We can't say for sure. We guess he was born somewhere in Kerala.' It is all like child's play. What gives us happiness, what gives us misery, we think, gives happiness or misery to God. Our conception of Him is coloured by our own minds, and we imagine that He likes the same things we like. He comes to us in whatever way we like to think of Him. Sri Ramakrishna says that God assumes forms to please His devotees.

To explain this further, the Master says that from *Om* comes *Om Kālī*, *Om Kṛṣṇa*, and others. The meaning of this is that *Om*, the formless Brahman, manifests Itself as Śiva, Kālī, and other deities. These manifestations are only to help devotees grasp the significance of *Om*. *Om* is beyond thought and speech. We need something concrete to make God real to us.

But God does not only manifest Himself in images. He also takes birth as a human being. **His Essence can and does manifest itself through men by His mere will. . . . God incarnates Himself as man from time to time in order to teach people devotion and divine love.** (p.725) For the welfare of the world, Kṛṣṇa and others have been born on earth as *Avatāras*. Sri Ramakrishna also says: **It is undoubtedly true that God comes down to earth in a human form, as in the case of Kṛṣṇa. . . . A prayer in the *Bhāgavata* says: 'Thou walkest before us, O Lord, in the shape of man; again Thou hast been described in the Vedas as beyond words and thought.'** (p.191)

Sri Ramakrishna continues: **He has been described in the Vedas both as formless and as endowed with form. He is also described there both as attributeless and as**

endowed with attributes. (p.191) But as long as there is 'I-consciousness', it is very difficult for a person to think of God as formless and attributeless. **As long as man is conscious of 'I' and 'you', and as long as he feels that it is he who prays and meditates, so long will he feel that God is listening to his prayer and that God is a Person.** (p.635) If I am a person, God is also a person. He certainly has many more good qualities and better attributes than I have, but He is still a person. So, **One must say: 'O God, Thou art the Master and I am Thy servant. Thou art the whole and I am a part of Thee. Thou art the Mother and I am Thy child.' At that time there exists a feeling of difference: 'I am one and Thou art another.' It is God Himself who makes us feel this difference; and on account of this difference one sees man and woman, light and darkness, and so on. As long as one is aware of this difference, one must accept *Śakti*, the Personal God. It is God who has put 'I-consciousness' in us. You may reason a thousand times; still this 'I' does not disappear. As long as 'I-consciousness' exists, God reveals Himself to us as a Person. Therefore, as long as a man is conscious of 'I' and of differentiation, he cannot speak of the attributeless Brahman and must accept Brahman with attributes.** (pp.635-36)

If I have no I-consciousness or body-consciousness, then it is possible for me to think that Brahman is without qualities or form (*nirguṇa*, *nirākāra*). But as long as there is I-consciousness, I am compelled to think of Brahman as a Person, because how can I with my limited intellect, conceive of Him who is unlimited—beyond thought and speech? How can a one seer container hold four seers of milk? It can hold only one seer, though four seers exist. With my limited mind and intellect I can think of the unlimited only in a limited way. So Sri Ramakrishna says that though we often talk about God as without form or qualities, our minds are not able to grasp this conception. We cannot understand His real nature.

The mind cannot be fixed, all of a sudden, on the formless aspect of God. It is wise to think of God with form during the primary stages. (p.127) As long as you have body-consciousness, you cannot think of God as without attributes or form, so it is better to think of Him as with attributes and form. **This Brahman with attributes has been declared in the Vedas, the *Purāṇas* and the Tantra, to be Kālī, the Primal Energy.** (p.636)

Someone asked Sri Ramakrishna, **How, sir, can one have the vision of the Primal Energy and attain *Brahmajñāna*, the Knowledge of the attributeless Brahman?** In answer, Sri Ramakrishna spoke out forthrightly in favour of *Bhakti*: **Pray to Him with a yearning heart and weep. That will purify your heart. You see the reflection of the sun in clear water.** (p.636) Then he compared Brahman to the sun. He said, **The body is a plate, as it were, containing the water of mind, intelligence and ego. Brahman is like the sun. It is reflected in the water.** (p.416) If the water is turbulent or dirty, the reflection of the sun on it is not clear. Water that is still and pure gives a clear reflection. Our minds are now cloudy, so the reflection of Brahman is not clear. It is our innate attraction to sense-objects that causes this cloudiness.

Śaṅkarācārya says : *Bāhyaviṣayarāgādidoṣa kaluṣitam aprasannam aśuddham*—'Our attraction to external objects (*bāhyaviṣayarāga*) is called a defect (*doṣa*). As a result of this defect, or error, our mind becomes dissatisfied (*kaluṣita*), turbid (*aprasanna*), and impure (*aśuddha*).' The state of our minds now is *malāvanaddhamivādarśaṁ, vilulitamiva salilam*—'like a dirty mirror, or like water lashed into waves.' But, *nāvabodhayati nityasannihitamapi ātmatattvam*—'spiritual Knowledge is always within us in spite of the fact that we are not aware of it.'[17]

The *Kaṭha Upaniṣad* says :

Parāñci khāni vyatṛṇat svayambhūstasmāt—
parāṅ paśyati nāntarātman
Kaściddhīraḥ pratyagātmānamaikṣad—
āvṛttacakṣuramṛtatvamicchan—

'Our sense-organs are by nature outgoing. The Lord made them that way. That is why we are not able to see the Self within. We perceive only the outer objects. But a calm person, desiring Immortality, beholds the Inner-Self with his eyes closed.'[18]

It is not only the eyes—it is all the sense-organs that must be restrained from going outward. Only then can we see the Lord within ourselves. We must overcome our attraction to outer objects. Sri Ramakrishna tells us how: Pray intensely and cry. Your tears will wash away the dirt from your mind, then the reflection of Brahman will fall on your clear mind. And, **in the mirror of his 'I-consciousness' the devotee sees the form of the Primal Energy.** (p.636)

The Master continues: **As long as a man must see the Sun in the water of his 'I-consciousness' and has no means of seeing the real Sun except through Its reflection, so long is the reflected sun alone one hundred per cent real to him. As long as the 'I' is real, so long is the reflected sun real—one hundred per cent real.** (p.636) The reflected sun means Brahman with Attributes, Īśvara. As long as we have body-consciousness, it is good to think of Him as having attributes and form, to be a dualist. In the end this dualism must terminate in non-dualism. At first I am one person, and God (Īśvara) is another person. There is this consciousness of difference. But at last I find that I and God are one and the same. A devotee used to sing this song: 'The more I go towards you, the more I am like you. At last we will be together—eternally united. Then there will be no difference between you and me.' For most people the idea of Brahman with attributes (Īśvara) is good. How do we view Īśvara? We think that He is endowed with limitless power, that His mercy is without end. If I do something wrong, He punishes me; but if I repent, He forgives me. He listens to my prayers and protects me from calamities and adversities. He is the greatest support of all. This is how most of us think of God, Īśvara.

But Brahman has no qualities, no form; He does nothing. How can He be my support, my refuge? I can't pray to Him, I can't lean on Him, because He has no qualities (*guṇas*). How can I rely on Him? He does nothing; how can I believe that He will give me strength in my distress, courage in adversity? Because of this Sri Ramakrishna says that we should hold to Brahman with attributes, Īśvara, who listens to our prayers and always protects us. **If you seek *Brahmajñāna*, the Knowledge of the attributeless Brahman, then proceed to the real Sun through Its reflection. Pray to Brahman with attributes, who listens to your prayers, and He Himself will give you full Knowledge of Brahman; for that which is Brahman with attributes is verily Brahman without attributes, that which is Brahman is verily *Śakti*. One realizes this non-duality after the attainment of Perfect Knowledge.** (p.636)

Saguṇa Brahman will take us to *Nirguṇa* Brahman (Brahman without attributes). If you pray intensely to Īśvara,

He will give you Knowledge of Brahman. After attaining this Knowledge you will understand that Brahman with attributes is the same as Brahman without attributes. Just as a snake is the same snake whether it is at rest or whether it is wriggling, so is Brahman the same Brahman whether It is the formless Absolute or if It is manifesting Itself through *māyā*.

Sri Ramakrishna also says: **But it is extremely difficult to understand this. Naturally the doubt arises in the mind: if God is formless, how then can He have form? Further, if He has a form, why does He have so many forms?** (p.858) Such questions arise in our minds. But Sri Ramakrishna says that we should first try to reach God through spiritual practice, devotional singing, etc. **These things do not become clear until one has realized God.** (p.858)

If I have not come face to face with God, I cannot understand Him. Sri Ramakrishna gave an example: You know Jadu Mallik is very wealthy and you wonder how many stocks and bonds he possesses. How can you find out about all these things? You can make friends with Jadu, and then one day he himself may tell you all about his possessions. Become acquainted with God. Then He Himself will explain everything to you. He will clear up all the questions you have in your mind. It is not a matter of intellect or reasoning.

> **How are you trying, O my mind, to know the nature of God?**
> **You are groping like a madman locked in a dark room.**
> **He is grasped through ecstatic love; how can you fathom Him without it?**
> **Only through affirmation, never negation, can you know Him;**
> **Neither through Veda nor through Tantra nor the six *darśanas*.**

It is in love's elixir only that He delights, O mind;
He dwells in the body's inmost depths, in Everlasting Joy.
And, for that love, the mighty yogis practise yoga from age to age;
When love awakes, the Lord, like a magnet, draws to Him the soul.
He it is, says Rāmaprasāda, that I approach as Mother;
But must I give away the secret, here in the market-place?
From the hints I have given, O mind, guess what that Being is! (p.107)

How can you know Him? How can you understand Him? Like a madman in a dark room you are groping about trying to grasp Him. But He is not anything material. He is love and that is found in the innermost recesses of the heart. You cannot see Him through '*darśana*' (philosophy), because He delights most in love. He makes His abode in 'the body's inmost depths', the heart. Because of this, we can see God in the devotee—the heart of the devotee is God's drawing room. The best manifestation of God is in those who love Him. That is why Sri Ramakrishna says that the devotee-I is like a mirror. In that mirror God is reflected and we see God in the devotee.

Sri Ramakrishna says: **Do not reason. Who can ever know God. . . . Hazra is given to too much calculation. He says, 'This much of God has become the universe and this much is the balance.' My head aches at his calculations. I know that I know nothing. Sometimes I think of God as good, and sometimes as bad. What can I know of Him. . . . I only call on Him as Mother. Let Mother do whatever She likes.** (p.299) You may

discriminate for millions of years about God's attributes and still you will not know them. (p.463)

In a hymn to Śiva it is said:

Asitagirisamaṁ syāt kajjalaṁ sindhupātre
suratаruvaraśākhā lekhanīpatramurvī
Likhati yadi gṛhītvā sāradā sarvakālaṁ
tadapi tava guṇānāmīśa pāraṁ na yāti—

'If the goddess of learning were to write eternally, having the biggest branch of the celestial tree for Her pen, the whole earth for paper, the Blue Mountain for ink, and the ocean for the vessel thereof, even then, O Lord, Thy attributes cannot be fully described.'[19]

Premik, a Bengali saint, in one of his songs says, 'Mother, no one knows for certain who you are or what you are. You are such that even Brahmā, Viṣṇu and Śiva are not able to describe Your nature.' Another devotee asks: 'How can we say what Mother is? She is so vast—containing as many worlds as there are pores in the skin of the body. She is also smaller than an atom.' 'Smaller than the smallest, greater than the greatest.'[20] She is everything. We can never say about Her that She is only this and nothing more.

One devotee prays this way:

Rūpaṁrūpavivarjitasya bhavato dhyānena yatkalpitaṁ
stutyānirvacanīyatākhilaguro dūrīkṛtā yanmayā
Vyāpitvañca nirākṛtaṁ bhagavato yattīrthayātrādinā
kṣantavyaṁ jagadīśa tadvikalatādoṣatrayaṁ
matkṛtam—

'O Lord, in my meditation I have attributed forms to Thee who art formless. O Thou Teacher of the world, by my hymns I have, as it were, contradicted that Thou art indescribable. By going on pilgrimage I have, as it were, denied Thy omnipresence. O Lord of the universe, pray, forgive me these threefold faults.'[21]

Sri Ramakrishna says that you should never think that what has been said about Him is the last word. **God has form and He is formless too. Further He is beyond both form and formlessness.** (p.192) He is 'one' and He is 'two'; again, He is *dvaitādvaita vivarjitam*, 'free from dualism and nondualism'. He is *Nirguṇa*, without qualities, and *Saguṇa*, with qualities, and much more. **No one can limit Him.** (p.192) To try to define Him is only foolishness.

Sometimes we find in the Upaniṣads that what is said about Him is contradictory:

Tadejati tannaijati taddūre tadvantike
Tadantarasya sarvasya tadu sarvasyāsya bāhyataḥ—

'He moves, again He does not move. He is far, again He is near. He is in everything, again He is outside.'[22]

Apāṇipādo javano grahītā
Paśyatyacakṣuḥ sa śṛṇotyakarṇaḥ—

'He has no hands or feet, but going swiftly, he takes in everything. He has no eyes, yet He can see. He has no ears, yet He can hear.'[23]

The significance of all these contradictory statements is that we can never say anything about Him that is absolutely true. Everything is possible for Him. *Mūkaṁ karoti vācālaṁ paṅguṁ laṅghayate girim*—'By His will, the dumb become eloquent and the lame scale mountains.'[24]

Sri Ramakrishna told a story about this; Once the great sage Nārada was returning from a visit with God. On the way he met two men who asked him, 'What was God doing when you left Him?' Narada replied, 'When I last saw Him, He was passing elephants through the eye of a needle.' Hearing this, one of the men said, 'Impossible! How could He do that? I don't believe it!' But the other man, who was a devotee, said: 'You have seen correctly. Everything is possible for Him.' Nothing is impossible in His kingdom.

Mathur once said 'Sir, can God do whatever he likes? Must He not obey His own laws?' Sri Ramakrishna replied, 'Of course not. Is He who made the law obliged to obey it? If He wishes, He can break His own law.' Mathur Babu said, 'That never happens. A white flower never appears on a tree of red flowers.' Sri Ramakrishna disagreed, 'Yes, that can happen. If He wishes, it can happen.' The next day, Sri Ramakrishna found a white flower growing on a red hibiscus tree. He immediately picked it and showed it to Mathur Babu.

Sri Ramakrishna says that one must admit that, **God has form; again He is formless. How many aspects He has! We cannot comprehend Him. . . . One must accept everything; God with form and God without form.** (p.577) In this connection, he told about one of his own experiences. 'I was meditating in the Kālī temple when I saw that Mother had appeared in the form of the prostitute Ramani.' **I said, 'Mother, I see that Thou art in that form too.' Therefore I say one must accept everything. One does not know when or how God will reveal Himself. . . . A man reads a little of the *Gītā*, the *Bhāgavata*, or the Vedānta and thinks he has understood everything. Once an ant went to a hill of sugar. One grain of sugar filled its stomach, and it was returning home with another grain in its mouth. On the way it said to itself, 'Next time I go, I shall bring**

home the whole hill.' (p.577) We are so insignificant, but we are not aware of it; we think we can understand God fully.

Sri Ramakrishna says: 'Look, do not forget the goal of human life. The purpose of life is to see God. Try with all your might for that.' Mere reasoning is pointless; nothing is gained by it. With our limited consciousness we believe we can have the full Knowledge of God. This is impossible.

Who can fully know the infinite God? And what need is there of knowing the Infinite? (p.150) **But as for us, it is enough to know Him as much as we need.** (p.329) **If a jug of water is enough to remove my thirst, why should I measure the quantity of water in a lake? I become drunk on even half a bottle of wine—what is the use of my calculating the quantity of liquor in the tavern? What need is there of knowing the Infinite?** (p.150) About the ant who went to the hill of sugar he said, **Did it need the entire hill? A grain or two of sugar was more than enough.** (p.329)

God is that hill of sugar, and we are that ant. We must try to get 'a grain or two'—that is to say, we must try to have the direct perception of God. 'You go to a mango orchard to eat mangoes. Once there why do you ask, "How many trees are there; how many mangoes are on the trees?"' Those who are intelligent first eat the mangoes.

In the same way, those who are wise do not waste time in vain reasoning about God. They try with all their strength to attain Him. Sri Ramakrishna says: **Eat . . . mangoes . . . and be happy.** (p.463) **You have been born in this world as a human being to worship God; therefore try to acquire love for His Lotus Feet. Why do you trouble yourself to know a hundred other things?** (p.901)

References

1. *Mahānirvāṇa Tantra*, XIV. 113
2. *Kaṭha Upaniṣad*, II.3.3
3. *Śvetāśvatara Upaniṣad*, VI.14
4. *Taittirīya Upaniṣad*, II.7
5. *Ibid.*, III.6
6. *Ibid.*, II.4
7. *Jñānasaṅkalinī Tantra*, 52
8. *Śvetāśvatara Upaniṣad*, III.7
9. *Īśa Upaniṣad*, 1
10. *Śvetāśvatara Upaniṣad*, III.16
11. *Bṛhadāraṇyaka Upaniṣad*, II.4.14
12. *Kena Upaniṣad*, II.3
13. *Vedānta Sāra*, 36, 37
14. *Brahmavaivarta Purāṇa* (Kṛṣṇajanma Khaṇḍa), VII.56
15. *Kulārṇava Tantra*, VI.73
16. *Śāktānanda-taraṅgiṇī*, 3/14
17. *Śaṅkara Bhāṣya, Muṇḍaka Upaniṣad*, III.1.8
18. *Kaṭha Upaniṣad*, II.1.1
19. *Śivamahimnaḥ Stotra*, 32
20. *Śvetāśvatara Upaniṣad*, III.20
21. from *Universal Prayers*, Swami Yatiswarananda, verse 308
22. *Īśa Upaniṣad*, 5
23. *Śvetāśvatara Upaniṣad*, III.19
24. *Gītādhyāna*, 8

III

He is the Source of All Power

Sri Ramakrishna says, **It is He who is the Indivisible *Saccidānanda.* Again, it is He who has become the universe and its living beings.** (p.779) Those who follow the path of Knowledge (*jñānī*s) often reject the universe and its living beings. In their opinion, Brahman is the only Reality; the universe and its living beings are illusory. But devotees (*bhakta*s) accept everything. In their view, this world and all living beings are His *līlā*, *māyā*, the play of His *Śakti*, His Power. He Himself through His *māyā* has become all this. The universe and its living beings are in reality the Indivisible *Saccidānanda*.

In the Upaniṣads we find the Supreme Being saying, *Bahu syām*—'May I be many!' It seems that He did not like to be alone, that He was lonely. *Prajāyeyeti*—'I will be born in many forms.'[1] So from Him everything came. Because of Him the world exists, animals exist—all kinds of living beings exist, including human beings. He Himself is everything. In reality, I myself am Brahman.

Sri Ramakrishna tried to explain Brahman in many different ways. He once compared Brahman to the sun: **The body is a plate, as it were, containing the water of the mind, intelligence, and ego. Brahman is like the sun. It is reflected in the water.** (p.416) That reflection is in everyone and everything.

Brahman has also been compared to the moon.

Eka eva hi bhūtātmā bhūte bhūte vyavasthitaḥ
Ekadhā bahudhā caiva dṛśyate jalacandravat—

'The one Ātman is present in all beings. Though one, It is seen as many, like the moon which is reflected in the water.'[2] The moon is in the sky but the reflection of the moon falls on the ocean, the rivers, the ponds, even on the little basins. We see those reflections in various containers of water, so although there is only one moon, there seem to be many. In the same way, Brahman is one, but He is reflected in all creatures, so He seems to be many.

Sri Ramakrishna gives another illustration: 'There are various kinds of pillows—one for the head, one for the side, etc., but all the pillows have the same stuffing.' Still another illustration: 'You can make different kinds of candy from sugar. One will be shaped like an elephant, one like a horse, another like a camel—many kinds of candy can be made. But all the candies are made of the same substance, sugar.' In the same way, we see a great variety of creatures in the world, but they are all in reality one. In all beings there is one Brahman. 'One' seems to be 'many'.

A Sanskrit verse tells us what Brahman is in its essential nature and what the world is:

Asti bhāti priyaṁ rūpaṁ nāma cetyaṁśapañcakam
Ādyatrayaṁ brahmarūpaṁ jagadrūpaṁ tato dvayam—

'*Asti*, *bhāti*, *priya*, *rūpa* and *nāma*—these five things. Of them the first three signify Brahman, the other two mean the world.'[3] That is, the nature of Brahman is Existence (*asti*), Consciousness (*bhāti*), Bliss (*priya*). Saccidānanda is to be understood by *asti-bhāti-priya*.

And what is the world? *Nāma* and *rūpa*—name and form. We see multiplicity and variation in the world because of differences in name and form. You have one name; I have another name. You have one kind of body; I have another—so we appear to be different from each other. If this difference in name and form is removed, there will be no difference between us. We are in reality one Brahman. What is called 'name and form' is an aberration. Through this aberration, the one Brahman appears as created beings.

Clay horses, clay elephants, clay camels, etc., though they differ in name and form, all come from the same clay. *Yathā somyaikena mṛtpiṇḍena sarvaṁ mṛnmayaṁ vijñātaṁ syāt*—'By knowing one clod of clay, all that is made of clay is known. The modification is only a name arising from speech, while in reality, all is clay.'[4] The clay is the substance; name and form are just superimpositions. In the same way, through the superimposition of name and form on the Reality, Brahman, we see the many variations in the world. This diversity is not lasting, it is ephemeral; Brahman alone is the unchanging Reality. Because of this, those who take the path of Knowledge often reject the world. But, as we have seen, devotees do not.

Devotees say that the universe is a manifestation of God's power and glory. God has created all these—sky, stars, moon, sun, mountains, ocean, men, animals. They constitute His glory. He is within us, in our hearts. Again, He is outside. The most advanced devotees say that He Himself has become all this—the twenty-four cosmic principles, the universe, and all living beings. (p.133)

If you ask from what material this world-system was made, the *Sāṁkhya* philosophy will answer that it is composed of twenty-four principal elements. First *prakṛti*, then *mahat*, and after that egoism. From egoism the mind arises. Next come the five *tanmātra*s: sound, touch, form, taste, smell; after that, the five *mahābhūta*s: earth, water, heat, air and space. Then come the five sense-organs: eyes, ears, nose, tongue, skin; and finally the five organs of action: speech, hands, feet and the organs of evacuation and generation.

Altogether there are twenty-four principal elements which compose this world-system. The mind is the pivot around which the other elements revolve. If there were no mind, there would be nothing. Devotees say that God (Īśvara) created these elements.

In the *Gospel*, Sri Ramakrishna mentions Rāmānuja's philosophy. He says, **Brahman is qualified by the universe and its living beings.** (p.652) Rāmānuja formulated this doctrine, which is called 'qualified non-dualism'. He taught that the universe and living beings are not unreal—they are a part of Brahman. Theirs is the relation between the part and the whole. Sri Ramakrishna continues his explanation: **But, at the beginning, while following the method of 'Not this, not this', one has to eliminate the universe and its living beings.**(p.652) When you become a spiritual aspirant, you must give up the world. At the present time, your view of the world is erroneous. Now you do not see the world as a manifestation of God. You see the world as the world and are attracted to it. Because of this, you must withdraw your mind from the world completely and direct it to God.

But when you have attained God, when you have reached the goal, you will then see that, **It is God who has become all this. Then you see that God, *māyā*, living beings, and the universe form one whole. God includes the universe and its living beings.** (pp.327-28) Sri Ramakrishna gives an illustration of a bel-fruit: **Suppose you have separated the shell, flesh, and seeds of a bel-fruit and someone asks you the weight of the fruit. Will you leave aside the shell and the seeds and weigh only the flesh? Not at all. To know the real weight of the fruit, you must weigh the whole of it—the shell, the flesh, and the seeds.** (p.328)

He must accept the whole thing: seeds and flesh. Seeds and shell and flesh belong to one and the same fruit. (p.652)

Then he explains this metaphor: **The shell may be likened to the universe, and the seeds to living beings. While one is engaged in discrimination one says to oneself that the universe and the living beings are non-Self and unsubstantial. At that time one thinks of the flesh alone as the substance, and the shell and seeds as unsubstantial. But after discrimination is over, one feels that all three parts of the fruit together form a unity. Then one further realizes that the stuff that has produced the flesh of the fruit has also produced the shell and seeds. To know the real nature of the bel-fruit one must know all three.** (p.328)

After attaining God we understand that everything is God. No one is excluded and nothing is left out. We accept everything—the world together with its living beings. Sri Ramakrishna said: **I accept all—Brahman and also *māyā*, the universe and its living beings. . . . The *Nitya* and the *Līlā* belong to the same Reality. Therefore I accept everything, the Relative as well as the Absolute. I don't explain away the world as *māyā*. Were I to do that I should get short weight.** (p.652)

We find in one of the Upaniṣads: *Devātmaśaktiṁ svaguṇairnigūḍhām*—'The sages, absorbed in meditation through one-pointedness of mind, discovered the power (i.e., *māyā*) belonging to the Lord Himself and hidden in its own *guṇas*.'[5] *Māyā* is the Power (*Śakti*) of Brahman. Under the influence of this Power, everything is created, preserved and destroyed. Due to the activity of this Power, the whole world moves. Many Vedāntists do not accept *māyā* at all, but if you do not accept *māyā*, or *Śakti*, there is no explanation for creation. Brahman is qualityless, actionless. How will He create or move the world to action? Therefore one must accept *māyā*.

One of Sri Ramakrishna's gurus, a monk named Totapuri, also did not acknowledge *māyā*. He accepted Brahman, but the Power of Brahman, which was responsible for the entire world-process of creation, preservation, and destruction, he refused to accept. When Totapuri saw Sri Ramakrishna clapping his hands while chanting the name of God, he would tease him, saying, 'Are you making bread?' (*Sādhus* often make their bread this way, flattening it between the palms of their hands. He was sarcastically putting Sri Ramakrishna's hand-clapping in the same category.) But at last Totapuri had to accept *Śakti*.

He had been at Dakshineswar a long time, but the climate of Bengal did not agree with him, and he came down with blood-dysentery. If a person established in *samādhi* has pain, he dives deep into *samādhi*, withdrawing his mind from his body. Then he is no longer conscious of pain. But one night the pain was so severe that Totapuri could not take his mind from his body. Every time he tried, his mind would come back down to the body. He became very irritated and decided to free himself from his cage of flesh and bones once and for all by drowning himself in the Gaṅgā. But when he waded into the river, he found that however far he went, there was not enough water to cover him. Then Totapuri understood: It is all the play of *Mahāmāyā*, the Divine Mother. He realized that 'Mother is in water, Mother is on land, the body is Mother, the mind is Mother, pain is Mother, health is Mother, knowledge is Mother, ignorance is Mother, life is Mother, death is Mother—That Mother is everywhere.'[6] *Acintyaśaktirūpiṇī-mā*—'Mother in the form of inconceivable power,' and *Aghaṭanaghaṭanapaṭīyasī-mā*—'Mother skilled in bringing about the impossible.' Totapuri at last accepted *Śakti*. After bowing down to Mother Kālī in the Temple, he left Dakshineswar.

There is a similar story about Śaṅkarācārya. At first he accepted only Brahman and would not acknowledge *Śakti*. Once at Kāśī he was going along a narrow path on his way to bathe at the Maṇikarṇikā ghāṭ when he met a woman sitting beside her husband's corpse bitterly sobbing. The corpse was blocking the pathway. Śaṅkarācārya waited a long time and then he said to the woman, 'Mother, will you please remove the corpse and allow me to pass?' The woman replied, 'Father, you yourself should command the corpse to move out of the way.' Śaṅkarācārya said, 'Grief has obviously destroyed your good sense. How can I ask the corpse to move? If I ask it, will it respond? Where is its power to move?' At that, the woman frowned and said, 'Sannyasi, you do not accept *Śakti*. You say that only Brahman is real, that Brahman does everything. This corpse is also Brahman, so why is it unable to move?' Śaṅkarācārya said, 'How can it move? Who will move it?' Then the woman said, 'So Brahman is not everything?' Śaṅkarācārya could not say a word. He had to acknowledge *Śakti*. *Mahāmāyā*, the Divine Mother Herself, had come to teach him.

After this, Śaṅkarācārya accepted *Śakti*, and in his discussions and debates he no longer rejected the world. In his Commentary on the *Brahma Sūtra*s he says, *Nahi tayā vinā parameśvarasya sraṣṭṛtvaṁ sidhyati. Śaktirahitasya tasya pravṛttyanupapatteḥ*—'Without Śakti it is not possible for Brahman to be a Creator.'[7] Brahman is actionless, independent. How can He be engaged in the work of all this creation - preservation - destruction? If you do not acknowledge the power of Brahman, *Śakti*, you cannot give any reasonable explanation for this.

How full of astonishing achievements Śaṅkarācārya's short life was! He travelled on foot from one end of India to the other, defeating many scholars in debates. In this way he re-established the *Sanātana Dharma* (the Eternal Religion, i.e., Hinduism). He wrote many commentaries on the scriptures, treatises on Vedānta, and hymns to gods and goddesses. He also revived holy places which had been destroyed or allowed to deteriorate. At each of the four corners of India he established a monastery to preserve the Hindu religion. He was not born to serve himself; his work was for the welfare of the world.

Although Śaṅkara repeatedly emphasized that 'Brahman is the only Reality', he recognized two aspects of Brahman. In his *Commentary* on the *Brahma Sūtra* (I.1.11), he states: 'Two kinds of Brahman are stated [in the Upaniṣads]: the one having as its adjuncts the diversities of the universe, the modifications of name and form; the other its contrary, completely free from all adjuncts.' He did not deny the empirical reality of the world (Brahman with its adjuncts); he only denied its ultimateness. Brahman alone is ultimately Real.

Sri Ramakrishna has a different approach to Ultimate Reality. He stresses the identity of both aspects of Brahman. He calls the pure Brahman *without* attributes, *Brahman*, and Brahman *with* attributes, *Kālī*. He says, **That which is Brahman is also Kālī, the Mother, the Primal Energy.** (p.634) Kālī is the *Śakti* (Power) of Brahman. The one who contains the power (Brahman) cannot be conceived of without the one who manifests the power (Kālī). **I have realized that Brahman and *Śakti* are identical; like water and its wetness, like fire and its power to burn.** (p.550) **They are**

like milk and its whiteness. Thinking of one, you must also think of the other. (p.635) *Prakṛti* (nature) is always united with *Puruṣa* (the Supreme Soul), *Śakti* (or Kālī) with Śiva, *māyā* with Brahman. In the *Purāṇas* we find Thakur's own words :

Yathā dugdhe ca dhāvalyaṁ yathā jalaṁ tathā śaityam
Yathā vahnau ca dāhikā na tayorbhedaḥ—

'Where there is milk, there is the colour white. Where there is water, there is coolness. Where there is fire, there is its power to burn. There is no difference between the two.'[8] The Master explains this further: **When inactive It is called Brahman. Again, when creating, preserving, and destroying, It is called *Śakti*. Still water is an illustration of Brahman. The same water moving in waves may be compared to *Śakti*, Kālī.** (p.634)

The Pure Brahman is sometimes called Śiva. In Indian icons, Śiva lies like a corpse under the feet of Kālī. He is actionless, unattached. Looking at the face of Kālī the Mother, He does nothing. But she who is Kālī is ever-moving, ever-playful. With one of Her four hands Mother Kālī grants safety to her devotees; with another she threatens with a sword. With her third hand She gives fearlessness, and with the fourth, She terrorizes. She is full of compassion, yet She is the Terrible. All these contradictions are found in one image.*

---

* Some people have a strong aversion to the Kālī image. In the *Gospel* we find Dr Mahendralal Sarkar, a famous scientist and physician, saying, 'Kālī? She was a Santhal woman.' Sister Nivedita once gave a lecture on Kālī at Albert Hall in Calcutta which created an uproar. One part of the audience was pleased and called it 'A wonderful incident'. But the other part, headed by Dr Sarkar called it 'Abominable in the extreme!' These people did not approve of a foreign lady defending Mother Kālī. Many members of the upper educated classes of that time believed that Kālī was only a Santhal woman. This may be one reason that Sri Ramakrishna revived the worship of Mother Kālī.

The world is made up of these contradictions. There is creation, but also destruction. There are great souls like Buddha and Caitanya, and then there are ruthless aggressors like Genghis Khan and Tamerlane. Someone once said to Sri Ramakrishna that God was merciful. The Master replied, 'Why do you say he is merciful? Because He gives us so much? But He also takes away so much.' He gives rain, but sometimes too much, or too little rain. Someone may be young, with a bright future before him; then suddenly he dies. Another person is old and sick, and wants to die, but he continues to live. How can you call God merciful? Then again, there is a terrible calamity; death seems certain, but in a superhuman way your life is saved. So is He not merciful? In reality, He is both merciful and merciless because He is everything.

Another thing we find in this world is that there is always evil along with good, good along with evil. They are always mixed together. Nothing is absolutely good: nothing is absolutely bad. In 1978 there was a terrible flood in West Bengal causing much devastation. Yet, as a result, there was an excellent harvest in all the flooded areas. I visited the site of greatest flooding afterwards. People there said that they had not had such good crops in many years.

In this world of *māyā* everything happens this way—this constant making and breaking. We call something good or bad from our own angle of vision. In reality, good and bad are relative. God is good, and also bad. He is merciful and again He is merciless. When two countries go to war, the people of both countries pray to Him. God is one and the same Person, and the winner of the war can only be one. If our country wins the war, we say He is merciful. But those who lose the war will not say that. What happened seemed good to us; but to those in the other country it seemed bad. For the same thing I call

Him good and another calls Him bad. In reality, He is both good and bad. He is everything.

The great poet-saint Rāmaprasāda sang, 'O Mother, it is written in the *Caṇḍī* that You are misery and You are happiness.' A remarkable thing—his calling Mother 'misery and happiness'. But he does not call Her Brahman. Brahman is above all this. She who is called 'the power of Brahman', is everything—good and evil. 'It is written in the *Caṇḍī*'—What do we find in the *Caṇḍī*? 'Mother, You are peace, You are forgiveness, You are illusion, You are creation, You are destruction—You are everything.'

Viśvasya bījaṁ paramāsi māyā
Tvamīśvarī devi carācarasya
Ādhārabhūtā jagatastvamekā—

'You are the seed, or root of everything. You are the Goddess of the moving and the unmoving. You are the source of all; You are verily One—You exist, therefore everything exists.'[9] Sri Ramakrishna gives this illustration: 'If you place zeros after the number "one", you will have a large figure. But if you erase the "one", there will be nothing.' Mother, You are that 'one'. You are *adhiṣṭhān*—the substratum. You exist, therefore everything exists.

Sri Ramakrishna said: 'One day at Dakshineswar I saw a woman suddenly rise up out of the Gaṅgā. Right before my eyes she gave birth to a baby. For a little while she nursed it lovingly; then she suddenly started to devour it.' She is the Creator, the Nourisher and the Destroyer—one *Śakti* in various forms.

This can be explained by the example of electricity. Much good can be done through electricity, as well as much destruction. It helps us in many ways, such as providing us light and heat. On the other hand, someone may touch a live-wire and be accidentally electrocuted. Can we call that electricity good or bad? Is God good or is He bad? Swamiji wrote a poem in which he said, 'Mother, this world is Your playhouse. You built it Yourself, and You are always playing with various things in it—sometimes with happiness, sometimes with misery.' Whenever there is happiness, whenever there is misery—it is happiness or misery to us. To Her it is all play.

This is the nature of the world—*dvandva*, pairs of opposites—day/night, light/dark, good/bad, birth/death. But because this is all the play of His *Śakti*, His Power, it ultimately all comes from Him, Brahman.

Sri Ramakrishna says, **It is God who manifests Himself as the atheist and the believer, the good and the bad, the real and the unreal; . . . it is He who is present in waking and in sleep**. (p.236) Again he says, 'As the snake I bite; as the exorcist, I remove the poison. As the judge, I pass sentence; as the executioner I carry out the punishment.' As the snake, He bit; as the exorcist, He came to remove the poison. As the judge, He gave the verdict; and as the executioner He carried out the orders. **And He is beyond all these.** (p.236)—When He is Infinite, Pure Existence, Actionless, He is then like Śiva, appearing to be a corpse. But when He is in a state of activity, He builds and breaks—He does everything. He who is the Absolute is also the Relative.

In the *Gospel* we again and again come across the words *Prakṛti*, *māyā*, and *Śakti*, and we find that these words have about the same meaning. In the Vedānta philosophy, the words Brahman and *māyā* are used; in *Sāṅkhya*, the words *Puruṣa* and *Prakṛti*; and in the Tantras, the words Śiva and *Śakti*, or Śiva and Kālī. In the *Brahmavaivarta Purāṇa* the Lord has said, *Prakṛtirmadvikārā*—'My deviation from the normal state, or my change of condition is this *Prakṛti*.'[9] Sri Ramakrishna said, ***Prakṛti* is the embodiment of the three *guṇas*. *Sattva*, *rajas* and *tamas* are in her.** (p.608) By the action of the three *guṇas* i.e., *Prakṛti*, the whole world process is created and moves along.

A question may arise: Is *māyā* (*Prakṛti*) the ruler of Brahman also? The answer is: No. Everything is under the command of *māyā*, but Brahman is not. Brahman is the Lord, or ruler, of *māyā*. Sri Ramakrishna gives an example: **There is poison in the snake, but it doesn't harm the snake. It is poison to him who is bitten by the snake. Brahman Itself is unattached.** (pp.608-09) The *Śvetāśvatara Upaniṣad* says, *Māyāṁ tu prakṛtiṁ vidyānmāyinantu maheśvaram*—'Know then that *Prakṛti* is *māyā* and that the Great God is the Lord of *māyā*.'[10]

Sri Ramakrishna continues: **She plays in different ways. It is She alone who is known as *Mahā-Kālī*, *Nitya-Kālī*, *Śmaśāna-Kālī*, *Rakṣā-Kālī*, and *Śyāmā-Kālī*. *Mahā-Kālī* and *Nitya-Kālī* are mentioned in the Tantra philosophy. When there were neither the creation, nor the sun, the moon, the planets, and the earth, and when darkness was enveloped in darkness, then the Mother, the Formless One, *Mahā-Kālī*, the Great Power, was one with *Mahā-Kāla*, the Absolute.**

***Śyāmā-Kālī* has a somewhat tender aspect and is worshipped in the Hindu households. She is the Dispenser of boons and the Dispeller of fear. People worship *Rakṣā-Kālī*, the Protectress, in times of epidemic, famine, earthquake, drought, and flood. *Śmaśāna-Kālī* is the embodiment of the power of destruction. She resides in the cremation ground, surrounded by corpses, jackals, and terrible female**

spirits. From Her mouth flows a stream of blood, from Her neck hangs a garland of human heads, and around Her waist is a girdle made of human hands. (p.135) Kālī, or *Śakti*, works in various ways, and according to her different aspects, various kinds of Kālī images have been created.

After the destruction of the universe, at the end of the great cycle, the Divine Mother garners the seeds for the next creation. (p.135) Creation, preservation, destruction—all these are Her activities. When there is destruction, when the world is destroyed, she carefully preserves the seeds of creation. **She is like the elderly mistress of the house, who has a hotch-potch pot in which she keeps different articles for household use**. In it are found **'sea-foam', blue pills, small bundles of seeds of cucumber, pumpkin, and gourd, and so on. She takes them out when she wants them**. Afterwards she plants those seeds in the earth and from those seeds, plants appear again. **After the destruction of the universe, my Divine Mother, the Embodiment of Brahman, gathers together the seeds for the next creation.** (p.135) Then she again creates a new world from them.

Sri Ramakrishna said, **It is the process of evolution and involution.** (p.328) We call it involution when She withdraws the world, when it is destroyed, and evolution when She creates, as if expanding Herself. The Spider with its own saliva constructs the web and then withdraws it into itself. In the same way the processes of evolution and involution go on. The Primal Energy or Kālī, manifests Herself, and then She goes into an unmanifested state. Sri Ramakrishna said, **After the creation the Primal Power dwells in the Universe itself. She brings forth this phenomenal world and then pervades it.** (p.135) It is She who has created the world and living beings, and She is in the world and living beings. *Tat* *sṛṣṭvā tadevānuprāviśat*—'Having created all this, He entered into it.'[11]

In the Hindu scriptures, there are many attempts to explain Brahman, and Brahman is viewed from various angles. Sometimes It is said to be the Instrumental Cause and also the Material Cause of the world. For example, take a wooden table. A carpenter made it—he was the instrumental cause. Then again, the table is made of wood—the wood is the material cause. Here the material cause and the instrumental cause are different. But in regard to the world, God is both the Instrumental Cause and the Material Cause. He has created this world and living beings through His *māyā*, and again, His *māyā* is the material of which this world and living beings are made.

Sri Ramakrishna gives the highest conception of Brahman when he says: **He alone has become father and mother, child and neighbour, man and animal, good and bad, holy and unholy, and so forth.** (p.328) This is in agreement with a verse from the *Śvetāśvatara Upaniṣad* :

> *Tvaṁ strī tvaṁ pumānasi*
> *Tvaṁ kumāra uta vā kumārī;*
> *Tvaṁ jīrṇo daṇḍena vañcasi*
> *Tvaṁ jāto bhavasi viśvatomukhah*—

'Thou art woman, Thou art man; Thou art youth and maiden too. Thou as an old man totterest along on a staff; it is Thou alone who, when born, assumest diverse forms.'[12] One day at Belur Math Swamiji was discussing this concept. As he talked he became so inspired that, looking at those seated in front of him, he exclaimed, 'There is Brahman! There is Brahman!' All those present then had the same realization. They felt that Brahman was everywhere, that God was actually present.

It is said, *Jīvo brahmaiva nāparaḥ*—'The individual soul is verily Brahman.' We bow down to God in the temple. Then seeing someone we say, *Namaskār*!—'Salutations!' Why do we say this? Because Brahman is present in everyone. We salute Him who is in the person. We try to see God in everyone because He in fact dwells in everyone. He is in the good, and He is in the most despicable sinner. The Master said, **I know that just as God takes the form of holy men, so He also takes the form of cheats and rogues. . . . All are God.** (p.766)

Swamiji used the expression, 'God the wicked, God the sinner'. Who can I ignore? If I see a person merely as a human being, I might question whether he is good or bad, pure or impure. But if I see God in that person, how can I look down on or hate him? We hear the words *same-sightedness, equality*, etc., but there will be true same-sightedness or equality only when people learn to see God in all creatures.

Sri Ramakrishna said, **Once, while listening to the various incidents of the life of Caitanya, Hazra said that these were manifestations of *Śakti*, and that Brahman, the All-pervasive Spirit, had nothing to do with them. But can there be *Śakti* without Brahman? Hazra wants to nullify the teachings of this place.** (p.550) (He did not like to use the words *I* and *my*, so he would say instead, 'the teachings of this place', e.g.) In Sri Ramakrishna's view, could there be *Śakti* without God? Hazra had said that in the play of *Śakti*, there was no God. He accepted *Śakti* but rejected Brahman. He accepted the Relative but not the Absolute. Sri Ramakrishna said that this was not right. Without the Absolute there cannot be the Relative. Without Brahman there cannot be *Śakti*.

It must be noted that Brahman and *Śakti* are not equal. Although *Śakti* cannot exist without Brahman, Brahman does not depend on *Śakti* or anything else, as the ocean does not depend for its existence on the waves. We generally think of *Śakti* in its manifest state, as waves, but the ocean is the same whether it has waves or not. It can become perfectly calm and waveless; at that time, the waves are only potentially present. In the same way, *Śakti* is sometimes in a potential state in Brahman; then there is no creation—no world, no creatures. Śaṅkara confirms this when he says, 'The waves belong to the ocean, but the ocean does not belong to the waves.' Brahman always is, though it is not always manifesting Itself through *māyā*.

Brahman is the eternal substratum of the world. Philosophers call It the *Ground*. The book is on the table. It cannot rest on nothing. It must be on something, so it is on the table. The table is the *Ground*. In the ocean many waves rise and break, but there is the *ground*, the substratum of the waves, and that is the ocean. There is another illustration : At the cinema, pictures are projected on the screen. We see many things happening, but at the back of all this movement is something which does not move—the screen, the substratum. In the same way, many things are happening in this world, but in back of everything there is one unchangeable substance. We call It Brahman. He is the Eternal Substratum, the Absolute. Because of Him, the Relative, (*Līlā*) comes into being.

Again, Sri Ramakrishna says, **God exists in every being as the All-pervading Spirit. He is in the ant as well as in me.** (p.625) Why are there so many variations in nature (*Prakṛti*)? Why do we find one person so different from another? Because, **There are different manifestations of His Power in different beings.** (p.625) **It is He, undoubtedly, who has become everything; but in some cases there is a greater manifestation than in others.** (p.319)

In a stone there is very little manifestation, as it is inanimate. In a person there is a much greater manifestation because he is a human being. Furthermore, there are beings like Buddha, Caitanya, Jesus Christ, Sri Ramakrishna, who are His highest manifestations. They are called *Avatāras*. They are, in reality, the same God, the one Brahman, though in different forms. Vidyasagar once asked Sri Ramakrishna if God had given some people more power than others. Sri Ramakrishna replied, 'Why is it that we have come to see you? Have you grown two horns?' Though in reality everything is one, we must acknowledge that there are differences in manifestation. **It is said in the *Gītā* that if a man is respected and honoured by many, whether it be for his scholarship or his music or his oratory or anything else, then you may know for certain that he is endowed with a special divine power.** (p.625)

Śrī Kṛṣṇa said to Arjuna:

Yad yad vibhūtimat sattvaṁ śrīmadūrjitameva vā
Tattadevāvagaccha tvaṁ mama tejo'ṁśasambhavam—

'Whatever being there is endowed with glory, grace or power, know that to have sprung from but a spark of My splendour.'[13]

In revealing His own nature to Arjuna Śrī Kṛṣṇa said:

Ahamātmā guḍākeśa sarvabhūtāśayasthitaḥ
Ahamādiśca madhyaṁ ca bhūtānāṁ anta eva ca—

'I, O Guḍākeśa, am the self seated in the hearts of all creatures. I am the beginning, the middle and the very end of beings.' I am ageless and immortal. Many living beings come and go, but I exist eternally.

Ādityānāmahaṁ viṣṇurjyotiṣāṁ raviraṁśumān
Marīcirmarutāmasmi nakṣatrāṇāmahaṁ śaśī—

'Among the Ādityas (a group of heavenly beings), I am Viṣṇu. Of the luminaries, the radiant sun. Of the Vāyus, I am Marīci. Among the night-luminaries, I am the moon.'

Vedānāṁ sāmavedo'smi devānāmasmi vāsavaḥ
Indriyāṇāṁ manaścāsmi bhūtānāmasmi cetanā—

'Among the Vedas, I am the Sāma. Among the gods, I am Indra [the king of gods]. Of the senses, I am the mind. Among living beings, I exist in the form of consciousness.'[14]

Whatever is great, whatever is beautiful, it is His power that is manifested. *Tasya bhāsā sarvamidaṁ vibhāti*—'By His light all this is lighted.'[15]

Sri Ramakrishna said: 'When rice, potatoes and eggplant are put in a pot and placed over a fire, the water boils and bubbles up, making the vegetables dance about. Little children seeing this believe the vegetables are alive, but the truth is, it is the fire beneath the pot that is making them dance. They cannot move by their own will. If the fire is removed, the rice, potatoes and eggplant will no longer dance about.' In the same way, **Men are powerful because of the power of God. All becomes quiet when the burning wood is taken away.** (p.893)

In the *Kaṭha Upaniṣad* it is said:

Bhayādasyāgnistapati bhayāttapati sūryaḥ
Bhayādindraśca vāyuśca mṛtyurdhāvati pañcamaḥ—

'For fear of Him, fire burns; for fear of Him, the sun shines. For fear of Him, Indra and Vāyu, and Death, the fifth, run.'[16] They all receive their power to work from His Power. Even Indra and Vāyu, the King of the gods and the god of the wind, are powerful because of His Power. This Upaniṣad also says that the sense-organs carry out their functions because He is in back of them. These eyes do not see; behind them are other eyes. These ears do not hear; behind them are other ears. All the sense-organs perform their actions with Him behind them.

In reality, all power ultimately comes from Him, just as the electricity that illumines our lights and makes our fans revolve comes from the power-plant. If the power-plant shuts off the supply of power, the lights don't come on, and the fan doesn't revolve. In the same way, all the many activities of our ever-changing world are carried on through the Power of God. He is the Power-plant. Whether I know it or not, whether I have faith in it or not, I am always ruled by that Power. Those who understand this and are able to see clearly that behind them is that eternal Power, can do the impossible. Their self-confidence and mental strength go on increasing day by day.

We can see this in the life of Jesus Christ. He was poorer than the poorest. His only disciples were a few fishermen. He endured so much suffering and allowed Himself to be crucified. Yet today He is victorious everywhere. The Christian religion has spread all over the earth because the Power of God is behind it.

In this age we find the same thing in Sri Ramakrishna's life. He was poor, almost illiterate, yet scholars showed him much respect. Today he has many devotees all over the world. Not only Hindus, but people of all religions honour and accept him. It is really true that if you rely on God completely, under all circumstances, you can accomplish seemingly impossible things, because the Power of God becomes manifest in you.

When Swami Vivekananda went to the first session of the Parliament of Religions in Chicago, he was an unknown monk. He gave a short talk, and by the end of the evening he had become famous. After that everyone knew about him. He himself had said, 'One day I will burst upon society like a bomb.' And he did burst like a bomb. This one man aroused the entire country of India from sleep. Today we find he is arousing the whole world. How did he make the impossible possible? It was through the Power of God. Swamiji once said, 'I am aware of a great power behind me—a power greater than any man or any thing.' By the force of that power he accomplished the impossible.

The great German monk, Meister Eckhart, said, 'If someone tells me to carry stones, he could tell me to carry a thousand stones—if he intends to do it all himself. . . . God wants to do your work Himself, and will if you will only obey and resist Him not at all. Let your soul stay where it belongs and then everything will be with you.'[17] Your heart and mind should always be at His feet. That is 'where they belong'. Then you will find everything coming to you. Suddenly everything will be as it should be. He will make you an instrument for His work. You will be the machine; He will be the operator of the machine. He will gather everything needed for His work and place it in your hands. Then the impossible will become possible for you. In reality, the words possible and impossible apply only in the life of the world. They do not apply to Him.

Jesus Christ said, 'If you have faith in God, you can move mountains.' One day Sri Ramakrishna said, 'Mother, if all my visions are true, then let me see this stone jump three times.' And the stone did jump three times. What is meant by these incidents? These great teachers are telling us that for those who completely rely on God and love Him, the impossible becomes possible. Their will becomes joined to God's will and the power of God is manifested in them. In the midst of a hundred blows they are unmoved; in spite of countless obstacles they continue on their way.

Swamiji said, 'You may be a little bubble, someone else a big wave, but behind you both is the same ocean.' The same source of all power is behind everyone. Anyone can be united with that source and become great. Swamiji said that the aim of his life was to teach everyone their essential divinity, to make them understand that they are not small, they are not ordinary, they are not weak. 'You are perfect. You are God. You are Brahman.'

An American teacher once said to me, 'You preach religion at the Ramakrishna Mission, but what social work do you do?' I answered him briefly, telling him some of the things we were doing. Then I said, 'Look, our country has many needs. Compared to those needs, our work is not very large, but we are working. To use the words of Swamiji, we are trying to arouse people's faith in themselves, their self-confidence. We tell them that they are not dependent on anyone. Yes, it is true there are many problems, but the question is, how can we get the power to solve them. No one can solve our problems for us.' Then I said to him, 'The central principle of religion is faith in one's own self. We teach people that they are not poor or weak. They have the support of God, and by His grace they can do the impossible. Trusting in God and relying on Him does not mean running away from life's struggles. It means facing life with great strength and courage.'

Swamiji said, 'If you gave the wealth of the whole world to one poor village, even then there would be no improvement in its miserable condition if the people in that village lacked confidence in themselves.' There is undoubtedly much monetary aid coming to our country today from foreign countries, but we don't know how that money is being used.

There are reports that it is not being used wisely. If someone puts money in my hand and I have no faith in myself, if I am not self-reliant, I will not be able to use that money wisely. The Ramakrishna Mission tries to arouse people's self-confidence, because that confidence in themselves gives them great power. And that power is the Power of God.

I once read an article about Hitler's tyrannical regime. Many people were confined in his concentration camps where various kinds of torture were used. They were given so little to eat that many became emaciated and died. Among those who stayed alive, those who had faith in God were always praying. And not only praying—they would give some of their own meagre pieces of bread and watery soup to those who were weak, sick or old. They had to do this secretly; because if they were discovered the guards would beat them. But still they continued to give, risking their lives. They had that much inner strength. They gave courage to others and tried to tell them the truths of religion. Despite dangers and against all odds, power comes to those who rely completely on God. *Dharma* (religion) has been defined as 'that which holds fast'—meaning that it gives one power and strength. Real greatness does not mean physical strength; it means strength of mind and soul.

Many great civilizations of the past—Greek, Roman and others—were destroyed, yet the Indian civilization is still living. Many blows were inflicted on this country, still it survives. What is the secret? It is that this country, this civilization, has stood firm on the foundation of *dharma*. It has always given the highest place to the power of the Self, to the power of God.

Several years ago I met a German gentleman who had come to this country. In the course of conversation I asked him, 'Are you going to Durgapur?' He said, 'Durgapur! What is there?' I answered that there was a big steel plant there. Then the gentleman laughed and said, 'Swamiji, you have probably forgotten that I come from Germany. There are huge steel plants there. No, Swamiji, I did not come to your country to see all that. I have travelled in many countries and seen many things. Instead of Durgapur, take me to Kamarpukur where the real power of India is stored. In your temples and mosques is still the power which has kept your country alive for thousands and thousands of years. If I can carry back even a small fraction of that power, my coming so far will not have been in vain. That is why I have come to your country.'

Swami Vivekananda once said, 'The life of India is in its spirituality.' In age after age, many people born in this land have renounced everything for God, and this is why India still lives in spite of the many, many blows it has received. India must continue to live because it has this message to give to the world—that behind this material world is something much more real. It is that One Reality which moves the entire universe through Its Power. Through the strength of that Power, India still lives.

Swamiji said, 'India will rise again.' And when India rises, it will not be by the power of physical might, but by the power of Consciousness, of spirituality. So before everything, India must be flooded with a deluge of spirituality which will manifest its power in everything. That Power is the manifestation (*Śakti*) of Brahman. Taking refuge in the Power, India will rise, and with it, the whole world.

References

1. *Chāndogya Upaniṣad*, VI.2.3; *Taittirīya Upaniṣad*, II.6; *Aitareya Upaniṣad*, I.1.1
2. *Amṛtabindu-Upaniṣad*, 12
3. *Dṛg-dṛśya Viveka*, 20
4. *Chāndogya Upaniṣad*, VI.1.4
5. *Śvetāśvatara Upaniṣad*, 1.3
6. *Līlāprasaṅga*, 1st part, 'In the Mood of a Teacher', 1st half, p.262
7. *Śaṅkara Bhāṣya, Brahma Sūtra*, I.4.3
8. *Brahmavaivarta Purāṇa* (Kṛṣṇajanma Khaṇḍa), 73, 46-47
9. *Ibid*., 73.46
10. *Śvetāśvatara Upaniṣad*, IV.10
11. *Taittirīya Upaniṣad*, II.6
12. *Śvetāśvatara Upaniṣad*, IV.3
13. *Gītā*, X.41
14. *Ibid*., X.20-22
15. *Śvetāśvatara Upanisad*, VI.14
16. *Kaṭha Upaniṣad*, II.3.3
17. *Meister Eckhart, A Modern Translation*, Raymond Bernard Blakney, 1941, p.135

IV

The Unripe I and the Ripe I

In the *Gospel* we find Sri Ramakrishna using two expressions again and again, the 'unripe I' and the 'ripe I' (*Kāncā āmi and pākā āmi*). These words are Sri Ramakrishna's coinage. No one before had used them. We find him using these words also while speaking to Keshab Sen, leader of the Brāhmo Samaj. He himself narrated the incident:

I said to Keshab: "'I" and "mine" indicate ignorance. Without ignorance one cannot have such a feeling as "I am the doer; these are my wife, children, possessions, name and fame." Thereupon Keshab said, "Sir, if one gave up the 'I', nothing whatsoever would remain." I reassured him and said: "I am not asking you to give up all of the 'I'. You should give up only the 'unripe I'. The 'unripe I' makes one feel: 'I am the doer. These are my wife and children. I am a teacher.' Renounce this 'unripe I' and keep the 'ripe I', which will make you feel that you are the servant of God, His devotee, and that God is the Doer and you are His instrument.'" (p.269)

To feel united with God—that is the 'ripe I'. One thinks, 'I am His servant, I am His child, I am His parent.' Or one can say, 'I am He.' These all indicate the 'ripe I'. But the pride of learning, of wealth, of virtuousness, of family or position is the 'unripe I'. This is sheer egotism.

This 'unripe I' is everything to us, but this 'I' is not free. It is enclosed within the bonds of the body, mind and intellect. We are unaware that there is another 'I' beyond this bound 'I'. Yet it is only because of the existence of this other 'I', the 'ripe I' that the body, mind and intellect are able to do their allotted duties. The 'unripe I' says, 'I am doing everything.' This is ignorance. In reality I am the 'ripe I', the Supreme Being. The 'ripe I' is real, eternal; the 'unripe I' is impermanent, ephemeral. It may disintegrate today or tomorrow; it may disintegrate after a few births, but it will be destroyed because it is non-eternal. If it breaks down quickly, so much the better, because that 'I', the 'unripe I', the insignificant 'I', is the source of all our suffering.

In the *Muṇḍaka Upaniṣad* there is the imagery of two birds. They look alike, and they are seated in the same tree. One is sitting still. There are various kinds of fruit on the tree, but he doesn't eat them. He just sits quietly; he is at peace, satisfied in his own Self. And thc other bird? He restlessly jumps from one branch to another. He is always on the go and impatient. Whenever he eats a sweet fruit, he is happy; whenever he eats a bitter fruit, naturally he is unhappy. But still he continues to eat the fruit—sometimes bitter, sometimes sweet.

A human being (*jīva*) is like this bird. How many sweet and bitter experiences he has to go through! The other bird is the Supreme Self, free from attachment. He is the witness, always unperturbed, withdrawn from worldly life. The joys and sorrows of the world cannot touch him. Both birds are in reality, one. The *jīva* (the individual self) is nothing but Brahman or Ātman (the Supreme Self), but because of ignorance, he thinks he is different from Brahman—that is, from his own true Self. Impelled by desires, he imposes his ego, his 'unripe I', on his true Self. Worldly life then binds him. He does not know that he is the eternal, free, blissful Brahman. He has forgotten his real self, the 'ripe I'. So he gets involved in the affairs of the world, its happiness and misery. The 'unripe I' is not my true self; my true self is that 'ripe I'.

Sri Ramakrishna says: **The 'servant ego', the 'Knowledge ego', or the 'devotee ego' may be called the 'ripe ego'. It is different from the 'unripe ego', which makes one feel: 'I am the doer, I am the son of a wealthy man. I am learned. I am rich. How dare anyone slight me?' A man with an 'unripe ego' cherishes such ideas.** (p.860) Putting yourself first, thinking you are very special—these are signs of the 'unripe ego'.

A Sanskrit verse says, *Ahaṁkārasya dve vṛttī ahantā mamatā ceti*—'Two propensities arise from egotism, "I-ness" and "my-ness"'.[1] 'I' and 'mine'—'I do,' not 'We do'; 'My house', not 'Our house'. Egotistical people do not like to say 'We', but always 'I'—never plural, always singular—'I' and 'Mine'. Sri Ramakrishna did not like the words, 'I' and 'My'. He said, 'Saying "our" is good; saying "I" and "My" is not.' He liked a humble attitude: **It is only the humble man who attains Knowledge. In a low place, rain-water collects. It runs down from a mound.** (p.633)

The Knowledge the Master referred to means Self-Knowledge, knowing your true identity. The 'ripe I', the 'I' of the child or servant of God, leads to Self-Knowledge, to liberation. The 'unripe I', the proud 'I', is the cause of bondage; it keeps us from knowing our true Self, God.

It keeps us away from the true joy we could find in God. God Himself wants to dwell in my heart, but I have installed myself there, dressed with great pomp and display. When God arrives He finds there is no place for Him, so He goes away. This is why Rabindranath has said, 'Break open the door and come into my heart.' My nature is such that I keep the door shut, but don't go away, Lord. Push open the door and enter my heart. Shatter my ego, my 'I'.

But this 'unripe I', this ego, is not easy to get rid of. Sri Ramakrishna says that you can reason a thousand times, still the ego remains. He uses the illustration of the peepal tree: You may cut off a branch from the peepal tree, but in a few days you will find a sprout coming from the place where it was cut. Egotism is like that. In how many ways it appears! Suppose you get rid of the ego through reason. You believe it to be gone, but soon you discover it is back in its place. This egotism comes from many sources—from being handsome or beautiful, from being a good musician, from scholarship, etc. There is also religious egotism, the 'holier than thou' attitude: 'I am more spiritually advanced than others.' This self-righteous religious egotism is very subtle, and for that reason the most difficult of all egotisms to get rid of. It makes one think, 'Mine is the only path to Truth' and leads to self-deception. It takes one far from the path to God.

Modesty can be another source of pride. Real modesty comes from within, it is spontaneous. If it is a matter of display, it is ludicrous. Modesty is good, but egotism can bring about an immodest pride in one's own modesty. The 'unripe I' is extremely crafty and difficult to eradicate.

Rabindranath has given a good picture of egotism in his poem about the *Rathayātrā*:

Rathayātrā, vast crowd, great pageantry—
Devotees do obeisance, rolling in the dirt on the road.
The road thinks, 'I am being worshipped'
The chariot thinks, 'It is I.'
The idol thinks, 'I am the Lord.'—the Inner Self smiles.

A Gujarati poem says: 'The dog trots in the shadow of the bullock-cart thinking that he is pulling it, not knowing that it is the bullock who is pulling the cart.' In the same way, behind all our efforts is the power of God. Not even a leaf moves without His will. Still, because of our egotism, we think we do everything.

A story from the *Kena Upanisad* tells about a war between the gods and the demons. The gods won and were very happy, but they became egotistical thinking they were more powerful than anyone. Suddenly a strange figure appeared. No one knew who or what it could be, so Indra, the King of the gods, sent Agni, the god of fire, to find out. As Agni approached the figure, it asked, 'Who are you? What can you do?' Agni said by way of introducing himself, 'I can burn anything to ashes.' The figure said, 'Is that so? Let me see you burn this straw.' Agni thought, 'This is no test at all!' He was sure he would be able to burn the straw. But though he tried very hard, he was unable to burn it. Hanging his head in shame, he returned to Indra.

Indra then sent Vāyu, the god of wind. The figure also showed him a straw and asked him to blow it away. But Vāyu could not budge it, and he too hung his head and left. Indra then decided that he must go himself. As he approached that strange figure, it suddenly vanished and in its place a goddess appeared. It was Umā, daughter of the Himalayas. She said to Indra, 'The figure you saw was Brahman. It is the source of everything. You thought you won your battle against the demons by your own power. You were mistaken; you won by the power of Brahman.' All our power comes from Brahman, yet: *Ahaṁkāravimūḍhātmā kartāhamiti manyate*—'With the understanding clouded by egotism, man thinks, "I am the doer".'[2]

This egotism, which comes from ignorance of our true Self, makes us think that we do everything, and there is no end to the ways that it asserts itself. When there is praise for something that has happened, we eagerly claim that we did it. But when something turns out badly, when there is an error or some disgrace, then someone else is responsible. If we can't find anyone else, then 'It is Thou, O Lord!' Sri Ramakrishna used to tell about the Brahmin who took the credit for making a beautiful flower garden, but wanted to lay his sin of killing a cow on Indra.

We are constantly engaged in a competition of 'I's, one ego clashing with another. As Swamiji said, 'Only "I", "I"—this way egotism is always active.' This 'I' runs through everything we do.

All our desires express themselves in the form of 'I'—'I want to eat well,' 'I want to dress well,' etc. Swamiji said, 'Our desires arise in beautiful forms. They have great power. They are like a river in flood, all centred around "I".' It is desires that keep our 'unripe I' alive. If there were no desires, there would be no birth or death; and that would be liberation, *mukti*—the end of all sorrow. Sri Ramakrishna says, **All troubles come to an end when the ego dies.** (p.168) And he links egotism with *māyā*: ***Māyā* is nothing but the egotism of the embodied soul. This egotism has covered everything like a veil.** (p.168)

Then he says: **The *jīva* is nothing but the embodiment of *Saccidānanda*. But since *māyā*, or ego, has created various *upādhi*s, he has forgotten his real Self.**

Each *upādhi* changes man's nature. If he wears a fine black-bordered cloth, you will at once find him humming Nidhu Babu's love-songs. Then playing-cards and a walking stick follow. If even a sickly man puts on high

boots, he begins to whistle and climbs the stairs like an Englishman, jumping from one step to another.

Sri Ramakrishna continues his discussion of egotism **Money is also a great *upādhi.* The possession of money makes such a difference in a man! He is no longer the same person. . . . A frog had a rupee, which he kept in his hole. One day an elephant was going over the hole, and the frog, coming out in a fit of anger, raised his foot, as if to kick the elephant, and said, 'How dare you walk over my head?' Such is the pride that money begets!** (p.169)

A Brahmin who was very modest and respectful to Sri Ramakrishna used to frequent the Dakshineswar Temple Garden. Then one day Sri Ramakrishna went to Konnagar with Hriday and met that Brahmin on the ghat of the Gaṅgā. Seeing Sri Ramakrishna, the Brahmin called out, **'Hello there priest! How do you do?'** When the Master heard his tone of voice he said to Hriday, **The man must have got some money. That's why he talks that way.** (p.169) His previous modesty had disappeared. Egotism causes this kind of change in behaviour. Success can also be a cause of egotism, changing a sweet and simple person into a disagreeable boor. He begins to think that no one knows as much as he does, that no one is superior to him.

This is how egotism is playing all the time. As the 'unripe I', it deceives and entangles us in so many ways that it is impossible to list them all. The only way to get out of this bondage is to take refuge in God. Take refuge in Him and say, 'Thou art All, I am nothing.'

People today are thought to be exceptionally egocentric, but people have always been egocentric. If a man's ego is offended, the man immediately reacts. He hits back. He may even disown a long-standing friend because of a wounded ego. I know of an incident in which this actually happened.

Two long-time friends were going on a pilgrimage to Manas-Sarovar, a holy place in Tibet. One of our monks was with them. After spending the night at an inn, they were preparing to continue their journey. As they folded up their bedding, one friend said to the other,

'Why did you take my string?'

'Why did I take your string? That is *my* string.'

'How can that be your string? It is *my* string.'

Friends sometimes quarrel like this and then are soon reconciled. In this case, however, they became more and more hostile. The second friend sat down and said, 'You are calling me a thief?' Then they stopped speaking to each other.

The monk came in at this moment and saw what had happened. He tried to reason with the two, but they refused to speak to each other. Seeing that their feelings were hurt, he prepared some food for them, but one of the friends would not eat. He walked outside and sat down. It was late before they could continue their pilgrimage—the delay caused everyone much inconvenience. A tactless remark, and a long-standing friendship was broken—all because of egotism. Sri Ramakrishna says that egotism is *māyā*, and *māyā* is inexplicable. We do not know why this 'unripe I' is always with us.

Sri Ramakrishna says: **This *māyā*, that is to say, the ego, is like a cloud. The sun cannot be seen on account of a thin patch of cloud; when that disappears one sees the sun.** (p.169) The sun, that is, *Saccidānanda*, is within us. God is always here, but because of our ego he seems to be hidden, as the cloud hides the sun. We see the sun. when the cloud is blown away. In the same way, **If by the grace of the guru one's ego vanishes, then one sees God.** (p.169)

In the Upaniṣads we find:

Sarvājīve sarvasaṁsthe bṛhante
asmin haṁso bhrāmyate brahmacakre
Pṛthagātmānaṁ preritāraṁ ca matvā
juṣṭastatastenāmṛtatvameti

'In the great wheel of Brahman, in which all things abide and finally take rest, The *jīva* wanders about so long as it thinks that it is separate from the Controller. When blessed by Him, the Self attains Immortality.'[3]

Why do I who am in Brahman's Circle suffer so much. It is because I imagine that I am separate from the Ātman, Brahman; I myself am Brahman; still I don't understand this. I am infinite, eternal—yet *māyā* leads me to believe that I am limited, finite. Psychologists use the word *alienation*—being foreigners (aliens) to our own self. That is exactly the case. Or you can say that we are like a star fallen from its orbit; we are out of place. We feel there is something wrong, but we don't know exactly what it is. The problem is that I am eternal, pure, awakened, free, and perfect—still I think I am bound. This is due to *māyā*, the 'unripe I', the ego.

Sri Ramakrishna says: **The intervention of this ego creates the difference between the *jīva* and Ātman. Water appears to be divided into two parts if one puts a stick across it. But in reality there is only one water. It appears as two on account of the stick. This 'I' is the stick. Remove the stick and there remains only one**

water as before. (p.170) Get rid of the 'unripe I' and you will find yourself in the Self, the Ātman—no difference will remain.

According to the *Vedāntasāra*: *Ayaṁ kartṛtva - bhoktṛtva - sukhitva - duḥkhitva - ādi - abhimānitvena ihaloka - paralokagāmī vyavahāriko jīva iti ucyate*—'It is the *jīva*, the embodied being, which says, "I am working," "I am enjoying," "I am happy," "I am unhappy," etc. It has this egotism. It is with us at birth and because of it we must be reborn.'[4]

As long as this 'I-consciousness' persists, my 'I' is the *Jīva*. When it vanishes, my 'I' becomes Śiva. The Tantras explain this clearly:

Dve pade bandhamokṣāya mameti nirmameti ca
Mameti badhyate janturna mameti vimucyate—

'There are two things. One is bondage, the other liberation. Bondage comes through consciousness of "I" and "my", the sense of attachment. And liberation comes through non-attachment'.[5]

Sri Ramakrishna says again and again that the 'I' should be trampled on and destroyed like rubbish. We understand that. The problem is, how to get rid of this terrible 'I'. The Master tells us how. He says that the 'I' need not be destroyed, but make that rascal the servant of God, or His child. Or, if you are a non-dualist, you can say, 'I am God Himself.' Thus your 'I' becomes the 'ripe I'.

This does not injure anyone. Sweet things cause acidity of the stomach, no doubt, but sugar candy is an exception. . . . The 'servant I'—that is the feeling, 'I am the servant of God, I am the devotee of God'—does not injure one. On the contrary, it helps one to realize God. (pp.170-71)

Now the question arose: **What becomes of the lust, anger, and other passions of one who keeps the 'servant I'?** Sri Ramakrishna said: **If a man truly feels like that, then he has only the semblance of lust, anger and the like. If, after attaining God, he looks on himself as the servant or devotee of God, then he cannot injure anyone. By touching the philosopher's stone a sword is turned into gold. It keeps the appearance of a sword but cannot injure. . . .**

The devotee says: 'O God, Thou art the Master and I am Thy servant; Thou art the Lord and I am Thy devotee.' He feels that way even after the realization of God. His 'I' is not completely effaced. Again, by constantly practising this kind of 'I-consciousness', one ultimately attains God. (p.171)

This is an important truth. Even after attaining God, you still have your 'I', but it is the'ripe-I', the 'servant-I'. However, until you attain God, you should practise the 'ripe-I' as a spiritual discipline. You should constantly remind yourself, 'I am God's servant and He is my Master,' or 'God is my Mother and I am Her child.' **This is called *Bhaktiyoga*.** (p.171) If you keep practising this way, you will attain God.

The path of Knowledge—'I am the eternal, pure, awakened, free Self; I am the witness, unattached, actionless'—is comparatively difficult. But whether you follow the path of Knowledge or the path of Devotion, you must have the conviction that 'I am not the doer.' The devotee says, 'I do not do anything; You do everything.' 'I am the machine; You are the operator of the machine.' Those following the path of Knowledge think, 'I am the actionless Self; I do not do anything.' These are the two different manifestations of the 'ripe ego'.

Sri Ramakrishna says, **'Thinking "I am the doer" is ignorance. But "O Lord, Thou art the driver and I am the machine"—This is knowledge.' If by the grace of God, a man but once realizes that he is not the doer, then he at once becomes a *jīvanmukta*. Though living in the body, he is liberated. He has nothing else to fear.** (p.169) The devotee thinks, 'Whatever you give me to do, I will do. As you move me, so will I work. I am nothing, You are everything. I have no existence apart from you.'[6]

Sri Ramakrishna used to sing,

> **O Mother, all is done after Thine own sweet will;**
> **Thou art in truth Self-willed, Redeemer of mankind!**
> **Thou workest Thine own work; men only call it theirs.**
> (p.818)

He said: **A true devotee says 'O God, Thou alone art the Doer. All these—wealth, possessions, nay, the universe itself—belong to Thee. This house and these relatives are Thine alone, not mine. I am Thy servant; mine is only the right to serve Thee according to Thy bidding.** (pp.900-01)

It is the complete denial of our egotistical self that is demanded of us. A Muslim poet has written, 'The inn is full of people. Rahim [God] has come. He sees that the inn is full and goes away, disappointed.' The inn is our heart. God tries to enter, but He sees that we are sitting there ourselves in great pomp, so He goes away. The 17th Century monk, Brother Lawrence, knew how important it was to give up our egotistical selves completely. He says in *The Practice of the Presence of God*, 'We must devote ourselves to Him in good earnest, casting everything else out of our hearts; He wishes to be alone therein.'[7] We must make our hearts completely empty, then He will enter. God loves to be alone in us. He cannot endure to have someone else there. He cannot endure our egotism. Sri Ramakrishna says that if there is even a little fiber sticking out of the thread, it cannot go through the eye of the needle. If there is even a trace of egotism, you cannot attain God. Jesus Christ wanted his followers to give up all ego. He said, 'If any man will follow me, let him first deny himself.'[8]

Swami Vivekananda revealed his own lack of egotism when he wrote in a letter, 'Do I plan what work I will do? No, I do not.' Then he continued, 'I am Mother's child. She works, She plays. Why should I plan? What should I plan? Things came and went just as She liked, without my planning.'[9] When he returned from his first trip to America and went to offer his *praṇāms* to Holy Mother, she said, 'Child, no one else could do what you have done.' Swamiji replied, 'What nonsense! Have you not done all I have done? By a mere wish, you can create lakhs of Vivekanandas like me. Do I not know that?'[10]

Sri Ramakrishna was so lacking in egotism that he rarely used the word 'my'. Instead of saying 'my words' or 'my views', he would say, 'the words of this place', or 'the views of this place'. Swami Saradananda has written about Sri Ramakrishna's attitude toward egotism in his book, *Sri Ramakrishna The Great Master*:

> Always depending entirely like a boy on the universal Mother in all respects, the Master had a reliance upon Her, so easy, natural and inward, that he felt a great pain to see or hear any person doing or intending to do anything under the impulse of egoism, let alone himself doing anything that way. Therefore, besides using the word 'I' as a servant of God on rare occasions, he could never use that word in any other mood, as we do. Anyone who saw the Master even for a short time was charmed and astonished to see that trait of his, or to see his

great annoyance at such apparently harmless egotistic expressions used by any one else as 'I'll do such and such an action.' He would be led to wonder what great offence he had committed to provoke such annoyance.[11]

Sri Ramakrishna even scolded the highly revered leader of the Bengal Vaiṣṇava community, Bhagavan Das Babaji, for his egotism. When he and Hriday went to see him, the Master did not at first introduce himself, but stood behind Hriday. He noticed that Babaji was scolding a Vaiṣṇava monk and threatening to expel him from the community.

After they were seated, Hriday asked Babaji, 'Sir, since you are a perfected soul, why do you keep using your rosary?' Babaji replied, 'It is not for myself, but to teach others.' Sri Ramakrishna had not liked Babaji's threat to expel the monk. Now when he heard Babaji talking about teaching people, he could no longer restrain himself and became very angry. Standing up, he said to Babaji, 'What? You will expel someone? You will give and you will take away? You will teach people? Who are you to teach anyone? If He whose world this is does not teach, you will teach!' As he continued to speak, he went into *samādhi*. Amazingly, Bhagavan Das Babaji was not offended at these words; rather, he listened respectfully. Even then, he did not know who Sri Ramakrishna was.

It is not only in our spiritual life that we must overcome our egotism, our self-centredness. In doing any kind of work, we must forget ourselves. The scientist is engrossed in his research. We say he 'loses himself' in his work. We do not use that expression lightly. 'Losing himself' means 'forgetting himself.' Forgetting himself, a scientist discovers many things.

We cannot live only in and for ourselves. The more we are able to forget ourselves, to open ourselves up to others, the more peaceful we become. The root of much of our suffering is this 'I'. As long as the little 'I' exists, **he comes back again and again to this world.** (p.633) When a person completely forgets this 'I', his sufferings are over. He no longer goes round again and again on the wheel of birth and death. He is liberated.

Sri Ramakrishna used the simile of a calf. **The misfortune that befalls a man on account of his egotism can be realized if you only think of the condition of the calf. The calf says, '*Hamma*! *Hamma*!', that is 'I! I!'. And just look at its misfortune! At times it is yoked to the plough and made to work in the field from sunup to sundown, rain or shine. Again, it may be slaughtered by the butcher. In that case the flesh is eaten and the skin tanned into hide. From the hide shoes are made. People put on these shoes and walk on rough ground. Still that is not the end of its misfortunes. Drums are made from its skin and mercilessly beaten with sticks. At last its entrails are made into strings for the bow used in carding cotton. When used by the carder the string gives the sound '*Tuhu*! *Tuhu*!', 'Thou! Thou!'—that is, 'It is Thou, O Lord! It is Thou!' It no longer says, '*Hamma*! *Hamma*!', 'I! I!' Only then does the calf's trouble come to an end, and it is liberated. It doesn't return to the world of action.** (p.451)

Likewise, when the embodied soul says: 'O God, I am not the doer; Thou art the Doer. I am the machine and Thou art its Operator', only then does its suffering of worldly life come to an end; only then does it obtain liberation. It no longer has to be reborn in this world of action. (p.451) When we find that constantly thinking 'I! I!' brings only suffering and more suffering, we at last completely surrender to the Lord saying, 'I have left everything in Your hands. Do what You will.' Peace come with this consciousness.

In all our work, in all our actions, we must practise this with all our strength of body, mind and soul: I am nothing, Lord, Thou art all. In place of 'I'— 'Thou'. Not 'I', but 'Thou'.

References

1. *Śrīmādhurya-kādambinī, Aṣṭamī Vṛṣṭiḥ*
2. *Gītā*, III.27
3. *Śvetāśvatara Upaniṣad*, I.6
4. *Vedāntasāra*, 73
5. *Kulārṇava Tantra*, I.111
6. *Gargasaṁhitā*, Aśvamedha khaṇḍa, 50.36
7. *The Practice of the Presence of God*, Brother Lawrence, Allahabad St. Paul Society, 1981, p.64
8. *St. Luke*, IXV.33
9. *C.W.*, Vol. VIII, 1977, p.517
10. *Śrī Śrī Sāradā Devī*, Brahmachari Aksayachaitanya, 1388, p.228
11. *Sri Ramakrishna the Great Master*, p. 579

V

Plunge Deep into the Ocean of Immortality

Sri Ramakrishna says, **This shrine of the body should not be left dark; one should illumine it with the lamp of wisdom.** (p.205) The human body is the holiest temple of all. Swamiji said that temples have been built for gods, but there is a better temple—a human being. A human being is the Taj Mahal of temples. That temple should not be left in darkness; a lamp must be kept lighted there—the lamp of knowledge.

Sri Ramakrishna says: 'How can you know if a person is rich? Lamps are lit in all the rooms. A poor person cannot afford to buy oil, so his rooms are dark.' On another occasion he said, **A house without light indicates poverty.** (p.174) In the same way, if the lamp of Knowledge is not lit in the temple of the body, that person is truly poor. He may be wealthy, he may be very influential; still he is poor. His 'house' is dark. His life is a failure. **One must light the lamp of Knowledge in one's heart.** (p.174) That is the purpose of our human birth—to light that lamp of Knowledge, to attain God.

Lighting the lamp of Knowledge in the chamber of your heart,

Behold the face of the Mother, Brahman's Embodiment. (p.174)

That Knowledge is the real sign of a 'rich person'. If you see that person you will immediately understand that the Blissful Mother dwells in his heart. He is joyful himself and also gives joy to others. 'To install that Blissful Mother in one's heart', 'to see the face of Brahman's Embodiment', 'to light the Lamp of Knowledge'—these all indicate the same thing, the attainment of perfection, and that is the goal of life.

Sri Ramakrishna says: **Everyone can attain Knowledge. There are two entities: *Jīvātmā*, the individual soul, and *Paramātmā*, the Supreme Soul.** (p.205) The 'little I', the 'I' that identifies itself with one body and mind is the *Jīvātmā*. And the Supreme Soul is the 'I' that is not attached to any one particular body, the 'I' which exists in all beings. Everyone has his own limited 'I-consciousness', but the 'I' in all, the sum-total of all 'I's, is the Supreme Soul. Devotees refer to this Supreme Soul as the Lord, or God. Yoga is the union of the individual soul with the Supreme Soul. **Through prayer all individual souls can be united with the Supreme Soul.** (p.205)

In different words, by various similes, Sri Ramakrishna tells us again and again that the only aim of human life is God-realization—that the attainment of Knowledge or Self-realization is the only reason for human existence. That is everyone's birthright. God-realization or Knowledge of Brahman is not anyone's monopoly. We find differences in regard to all other matters, but in this one thing everyone has the same right—all have the same claim on God. Anyone who has great longing can see Him. Sri Ramakrishna once told Holy Mother, 'Uncle Moon is everybody's uncle. Those who call on Him see Him. If you call on Him you also will see Him.'

Every house has a connection for gas, and gas can be obtained from the main storage of the Gas Company. Apply to the Company, and it will arrange for your supply of gas. Then your house will be lighted. (p.205) If the lamp of Knowledge is lit, the Embodiment of Brahman will be manifest in the temple of my body; my Chosen Ideal will be present there. I will realize the truth that I am not poor or weak; I am above everything— the body, the mind, the senses. No power in the whole universe is greater than I.

There are two ways to 'light the lamp of Knowledge' in your heart. If you are a devotee, you can say, 'I am the child of God or His servant.' You are closely related to Him. God is unlimited, so if you realize your relationship with him, you begin to lose your limitations. This is from the standpoint of Devotion.

The second way is the way of the *jñānī*, one who follows the path of Knowledge. The *jñānī* says, 'I myself am God, I myself am Brahman.' Swami Vivekananda said: Either you say, 'I am the All' or say 'You are the All'. Devotees say 'O Lord, You are everything.' *Jñānī*s say, 'I am everything—everything is Brahman, so I am also Brahman.' This is my true identity. We have so many identities that we forget this one real identity. We forget we are essentially Brahman. Because of this we suffer and make other suffer. Our misery comes from forgetting our true identity.

God is within us; that is why the body is called a temple. Within that temple-body is He who is beyond the body. This truth was expressed in a poem Swami Vivekananda wrote for his American friend, Professor Wright:

> My love, my love, you are here,
> And you are here, my love, my all!
> And I was searching Thee!
> From all eternity you were there
> Enthroned in majesty![1]

Śrī Kṛṣṇa says, *Iśvaraḥ sarvabhūtānāṁ hṛddeśe'rjuna tiṣṭhati*—'The Lord dwells in the hearts of all beings, O Arjuna.'[2] He is always there in His royal splendour, but we do not know it. Some hunt for Him outside and others do not search for Him at all. Sri Ramakrishna once said that the great philanthropist Vidyasagar had much inner wealth, but that wealth was hidden and he was not searching for it. **Gold lies hidden within him. Had he but found it out, his activities would have been reduced; finally they would have stopped altogether. Had he but known that God resides in his heart, his mind would have been directed to God in thought and meditation.** (p.267)

'Gold' lies within all of us. God is always there, yet we are not aware of Him. We restlessly indulge ourselves in outer enjoyments. A Bengali song tells of the musk deer which is intoxicated by the scent of musk and wanders around the forest searching for it. It does not know that the musk is in its own navel.

We are all in the same condition as that deer; we don't know that what we are searching for is within us. But if we are fortunate, we find a *sadguru*, a real spiritual teacher. The guru opens our eyes and teaches us to see the God that is within us. It is not that the guru takes something from outside and gives it to us. Rather, he awakens the power that is already within us, and guides us to perfection. This is why we revere the guru so highly.

Ajñānatimirāndhasya jñānāñjanaśalākayā cakṣurunmīlitaṁ yena tasmai Śrīgurave namaḥ—'Salutations to the Guru who with the collyrium stick of Knowledge has opened the eyes of one blinded by the disease of ignorance.'[3] The guru says, 'Look! Thou art That! This is your true identity. You are not miserable; you are not weak; you are not a sinner. You are pure, perfect, infinite, limitless. You have infinite power.' Then I learn to see what is. I learn to see

Him who is within me and I discover that in me is a vast treasure-house. I recognize a new self. Now I know my way; I am no longer miserable. The guru has given me life.

A poem by the English poet Shelley tells of that inner treasure.

> That content surpassing wealth
> The sage in meditation found
> And walked with inward glory crowned.[4]

What the sage finds within himself through meditation is more valuable than all the wealth in the world. He walks with a crown of glory on his head; that glory has come from within. Having known outer riches to be worthless, he is radiant with divine majesty. In every country, in every religion, we find this teaching: God, Knowledge, is not outside, but within.

Then why don't we see God? Why isn't everyone inspired and eager to see Him who dwells within? Hindus say that we cannot see Him because of *māyā*. Sri Ramakrishna says, ***Māyā* entangles a man and turns him away from God.** (p.456) Again, **God is the nearest of all, but we cannot see Him on account of this covering of *māyā*.** (p.169) A song in the Gospel describes how *māyā*'s spell deludes everyone.

> **When such delusion veils the world, through**
> ***Mahāmāyā*'s spell**
> **That Brahmā is bereft of sense**
> **And Viṣṇu loses consciousness,**
> **What hope is left for men?** (p.325)

All beings, even Brahmā and Viṣṇu are under the spell of *māyā*, such is her power. A story about this is found in the *Gospel*:

Viṣṇu once took on the form of a boar in order to kill the demon Hiraṇyākṣa. However, after accomplishing his mission he did not return to his celestial abode. He was very happy in his boar-form with his pig-wife and pig-children and forgot that he was really God. The gods became worried because if Viṣṇu were not in heaven, creation could not continue. Finally they went to Śiva and asked him to deal with the problem. Śiva agreed to help them and went to have a talk with the boar. But the boar refused to listen to him having completely forgotten that he was Viṣṇu. He said that he was quite happy with his pig-family. Then Śiva struck the boar's body with his trident, killing it. Viṣṇu came out laughing and returned to his abode in heaven. So it is said that even Viṣṇu is bereft of consciousness because of *māyā*, what to speak of man.

The song continues:

The narrow channel first is made, and then the trap is set;
But open though the passage lies,
The fish, once safely through the gate
Do not come out again.
Yet even though a way leads forth,
Encased within its own cocoon,
The worm remains to die. (p.325)

As the fish are ensnared in the trap, so are we ensnared by *māyā*. In the trap there are two gates, one for entering and the other for going out. The fish enter but do not try to escape. Then there is the example of the worm. From its mouth the worm secretes saliva from which a cocoon is made. It enters that cocoon and stays there. It can escape but it doesn't want to. We also are bound in the *māyā*-cocoon which we ourselves have created. We can't escape; *māyā* keeps us bound. Sri Ramakrishna says, ***Māyā* robs him of his knowledge to such an extent that he cannot find the way of escape, though**

such a way exists. (p.325) For this reason *māyā* is called magic, or sorcery. We seem to be hypnotized. It is difficult to understand—either we do not wish to know God or we are not prepared to know Him. Such is *māyā*!

According to Hindu scriptures, *māyā* has two aspects. One is the power of concealment, and the other the power of projection. *Māyā* conceals as the cloud covers the sun. And what does *māyā* conceal? That which is within us, our Inner-Self—God. It is not that God is sometimes present and sometimes absent. He is always there, but because of the covering of *māyā* we do not see Him.

The other aspect of *māyā*, its projecting power, causes us to see wrongly. In the darkness a rope appears to us to be a snake and we are frightened. Then someone brings a lamp and we see that it was only a rope. This is the well-known 'fallacy of mistaking a rope for a snake'. In the same way, because of *māyā* we do not see rightly; we see only the changeable universe and believe it to be the sole reality. We do not understand rightly, so we live in fear. **Through *māyā* one feels the Real to be unreal and the unreal to be the Real.** (p.583)

Nārada once asked Śrī Kṛṣṇa to explain *māyā*. Śrī Kṛṣṇa said, 'Very well, but first go and bring me a little water to drink.' Nārada went to a nearby village to get the water and there met a young woman to whom he was at once attracted. The two were soon married, had several children and were very happy. Then came a terrible flood. All the houses were being washed away. Nārada was struggling in the water holding on to his wife and children, but they slipped from his arms. He himself was trying to stay afloat when he suddenly heard Śrī Kṛṣṇa's voice, 'O Nārada, where is my water?' Twelve years had passed in just ten minutes! Now he knew what *māyā* is.

Because of her incomprehensible nature, *māyā* is called 'Skilled-in-making-the-impossible-possible'.

Māyā can't be ignored. Sri Ramakrishna says that if *māyā* does not set us free, we cannot attain Self-knowledge. By way of illustration he told about what happened one time when Rāma, Sītā and Lakṣmaṇa were walking single file along a narrow path. Rāma led the way, Sītā was in the middle and Lakṣmaṇa was at the rear. Because Sītā was in the middle, Lakṣmaṇa could not see Rāma. At last Sītā moved to one side so that he could see him.

In the same way *māyā* comes between God and the individual soul. Unless She stands aside the individual soul can't see God, so he suffers. It is by Her grace that one can see God, and all troubles and sufferings come to an end. You may reason a thousand times, but nothing comes about unless *māyā* is propitious. Swami Brahmananda said that the Divine Mother has the key to the Knowledge of Brahman. The door can't be opened without the key of Mother's grace. Whether you take the path of Knowledge or the path of Devotion, you must first propitiate *māyā*.

Sri Ramakrishna says: One must propitiate the Divine Mother, the Primal Energy, in order to obtain God's grace. God Himself is *Mahāmāyā*, who deludes the world with her illusion and conjures up the magic of creation, preservation and destruction. (p.116) This agrees with a verse in the *Caṇḍī*; *Saiṣā prasannā varadā nṛṇāṁ bhavati muktaye*—'When *Mahāmāyā* in the form of the Divine Mother, the Primal Energy, is propitiated, She grants liberation.'[5] And the *Gītā* says:

Daivī hyeṣā guṇamayī mama māyā duratyayā
Māmeva ye prapadyante māyāmetāṁ taranti te—

'Verily this divine illusion of Mine, made up of the *guṇas*, is hard to surmount. But those who take refuge in Me alone cross over this illusion.'[6]

This is the way—taking refuge in God and praying intently, 'Lord, protect me from Your *māyā*.' Sri Ramakrishna prayed, 'Thou, the *māyā* who captivates the minds of all people in the world, do not tempt me.' We should never be proud and say, '*Māyā* has no power over me.' If She is not gracious, we forget God.

Sometimes we find someone trying to stay on the path of Truth, trying to go to God, but *māyā* bars the way. All his efforts are fruitless. But when *māyā* is gracious, everything becomes favourable.

Good and bad tendencies in us are both His *māyā*. His *māyā* is good as well as bad. Sri Ramakrishna spoke of *vidyāmāyā* and *avidyāmāyā*—the *māyā* of Knowledge and the *māyā* of Ignorance. **The world consists of the illusory duality of knowledge and ignorance.** (p.101) ***Śakti*** **alone is the root of the universe. That Primal Energy has two aspects:** ***vidyā*** **and** ***avidyā*****.** (p.116) She is existence and also non-existence; good and also evil. Sometimes lofty thoughts arise in our mind and we think ourselves to be very great. But then bad thoughts come and we laugh at our pretensions. All thoughts are in the domain of His *māyā* of Knowledge or His *māyā* of Ignorance.

Avidyā **deludes . . .** ***vidyā*** **begets devotion, kindness, wisdom and love, which lead one to God.** (p.116) So we must first pray to God so that He will protect us from his *māyā* of Ignorance, but we must hold fast to His *māyā* of Knowledge. **A man can realize God if he takes shelter under His** ***vidyāmāyā*** **and follows the path of**

righteousness. (p.893) At first we must give up the *māyā* of Ignorance, and then we attain God through His *māyā* of Knowledge. After attaining Him, we go beyond both—the *māyā* of Knowledge and the *māyā* of Ignorance. **He who knows God and realizes Him is able to go beyond *māyā*.** (p.893)

How do we know that a person is near to God-realization? The Master says that the glory of longing for God (*anurāga*) appears in him. **The man in whom longing for God manifests its glories is not far from attaining Him.** (pp.202-03) He used the term 'the glories' (*aiśvarya*) of longing for God. As a result of spiritual disciplines practised through many births, one attains something very rare—longing for God. **What are the glories of that longing? They are discrimination, dispassion, compassion for living beings, serving holy men, loving their company, chanting the name and glories of God, telling the truth and the like.** (p.203)

It is said of Sri Ramakrishna that, though other *Avatāra*s came with many wonderful attributes—scriptural knowledge, beauty, miraculous powers, etc.—he was completely bereft of all these. That is true. Sri Ramakrishna was not a scholar, nor did he possess yogic powers. He did not have the support of many followers or wealthy disciples. Outwardly he was very ordinary—he looked like any other person. But in reality, did he not come with even greater qualities? This time he came with the grandeur of love, devotion, renunciation—the glory of longing for God.

Love, dispassion, renunciation, etc.—all these followed in the wake of his intense longing for God. Do holy persons desire anything else? This longing is their only desire. Discrimination, renunciation, love for all creatures, service to holy persons, the company of devotees, chanting God's name, firmness in vows—all these accompany the devotee's longing for God. These are difficult to master, but they arise spontaneously in those who have true longing for God. **When you see those signs of longing in an aspirant, you can rightly say that for him the vision of God is not far to seek.** (p.203)

God is manifested in the heart of the devotee. We can recognize this through his behaviour and way of living. We find that his life is gradually being transformed, and that God is living in Him. Sṛi Ramakrishna used a simile to illustrate this: **The state of a servant's house will tell you unmistakably whether his master has decided to visit it. First, the rubbish and jungle around the house are cleared up. Second, the soot and dirt are removed from the rooms. Third, the courtyard, floors, and other places are swept clean. Finally the master himself sends various things to the house, such as a carpet, a hubble-bubble for smoking and the like. When you see these things arriving, you conclude that the master will very soon come.** (p.203) In the same way, whenever devotion, faith, discrimination, dispassion, etc. gradually become manifest in the devotee, we can tell that God-realization is not far off.

What are the signs of God-realization? Sri Ramakrishna says: **There are such signs. It is said in the *Bhāgavata* that a man who has seen God behaves sometimes like a child, sometimes like a ghoul, sometimes like an inert thing, and sometimes like a madman.** (p.451) The *Śrīmad Bhāgavatam* says, *Budho bālakavat krīḍet*—'He may be a man of Knowledge, but he plays like a child.'[7] Those who attain God take on His nature and behave like a little child. The

God-realized soul may seem whimsical and capricious—not concerned about rules and regulations. **Through Perfect Knowledge, a man becomes like a child five years old.** (p.857) **The child is not under the control of any of the *guṇas*. He is beyond the three *guṇas*. He is not under the control of any of the *guṇas—sattva, rajas* or *tamas*.** (p.860)

As Sri Ramakrishna continues his conversation, he discusses the three *guṇas*. One sign of *tamas* is anger, but what does a little child do? **One moment he quarrels with his chum or even fights with him, and the next moment he hugs him, shows him much affection and plays with him!** (p.860)

He is not even under the control of *rajas*. (p.860) The signs of *rajas* are activity, eagerness for work and great interest in worldly affairs. But the child is beyond *rajas*. **Now he builds his playhouse and makes all kinds of plans to make it beautiful, and the next moment he leaves everything behind and runs to his mother. Again, you see him wearing a beautiful piece of cloth worth five rupees. After a few moments the cloth lies on the ground; he forgets all about it. Or he may carry it under his arm.** (p.860)

Sattva is characterized by compassion, love, etc. In a little child you will also find love and attraction for some person, but this cannot bind him. **You may find him today very fond of his playmates in the neighbourhood; he doesn't feel happy for a moment without seeing them; but tomorrow, when he goes to another place with his parents, he finds new playmates; all his love is now directed to his new friends, and he almost forgets his old ones.** (p.861) If you attain God, you rise above the three *guṇas*. You become like a child.

Another verse in the *Bhāgavatam* says, *Kuśalo jaḍabaccaret*—'A person may be very intelligent and judicious, yet he behaves like an imbecile.'[8] Realized souls sometimes behave like fools. An example of this is found in the life of Śaṅkarācārya. A brahmin and his wife had a son who grew up to be mute, dull and foolish. They were very worried about him. One day, Śaṅkara, who was travelling across India reviving its ancient spiritual traditions, arrived at the place where the couple lived. They had heard of his great powers so they took their son to him to see if he could help the boy. Śaṅkara immediately understood that the son was not stupid but was a realized soul. When Śaṅkara asked him, 'Who are you?', the boy, who had never spoken a word in his life, answered clearly, 'I am the Ātman.'

He had the realization of God 'like a *hastāmalaka*—like a plum (*āmalaka*) in his hand (*hasta*). If you have a plum in your hand, you will know beyond any doubt that you have a plum in your hand. In the same way, the boy knew without any doubt that he was the Ātman, the Divine Inner Self. Śrī Śaṅkarācārya initiated him into monastic life and gave him the name Hastāmalakācārya—'the teacher with the plum in his hand.' Since his birth he had behaved like an idiot, but Śaṅkara recognized him as a great soul.

A great soul also sometimes behaves like a madman. *Vadet unmattavad vidvān*—'He may have wisdom and be learned in the scriptures, still he talks like a madman.'[9] His talk does not fit in with that of other people. He seems to speak a different language. We cannot understand him. Sri Ramakrishna says: **Again, like a madman he sometimes laughs and sometimes weeps. Now he dresses himself like a dandy and the next moment he goes entirely naked and roams**

about with his cloth under his arm. Therefore he seems to be a lunatic. (pp.451-52)

We see these very same things in Sri Ramakrishna's life. He could not wear his cloth properly. He would often speak with the Divine Mother, who was in his own mind. Sometimes he would laugh, sometimes cry, sometimes sing. Anyone seeing all this would think he was crazy. Shivanath Shastri once said that Sri Ramakrishna's head had become deranged. When Sri Ramakrishna heard about this he said: He remains perfectly safe keeping his mind immersed in worldly affairs, and I become unconscious thinking of Divine Consciousness? The truth is, our vision is so clouded that we can't understand great souls. But if a person keeps his mind on God, he can never be mentally unbalanced.

He maintains the same attitude towards things holy and unholy. (p.451) A song by Rāmaprasāda says that only after distinctions between the holy and the unholy are rooted out of our minds will God be revealed to us. Something may seem holy or unholy to us, but great souls see everything from a higher plane. Holiness and unholiness are the same to them. Sri Ramakrishna was at one time in that state—he was not aware of the difference between the holy and the unholy.

The *Bhāgavatam* continues its description of a great soul: *Gocaryaṁ naigamaścaret*—'He has abundant knowledge of the scriptures, so he can be a guru, yet he may act like a stupid person.'[10] Again, we find this in the life of Sri Ramakrishna. He once threw coins and clods of dirt into the river saying, 'Money is dirt, dirt is money.' Another time Mathur Babu wanted to deed him some land. When Sri Ramakrishna found out about it, he was about to beat Mathur. Is this not foolishness? It may seem foolish to us, but great souls are of another world. They do not conform to our ideas of propriety. We judge them with our limited reason, so we do not understand them. We think they are stupid or foolish, but in reality, their lives are completely surrendered to God. They have given their all to Him and are utterly indifferent to society and to what it judges to be good or bad.

Swami Vivekananda sometimes showed the same disregard for people's opinions. One day at Belur Math he put on long stockings and high boots and nothing else but a loin-cloth. Dressed like this and carrying a hookah with a large water-bowl, he strolled around the grounds of the Math. Everyone stared at him in astonishment, but he did not even glance at anyone. Swami Vijnanananda ordinarily dressed in a strange way, wearing a coat with many, many pockets. He looked so odd that mischievous little children would jeer at him as he walked down the street. He would turn to them and say, 'Do you want to see a monkey? Look at me, I am a monkey—Rāma's monkey.' He was very disorderly, but if any servant or *brahmacārin* would try to straighten up his room, he would be extremely irritated.

Knowers of Brahman are not bound by ordinary rules. They are utterly unique. It must be remembered, however, that what they say and do conforms to the scriptures. But what are the scriptures? Are they not records of what seers of Truth or Knowers of Brahman have done, what they have realized? The behaviour of great souls may be childlike, it may be like that of a madman, or like a fool, or even like a ghoul, but however they behave, however they live their lives, they set an ideal to be followed. By honouring them, people enrich their own societies and civilizations. In every country, in every age, they come to protect righteousness and culture.

There are two kinds of realized souls. Those in one group are satisfied and happy with their own liberation. The other great souls want to share their joy with others. Sri Ramakrishna gives an analogy: 'Some persons after eating wipe their mouths to conceal what they ate. But others invite everyone to come and join them: "Come, come and eat! How good the food is!"' They are like the great souls who after God-realization keep their bodies for the welfare of others. Sri Ramakrishna says: **Generally the body does not remain alive after the attainment of *samādhi*. The only exceptions are such sages as Nārada, who keep their bodies alive in order to bring spiritual light to others. It is also true of Divine Incarnations, like Caitanya. After the well is dug, one generally throws away the spade and basket. But some keep them in order to help their neighbours.** (p.152)

Rāmānuja was such a great soul. His guru told him that he must never tell his mantra to anyone else—that if he gave it to another person, that person would be liberated but he himself would go to hell. Hearing this Rāmānuja thought, 'If I go to hell, others will be liberated.' So he went to a high platform, and standing on it cried out, 'Listen, everyone! I am going to give you a great *mantra* hearing which you will all be liberated—*Oṁ Namo Nārāyaṇāya.*' All who heard the *mantra* were very happy. When his guru found out about this, he was about to curse Rāmānuja. But Rāmānuja did not repent. He said, 'You are my guru and I have disobeyed your command, so your curse is justified. I am ready to go to eternal hell, but my going there will be for the good of others so I will not suffer.' When the guru heard these words, he warmly embraced Rāmānuja.

Sri Ramakrishna says: **The great souls who retain their bodies after *samādhi* feel compassion for the suffering of others. They are not so selfish as to be satisfied with their own illumination.** (p.152) He told the story of four friends who were walking together when they came to a high wall. One of them climbed up the wall to see what was on the other side. What he saw gave him such great joy that he went on over the wall and never returned. The second man then climbed the wall and was also filled with joy and went over to the other side. The third man did the same. But the fourth, after climbing the wall and seeing the other side, decided to return. He wanted to tell others: 'Look, behind this wall there is a wonderful field. If you climb over the wall, you can jump into that field and be very happy.' The fourth man was concerned about other people so he came back. Sri Ramakrishna said that he was like an *Avatāra* or *Iśvarakoṭi* who after attaining illumination keeps his body for the welfare of others.

After attaining *samādhi*, Nārada, Śukadeva, and others came down a few steps, as it were, to the plane of normal consciousness and broke their silence out of compassion for the suffering of others and to help them. (p.276) Nārada is a *nityajīva*, an Eternal Soul. He is said to be still living and will never be liberated. With a *vīṇā* in his hands, he wanders about the world eternally, singing the name of God. Śukadeva was born as the result of Vyāsadeva's hard austerities in the Himalayas. He was as bright as fire and as pure as the sky. It is believed that after birth, while being bathed in the Gaṅgā, Śiva himself came to invest him with the sacred thread. From heaven Indra sent him a water-pot, loin-cloth, etc. Śukadeva came to earth as a world-teacher and did not need liberation for himself. For the good of others, he recited the *Bhāgavatam* to King Parīkṣit.

Swami Vivekananda at first wanted liberation for himself, but Sri Ramakrishna scolded him. He said, 'What! You are so low? I thought you would be like a huge tree in the shade of which travellers going along the road could take refuge from the heat of the sun. And now I see that you want only your own liberation!' Afterwards, what a great change came about in Swamiji! He said, 'As long as there is one starving dog in this country, it is my religion to feed it.' He told a disciple, 'If you seek liberation for yourself, you will go to hell. You must seek liberation for others. If you work for yourself, you will go to hell; if you work for the liberation of others, that is better than going to heaven.'

In one community of Buddhists, the members do not seek *nirvāṇa* or the state of Buddha. Theirs is a different goal: 'I will sacrifice my life for the good of others,' they say. Among Buddhists there are two major schools, the Hīnayāna and the Mahāyāna. *Yāna* means vehicle or carriage. The Hīnayānists want liberation only for themselves, so they are called *hīna*—low or small, because their *yāna*—carriage, is small. Mahāyāna means *Great Vehicle*. Those who belong to this school want liberation for all, because 'Everyone's liberation is *my* liberation.'

Sri Ramakrishna's life also exemplifies this. He felt the suffering of others as his own and longed to help them. He said: Even if I fall sick and live only on sago, I shall continue to do good to others. It bothered him that Nitai, one of Caitanya's companions, had wandered about on foot chanting the Lord's name, 'but I cannot move about without a carriage.' Even after his body had become emaciated from cancer of the throat, he continued to speak. It was very painful for him yet he went on talking about God, even when death was imminent. He wanted to remind everyone of their ultimate goal in life, God-realization. He knew that only God-realization would permanently remove people's sufferings.

We notice the same thing in the life of Swami Shivananda, a disciple of Sri Ramakrishna and the second President of the Ramakrishna Math and Mission. Toward the end of his life he was paralyzed and unable to speak. A devotee who had been told in a dream to take initiation from him arrived from a distant place. When Swami Shivananda was informed of this, he understood everything. He indicated by a gesture that the man should come inside. How he gave initiation no one knew, because the door was shut. But the man was satisfied. Out of compassion, Swami Shivananda had in some way initiated him. On a previous occasion, when the Swami was still able to speak, someone asked him for a blessing. He answered, 'Always flowing, flowing, flowing,'—his blessings would always be there. As the river current flows along, as the breeze is always blowing, silently but continuously moving—in the same way the blessings of holy persons are constantly and indiscriminately at work. Swami Shivananda wanted everyone's welfare. He lived for nothing else.

We remember the wonderful words of blessing that Holy Mother spoke towards the end of her life—perhaps unprecedented in the history of religion. She said, 'My blessings are for everyone—for those who have come, for those who have not yet come and for those who will come in the distant future.' She was one of those few who live only for the welfare of all—*lokasaṁgrahārtham*—for the good of the whole world.

In the *Gospel* we find Sri Ramakrishna saying again and again, 'You must realize God. Move forward!' In all the Hindu religious texts there is that teaching—'Move forward!' Move on from wherever you are. Don't stop. March onward until you reach the goal. Swamiji said, 'Stop not till the goal is reached.' What is that goal? It is God, or Brahman. But why should I go there? I am here; why should I go there? You go to God for happiness. Brahman is called *Saccidānanda*—Existence-Consciousness-Bliss absolute. One of the names of Durgā is *Ānandamayī*—full of bliss. All bliss comes from God. We all want happiness and we do anything to get it. We eat *rasagolla*s—to be happy. We go to the cinema—to get joy. We dedicate our lives to a great ideal—to get happiness. But all bliss comes from one source—from God.

All worldly happiness has a reaction. It is momentary—it comes to an end, and it is mixed with pain. But the bliss of God-realization never ceases. Worldly happiness is trifling compared to it. If you taste a drink made of sugar candy, you no longer care for one made of molasses. Sri Ramakrishna says, **If a man once tastes the Bliss of Brahman, then his mind no longer runs after the enjoyment of sense pleasures or wealth or name and fame. If the moth once sees the light, it no longer goes into the darkness.** (p.653)

In every country and in every age we find men and women renouncing everything and practising many difficult austerities in their search for God. Buddha gave up his kingdom. Mīrābāī left her palace. Śrī Caitanya took the vows of a sannyasi in spite of the fact that he had received great honour as an erudite scholar. Youth and beauty, honour and recognition, wealth and high position—everything anyone would desire was theirs, yet they left it all behind when they went searching for God. They believed that the greatest happiness was God-realization. In truth, their renunciation was not anything negative. It meant giving up small things for large things—renouncing the little happiness for the great happiness, renouncing worldly pleasures for the Bliss of God.

Sri Ramakrishna said that the happiness one gets from worldly pleasures is trifling compared to the Bliss of Brahman. Mahendranath Datta, Swami Vivekananda's younger brother, was eye-witness to one incident relating to this, and has described it. Habu Datta, Swamiji's elder cousin was an accomplished musician. He was also without peer in his addiction to drugs and alcohol. There was no drug or liquor which he had not tried. On a sudden impulse, Swamiji brought him to Cossipore to see Sri Ramakrishna. Sri Ramakrishna was in the last stages of his illness and very weak. Despite all this, Swamiji told him that he must touch Habu, perhaps thinking that his touch would change Habu's character as it had that of others. Sri Ramakrishna, however, was reluctant to use his power in Habu's case. He said, 'Have you no sense? Don't you see my condition? Any moment I can die.' But Swami Vivekananda would not listen—he kept insisting. Then suddenly Sri Ramakrishna touched Habu, and Habu at once was lost in *samādhi*. The *samādhi* was so deep that it continued for hours. Habu sat inert as a stone. Swamiji became worried. Perhaps that touch had killed Habu! He started to push and shove Habu, telling him, 'Stand up! I've prepared some *gānjā* (marijuana) for you. Will you smoke it?' After a long time Habu said slowly, 'Why do you speak of *gānjā*? I was absorbed so long in that intoxicant, not some drug like *gānjā*. I do not want *gānjā* any more.' He had discovered that compared to the Bliss of Brahman, worldly bliss is nothing.

Buddha, after attaining illumination wandered around for seven days—he could not contain so much bliss. One of the

Upaniṣads says, *Ānando brahmeti vyajānāt*—'Bliss is Brahman.'[11] Bliss is also the nature of Īśvara. That bliss is unconditioned—it is not dependent on anything else. And there is no end to that Bliss. Holy Mother in describing her life at Dakshineswar once said: 'There was so much hardship. I was always confined to the tiny room in the Nahabat, but still I was never conscious of any difficulties. I felt as if a pitcher of bliss had been installed in my heart.'

We see that bliss on the shining faces of those who have realized God. They seem to be immersed in that bliss. In the *Gospel*, M. depicts Sri Ramakrishna in many different places and with many different people, but he is always full of bliss. It is as if he has opened a market of bliss and is sitting there waiting for people to come. He himself has made that bliss and now he is distributing it to all.

A verse from the *Prapannagītā* says:

Nityotsavo bhavetteṣāṁ nityaśrīrnityamaṅgalam
Yeṣāṁ hṛdistho bhagavān maṅgalāyatanaṁ hariḥ—

'Where Hari, of the nature of Goodness, is ever seated in the heart, there is an eternal festival, an eternal well-being. There everything is beautiful, everything is good, everything is full of bliss.'[12]

That was Sri Ramakrishna. He was always immersed in the Ocean of Bliss and he distributed that Bliss to all. He called to everyone : Come! You think that happiness from worldly objects and from the senses is so wonderful. You do not know what you are missing! The Bliss of Brahman, of God-realization, brings the greatest joy. I am the proof—look at me and understand! How long will you remain satisfied with trifling worldly pleasures? I have come to show you the way. In whatever way you want, go to Him. **Now it is your bounden duty to give your entire mind to God, to plunge deep into the ocean of His love. . . . There is no fear of death from plunging into this Ocean, for this is the Ocean of Immortality.** (pp.455-56)

References

1. *C.W.*, Vol. VII, 1964, p.449
2. *Gītā*, XVIII.61
3. *Hymn to the Guru. Viśwasāra Tantra, Altar Flowers*, Advaita Ashrama, p.3
4. Stanzas Written in Dejection, P.B. Shelley
5. *Caṇḍī*, 1/56
6. *Gītā*, VII.14
7. *Bhāgavatam*, XI.18.29
8. *Ibid.*
9. *Ibid.*
10. *Ibid.*
11. *Taittirīya Upaniṣad*, III.6
12. *Prapannagītā*, 44

VI
No One Is a Sinner

Sri Ramakrishna used to say that we should not think of ourselves as sinners or consider ourselves to be worthless. **The fool who says only, 'I am a sinner, I am a sinner', verily drowns himself in worldliness. One should rather say: 'I have chanted the name of God. How can I be a sinner!'** (p.274)

One day Sri Ramakrishna was talking to some Brāhmo devotees about religion when one of them interrupted him to say : 'I am a great sinner. How can I say that God is in me?' At this the Master became annoyed and said: **With you it is always sin and sin! That's the Christian view, isn't it? Once a man gave me a Bible. A part of it was read to me, and it was full of that one thing—sin and sin!** (p.617)

Consciousness of sin is the basis of the Christian religion. Christians believe in 'original sin'. They believe that Adam and Eve were the first man and woman and that they lived happily in Paradise, in the Garden of Eden. God told them, 'You can eat all the fruit in the garden except that which grows on one tree, the Tree of Knowledge. Never eat that.'

But Satan made his appearance in this paradise. To Christians, Satan is the personification of sin, and he is believed to be all-evil.

According to Hinduism, there is one power behind both good and evil, happiness and misery. But Christians believe that there is one creator of good—God, and one creator of evil—

Satan. It is Satan's job to always act in opposition to what God wants.

One day Satan said to Eve: 'Why are you not eating the fruit from the Tree of Knowledge? You don't know what you are missing. Don't listen to what God says—eat this delicious fruit!' Tempted by Satan, Eve ate half of one fruit from the forbidden tree and gave the other half to Adam, who also ate it.

Before this Adam and Eve had never been aware of their bodies though they were naked. But after eating the fruit, they at once became conscious of their nakedness. In shame, they hid themselves behind a bush. Just then God appeared in the garden and called to them, 'Adam, Eve, where are you?' From behind the bush they answered, 'We are here.' Then God asked, 'Why are you hiding?' They answered, 'How can we come to you? We don't have any clothes.' At this God said: 'Ah, I see that you have eaten the forbidden fruit! You have disobeyed me. You can no longer stay in the Garden of Eden but must go out into the world.' So they left Paradise to live in the world.

This is what is known as 'original sin'. We are all descendants of Adam and Eve and have inherited their sin. Like them, we are sinners. Only *Jesus* Christ can save us from sin. The word Jesus means *saviour*. God sent him to save us. He is God's son, God's 'only begotten son' according to Christian doctrine. We will be saved from sin only if we worship Jesus Christ and accept him as our saviour. Without this, there is no salvation. This is the central doctrine of Christianity.

But the Hindu belief is different. Hindus say: 'Yes, it is true that people make mistakes, commit crimes and are often impure, but that is only a passing phase. After some time a person changes. "Sin" is a condition temporarily imposed on us, like a cloud that covers the sky. The sky appears to be dark, but after some time the cloud passes and we see that the sky is really a translucent blue. This is also true of us. Something like a cloud covers our true nature, but that cloud is blown away after a time. Then our real self is revealed.'

The river's destination is the ocean. From the mountains it rushes forth and makes its way through villages, meadows, valleys—forcing its way through many obstacles. One day it reaches the sea. Nothing can stop it. That is what happens to us. We will all finally reach our destination and know our true, divine nature. Some travel along a straight path and reach their destination quickly, while others take a winding, circuitous route and take a longer time to arrive. If I consciously try to reach the goal through the practice of spiritual disciplines, I will arrive quickly. If I don't try, I will arrive after a long time and will suffer more. But we will all some day reach our destination and find perfect fulfilment.

Swami Vivekananda said that we are all trying to become liberated, and attaining liberation means realizing our own true identity, realizing that 'I am Brahman'—the Supreme Self. None of us are happy in our present state. We are always conscious of something lacking, an emptiness, which is why we distract ourselves with different activities. From this feeling of something lacking, the thief steals, the poor run after money, and the sannyasi calls on God. Those who steal or run after money are not taking the right path to liberation, so there is some delay for them. But one day or other they will find the path and reach the goal. And the sannyasi, who takes the right path, will quickly arrive at his destination.

So you should not constantly think of sin. The way to remove sin is to think of yourself as pure; the way to remove bondage is to think of yourself as free. What you think you become. When do you make mistakes? When you think you are separate from God, when you are Self-forgetful. Self-forgetfulness means forgetting your true identity. We have all forgotten who we really are.

Sri Ramakrishna told a story to illustrate this: A lion cub grew up amidst a flock of sheep. Like them, he ate grass and bleated, 'Baa, baa'. One day a lion attacked the flock. All the sheep fled in fear, and along with them, the lion cub. The lion chased them, but to his great surprise saw the little lion cub among the sheep! He seized it with his teeth, dragged it to a pond and showed it its reflection in the water. 'Look at your face,' he said, 'and look at mine. Can't you see we are the same?' At first the cub trembled in fear, but as it continued to look at its reflection, it realized its real identity. It was a lion! Suddenly the cub gave a mighty roar, and leaping in joy, scampered off to its real home in the jungle.

The lion cub behaved like a sheep as long as it thought it was a sheep. We are like that. When we think we are weak, worthless and powerless, we become weak, worthless and powerless. Swami Vivekananda said, 'The remedy for weakness is not brooding over weakness, but thinking of strength.'[1]

It is true that at times very depressing thoughts arise in our minds. Sometimes a foul odour suddenly comes into a house. Where it comes from nobody knows. Does it stay there forever? No, after a little while it goes away. In the same way, some impurity comes into my mind, but then it goes away. Do I need to get a headache over it? Bad thoughts come to my mind, but so do lofty thoughts—such great thoughts that I no longer regard myself as human. I seem to be divine! If my falling is true, is not my rising up and dusting myself off also true? If I acknowledge one, I must also acknowledge the other.

You must have the confidence that you can become great, immeasurably great—that you can rise higher and higher till you reach the highest. Whenever some impurity enters your mind, do not think that *you* are impure. Impurity is like a garment, a covering. Your clothes have become soiled; that does not mean *you* are dirty. You remove your clothes and find that you yourself are clean and pure.

The *Śvetāśvatara Upaniṣad* says, *Sṛṇvantu viśve amṛtasya putrā ā ye dhāmāni divyāni tasthūḥ*—'May the sons of the Immortal, who occupy celestial positions, hear it!'[2] We are all 'sons of the Immortal.' At the Parliament of Religions in Chicago, Swamiji told the people in the audience, 'You are children of immortal bliss.' He went on to say, 'Sinners! It is a sin to call a man so.'[3] Those who heard those words thought, 'This is a new conception. Now we know we are not sinners—we have gotten the taste of freedom.'

Swamiji said many things about the concept of sin :

'Vedānta believes in only one sin, only one in the world, and it is this: the moment you think you are a sinner or anybody is a sinner, that is sin. . . . From that follows every other mistake or what is usually called sin. ...Take a long look at your past life. If your present condition is good, it has been caused by all the past mistakes as well as successes. Glory be unto success! Glory be unto mistakes! Do not look back upon what has been done. Go ahead!'[4]

'Be not deluded by your religion teaching original sin, for the same religion teaches original purity. When Adam fell, he fell from purity. Purity is our real nature and to regain that is the object of all religion.'[5]

'Education is the manifestation of the perfection already in man.'

'Religion is the manifestation of the divinity already in man.'[6]

Swamiji also said, 'No one was ever really taught by another; each of us has had to teach himself. The external teacher offers only the suggestion which rouses the internal teacher to work to understand things."[7]

A real teacher reminds me of the perfection already in me. His duty is merely to remove the obstacles that prevent me from manifesting that perfection. What is called sin is simply those obstructions that prevent the manifestation of that perfection.

A real teacher does not tell me, 'You are nothing!' Rather he tells me: 'You also can be great. In you is infinite power, only that power is hidden.' He will not criticize me for my impurities, for my faults, but will sympathize with me. He will remove my impurities and help me manifest the divinity, the perfection that is always present in my heart. Divinity is within me. He only awakens it. The Upaniṣads affirm, *Tattvamasi*—'That thou art.' And, 'Arise, awake—be established in your own true nature!'

Brooding over my past and present, I may think myself to be worthless, but I am not worthless. No one is worthless. Anyone who wishes can make himself perfect and discover his innate purity.

Swami Vivekananda once said that even the most hardened criminal is the very picture of love when he caresses his child. That love comes from within the criminal; he does not manifest anything external to his nature. It is the man's criminality that lies like a shadow over his real nature. The shadow is ephemeral, someday it will disappear. Someday he will become good. He will manifest the beauty that lies within him.

There are many examples of this type of transformation. Ratnākar, the king of the robbers, became Vālmīki, the great poet who wrote the *Rāmāyaṇa*. The infamous Aṅgulimāla also led a wicked life. His name means 'garland of fingers' because of his habit of adding a finger from each of his victims to the garland of fingers he wore around his neck. No one could capture him, not even the king. But one day Lord Buddha met him and showered his grace on him. Aṅgulimāla's life was transformed and he became a monk.

No one remains the same forever. A person may be wicked today, but good tomorrow. We may find someone weak and frail today, and tomorrow strong and self-confident. A person's destiny can be changed in a moment. An incident, a word, a song, can propel a person towards a new life. An ordinary event can awaken the sleeping God in him.

One day, a famous devotee of 18th Century Bengal, Lalababu, was riding in a palanquin when he heard a washerman's daughter say : 'Father, it is evening. Please set fire to the *vāsanā*.' (*Vāsanā* means dry banana leaves and also desire.) Suddenly Lalababu thought: 'That is true. It is the evening of my life. Should I not set fire to my worldly desires?' That very moment Lalababu got down from the palanquin and renounced the world.

This can happen. It is like a spring of water long suppressed under a rock. One day someone lifts the rock and the water gushes forth. It happens like that with us. Something covering our mind is removed, and we know who we really are.

One of Sri Ramakrishna's stories illustrates this. One night a thief went out to steal, as was his custom, but this time he was caught in the act and chased by a group of angry people. What could he do? In desperation, he hit upon a plan. He suddenly entered a garden, sat down on the ground, smeared his body with ashes and pretended to be a holy man. No one recognized him. As days went by, people in the village heard that a holy man was living among them. They flocked to see him and bow down to him. They showed their devotion in many ways, bringing fruits, sweets and other things for him to eat. One day it dawned on him that if he got so much honour from being a fake holy man, how much more honour he would get if he became a real holy man. So he decided to become a real holy man. He who had been a thief, became a holy man.

One night a thief entered the hut of the saint, Pavhari Baba, while he was sleeping. The thief had picked up a few things and was putting them in a bundle when Pavhari Baba woke up. The thief in fright dropped the bundle and fled. Pavhari Baba picked up the bundle and ran after the man. When he finally caught up with him he said, 'Lord, you were gracious enough to come to my house, but why did you go away leaving these things behind?' In Pavhari Baba's eyes, the man was not a thief, but God, his own Chosen Ideal. He insisted that the man take the things he had tried to steal. Seeing Pavhari Baba's loving behaviour, the thief felt repentant. From that day he gave up his criminal activities and eventually became a holy man.

When Swami Vivekananda was wandering in the Himalayas he came upon a group of holy men. Among them he noticed one of exceptionally serene appearance who seemed to be a great saint. After Swamiji had conversed with him for some time, he realized that this was the man who had tried to steal from Pavhari Baba. He was speechless with wonder. As Swamiji continued to talk with him, he understood that the man was indeed a man of high spiritual attainments. Because of this incident, Swamiji would often say that even in the worst sinner there is the seed of sainthood.

The writer Oscar Wilde has said, 'The only difference between the saint and the sinner is that every saint has a past and every sinner has a future.' Many great souls were very immoral when they were young, but their lives were changed.

The darkness of their past was removed and they became enlightened, pure, perfect. A wicked person can become a saint. This point is stressed in many places in Hindu scriptures.

Śrī Kṛṣṇa says in the *Bhagavad Gītā*:

Api cet sudurācāro bhajate māmananyabhāk
Sādhureva sa mantavyaḥ samyagvyavasito hi saḥ—

'Even if a man of most vile conduct worships me with undistracted devotion, he must be reckoned as righteous for he has rightly resolved.'[8]

From the *Bṛhadviṣṇu Purāṇa*:

Nāmno'sya yāvatī śaktiḥ pāpanirharaṇe hareḥ
Tāvat kartuṁ na śaknoti pātakaṁ pātakī janaḥ—

'If one takes the name of the Lord, so many sins are destroyed that even the worst of sinners is unable to commit.'[9]

The poet-saint Rāmaprasāda sang:

If you have no head,
How can you have a headache?
If you chant the name of Kālī,
How can you be a sinner?

Fire can burn heaps of cotton,
In the same way, the name of God
Can burn up all accumulated sins.

In another song Rāmaprasāda said:

If only I can pass away repeating Durgā's name,
How canst Thou then, O Blessed One,
Withhold from me deliverance,
Wretched though I may be?
I may have stolen a drink of wine, or killed a child unborn,
Or slain a woman or a cow,

Or even caused a Brahmin's death;
But, though it all be true,
Nothing of this can make me feel the least uneasiness. . .
My wretched soul may still aspire
Even to Brahmanhood. (p.88)

Rāmaprasāda was trying to awaken hope in people's mind. He was not trying to condone evil. But if you have done something wrong, you should not think you are hopeless. Have faith in yourself; there is a bright future ahead for you. It is never too late. Vow that whatever you have done, you will never do again. Have faith in yourself and faith in God. Hold your head high and continue along the path. The journey is long. You may now and then stumble. So you stumble! Rise again and move onward. Continue on your way.

Swami Vivekananda said, 'Negative thoughts weaken men. Do you not find that where parents are constantly taxing their sons to read and write, telling them they will never learn anything, and calling them fools and so forth, the latter do actually turn out to be so in many cases? If you speak kind words to boys and encourage them, they are bound to improve in time. . . . If you can give them positive ideas, people will grow up to be men and learn to stand on their own legs.'[10]

Swamiji continued, 'We have seen how Sri Ramakrishna would encourage even those whom we considered as worthless and change the very course of their lives thereby!'[11] Sri Ramakrishna did not like negative thinking. He said 'Christian preachers only say "Sin, sin, sin"! Why do they talk so much about sin? Let them talk about God.' He also said, 'When you clap your hands, the birds fly up from the tree. In the same way, if you chant the name of God sins fly away from you.'

The attitude of Jesus Christ to so-called sinners is revealed in one episode in his life. Some men wanted to punish a woman who had committed adultery by stoning her to death. Jesus was present and said to them, 'Wait—is there any one of you who has not committed sin? If there is, let him be the first to throw a stone.' No one said a word. Then one by one, the men went away. There was no one who had not committed a sin. Jesus gave a few words of advice to the woman and bade her farewell. Great teachers act like this. They forgive everyone. They forgive, but do not condone evil. They help people go forward on the path to perfection.

Someone once asked me, 'Swamiji said that God is in all beings—"God the wicked, God the sinner". If this is true, then if a thief enters my home and in front of my eyes tries to steal something, should I let him go ahead and steal since he is God? Why should I take God to the police? When the thief came to rob Pavhari Baba, he gave him everything he wanted. Should I do the same?'

The answer to this question lies in the fact that what a saint like Pavhari Baba can do, ordinary people cannot do. Pavhari Baba was a *siddha purusa*, a Realized Soul. He saw God in all beings. To him the thief was not a thief—he was God. But in our sight, a thief is a thief. We can force ourselves to say, 'He is not a thief; he is God', but we do not believe it.

Sri Ramakrishna's story of the elephant-god and the *māhut*-god explains this. A guru told a disciple that God is in everything and everyone. The next day as the disciple was walking down the road, a mad elephant came rushing towards him. The *māhut* yelled, 'Get out of the way! Get out of the way!' But the disciple did not move; he wanted to put into practice what he had been taught. So with palms together he greeted the elephant saying, 'O Lord! O God!' The elephant paid no heed to these reverent salutations and with his trunk grabbed the disciple and threw him to the ground. He was severely injured with wounds all over his body. His brother disciples carried him back to the ashram. When his guru heard what had happened he said, 'Child, why did you see God only in the elephant? Don't you know that God is also in the *māhut*? The *māhut*-god told you to get out of the way. You should have listened to him.'

In everyday life we must make a distinction between the *māhut*-god and the elephant-god. Everything is God; He is in everyone, in the good and in the wicked. But we should associate only with good persons, not with the wicked. Sri Ramakrishna says: '*Āpo Nārāyaṇah*—"Water is God", that is true. But one kind of water is used for worship, another for drinking, and another kind can only be used for washing one's feet.' He also said, 'Be a devotee, but why should you be a fool?' We must make distinctions in everyday life; social and cultural norms are not to be ignored.

Swami Vivekananda was aware of this. When he and Swami Turiyananda were travelling by ship to America, Swami Turiyananda one day left their cabin door open when he went out on the deck. Swamiji knew that he had left his valuable watch on the table in the cabin, and felt very uneasy. He said to Swami Turiyananda, 'Brother, what right have you to tempt some man? There are poor men constantly going in and out of the cabin, and if you keep some valuable in front of their eyes, they will be tempted to take it. I would not blame them. They are not holy men. Why should they not steal if they think they won't be caught? That is their very nature.'[12]

If we are really concerned about others, we should take precautions to prevent anyone from stealing. We must take care that our actions do not incite others to do something wrong. We have a duty to those who are weak. If we leave money lying around, we will be partly responsible if some weak person steals it. But if, in spite of our precautions, someone steals or commits any other misdeed, we should certainly discipline him. We must treat the wicked as the wicked-god, always remembering that he is God. Divinity, Brahman is also in him, though it is sleeping. When the time is ripe, he will manifest that divinity. In the meantime we will try to do whatever we can for him. If we cannot help him in some way, we can pray for him. We will not look down on him. God is in him—that is his true nature. Some day he will manifest that divinity.

Jean Valjean is a character in Victor Hugo's novel *Les Miserables*. He and his widowed sister and her children were very poor. One morning there was nothing to eat and the children were crying for food. What could he do? He did not have a cent in his pocket and he could not get any work. He went out to try to find something for them. Walking along the road, he saw some warm bread in a shop window. He entered the shop and started to run off with a loaf of the bread, but someone saw him and he was arrested. For stealing one loaf of bread for starving children he was sentenced to the galleys of a ship. There, along with other convicts, he was forced to ply the oars day after day. He tried again and again to escape but was caught each time and given more punishment. After twenty years, he was at last released.

But people regarded Jean Valjean as a dangerous criminal and were afraid of him. Every door was shut in his face. Exhausted and starving, he was finally given refuge in the house of the bishop. The bishop knew all about him, but he took loving care of him and put him to bed in a pleasant room. In the middle of the night Jean Valjean stealthily got out of bed, put two costly candlesticks in his bag, and ran off. The next day he was found with the candlesticks in his possession and taken to the bishop. But the bishop refused to charge him. He said: 'Jean Valjean did not steal anything. I gave him those candlesticks because he was poor.'

This incident brought about a complete change in Jean Valjean's life. He had been regarded for so long as a criminal that he was convinced that he *was* a criminal. But the bishop saw something else in him and loved him. This gave Jean Valjean a new conception of himself. And he who everyone thought was a criminal became a great man. He used his wealth to aid the poor and distressed. Everyone in the city loved and trusted him, and eventually he was elected mayor. Such a transformation in a man's life is possible.

In some countries in recent years, humane laws have been passed that are designed to reform the criminal rather than punish him. He may be given psychiatric help, his condition being regarded as an illness. He is sick, not evil. This is the right approach.

We should 'hate the sin, but not the sinner'. Man's present and past are not everything. In your inner nature, you are beautiful. Given the opportunity, you can manifest this beauty. If you are constantly encouraged and reminded of your own innate goodness, all obstructions will gradually be removed and you will become a new man or woman.

Swami Vivekananda always emphasized the importance of positive ideas. He said, 'Calling a person a sinner is a great sin because it makes him feel he really is a sinner.' His self-confidence is destroyed. Teaching a person to hate himself is the greatest injury that you can inflict on him.

To illustrate this, Swamiji told a story about Pat, a young Irishman. Everyone would tell him: 'Pat, there is no hope for you. You were born a drudge and you will always be a drudge.' Pat believed them. He thought he was worthless. In Pat that divine consciousness, Brahman, was present, but it was all covered over by negative thoughts.

Then Pat emigrated to America. At first he was benumbed, frightened, but slowly he discovered that he was in a different kind of place. Everyone in the country seemed to be saying to him : 'Pat, you are a man. We also are men and look what we have done! If you want, you too can accomplish great things.' After some days a change could be seen in Pat's demeanour and movements. There was no fear, no inertia; he walked with his head held high. Swamiji said that Pat had learned to have faith in himself. The power that had been sleeping in him was aroused. Brahman became manifest in him.

Our scriptures say that he who regards himself as weak, powerless and worthless, is a killer of the Self, another name for suicide. We should not be the cause of someone committing suicide. Our thoughts, actions and words must not make anyone feel worthless or inferior. Truly great men never regard others as insignificant. Only small-minded people see others as small.

Holy Mother said, 'Learn to make the whole world your own. No one is a stranger, my child.' In Jesus Christ, Buddha, Caitanya—in all great souls—we find this large-heartedness. They are pure, so they can't see impurity in others. They embrace everyone in their infinite love.

We previously mentioned the story of Pavhari Baba. The same kind of compassion is found in Sri Ramakrishna. He showered his grace on Binodini the actress and on Girish Ghosh. Girish used to say that there was no sin that he had not committed, yet the Master forgave him and blessed him.

One day Girish was very drunk and made an extraordinary demand. He said to the Master, 'You must be born as my son.' Sri Ramakrishna replied, 'I cannot do that. Why should I be your son?' This enraged Girish and he began to insult the Master, using the most obscene language. When the other devotees heard about this they said to the Master, 'You should never visit him again.' But the very next day, the Master went to Girish's house. Girish fell at his feet, and crying bitterly said, 'Thakur, if you had not come today, I would not have believed you are an *Avatāra*. I would not have known that praise and blame are the same to you.'

When Swami Vivekananda was in the West, he received a letter from India saying, 'You will be sad to hear that immoral women now frequent the room that the Master used to live in.' Swamiji wrote in reply, 'They may certainly go into Thakur's room. He came just for the fallen.'

These words are echoed in a song dedicated to the Master:

You have come like a beggar
 to show mercy to the poor;
You have come to shower love
 on those whose lives have become like a desert;
You have come to raise
 those who have fallen.

Perhaps the most prominent trait of Holy Mother was her never seeing anyone's faults or sins, and her acceptance of all—the virtuous and the unvirtuous. She said, 'Did the Master come only to eat *rasagollās*? No, he came just for this—to raise the fallen.' A woman once said to her, 'I have done so many bad things that I am not worthy to enter your room.' Holy Mother embraced her and said, 'What if you have done something wrong? Come, I will give you a *mantra*.' And she gave the woman a *mantra* and showered her blessings on her.

On another occasion, Holy Mother said, 'As Sarat [Swami Saradananda] is my son, so also is Amjad [a Muslim dacoit].' In Mother's eyes they **were** the same. It was not that she was unaware of Amjad's misdeeds. She knew all about him, but she would say, 'I am the mother of the virtuous and I am also the mother of the wicked.' Further, 'Anyone can destroy. Who is able to build? Everyone can criticize bad people, but how can you make them good? Who can tell us how?' She also said, 'If my child becomes smeared with dirt, is it not my duty to wash him? Our coming is just for that.' To make the world better, to put the wicked on the path to good, to make the sinner free from sin—for this Sri Ramakrishna and Holy Mother took birth.

Swami Vivekananda said, 'When I was twenty years old, I was so narrow-minded that I would not walk on the footpath leading to the theatre. But now that I am thirty I cannot criticize even prostitutes. The idea of censuring them never enters my mind.'

When Swamiji was returning to India from his second trip to the West, he stopped at Cairo. With him were several of his Western disciples. One day while they were out walking, they wandered off and by mistake entered a district where prostitutes lived. It did not take them long to realize where they had come. Swamiji walked towards several women who were sitting together. At first they taunted him with obscenities, but they soon understood that this was not an ordinary man. Kneeling reverently at his feet, they touched his robe and said, 'Man of God! Man of God!' Tears of compassion flowed down Swamiji's cheeks.

Those who are genuinely religious do not ignore or slight anyone. They do not regard anyone as unworthy. True religion awakens hope in men and women. It tells you to rise. Wherever you are, don't stop there; go higher and higher.

I can begin this very moment. If not now, I will never begin. I will not believe that I am wicked, weak, or sinful. Sri Ramakrishna forbade anyone to regard himself as a sinner. Swami Brahmananda once said, 'Something may be a big sin in man's eyes, but to God it is nothing.' Swamiji did not like anyone to use the word *sin*. He said that man does not sin, he makes mistakes. He said that it is man's nature to make mistakes, that only human beings can do wrong. Man can steal and lie, but he can also become divine.

Why say 'become divine'? We are already divine, but that divinity is sleeping in us. When that sleep is ended, our divinity will be manifest. That is the goal in life for everyone of us.

References

1. *C.W.*, Vol.II, 1976, p.300
2. *Śvetāśvatara Upaniṣad*, II.5
3. *C.W.*, Vol. I, 1962, p.11
4. *Ibid.*, Vol.VIII, 1959, pp.126-27
5. *Ibid.*, Vol.VII, 1964, p.418
6. *Ibid.*, Vol.IV, 1962, p.358
7. *Ibid.*, Vol.I, p.93
8. *Gītā*, IX.30
9. *Haribhaktivilāsa*, Sanātana Goswāmī, 11/342
10. *C.W.*, Vol.VII, p.170
11. *Ibid.*, pp.170-71
12. *Udbodhan*, Vol.66, p.121

VII

What is there in Mere Scholarship?

It was the day of the *Rathayātrā*, the Car Festival of the Hindus. At Ishan's invitation Sri Ramakrishna went to his house in Calcutta. For some time the Master had had a desire to meet Pundit Shashadhar Tarkachudamani, who had been staying with one of Ishan's neighbours. (p.462)

Sri Ramakrishna liked to meet outstanding or prominent people of his day. He would go on his own initiative, uninvited, to see them because he knew that they could be instruments for the Divine Mother's work. These people were leaders of society and had many good qualities, but most of them had some narrowness or other defects in their outlook. Sri Ramakrishna thought that if he could remove these, many people would benefit. He would not argue with them, but would try by other means to remove these defects. This was especially noted in his influence on Keshab Chandra Sen and other members of the Brāhmo Samāj, who accepted only the formless deity. He helped to remove this narrow conception from their minds, and eventually Keshab and others accepted the reality of *Sakti*, the power of Brahman, and understood that God is also with form.

The well-known Brāhmo periodical of the time, *Dharmatattva*, said in one of its articles:

> The way the Paramahamsa views God as Mother has aroused the interest of the Brāhmo Samāj. Like a simple child,

he calls God by the sweet name of 'Mother' and makes demands on her. This is the paramahamsa state which the acharya (i.e., Keshab Sen) has achieved in a special way. Formerly the Brāhmo religion was dry reasoning and a religion of knowledge. Coming under the influence of the Paramahamsa, the Brāhmo religion has become sweet.[1]

Sri Ramakrishna had heard about Shashadhar Tarkachudamani, a famous scholar of that time, and was eager to meet him. **So it was decided that he would visit the pundit in the afternoon.** (p.462)

It was about four o'clock. **As soon as Sri Ramakrishna got into the carriage he went into *samādhi*. . . . It was the rainy season, and a fine drizzle of rain had made the road muddy. The sky was overcast.** The devotees followed on foot. **As the carriage stopped in front of the house, the host and his relatives welcomed the Master and took him upstairs to the drawing room. There the Master met the pundit. Pundit Shashadhar, a man of fair complexion and no longer young, had a string of *rudrākṣa* beads around his neck. . .**

The pundit saluted the Master with reverence. Narendra, Rakhal, Ram, Hazra, and M., who had come with the Master, seated themselves in the room as near the Master as they could, anxious not to miss one of his words.

At the sight of the pundit the Master again went into *samādhi*. After a while, still remaining in that state, he looked at the pundit and said with a smile, 'Very well, very well!' (p.464)

Then Sri Ramakrishna asked him what kind of lectures he gave. The pundit replied, 'Sir, I try to explain the words of the scriptures.' Perhaps the Master did not agree with this because he said, 'Devotion according to Nārada is best for the *Kali Yuga*.'

The celestial sage Nārada who eternally wanders around the world singing the names and glories of God asks for nothing—he is simply intoxicated with the name of God. Devotion according to Nārada is pure love which desires nothing. Sri Ramakrishna continued, **Where can people find time now to perform their duties according to the scriptural injunctions?** (p.464)

People today are involved in many activities. Formerly they had more leisure; their lives were not so hurried. They had time to worship, observe vows, perform elaborate sacrifices and other things. But Sri Ramakrishna was not only concerned about people's busy lives, he also objected to the idea that merely by reading the scriptures and strictly observing their injunctions, one could realize God.

Once someone said to Sri Ramakrishna, **There is so much to read! The scriptures are endless.** The Master answered, **How much of the scriptures can you read? What will you gain by mere reasoning? Try to realize God before anything else. Have faith in the guru's words, and work. If you have no guru, then pray to God with a longing heart. He will let you know what he is like.** (p.645)

Sri Ramakrishna was not criticizing the scriptures. He only objected to the idea that those who study them are thereby nearer to God than others. He said, 'Knowledge of the scriptures is one thing, and experience another. Direct experience is the goal—not scriptural knowledge.' Scriptural knowledge is dry. We have many teachings about this in the scriptures themselves. They warn us, 'You will not find God in the forest of the scriptures. Learn from them, and then practise whatever they teach you. Your goal is God—not the scriptures.'

In the words of the *Vivekacūḍāmaṇi*:

Śabdajālaṁ mahāraṇyaṁ cittabhramaṇakāraṇam
Ataḥ prayatnājjñātavyaṁ tattvajñaistattvamātmanaḥ—

'A network of words is like a dense forest that causes the mind to wander hither and thither. Therefore, those who know this truth should struggle hard to experience Brahman.'[2]

And from the *Kulārṇava Tantra*:

Ṣaḍdarśanamahākūpe patitāḥ paśavaḥ priye
Paramārthaṁ na jānanti paśupāśaniyantritāḥ—

'Those who study the six systems of Indian philosophy but do not direct their minds to God, do not know the highest goal. It is as if they have fallen into a deep well. They are bound, their lives are despicable—like animals.'[3]

Sri Ramakrishna had some hard words to say about mere scholars. Before going to see any scholar he would first find out if he kept his mind on God, if his character was good, etc. If these questions were answered in the affirmative, he would visit him, otherwise not. He went to see the pundit Vidyasagar because he had heard of his great compassion.

The Master said to Pundit Shashadhar: **When I first heard about you, I inquired whether you were merely erudite or whether you had discrimination. A pundit who doesn't know how to discriminate between the Real and the unreal is no pundit at all.** (p.465)

Sri Ramakrishna said that some scholars are like vultures. They soar very high in the sky but always have their eyes fixed on the carrion below. They may study the scriptures and lecture on God, but their minds are not on God but on sense objects. Again from the *Vivekacūḍāmaṇi*:

Vāgvaikharī śābdajharī śāstravyākhyānakauśalam
Vaiduṣyaṁ viduṣāṁ tadvadbhuktaye na tu muktaye—

'Erudition, well-articulated speech, a wealth of words, and skill in expounding the scriptures—these things give pleasure to the learned, but they do not bring liberation.'[4]

A similar verse is found in the *Kulārṇava Tantra*:

Vedāgamapurāṇajnaḥ paramārthaṁ na vetti yaḥ
Viḍamvakasya tasyāpi tat sarvaṁ kākabhāṣitam—

'A person may read the Vedas, *Āgamas*, and *Purāṇas* and study all the scriptures, but still not know God or the highest good verified by the scriptures. His words are not from his own realization. (*Viḍamvak* means one who imitates or copies.) They are worthless, like the *kā kā* of a crow.'[5] They make no impression on those who hear them.

Sri Ramakrishna used the simile of a water pitcher. When you put an empty pitcher in a pond, at first there is much noise, *bhak bhak*, as the water enters the pitcher. But when the pitcher is filled, there is no sound at all. 'Empty vessels make a big noise', in the words of an English saying. When a person is filled with true knowledge, he becomes silent.

Another illustration Sri Ramakrishna used was about guests at a dinner. They sit down to eat and there is much chatter. The host is shouting, 'Have some *lucis*! Have some dal! Have some curry!' Then the guests become absorbed in eating and there is less noise. Finally curd is served and all that is heard is *sup sup*. At last sleep, and perfect silence. In the same way, we at first engage in much reasoning and discussion of the scriptures. But when God is realized, all reasoning and argumentation disappear. Our character is changed. Whatever we say comes from God because our minds have become pure. The Master says, 'The words of God arise in a pure mind.'

We think that if someone speaks beautiful, poetic words, people will be impressed. It is not so. The power of the words comes from the speaker's life and character. When Swamiji first addressed the Parliament of Religions saying, 'Sisters and brothers of America', there were two minutes of spontaneous applause. Only five ordinary words—we ourselves can easily say them, but they do not come from our heart. Swamiji's words had behind them the force of the man. Romain Rolland said, 'I cannot touch these sayings of his, scattered as they are through the pages of books at thirty years distance, without receiving a thrill through my body like an electric shock. And what shocks, what transports must have been produced when in burning words they issued from the lips of the hero!'[6]

That is true : Swamiji's words are such that we cannot fail to be inspired by them. It is the same with the words of Sri Ramakrishna and Holy Mother. They leave a deep impression on our minds because they carry with them the power of direct God-realization. In all religions the value of direct experience is emphasized. Jesus Christ said, 'Beware of the doctors of the law, who love to walk up and down in long robes, receiving respectful greetings in the street; and to have the chief seats in synagogues, and places of honour at feasts. These are the men who eat up the property of widows while they say long prayers for appearance's sake.' At last he says, 'and they will receive the severest sentence.'[7]

Sri Ramakrishna often warned people not to put too much emphasis on book-learning. He said, **Do you know my attitude? Books, scriptures, and things like that only point out the way to reach God. After finding the way, what more need is there of books and scriptures?** He illustrated this point with a story:

A man received a letter from home informing him that certain presents were to be sent to his relatives. The

names of the articles were given in the letter. As he was about to go shopping for them, he found that the letter was missing. He began anxiously to search for it, several others joining in the search. For a long time they continued to search. When at last the letter was discovered, his joy knew no bounds. With great eagerness he opened the letter and read it. It said that he was to buy five seers of sweets, a piece of cloth and a few other things. Then he did not need the letter any more, for it had served its purpose. Putting it aside, he went out to buy the things. How long is such a letter necessary? As long as its contents are not known. When the contents are known one proceeds to carry out the directions. (p.729)

The *Kulārṇava Tantra* says:

Na vedāḥ kāraṇaṁ mukterdarśanāni na kāraṇam
Tathaiva sarvaśāstrāṇi jñānameva hi kāraṇam—

'The Vedas do not bring about liberation. They do not have the power of sight. Knowledge alone gives liberation. That knowledge does not mean knowledge of the material world, but knowledge of Reality.'[8]

And the *Vivekacūḍāmaṇi* says:

Na gacchati vinā pānaṁ vyādhirouṣadhaśabdataḥ
Vinā'parokṣānubhavaṁ brahmaśabdairna mucyate—

'Illness is not cured by saying the word *medicine*. You must take the medicine. Similarly, liberation does not come by merely saying the word *Brahman*. Brahman must be actually experienced'.[9]

Without direct experience, there is no liberation. Sri Ramakrishna says that by merely saying '*Siddhi, siddhi*!', you will not become intoxicated. You must pound the *siddhi*, mix it with milk, and drink it—then you will be intoxicated. Our scriptures emphasize over and over again the necessity of direct, personal experience.

Sri Ramakrishna said, **I do not accept anything unless it agrees with the direct words of the Divine Mother.** (p.773) In the scriptures sugar is mixed with sand, so to speak. What part is accepted as sugar and what rejected as sand? The Master said that he would accept only whatever is in agreement with the words of the Divine Mother and his own direct experience—nothing else. He stressed the necessity of having direct perception of Reality.

All Sri Ramakrishna's experiences agree with what is in the scriptures. We can verify the truths of the scriptures by his life. Seeing him we can believe that they are not false or designed to hoodwink us. They speak the truth. The Master said that his experiences have gone even beyond the Vedas and Vedānta. It seems that the scriptures were too small to hold him. They fail to describe what he directly experienced. Scholars would be awe-struck listening to him. They would say, 'We have studied the scriptures, but we find them trifling compared to you.' For example, *samādhi* is mentioned in the scriptures, but who has experienced *samādhi*? Yet Sri Ramakrishna was in the state of *samādhi* again and again. Those who came to see him were able to understand what *samādhi* is and that it is possible for a person to directly experience it.

In the Tantras we read:

Mathitvā caturo vedān sarvaśāstrāṇi caiva hi
Sārantu yogibhiḥ pītaṁ takraṁ pivanti paṇḍitāḥ—

'Churning the four Vedas and the scriptures, cream and butter rise. This is consumed by *yogis* who practise spiritual disciplines. Scholars only drink what remains, the whey. They are cheated.'[10]

After seeing Sri Ramakrishna in *samādhi*, Dayananda Sarasvati, the founder of the Ārya Samāj, said the same thing: 'We have only read the Vedas and Vedānta, but this great soul has found the fruit. Seeing him we have direct evidence that scholars by churning the scriptures get only whey. Great souls take all the butter.'

Swami Virajananda, the sixth President of the Ramakrishna Order, referred to Sri Ramakrishna in a hymn as 'the illiterate-yet-all-knowing-perceiver-of-the-essence-of-the-scriptures'. Of course the Master was not completely illiterate, but in the common meaning of the term he was, as he was unschooled. Still we find in the *Gospel* what vast knowledge of the scriptures he had. He could clearly explain abstruse passages. Moreover, the essence of all the scriptures can be found in his words collected in the *Gospel*. Where did he get such knowledge? Through his direct spiritual realizations. Knowing *That* (the Divine Reality, Brahman), you have knowledge of everything—and he knew *That*. So though he was almost illiterate, he was 'All-knowing'.

Again and again the Master would tell people, 'You must realize God. That is the purpose for which you were born—not for scriptural knowledge or mere book-learning. God realization is the goal of life.' He said, 'The words in a letter and the words from the mouth of the person who wrote the letter are very different. The scriptures are like the words of the letter; the words of God can be directly heard from His mouth.' If you spend your time only in studying the scriptures, your life will be in vain.

The *Kulārṇava Tantra* says:

Paṭhanti vedaśāstrāṇi vivadanti parasparam
Na jānanti paraṁ tattvaṁ darvī pākarasaṁ yathā—

'Scholars read the Vedas and other scriptures, arguing about them among themselves. A scholar is like a ladle with which food is stirred and served. Everyone eating the food is gratified, but the ladle can never get the taste of the food. In the same way, scholars only study the scriptures and quarrel over them. They are deprived of the bliss of God-realization which the scriptures are describing.'[11] They are unfortunate; they do not know what they are missing. Their knowledge is not true knowledge. Direct God-realization is true knowledge. That knowledge is based on devotion, faith, renunciation, love and purity.

In the *Caitanya Caritāmṛta* we find an interesting incident relating to this. One day Śri Caitanya noticed a man reciting the *Gītā*. The man could not pronounce the Sanskrit words properly, yet tears of joy trickled down his cheeks. Śri Caitanya asked him what it was that gave him so much joy. The man replied, 'I do not understand any of the words of the *Gītā*. I only read it at the command of my guru. But when I read it I see before me Lord Kṛṣṇa and Arjuna and am filled with joy.' That man was blessed. He had no knowledge of the scriptures, but he had devotion, faith, and love of God. He was much greater than those who have only scriptural knowledge.

Sri Ramakrishna says: **In the scriptures you will find the way to realize God. But after getting all the information about the path, you must begin to work. Only then can you attain your goal.**

What will it avail a man to have mere scholarship? A pundit may have studied many scriptures, he may recite

many sacred texts, but if he is still attached to the world and if inwardly he loves 'woman and gold', then he has not assimilated the contents of the scriptures. For such a man the study of the scriptures is futile.

The almanac forecasts the rainfall for the year. You may squeeze the book, but you won't get a drop of water—not even a single drop. . . . The pundits talk big, but where is their mind fixed? On 'woman and gold', on creature comforts and money.

***The vulture soars very high in the sky, but its eyes are fixed on the charnel-pit.* (pp.729-30)**

Sri Ramakrishna always taught that the false, the counterfeit, should be shunned. Even as a child he would mimic the village pundits—their gestures, their recital of sacred texts. He understood that their expounding of the scriptures was futile. They were not worthy of respect because their only aim was to earn money. He honoured only those scholars who had real knowledge and devotion. He said, **If I see a pundit without discrimination and love of God, I regard him as a bit of straw.** (p.889)

Through learning one may get name and fame and money. But Sri Ramakrishna measured the worth of a person by something else—how much love he had for God. Again and again he emphasized this. He said, **You may read scriptures by the thousands and recite thousands of texts; but unless you plunge into God with yearning of heart, you will not comprehend Him. By mere scholarship you may fool man, but not God.** (p.625)

To Shashadhar he said, **Add a little more of your strength. Practise spiritual discipline a few days more. You have hardly set your foot on the tree, yet you expect**

to lay hold of a big cluster of fruit. (p.465) But it was not only Pundit Shashadhar that he was addressing. He was speaking to all preachers of religion: 'First add a little more to your strength. Are you able to love God? If you do not have devotion within you, can you give it to anyone else? Without that love, you may try to preach, but your words will have no effect on others.'

He did not forbid anyone to speak. Elsewhere in the *Gospel* we find the Master visiting the Brāhmo Samāj when Vijaykrishna Goswami was to speak on some religious topic. Vijay was hesitant to speak in the presence of the Master, but Sri Ramakrishna said to him, 'Go ahead and preach as you normally do, but don't think you are teaching anyone. Think that God Himself is speaking through you, that His power is being expressed through you.'

Years later a similar incident occurred when Swamiji wanted to send Swami Virajananda to speak in Dhaka. Swami Virajananda protested, 'I have not realized God, how can I preach?' At first Swamiji tried to reason with him, telling him that he should regard this as he would any other work, as a service to God in man. Still Swami Virajananda persisted, 'I do not know anything, so what can I say?' Then Swamiji said: 'That is true, so stand up and say, "I do not know anything." That will be a great teaching'. 'I know everything' indicates ignorance. Indeed, anyone who really believes that he knows nothing has annihilated his ego. Thus, he receives God's grace and the power of God works through him.

Another president of the Ramakrishna Order, Swami Madhavananda, was also reluctant to speak. If anyone wanted instruction from him, he would say, 'It has all been written in the books.' If repeatedly urged, he would say a few words, and if we still pestered him, he would say a few more words—all invaluable. He was a very good speaker, yet he never wanted to speak. Once at Belur Math on Swamiji's birthday, after many entreaties, he gave a wonderful speech—a kind seldom heard. I noticed that no matter whether he was to speak before a large or small gathering, he would meditate in the Master's shrine before speaking. I imagine he prayed something like this : 'How can I speak? I know nothing. Do Thou speak through me!' And we felt that God was truly speaking through him when he gave his talk.

Sri Ramakrishna would say to religious teachers and preachers: 'Let there be no egotism. When you give a lecture or any kind of teaching, always remember that you are the machine and God is the operator of the machine. If by His grace He gives you something to say, say that.' In reality, only God can teach the love of God. Those whom God chooses, to whom he gives His power, are able to teach religion. People feel that it is really God Himself who is preaching through them—that they are only His instrument.

Swamiji was such a speaker. He once said, 'I am a voice without a form.'[12] Whatever he said came from God. He was only an instrument.

Sri Ramakrishna says, **There is no teacher except *Saccidānanda*. There is no refuge except Him. He alone is the Ferryman to take one across the ocean of the world.** (p.633)

God alone, the Creator of this world-bewitching *māyā*, can save men from *māyā*. . . . How is it ever possible for men who have not realized God or received His command, and who are not strengthened with divine strength, to save others from the prison-house of the world? (p.168)

We think that if we say a few words we can help a person. That is not so. We may say the right things, but after a short time he will forget what we have said. And, one who has true wisdom, who has seen God, does not even need to speak. A touch, even a glance from him is enough to transform others. Whatever he says, though it may be in ordinary conversation, is for the good of all. Behind his words is such power that he is able to arouse the spirituality in others. People by the hundreds, unable to resist that power, flock to him, and their lives are changed.

Some holy persons take a vow of silence, yet people somehow hear about them and go to them. Such a person was Trailangaswami, who lived in Vārāṇasī. People there regarded him as the 'moving Viśvanātha' in contrast to the 'unmoving Viśvanātha' in the temple. Sri Ramakrishna visited him, as did Swamiji.

Truly speaking, a holy person's life is his best 'sermon'. People are attracted to a person whose life is built on a strong spiritual foundation. The Master said to Pundit Shashadhar: **When the lamp is lighted the moths come in swarms. They don't have to be invited. The preacher who has a commission from God need not invite people to hear him. He doesn't have to announce the time of his lectures. He possesses such irresistible attraction that people come to him of their own accord.** (p.466) This was true of Sri Ramakrishna himself. People came to him drawn by his immense spirituality. No one had to invite them.

Continuing his conversation with the pundit, the Master said, **There is no harm in teaching others if the preacher has a commission from the Lord. Nobody can confound a preacher who teaches people after having received the**

command of God. Getting a ray of light from the goddess of learning, a man becomes so powerful that before him big scholars seem mere earthworms. (pp.465-66)

We find this in Sri Ramakrishna's life. Great scholars would seem like earthworms compared to him. Pundit Gauri was considered to be a great scholar. When he entered a meeting-place to engage in debate, like a wrestler challenging his opponent he would shout, '*Hā*, *re*, *re*, *re*! Helpless I take refuge in the Mother of Gaṇeśa!' Then no one could defeat him. When he first came to see Sri Ramakrishna, he did the same thing. Entering the temple compound he shouted, '*Hā*, *re*, *re*, *re*!' But the Master shouted even louder, '*Hā*, *re*, *re*, *re*!' Gauri raised his voice to a louder pitch and the Master again shouted louder. At this the gatekeepers of the temple came running with their sticks. After a time, Gauri realized that he could not compete with Sri Ramakrishna. Distressed and baffled, he became silent. Gradually he came to recognize the Master's greatness and surrendered himself to him.

Another well-known scholar who came to Dakshineswar was Vaishnavacharan. One day Sri Ramakrishna sat on his shoulders in a state of ecstasy. The scholar felt blessed and on the spur of the moment composed a hymn to him.

Sometimes Sri Ramakrishna saw that a scholar was not really interested in finding the truth, but only in displaying his learning. Then he might give the man a little touch. That would be enough. At once the scholar would come to his senses.

Many great scholars have come and gone in this world, but they are now forgotten. It is great souls like Christ, Buddha, Caitanya and Sri Ramakrishna who have given us what we need to build our lives. Most of them were not scholars and had little knowledge of the scriptures. Still they had the one essential thing: they had seen God. Because of that, their words kindled the minds of their followers.

Truth is floating around us in space, as it were, yet we cannot grasp it. But when your mind reaches a certain state, when it becomes very pure and your egotism dwindles to almost nothing, when you become eager to realize God—then your mind becomes united with Truth. And when you speak, people become spellbound: they feel their lives are being transformed.

The words of those who have had direct spiritual experience carry great power. A Sanskrit verse uses the expression *karāmalakavat*—'Like the *āmalaka* fruit in my hand'. If I have an *āmalaka* fruit in my hand, everyone on earth can tell me there is nothing in my hand, still I will not believe them. Realized souls have the direct experience of 'the *āmalaka* in their hands'. They know they have seen God, and they speak with such confidence, with such force, that they move the minds of others. This great conviction they pass on to their followers.

Sri Ramakrishna said, 'Yes, I have assuredly seen God, just as I am seeing you—only more intensely.' He wanted everyone to see God. 'If you wish, I can show Him to you,'—these are words of great assurance. Only a person established in Truth can speak like that; a divine light exists in him.

In the *Caitanya Caritāmṛta* we find,

> To teach religion, you yourself must be religious:
> This is the conclusion of the *Bhāgavatam* and the *Gītā*.[13]

If we ourselves do not live righteously, how can we teach others? We ourselves must know and understand the Truth and apply it in our lives. Only then can we teach others. Mere lip-service is worthless.

Once someone said to Muhammad: 'My son likes to eat too many sweets. Please explain to him that that is not good for him.' Muhammad replied, 'You are right, but come again after a week.' The next week the man again brought his son to Muhammad, who said to the boy: 'See here, don't eat so many sweets. They will make you sick.' He said only these few words. The man was surprised and said, 'Why did you not say those same words last week when we were here?' Muhammad said: 'The reason is, I myself eat many sweets. How could I tell the boy not to eat them? But for a whole week now I have not eaten a single sweet, so my words will be effective.' It is one's conduct that teaches others.

Sri Ramakrishna says: **Does the magnet say to the iron, 'Come near me?' That is not necessary. Because of the attraction of the magnet the iron rushes to it**. And referring to a God-realized soul: **Such a preacher may not be a scholarly person, but don't conclude from that that he has any lack of wisdom. Does book-learning make one wise? . . . He who has a commission from God never runs short of wisdom. That wisdom comes from God; it is inexhaustible.** (p.466)

We find proof of this in Swami Vivekananda's experience in America. He often had to deliver lectures there and would sometimes wonder what he could say next. But at night when he went to bed, it seemed to him that someone was talking to him, telling him what to say at the next day's lecture. The Master had said, 'Naren will teach people.' Now it seemed that the Master himself was pushing towards him portions from his great store of knowledge.

Swamiji was so young, barely thirty, but what beautiful words, what original thoughts he gave to the world! Scholars were astonished at his brilliance and showed him much honour and respect. Where did his power come from? From Sri Ramakrishna. Swami Premananda once said, 'If you write the words "Sri Ramakrishna" on a stick, that stick will become a world conqueror.'

Sri Ramakrishna shows us what a true teacher of religion is. Pratap Chandra Mazumdar, himself a well-known orator, would sit listening to Sri Ramakrishna hour after hour. His remarks about the Master are found in chapter XVIII.

Another famous person, Keshab Sen, came by steamer to Dakshineswar one day, accompanied by some of his friends. As Sri Ramakrishna boarded the steamer, everyone stood up. Keshab led him by the hand to his seat and then sat down beside him. Everyone stopped talking, not wanting to miss one of the Master's words. Nagendranath Gupta, one of those present, has described the incident.

> Practically all the talking was done by the Paramahamsa, and the rest, including Keshab himself, were respectful and eager listeners. I have never heard any other man speak as he did. It was an unbroken flow of profound spiritual truths and experiences, welling up from the perennial spring of his own devotion and wisdom.[14]

Sri Ramakrishna was a real preacher of religion. He did not like miracles, but what can be more miraculous and superhuman than his ability to attract so many people by his simple yet profound words? How was it possible? It was possible because he had realized God. That is what made his words so full of fire and his personality so attractive.

Sri Ramakrishna said to Shashadhar, **Can a preacher ever lack knowledge if but once he is favoured with a benign glance from the Divine Mother? Therefore I ask**

you whether you have received any commission from God. Shashadhar replied, **Commission? No, sir, I am afraid I haven't received any such thing.**

At that, the Master said: **What will a man accomplish by mere lectures without the commission from God? Once a Brāhmo preacher said in the course of his sermon, 'Friends, how much I used to drink!' and so on. Hearing this the people began to whisper among themselves: 'What is this fool saying? He used to drink!' Now these words produced a very unfavourable effect. This shows that preaching cannot bring a good result unless it comes from a good man.** (p.466)

Sri Ramakrishna put great emphasis on 'being'. Swamiji said, 'Religion is being and becoming.' I am devoted to one ideal and am trying to embody that ideal in my life. Little by little I am moving towards that ideal, and gradually it will become manifest in my life. This is religion. I will not have to tell others that I am religious. My religion will be intimately united with my life. I will become a new person. My life, my character—all the trifling things I am involved in—will show that I am following the path of religion.

Swamiji said that learning does not mean acquiring information or knowing so many facts, so many words. If that were so, encyclopedias would be the greatest scholars and libraries would be *Ṛṣis*. But one idea must dominate my life in such a way that it becomes part of me. I will not be able to behave in another way, even by mistake. If I am good, I am good—not for praise or fear of punishment—but because I can't help being good. Only those whose characters are formed in this way can truly teach.

The Master told a story about this: **In Kamarpukur there is a pond called the 'Haldarpukur'. . . . People used to**

dirty the bank of the Haldarpukur. This was stopped only when a constable, armed with authority from the government, put up a notice prohibiting it. (p.466) One needs this authority. Where does it come from? 'The government'—from direct realization, from God Himself. A person can speak with authority only if he can say with the Upaniṣad, 'I know the great *puruṣa*', if he can say, 'Look at me, see my life. I have seen God. The proof is in my character.'

Sri Ramakrishna said, **Caitanyadeva was an Incarnation of God. He brought a flood of devotion to the whole country. His influence spread everywhere; still that power slowly diminished, in spite of the fact that he was an *Avatāra*. How little is left of what he accomplished—not to speak of a lecturer who preaches without authority from God! What good will a lecturer do?** (p.467)

At that time, in the 1880's, Christian missionaries were giving lectures on every corner in Calcutta. They would tell the Hindus that their religion was false, that they were idol worshippers, etc. There were also many Hindu religious teachers and social reformers giving lectures. Sri Ramakrishna did not give lectures, but something much more effective. His life was more eloquent, more full of meaning than any lecture.

The title of Dhan Gopal Mukherjee's book on Sri Ramakrishna, *The Face of Silence*, is very suggestive. Sri Ramakrishna was silent in that he did not lecture or advertise himself. He only came, played with the Divine Mother and his companions, and departed. But his quiet power intoxicated everyone. Today his life and message are being discussed more and more, and many books are being written about him. By meditating on him people get peace and strength and hope. He is no longer silent but is being heard everywhere. His message reaches all those who sincerely long for God.

Holy Mother's life is even more amazing than the Master's. Sri Ramakrishna was a man and mingled with many people, but Holy Mother was always veiled. Some of the people at the Dakshineswar temple did not even know that she was there. Still, later on, many people came to her to quench their thirst for religion. She would sit in front of them, covered by her veil, and speak with them through her attendants, or sometimes she would remain silent. But all their doubts would disappear; they would be completely satisfied.

These marvellous persons—they did not advertise themselves, they did not give lectures—why then are they so greatly revered all over the world today? It is because of their lives, their characters. They saw God and talked with Him. It is because they had this direct experience that more and more people are being attracted to them and their teachings.

When Buddha was about to leave this world, his disciples gathered around him. His most beloved disciple, Ānanda, was crying. He said to Buddha, 'When you depart, all will be in darkness. Who will be our light?' Buddha answered, 'Be ye lamps unto yourselves.' The lamp of knowledge is within all of us. We must follow that light. And as we follow it, we can also show the way to others.

Sri Ramakrishna says, **Dive into the Ocean of *Saccidānanda*. Nothing will ever worry you if you but realize God. Then you will get His commission to teach people.** (p.467)

References

1. *Samasāmayik Dṛṣṭite Śrī Rāmakṛṣṇa*, p.61
2. *Vivekacūḍāmaṇi*, 60
3. *Kulārṇava Tantra*, 1/87

4. *Vivekacūḍāmaṇi*, 58
5. *Kulārṇava Tantra*, 1/89
6. *World Thinkers on Ramakrishna-Vivekananda*, Swami Lokeswarananda, Editor, 1983, p.50
7. New Testament, *St. Mark*, XII. 38-40
8. *Kulārṇava Tantra*, 1/106
9. *Vivekacūḍāmaṇi*, 62
10. *Jñānasaṅkalinī Tantra*, 51
11. *Kulārṇava Tantra*, 1/94
12. *C.W.*, Vol. VI, 1985, p.283
13. *Caitanya Caritāmṛta*, Ādilīlā, Chapter 3
14. Quoted in *A Bridge to Eternity* (Advaita Ashrama, 1986), p.78

VIII

Truth Alone Triumphs

Sri Ramakrishna said: **If a man leads a householder's life he must have unflagging devotion to truth. God can be realized through truth alone.** (p.418) And it is said in the *Muṇḍaka Upaniṣad, Satyena labhyastapasā hyeṣa ātmā*—'This Ātman is attained by unceasing practice of truthfulness.'[1]

Truth does not mean only truthful words; it means truth of body, mind—everything. One must behave truthfully, think truthfully, and speak truthfully. Sri Ramakrishna says, 'Make your mind and speech one.' A person's behaviour must not be in opposition to his thought.

Once a man came to see the Master wearing *geruā*, the mark of a monk, though he was not a monk. The Master did not like this. He said: **Why this *geruā*? Should one put on such a thing for a mere fancy?** (p.195) The man dressed like a monk, but did not live like a monk. That was not right. If a person dresses like a monk, he must sincerely try to live the life of renunciation as a monk does. Otherwise his behaviour is false.

Sri Ramakrishna said: **No lie of any sort is good. A false garb, even though a holy one, is not good. If the outer garb does not correspond to the inner thought, it gradually brings ruin. Uttering false words or doing false deeds, one gradually loses all fear. Far better is the white cloth of a householder. Attachment to worldliness, occasional lapses from the ideal, and an outer garb of *geruā*—how dreadful!** (p.195)

Śrī Kṛṣṇa says in the *Gītā*:

Karmendriyāṇi saṁyamya ya āste manasā smaran
Indriyārthān vimūḍhātmā mithyācārah sa ucyate—

'He who restrains his organs of action but continues in his mind to brood over the objects of sense, whose nature is deluded, is said to be a hypocrite (a man of false conduct).'[2]

If I take a vow of renunciation and do not enjoy anything physically, yet mentally crave things, my behaviour is false. My renunciation is not genuine. I must be the same inside and out. Whether anyone is watching or not, whether anyone knows what I am doing or not, I will hold to truth. I am devoted to truth for the sake of truth and not for people's praise. Even though the whole world stands against me, I will cling to truth because I value it more than life itself.

Swami Vivekananda once said, 'One can renounce everything for truth, but one should not give up truth for anything.'[3] He also said, 'Truth does not pay homage to any society. . . . Society has to pay homage to Truth. . . .'[4] There is nothing greater than truth. God is truth; truth is God. If I hold to truth, all my actions will be true. Why is *tapasyā*, austerity, called 'truth'? Because real austerity is truth of body, mind, and speech. If one is truly able to practise this austerity he will attain God, Self-realization.

Sri Ramakrishna placed truth above everything else. Even if by mistake he said he would do something, he would do it, no matter how inconvenient. He once said he would go to Jadu Mallik's garden house on a particular day, but as he had many visitors all day long, he forgot to go. When he finally remembered, it was late at night. No one else would think of going at that time, but he went, taking his attendant with him. They found the door of the house shut and everyone apparently asleep. Pushing open the door a crack, he put his foot inside and said three times, 'I have come.' Then he was at peace. One must keep one's word, and he had kept it.

If someone said he would do something and fail to keep his word, the Master would be annoyed. Once Shivanath Shastri forgot to visit him as he had promised. People often do things like that, but Sri Ramakrishna did not approve of this, though ordinarily he would praise Shivanath. He said: **I feel very happy when I see Shivanath. He always seems to be absorbed in the bliss of *bhakti*. Further, a man who is respected by so many surely possesses some divine power. But he has one great defect: he doesn't keep his word. Once he said he would come to Dakshineswar, but he neither came nor sent me word. That is not good. If a man clings tenaciously to truth he ultimately realizes God. Without this regard for truth, one gradually loses everything.** (p.312)

Satyameva jayate nānṛtam—'Truth alone triumphs, not untruth.'[5] One may gain a temporary victory through falsehood, but in the end truth is victorious. The Sanskrit word *ṛta* means moral order, or truth. We see much confusion in the affairs of the world, but behind it all is the moral order, *ṛta*. You may not believe in God or heaven, but you can't help being aware of something unchanging behind everything, something more powerful than anything in this changeful universe, *ṛta*. If we observe events over a long passage of time, we see that truth eventually wins out. So it is said:

Na hi satyāt paro dharmaḥ
Na pāpamanṛtāt param—

'There is no religion greater than truth; there is no sin greater than untruth.'[6] Truth is the highest religion.

Before the War of Kurukṣetra began, Duryodhana went to his mother Gāndhārī for her blessing. She could have said, 'May you be victorious!' But she did not. Instead she said, *Yato dharmastato jayaḥ*—'May *dharma* be victorious!' What is *dharma?* It is the highest religion, which is truthfulness. Gāndhārī knew this and that whoever holds to truth will be victorious. And that is what happened. Her son and his allies, who were unrighteous, were defeated. Their cousins, the Pāṇḍavas, were victorious because they were firm in their devotion to truth.

In the *Īśa Upaniṣad* we find:

Hiraṇmayena pātreṇa satyasyāpihitaṁ mukham
Tattvaṁ pūṣannapāvṛṇu satyadharmāya dṛṣṭaye—

'The door of the Truth is covered by a golden disc. Open it, O Nourisher! Remove it so that I who have been worshipping the Truth may behold It.'[7] What is this disc? *Saṁsāra*, the world. This *saṁsāra* is always attracting us, and we struggle to possess it. But behind it is something much more attractive—Truth, Brahman, God. We want to see that Truth and understand it.

Rabindranath Tagore in one of his songs says, 'O Lord, you are Truth, Bliss, and Love, a never-failing light in darkness. Those in whose heart you dwell forget all their burning grief.' To have the Lord always dwelling in our heart is the goal of life. Truthful speech is the first step to that goal. If a person always speaks the truth, such power will be produced in him that he will become a *vāk-siddha*—whatever he says will come true. God will not allow any of his words to be false.

Many great souls have spoken about truthfulness:

Tulasīdāsa said: 'Always speak the truth, take refuge in God, and look on all women as your mother. If you do not attain God by doing these three things, know that all the words of Tulasīdāsa are lies.'

Swami Brahmananda said much the same thing: 'Observe two things, speak the truth and look on all women as mother. There is nothing more.'[8] He also said, 'One must always be tethered to truth as to a stake.'[9]

Holy Mother said, 'One attains God in the *Kali Yuga* [modern age] if one is firmly established in truth.'[10]

Śrī Kṛṣṇa says in the *Bhagavad Gītā* (XVI.2) that truth is one of the endowments of those born with a divine nature.

And from the Upanisads:

Satyena panthā vitato devayānaḥ
Yenākramantyṛṣayo hyāptakāmā
Yatra tat satyasya paramaṁ nidhānam—

'By truth the path is laid out, the way of the Gods, on which seers, whose every desire is satisfied, proceed to the Highest Abode of the True.'[11]

In a conversation with Vijaykrishna Goswami and other devotees at a Brāhmo Samāj festival, Sri Ramakrishna said: **If by chance I say that I will go to the pine-grove, I must go there even if there is no further need of it, lest I lose my attachment to truth. After my vision of the Divine Mother, I prayed to Her, taking a flower in my hands: 'Mother, here is Thy knowledge and here is Thy ignorance. Take them both and give me only pure love. Here is Thy holiness and here is Thy unholiness. Take them both, Mother, and give me pure love. Here is Thy righteousness and Thy unrighteousness. Take them both, Mother, and give me pure love,' I mentioned all these, but I could not say: 'Mother, here is Thy truth and here is Thy falsehood. Take them both.' I gave up everything**

at Her feet but could not bring myself to give up truth. (p.312)

On another occasion he said, **Formerly I was very particular about telling the truth, though now my zeal has abated a little. If I said, 'I shall bathe', then I would get into the water of the Ganges, recite the *mantra*, and sprinkle a little water over my head. But still there would remain some doubt in me as to whether my bath was complete. Once I went to Ram's house in Calcutta. I happened to say, 'I shall not take any *luci*.' When I sat down for the meal I felt hungry. But I had said I would not eat *luci*; so I had to fill my stomach with sweets.**

But my zeal for truthfulness has abated a little now. Once I said I would go to the pine-grove, but then I had no particular urge to go. What was to be done? I asked Ram about it. He said I didn't have to go. Then I reasoned to myself: 'Well, everyone is *Nārāyaṇa*. So Ram, too is *Nārāyaṇa*. Why shouldn't I listen to him? The elephant is *Nārāyaṇa* no doubt, but the *māhut* asked me not to go near the elephant, then why shouldn't I obey him?' Through reasoning like this my zeal for truthfulness is slightly less strong now than before. (p.195)

Sri Ramakrishna used to say that the Divine Mother never puts false words in the mouth of one who is steadfastly devoted to truth, and she does not permit him to act falsely. In the Master's own life we find many examples of this.

One day he went to Sambhu Mallick's garden house. He happened to be suffering from a stomach-ache at that time. When Sambhu learned of this he said: 'When you leave, please take some opium from me. It will relieve your stomach-ache.' Sri Ramakrishna agreed, but at the time of leaving he forgot to take the opium. On the way home, the Master suddenly remembered and returned to Sambhu's. But Sambhu had gone to the inner apartments. Thakur wondered what to do. Should he call him? No, that would not be right, so he took some opium from one of Sambhu's employees. From Sambhu Mallick's garden house to the Dakshineswar temple is only a short distance. Sri Ramakrishna had gone that way many times, but this time he could not find the way back. He wandered here and there trying to get his bearings, but he was totally lost. Then it occurred to him that Sambhu had not told him to take the opium from his employee, but from him, and Sri Ramakrishna had agreed. He should have taken the opium only from the hand of Sambhu and not from anyone else. He understood that because of this, the Divine Mother had caused him to wander about and lose his way back to the temple. Returning to the garden house, he gave back the opium. Then he had no trouble finding his way back to his room.

Another example of the Divine Mother not permitting him to say or do anything false concerns Gopal-Ma. When Gopal-Ma came to Dakshineswar, she would sometimes bring something she had cooked for the Master. She was full of devotion and loved the Master very much, so he could enjoy eating what she had prepared. But one day she cooked some rice for him that was not properly boiled; it was a little hard. Sri Ramakrishna said like a peevish child, 'How can I eat this rice? I will never eat rice cooked by her any more.' Everyone thought that the Master did not really mean what he said, that he was just warning Gopal-Ma to be more careful in her cooking. He always looked after her so lovingly. Was it possible that he would never again take food cooked by her? But the Divine

Mother would not allow any untruth to come from his mouth. A few days after this, he started to have pain in his throat, the beginning of his cancer, and he was unable to eat any rice. No utterance of his could ever be false.

Another day, in a state of ecstasy he said to Holy Mother, 'Later on I will eat only *pāyes* (pudding).' At that time he was perfectly well; his illness had not yet begun. Holy Mother was frightened because she knew that whatever came from the Master's lips was always true. Shortly after, the cancer began to develop in his throat and he could not eat anything but *pāyes*.

Even in his childhood the Master was firm in his devotion to truth. When he was a little boy, he had promised Dhani Kamarni, a woman of low caste, that she could be his '*Bhikṣā* Mother' at the time of his sacred-thread ceremony, which meant that she would have the honour of giving him his first food after the ceremony. It was a great violation of orthodox tradition. He was the son of a brahmin—a very orthodox brahmin who never accepted gifts from anyone of a lower caste. Yet, after the ceremony the Master was adamant. He must keep his word and accept his first alms from the hand of Dhani Kamarni. People remonstrated with him and reminded him that he was a brahmin. But Gadai (that was his boyhood name) told them, 'You want me to be a brahmin. I will be a real brahmin!' How could he be a *real* brahmin if he did not keep his word? He was so young, only nine years old when he said these words, but he had his way. He took his first food from the hand of Dhani Kamarni.

In later years when young devotees came to him the Master would be very strict with them about truthfulness. One day he said to Rakhal (Swami Brahmananda): 'Why can't I look at your face? Have you done anything wrong?' Rakhal thought to himself: 'What wrong could I have committed? I have not robbed anyone or anything like that.' Then it occurred to him that he had jokingly told a lie. Sri Ramakrishna knew this because he could read others' minds, and he regarded that seemingly innocent lie as a serious moral lapse. Even jokingly one must not tell a lie, because if one repeatedly speaks this way, lying will become a habit. **It is not proper for a righteous person to tell a lie or do something false. . . . The mind is like white linen fresh from the laundry; it takes the colour in which you dip it. If it is associated with falsehood for a long time, it will be stained with falsehood.** (p.195)

In the Indian epics there are many stories illustrating the supreme importance of truthfulness. One of them tells of the great vow of Bhīṣma.

Bhīṣma was originally named Devavrata. To keep his word he made an extraordinary renunciation for which he became known as Bhīṣma, which means 'He who performs great deeds'. His father, King Śāntanu, became attracted to a fisherman's daughter named Satyavatī. But her father said, 'I will give you my daughter only if you promise to make her son king.' Śāntanu was in great difficulty. His son Devavrata was the rightful heir and worthy to inherit the throne. If he honoured the fisherman's request, Devavrata would be cheated of his rightful kingship. However, when Devavrata heard of his father's predicament, he went to him and said, 'I will do whatever you say. Let Satyavatī's son be our king.'[12] But the question arose: 'What if in the future Devavrata has a son and this son claims the right to the throne?' Then Devavrata made his second vow: 'I have previously vowed to renounce the throne. Now I promise that I will never have a son. Today I will begin a life of continence. I vow I will never marry.'[13]

The fisherman then consented to the marriage of Satyavatī to King Śāntanu. Satyavatī had two Sons by Śāntanu. The eldest was killed in battle, and the younger son became king. He neglected his duties, lived a life of dissipation and died at an early age without issue. Then Satyavatī said to Bhīṣma, 'You should now marry the widows of my son.' (At that time this kind of marriage was customary in some parts of India.) Bhīṣma replied: 'I cannot do that as I am bound to truth. For keeping my vows I can renounce the three worlds and the kingship of the gods. I can renounce even greater things than that, but I can never renounce truth!'[14] This is the ideal of India. Holding fast to truth, India has gone its own way age after age.

In the *Rāmāyaṇa* we find the story of King Daśaratha's adherence to truth. Kaikeyī, one of his three wives, one day said to him: 'Do you remember that long ago you promised me two boons? Perhaps you have forgotten.' Daśaratha answered: 'No, we do not forget our promises. This is the practice of the Raghus. Even at the cost of our lives we will not violate our given word. It is a great sin to break a promise. No sin is greater than untruthfulness. Millions of tiny seeds do not make a mountain. In the same way, millions of good deeds will not atone for untruthfulness. The Vedas, the *Purāṇas*, and great sages all say, "The root of all good deeds is truth".'[15]

Then Kaikeyī said: 'I now ask for those two boons. The first is that my son Bharata will become king. The second is that Rāma will be sent in exile to the forest.' Daśaratha felt as if the sky had fallen on his head, but there was no way out. He had made a promise to Kaikeyī and he had to remain true to his word. Rāma was sent to the forest and King Daśaratha died from grief. Bharata however refused to become king. Many have said that Daśaratha allowed himself to be dominated by Kaikeyī, but that is not true. Daśaratha held fast to truth, even at the cost of his life.

Karṇa was a fascinating character in the *Mahābhārata* who exemplified in his life both truthfulness and untruthfulness. What dire consequences followed from his lying! He had gone at first to Droṇa, the teacher of the Pāṇḍava princes, to learn the art of weaponry. But as he did not belong to the warrior caste, Droṇa refused to teach him. Then he went to Paraśurāma and introduced himself as a member of even a higher caste. He claimed to be a brahmin. Paraśurāma agreed to teach him, and Karṇa started to learn the art of weapons.

One day Paraśurāma became very tired and fell asleep with his head on Karṇa's knees. Suddenly an insect fell on one of Karṇa's legs and began to sting him. Karṇa was in agony but he would not move. He did not want to disturb his guru's sleep. When Paraśurāma woke up he saw that Karṇa's leg was bleeding. On asking he learned everything. Then he said to Karṇa: 'You are certainly not a brahmin. A brahmin could never endure such pain.' Karṇa then acknowledged his low birth. It might be thought that Paraśurāma would overlook Karṇa's previous lie and praise him for his heroic devotion to his teacher. But on the contrary, he cursed him. He said to Karṇa: 'The knowledge of weapons you learned from me you will forget at a moment when you are in great danger!' Speaking an untruth was the greatest offence. Neither devotion to one's teacher nor any heroic deed could atone for the forsaking of truth.

In the contradictory life of Karṇa there is another incident in which to hold fast to truth he made a great sac ifice. Once he made a vow that he would give to anyone who asked, anything he wanted. Śrī Kṛṣṇa came to him disguised as a brahmin and said to him: 'I am very hungry. I want you to kill your son Bṛṣaketu and have your wife cook him for me to eat.' What a terrible test! But Karṇa was unswerving in keeping his vow and carried out Kṛṣṇa's gruesome request. (Afterwards Śrī Kṛṣṇa brought Bṛṣaketu back to life.)

Another incident exemplifying Karṇa's truthfulness involves a similar promise. He vowed that after he came from his bath he would give any brahmin whatever he asked for. From his birth Karṇa had a suit of armour fixed on his body and an earring attached to one ear which protected him from ever being killed. Indra, the king of gods, came to him in the guise of a brahmin and asked him for the armour and earring. Karṇa, to keep his word, gave them to him. The Sun-god had told him this would happen and had warned him, 'When you give the earring to Indra, don't forget to demand in return his great weapon with which you can kill any enemy.' Remembering that, Karṇa said to Indra, 'I know who you are and what you came for. In return, please give me your powerful weapon.' Indra gave it to him saying, 'With this weapon I can kill many enemies, but you will be able to kill only one.' Karṇa thought, 'That is all right. I will kill my great enemy, Arjuna, with this weapon. I have enough weapons to kill other enemies.'

But in the War of Kurukṣetra, when all his other weapons had failed to kill Bhīma's son, Karṇa was forced to use the powerful weapon Indra had given him. Thus he was unable to use it when he fought Arjuna. When he at last faced Arjuna, the duel was long and fierce. Finally the wheel flew off Karṇa's chariot. At this critical juncture, Paraśurāma's curse fell on him, and he forgot his knowledge of weaponry. Helpless, he was killed by Arjuna.

How unpredictable was Karṇa's fate! His greatness lies in the fact that, knowing it would bring about his death, he gave his armour and earring to Indra—for the sake of truth. On the other hand, he was guilty of untruthfulness when he told Paraśurāma that he was a brahmin. The great evil of untruthfulness and the greatness of adhering to truth at all costs—both of these are exemplified in Karṇa's life.

The *Rāmāyaṇa* gives us another illustration of truthfulness. Rāma and his brother Lakṣmaṇa were so close that they could not bear to be separated. Yet for the sake of truth, Rāma banished Lakṣmaṇa.

Once Kāla, the god of death, came to see Rāma. Kāla told Rāma: 'I want to speak with you privately. We must go to a place where we can be alone. If someone else enters the room, you must kill him.' Rāma gave his word and said to Lakṣmaṇa, 'Guard the entrance to this place. If anyone enters, I have promised to kill him.' Rāma and Kāla went inside and began their secret conversation.

Before long the great sage Dūrvāsā arrived at the entrance where Lakṣmaṇa was standing guard. He said to Lakṣmaṇa, 'Where is Rāma? Take me to him immediately!' Lakṣmaṇa said: 'That is not possible. He is engaged in a very important conversation with Kāla.' At this Dūrvāsā became terribly angry. 'I will burn everything to ashes!' he threatened. 'Take me to Rāma at once!' Then Lakṣmaṇa thought, 'Only I will be killed if I take Dūrvāsā to Rāma. But if I refuse, everyone will die.'[16] And he took Dūrvāsā to see Rāma. The two engaged in light conversation; then Dūrvāsā took refreshments and left, satisfied.

Now Rāma was faced with a great dilemma. He had promised to kill anyone who entered the place where he and Kāla were talking, but how could he kill Lakṣmaṇa? He was silent and could not say a word. His face was pale and grave. Then Lakṣmaṇa said: 'O Brother, punish me—keep your word. Those who do not keep their promises go to hell.'[17]

Rāma knew that if one does not keep his promises, *dharma* (the moral order) will be destroyed. If *dharma* is destroyed, everyone will suffer. Remembering this, he said to Lakṣmaṇa: 'Lakṣmaṇa, I am banishing you. For a righteous person, banishment is the same as death, so I am fulfilling my vow.'[18] Thus, for the sake of truth, he sent away his beloved brother. Lakṣmaṇa then bade farewell to Rāma and went to the bank of the river Sarayu where, absorbed in yoga, he gave up his body.

We find this same devotion to truth in Sri Ramakrishna's father, Khudiram. Sri Ramakrishna's ancestral home was in the village of Dere, a short distance from Kamarpukur. Khudiram was virtuous and respected by everyone there. At one time the landlord of that village started a false litigation against someone and needed a witness, someone whose word would be accepted by the court. He chose Khudiram as that person because of Khudiram's unblemished reputation. Approaching him he said: 'You must give false evidence in court for me. I will tell you what you must say.' Khudiram said : 'I cannot do that. No untrue word will come from my mouth.' The landlord became very angry. 'I own this village,' he said, 'you must obey me!' Still Khudiram refused to lie. In revenge, the landlord brought a false suit against Khudiram and he and his family were forced to leave the village. They were given refuge in Kamarpukur where Sri Ramakrishna was later born. Who else but a man like Khudiram could have God for a son? Though Khudiram was very poor, everyone showed him great respect. When he went to take his bath in the pond, people would stop their conversations and move out of his way. They honoured Khudiram because he was the embodiment of all they held sacred—the Indian ideal, 'Truth above all.'

Swami Vivekananda often denounced the cult of untouchability and looked forward to the rise of the lower castes, but he insisted that the ideal person was the *real* brahmin—free from greed and pride, firmly established in truth, his senses under control. I myself have seen that kind of brahmin. He was a teacher in our primary school for many years, educating three generations of students. Though poor, almost destitute, he never accepted money from his students. How did he live? When the rice harvested, people would give him a portion, or if people had banana trees in their yard, they would give him some bananas.

Everyone liked to go to his house, and they would then bring him milk and other things to eat. On the occasion of a marriage, they might give him some clothing. Everyone showed him great honour. In appearance he was tall, heavily bearded and dark-complexioned. He usually wore only a dhoti, with his sacred-thread hanging across his chest. Like Khudiram, when he went to the pond to take his bath, everyone made way for him out of respect. He was often silent, but everyone was in awe of him. Swamiji said, This is our Indian ideal.

In the Upaniṣads it is said, *Satyaṁ jñānamanantaṁ brahma*—'Brahman is Truth, Knowledge, Infinity.'[19] Brahman is Truth, which is the highest knowledge, and infinite. Truthfulness is the special characteristic and ideal of India. People here have practised much austerity and renunciation for the sake of Truth. But this renunciation is not anything negative. It means giving up the lesser for the greater good. If I want to become a scientist I must give up many things. I may want to go to a football game, but instead I must stay in the laboratory and carry out my research. In this way, I am renouncing the lesser happiness for the greater, future good. Swami Vivekananda said that we proceed from the lower to the higher truth. In the same way, we renounce the ephemeral for the eternal. For God, for Truth, we renounce everything.

In a poem addressed to India, Swami Vivekananda does not say, 'O India!' He says 'O Truth!'[20] India and Truth were identical to him. When he was in the West, he gave a talk about India in which he told the audience that they would find many Indian customs strange. Indians judge people differently, he said. Some of India's most revered people would be considered insane in the West. In India, a man may be seen standing neck-deep in ice-cold water; another may be sitting naked on burning sand, in deep meditation. Why would people act in such an unnatural manner? Because they were trying to realize truth, Swamiji said.

Swamiji loved India—not because it was the land of his birth—but because of this great ideal. For that reason, India was a holy land to him. He held every particle of its dust to be sacred because India had practised the ideal of truth the most. Speaking of India's future, Swamiji said, 'Shall India die? Then from the world all spirituality will be extinct, all moral perfection will be extinct, all sweet-souled sympathy for religion will be extinct, all ideality will be extinct. . . .'

Swamiji once said, 'The *Satyayuga*, the Age of Truth, the Golden Age, has begun again with the advent of Sri Ramakrishna.' In the Age of Truth, people give the highest place to truth, not to wealth, power, or anything else. Sri Ramakrishna's whole life was one long austerity for the sake of Truth. He came to this world to establish that Truth.

References

1. *Muṇḍaka Upaniṣad*, III.1.5
2. *Gītā*, III.6
3. *C.W.*, Vol. V, p.410
4. *Ibid.*, Vol. II, p.84

5. *Muṇḍaka Upaniṣad*, III.1.6
6. *Mahānirvāṇa Tantra*, IV.75
7. *Īśa Upaniṣad*, 15
8. *Dharmaprasaṅge Swami Brahmananda*, Udbodhan Office, Calcutta, p.86
9. *Ibid.*, p.75
10. *Māyer Kathā*, 2nd Part, p.149
11. *Muṇḍaka Upaniṣad*, III.1.6
12. *Mahābhārata*, Ādiparva, 94/87
13. *Ibid.*, 94/95-6
14. *Ibid.*, 97/16
15. *Rāmacaritamānasa O Dohāvalī*, Tulasīdāsa, 2nd Chapter, 1980. *Ayodhyākāṇḍa*, 28, *Sampādanā* : Jyotibhushan Chaki
16. *Rāmāyaṇa, Uttarakāṇḍa*, 105/9
17. *Ibid.*, 106/3
18. *Ibid.*, 106/13
19. *Taittirīya Upaniṣad*, II.1.3
20. *In Search of God and Other Poems*, Advaita Ashrama, Calcutta, 1981, p.21

IX

Living in the World

In Indian society there are two distinct choices in life : a person can live either as a 'householder' (usually, but not always, married) and take part in the activities and duties of society, or he or she can renounce the world and become a monk or nun. The number of renunciates is naturally small. Sri Ramakrishna had many disciples who lived as householders, and he had particular instructions for them which differed in some respects from the instructions he gave to those who would renounce the world. The advice he gave to Indian householders has universal relevance. It is meant for all those who are not monastics, wherever they live.

The Master said: **I tell people that there is nothing wrong in the life of the world.**(p.456) He said that living in the world is like fighting from within a fortress. If you are in the world, why not stay in such a fortress? Living with your family, you will have relatives and neighbours and a regulated way of living. If you are about to make a mistake, your relatives will warn you, 'No, don't do that.' And you also learn from watching them. Some of them are older than you and can teach you. But if you live alone, you will have to learn from your own mistakes. Living in the world is like having a wall to protect you. It saves you from your own folly.

If you renounce the world, your reliance on God must he very strong. You must have razor-sharp discrimination and firm faith in yourself. Without these, there is every chance of falling.

It is difficult to live a life of renunciation. It is for the very few. Because of this, Sri Ramakrishna said that it was best for most people to 'fight from within a fortress.' It is easier to fight from a fortress than to fight in an open field. It is easier to call on God from within your home than to call on him while wandering about outside.

He told about a man who decided to renounce the world. When he told his wife about his plans, she said to him, 'Go if you wish, but first tell me one thing : Why are you leaving? Is it to call on God? If so, why don't you call on Him from here. I will not bother you in any way. If you become a monk, you will have to wander from house to house begging for alms. Rather than begging at a hundred doors, you can get your food from me. You can live a life of renunciation in your own home.'

From this we must not think that the Master did not value the ideal of renunciation. He himself was called the 'King of Sannyasis' and the 'Emperor of Renunciation'. Hindu scriptures say that as soon as dispassion for the world arises, you should renounce the world. But this kind of dispassion is awakened in the minds of very few. The ideal of complete renunciation (sannyasa) is difficult for most people to follow.

Yet the spiritual life is for everyone, whether they renounce the world or not. Those who live in the world can also develop their spiritual potential. The Master always encouraged those who lived in the world. He reminded them that the goal of life is the attainment of God, and that can be attained even while living in the world. **But they must live in the world as a maidservant lives in her master's house.**(p.456) He meant that we must rid ourselves of the idea of ownership. Children, house, money, etc., all belong to 'the master', to God. This mental renunciation of all possessions and relationships is true renunciation. Sri Ramakrishna emphasized this mental renunciation. A person may be living the life of a monk but still have strong desires. As the *Gītā* says,[1] this kind of renunciation is sheer hypocrisy.

If having nothing means renunciation, then the beggar on the street is the greatest renouncer of all. But what do we find? He has a cracked bowl and a tattered cloth, and he is fighting with another beggar over these. True renunciation is not external; it is inward, of the mind. If we are attached to anything or anyone; we do not have true renunciation. Sri Ramakrishna said we should live in the world without attachment, the way a maidservant lives. **Pointing out her master's house to others, she says, no doubt, 'This is our house', but in her heart she knows very well that it doesn't belong to her and that her own house is in a far-away village. She brings up her master's son and says, 'My Hari has grown very naughty', or 'My Hari doesn't like sweets'. Though she repeats 'My Hari' with her lips, yet she knows in her heart that Hari doesn't belong to her, that he is her master's son.** (p.325) Her own child is in some rural village and she does not know how he is or what he is doing.

On another occasion Sri Ramakrishna said, **Thus I say to those who visit me: 'Why don't you live in the world? There is no harm in that. But always keep your mind on God. Know for certain that house, family, and property are not yours. They are God's. Your real home is in God.' Also I ask them to pray always with a longing heart for love of God's Lotus Feet.** (pp.456-57)

While living in the world, you must remain aloof, unattached. But what is non-attachment? Non-attachment is attachment to God. If your mind is on God, it is naturally far from worldly attachments. The more you proceed towards God, the more the world recedes from you. In the words of the Master, 'The further you go towards the East, the farther you are from the West.' The more you go towards God, love Him and make Him your own, the more you find that the world has been left far behind.

Sri Ramakrishna's simple instruction is to love God. The more you love Him, the more tasteless worldly pleasures become. They seem like poison. This is true renunciation.

Sri Ramakrishna says, **It [the world] is unreal as long as one has not realized God.** (p.325) We do not want to give our minds to God. We do not understand that if we do not give our minds to Him, the world will cause us much suffering. Because the world has deluded us so much, we do not even want to know Him. **Through ignorance man forgets God and speaks always of 'I' and 'mine'.** (p.325)

Bound in *māyā*, we are enchanted by sense objects. ***Māyā* robs him of his knowledge to such an extent that he cannot find the way of escape, though such a way exists.** (p.325) The Master has used many examples to explain how *māyā* has kept us under its spell. He said: 'A camel continues to eat a thorny plant even though his mouth is bleeding. In the same way, worldly life gives us grief and pain; still we are attracted to it.' Then he told about a fisherman's wife who used to go every day to the market to sell her fish. One day, because of the rain, she was forced to spend the night in the home of a flower grower. She was given a place to sleep in a room full of flowers, but the lovely fragrance of the flowers made her restless. It was so disturbing to her that she got up in the middle of the night, got her fish basket and sprinkled a little water on it so that it gave off the smell of fish. Then she could sleep. The fish smell is worldly attraction. The scent of the flowers is the spiritual life. Most of us prefer the smell of fish to the scent of flowers.

Sri Ramakrishna tells us that we should know the world before entering it. If we do not understand it rightly, if we think the world is a sweet, beautiful place, we will suffer. Our scriptures say that worldly life is a forest ; in another place it is called an ocean. We can get lost in the forest of the world, or drown in the ocean of the world, if we don't know its true nature. We must remember that though there is some happiness in worldly life, there is also much suffering. The world is ever-changing; its happiness and misery are both momentary.

The Hindu scriptures also define the world in more positive ways. It is likened to a bridge between birth and death. I am crossing over that bridge. In a little while I will reach the other shore. If I try to make my home on that bridge, I will suffer.

Then the world is like an inn. I am here for only a few nights. I will rest here and in the morning go on to my destination.

You can also say that the world is a stage and we are all actors here. In a drama one man may play the role of a king and look very impressive with his royal dress. He seems to be a king in very way. Another man plays the role of the king's servant and carries out his orders. But it is all make-believe. The world is like that stage and we are all playing different roles. If we can remember that the role we play is not our true identity, that we are in reality the children of God who is our support, that we are the eternal, pure, awakened, free Self, then our attraction to the world will vanish. Our suffering will come to an end.

We often forget that we are in the world for a few days only. We see death all around us but don't remember that one day we ourselves will die. In the *Mahābhārata* the god *Dharma* asked Yudhiṣṭhira, 'What is the most amazing thing in the world?' And Yudhiṣṭhira answered, 'The most amazing thing is that though we see death everywhere, we do not believe that we ourselves will ever die.' We somehow have the idea that this life will exist forever, that we will be perpetually youthful and that our health and prestige will remain always. Because of this belief we suffer.

Sri Ramakrishna says: **This moment the world is and the next it is not. It is impermanent. Those you think to be your very own will not exist for you when you close your eyes in death. Again, you see people who have no immediate relatives, and yet for the sake of a grandson they will not go to Benares to lead a holy life. 'Oh, what will become of my Haru then?', they argue. . . . This . . . world is illusory and impermanent.** (p.325)

Because Hinduism faces the fact that the world is, as Sri Ramakrishna says, 'illusory and impermanent', people in the West often assume that the Hindu religion is pessimistic, that it is a doctrine of despair. But this is not so. Hinduism says : Recognize the truth about the world, then live in it. Be happy and enjoy life, but that doesn't mean that you should live recklessly and without restraint. There are rules for enjoying life. I like ice cream but if I indulge myself by eating five dishes of it, I may end up in the hospital. You must practise self-control if you want to enjoy anything in life.

It was the custom in ancient India for a student to live in the home of his guru. There he learned about the true nature of the world and what the aim of life is. After that he usually married and entered worldly life.

The great sages of India who formulated this way of life were aware that the vast majority of people have desires which cannot be wished away. So they acknowledged the four values of life: *dharma* (here meaning righteousness or morality), *artha* (worldly possessions), *kāma* (worldly happiness, pleasure), and *mokṣa* (liberation). First be established in *dharma*; after that seek *artha* and *kāma*. But always remember that the ultimate goal in life is *mokṣa*, freedom from all selfish desires—perfect joy and peace.

Thus, the Hindu religion does not forbid enjoyment, it only wants you to remember what worldly life is for. If you forget, you will suffer. The Master tells us that only after knowing what the world is and developing some spiritual strength should you enter it. He says, **Do your duty to the world after knowing God.** (p.325) But what is 'the world'? Is it really false, as some have called it?

Sri Ramakrishna said that though the world has been described as a mere 'framework of illusion', if one loves God then **This very world is a mansion of mirth; here I can eat, here drink and make merry.** (p.139)

If you have love for God, the world is no longer false or illusory, because you then see that the world is His manifestation. It is no longer a place of suffering but a place of bliss. The main thing is to keep firmly set on the path to the goal. If you are going somewhere, you must go in the right direction; you must be alert. A holy man used to say: 'I have purchased a ticket and have boarded the train. What have I to worry about?' What he meant was: 'The realization of God is my destination. I have prepared myself through spiritual disciplines and have taken shelter at the feet of the guru. I have no fear. Maybe today, or after a hundred years I will reach my destination. I will realize God, because I am headed in the right direction.'

Sri Ramakrishna emphasizes this concept—going in the right direction. His teaching was quite simple : you merely change the direction of your mind. The same mind that now is attracted to enjoyment, can be turned to God. All my thoughts, my desires that are now directed to sense objects, can be directed to God. I don't need to change my work, but whatever I am doing, my mind must be directed towards God. I may be cooking, I may be working in an office or a shop, but everything will be for God. If you think in this way, your mind gradually becomes free from attachment to sense objects and you reach your goal.

Swamiji urged people to live actively and energetically. He said: What do the Upaniṣads do? They make the teacher a better teacher, a fisherman a better fisherman. The Upaniṣads do not teach neglect of duty. 'I will sit idle, aloof from life's battles'—this is not what is meant by religion. The *Gītā* says, *Klaivyaṁ māsma gamaḥ*—'Yield not to this unmanliness.'[2] Whatever you are doing, try to do better by doing it for God.

Monks of the Ramakrishna Order do all kinds of work—typing, teaching, gardening, editing, nursing, etc. How are they different from ordinary householders? The difference is that the monks have changed the direction of their minds. All their work is directed towards the attainment of God. They worship God through their work with as much dedication as they worship Him in the temple. Work, for the time being, becomes their sphere of worship. Swamiji said, 'Work is worship.'

The same idea we find in the *Gītā* where Śrī Kṛṣṇa says to Arjuna:

Yat karoṣi yadaśnāsi yajjuhoṣi dadāsi yat
Yat tapasyasi kaunteya tat kuruṣva madarpaṇam—

'Whatever thou doest, whatever thou eatest, whatever thou offerest, whatever thou givest away, whatever austerities thou dost practise—do that, O Son of Kuntī, as an offering to me.'[3]

If a person is able to think: 'In all my work I am serving God', then that work will not be work, it will be worship. Sri Ramakrishna repeatedly reminds us that for such a person, the very appearance of the world changes. Lust and greed have vanished. The world has become a place of bliss.

Our teachers say that it is by our mind that we are bound, and by our mind we become free. Where is worldliness but in the mind? If there are desires in the mind, formal renunciation is meaningless. At any moment some desire may manifest itself and our renunciation will take flight. Sri Ramakrishna illustrated this with a story: A holy man had only one loincloth, but whenever he washed it and set it out to dry, a mouse would nibble at it. So he brought a cat to his hut to frighten away the mouse. Then he found that, he needed milk for the cat, so he bought a cow. The cow needed a pasture, fence, etc. Thus one thing after another was acquired till the holy man became a full-fledged householder. For the sake of a loin-cloth, he became a worldly man even in the forest. His renunciation was not strong enough to resist the lure of the world.

As long as there are desires in the mind, it is best to proceed towards God living in the world. It takes time for desires and old habits to fall away and genuine renunciation to arise in our minds. The Master said that when the fruit is ripe, it falls from the tree of itself. Renunciation occurs spontaneously this way. So stay in the world and do everything. There is no harm in it. Only change the direction of your mind so that it goes towards God.

One day a woman devotee came to the Master and said, 'I can't meditate. When I try to think of my chosen Ideal, the face of my nephew comes to my mind.' Sri Ramakrishna then told her to think of her nephew as God, as her chosen Ideal. 'Think that when you are caring for your little nephew, it is God you are caring for,' he said. The woman followed this advice and rose to a high spiritual state in a short time. She had changed the direction of her mind.

Sri Ramakrishna would always encourage people who had to live in the world. He said : **Why shouldn't one be able to realize God in this world? King Janaka had such realization. . . .**

> **Janaka's might was unsurpassed;**
> **What did he lack of the world or the Spirit?**
> **Holding to one as well as the other,**
> **He drank his milk from a brimming cup!** (p.139)

King Janaka was King of Mithilā, yet he was a sage. He lived in the world, yet he was a monk. The life of renunciation and the life of the world were joined together in his life. The great sage Vyāsa sent his son Śukadeva to King Janaka to learn about liberation. He said: 'King Janaka will show you the way to liberation. He is well-versed in the scriptures dealing with this subject. Do whatever he tells you to do unquestioningly.'

King Janaka was an ideal example of a *jīvanmukta*, a person who has attained liberation while living. We usually think of *mukti* as liberation after death. But according to Hindu scriptures, there is another kind of liberation called *jīvan eva muktiḥ*, free while living. Such a person is unattached to his body. He lives in the world and may have everything—sons, daughters, possessions, etc., but he is not attached to anything. King Janaka was that kind of person. If the city of Mithilā were burned to the ground, he would be unperturbed. He said:

Anantaṁ vata me vittaṁ yasya me nāsti kiñcana
Mithilāyāṁ pradīptāyāṁ na me dahyati kiñcana—

'Infinite indeed is my wealth of which nothing is mine; if Mithilā is burnt, nothing that is mine is burnt.'[4] He had no attachment whatsoever to his vast kingdom. He was utterly aloof from all the royal possessions. This is the Indian ideal.

But Sri Ramakrishna tells us how difficult this ideal is to put into practice. He says: **It is difficult to lead the life of a householder in the spirit of detachment. Once Pratap said to me : 'Sir, we follow the example of King Janaka. He led the life of a householder in a detached spirit. We shall follow him.' I said to him: 'Can one be like King Janaka by merely wishing it? How many austerities he practised in order to acquire divine knowledge! He practised the most intense form of asceticism for many years and only then returned to the life of the world.'**(p.313) **Do something first; then you may become a King Janaka.** (p.626)

It is possible to realize God while living in the world, but you must struggle hard. **Is there, then, no hope for householders? Certainly there is.**(p.313) You must call on Him in solitude whenever it is possible; otherwise you will not succeed. Speaking of householders who long to realize God, the Master said: **They must practise spiritual discipline in solitude for some days. Thus they will acquire knowledge and devotion. Then it will not hurt them to lead the life of the world.** (p.313) He made a concrete suggestion: **He**

should take a room near his house, so that he may come home only for meals.(p.626)

At first it is better to meditate on God in solitude, returning home for meals, medicine, etc. In this way you can develop some kind of relationship with God so that you are convinced that 'He is my own. He is always protecting me and watching over me. I can force my demands on Him.' Without practising spiritual disciplines in solitude this feeling does not grow to fruition. If you once attain this intense love for Him, you will have no more worries, and there will be no harm in living in the world.

The *Uttaragītā* says, *Putradārādisaṁsāro yogābhyāsasya vighnakṛt*—'Wife, son, family—this worldly life is an obstacle to the practice of yoga.'[5] But if you go into solitude, you do not face these obstacles. Sri Ramakrishna says. **Now and then one must go into solitude and practise spiritual disciplines to realize God.** (p.139)

You need to strengthen your mind through spiritual disciplines in solitude, because, 'The mind is always strong and powerful. One seems to have no control over it. Again the same mind becomes free from fluctuations—at peace.'[6] It seems that at one moment I am very happy, the next moment I am depressed. I may be thinking very lofty thoughts, but the next minute I am shocked by the low thoughts that come to my mind. This rising and falling of thoughts and feelings is often compared to waves in the ocean.

Sri Ramakrishna gives another example, which he got from the *Bhāgavatam*, about putting an elephant in the stable after washing it. The verse reads: 'Purifying the mind is like bathing and cleaning an elephant whose habit it is to always spray dust on its back. But if after bathing it is put in a stable, it will not be able to make itself dirty.'[7] In the same way, if you are once attached to the Lord ('put in a stable'), desires will be unable to cloud your mind. That is why you must become attached only to God by practising spiritual disciplines in solitude.

Sri Ramakrishna said: **A worldly man is suffering from delirious fever, as it were. Suppose there are pickled tamarind and jars of water in the room of such a patient. Now, how can you expect him to get rid of the disease? Just see, the very mention of pickled tamarind is making my mouth water. He must be removed for a few days to another place where there are neither pickled tamarind nor water-jars. Then he will be cured. After that if he returns to his old room he will have nothing to fear.**(p.626) You must live away from attractive sense objects for some time until you become devoted to the Lord. Then you can return safely to the world. Your delirious fever of worldliness will have been cured.

The Master gives this advice: **When you practise discipline in solitude, keep yourself entirely away from your family. You must not allow your wife, son, daughter, mother, father, sister, brother, friends, or relatives near you. While thus practising discipline in solitude, you should think: 'I have no one else in the world. God is my all.' You must also pray to Him, with tears in your eyes, for knowledge and devotion.**

If you ask me how long you should live in solitude away from your family, I should say that it would be good for you if you could spend even one day in such a manner. Three days at a time are still better. One may live in solitude for twelve days, a month, three months or a year, according to one's convenience and ability.

One hasn't much to fear if one leads the life of a householder after attaining knowledge and devotion. . . . While playing the game of hide-and-seek, you are safe if you but once touch the 'granny'. Be turned into gold by touching the philosopher's stone. After that you may remain buried underground a thousand years; when you are taken out you will still be gold. (p.313)

Sri Ramakrishna says that the mind needs a 'fence' at first. **While the trees on the footpath are young, they must be fenced around; otherwise they will be destroyed by cattle.The fence is necessary when the tree is young, but it can be taken away when the trunk is thick and strong. Then the tree won't be hurt even if an elephant is tied to it.** (p.140) At first you need to protect the mind; it needs a 'fence'.

As we advance along the path of spirituality, we must always guard our mind. We must keep vigilant. It has been said, 'The condition upon which God hath given liberty to man is eternal vigilance.'[8] The mind cannot be trusted. It is unpredictable. Because of this the Master says we must **Repeat God's name and sing His glories, and keep holy company; and now and then visit God's devotees and holy men.**(p. 81) These things all guard the mind and help it to be vigilant, but Sri Ramakrishna especially emphasizes holy company. He says, 'If one has holy company, attachment to sense objects is gradually removed.' He also says, 'Through holy company one's clock is set right.' Those who are living in the world need holy company. Holy persons are a constant reminder that we should not become entangled in the world.

In addition we must always practise discrimination. Discrimination means choosing wisely between truth and untruth, good and evil, the good (*śreyas*) and the pleasant (*preyas*). Many things seem pleasant at first sight, but later turn out to be a source of suffering. And many things seem to be unpleasant, but later give us joy by leading us to God. So we must always be discriminative.

The mind is everything. Sri Ramakrishna compares the mind to milk. He says: **The mind is like milk. If you keep the mind in the world, which is like water, then the milk and water will get mixed. That is why people keep milk in a quiet place and let it set into curd, and then churn butter from it. Likewise, through spiritual discipline practised in solitude, churn the butter of knowledge and devotion from the milk of the mind. Then that butter can easily be kept in the water of the world. It will not get mixed with the world. The mind will float detached on the water of the world.** (p.313)

It is amazing that the Master in his rustic language could give similes which are corroborated in the ancient scriptures, though he had not read them. The *Garuḍa Purāṇa* says:

Navanītaṁ yathā dadhno jyotiḥ kāṣṭhādapi kvacit
Manthanaiḥ sādhanairevaṁ paraṁ jñātvā sukhī bhavet—

'Butter comes from curd by churning; fire is lighted by rubbing sticks of wood together repeatedly. In the same way, by spiritual disciplines, you will come to know the Self and become blissful.'[9]

Sri Ramakrishna says, 'If you once acquire this intense love for God, you will no longer be entangled in worldliness.'

Nothing will disturb you. A Christian teaching says, 'Be in the world, but not of the world.' I maybe living in the world, but I am not worldly. The world is not my master; God is my master. Sri Ramakrishna says: 'There is no harm if the boat is in the water, but the water should not be in the boat.' I can be in the world, but the world must not be in me. This is non-attachment. From this, love for God is born.

Aldous Huxley discusses this concept in his book, *Ends and Means*, referring to non-attachment as detachment. The *Gītā* repeatedly emphasizes non-attachment. For example:

Brahmaṇyādhāya karmāṇi saṅgaṁ tyaktvā karoti yaḥ
Lipyate na sa pāpena padmapatramivāmbhasā—

'He who works, having given up attachment, resigning his actions to God, is not touched by sin, even as a lotus leaf [is untouched] by water.'[10]

This is how we must live in the world. If we are unattached to our work, we will not be bound by it. *Japa* and meditation, worship and prayer—these are very valuable if they are done without any selfish desire for results—with detachment. Sri Ramakrishna says, **To work in such a spirit of detachment is known as karmayoga.** (p. 452)

The *Sahajiyā*s have a song which describes detachment: 'I will cook, I will make curries—and everything else, but I will not touch the pot.' They mean to say, 'I will do all my work, but I will not be aware that "I" am working because "I" and "my" are the cause of bondage. It is better to say "Thou" and "Thine". "Thou, O Lord, art the doer. Thou doest everything; everything in the whole world is thine".' This is how the *Sahajiyā*s like to think. It is the way they practise non-attachment. They also say, 'Take your bath in the ocean of nectar but your hair should not get wet'— bathe in the ocean of His love.

But the *Sahajiyā*s also emphasize silence and secrecy. That is why they say not to wet your hair. Do not tell anyone about your spiritual practice. Silently, secretly, call on Him. The more your thoughts of Him are hidden, the better it is for you. Calling on God in secret has a special sweetness. Let everyone think that you are drowned in worldliness! In reality you are immersed in God, always remembering Him.

We find an example of this in the life of Holy Mother, Sri Sarada Devi. She seemed to be immersed in worldly activities. Some people would express their doubts and say, 'Mother, we find you are very much bound up in *māyā*'. Mother would answer: 'What can I do, child? We are women; we are made this way.' She wanted to avoid the subject. But one day she answered: 'What do you know? When lightning flashes, it lights up the window pane, but not the wooden shutters.' She meant: 'I am like the wooden shutters. Nothing can touch me; I am unattached.'

Swami Vivekananda in his Karma Yoga said that the ideal person is one who in the midst of intense activity remains utterly at peace. We see this perfectly exemplified in Holy Mother's life. How wonderful was her everyday life! On one hand she had Swami Saradananda, Swami Yogananda, and other great souls, and on the other, her mad sister-in-law and Radhu, and others who were also mentally disturbed. On one hand, those who had renounced all for God; on the other, those who were deeply immersed in worldly life. Holy Mother lived in the midst of all these, amid constant confusion and quarrelling over trifles. Still, she was always serene, unperturbed, unconcerned—the witness.

The *Gītā* describes such a person, *Duḥkheṣvanudvignamanāḥ sukheṣu vigataspṛhaḥ*—'One whose mind is untroubled in the midst of sorrows and free from eager desire amid pleasures.'[11] This is the ideal the Hindu scriptures extol.

Sri Ramakrishna explains the ideal of non-attachment in many ways: 'Smear your hands with oil before opening the jackfruit'. (Prepare yourself through spiritual disciplines before entering worldly life.) 'Live in the world like a mud-fish,' which stays clean even in the midst of mud. 'Be like the mother turtle that swims in the water but has her mind on the bank of the river where her eggs are.' These similes all illustrate one teaching— 'Live in the world but be unattached to it.' Do all the work that is expected of you, but keep your mind at the feet of the Lord. The Master said, **Hold fast to His Lotus Feet with one hand and with the other do your duties.** (p.627)

He emphasizes the importance of keeping our minds on God in the midst of our activities. He says, 'If you hold fast to the pillar while whirling round and round, you will not ever fall.' God is that pillar. If we hold on to Him while moving about in the world, we will never fall. Swami Brahmananda says, 'If you give three-fourths of your mind to God and the remaining one-fourth to your work, your work will be done well.'

Most of our work is done with our minds. If our mind is directed towards God, it becomes very pure, crystal-clear and tranquil. With that mind, whatever we do will be done well. Detachment does not mean neglecting our duties. It means keeping our mind on God; that way we do everything perfectly.

Sri Ramakrishna gives the example of the ancient sages. He says, **Sages like Janaka, Vyāsa and Vaśiṣṭha lived in the world after attaining Knowledge. They fenced with two swords, the one of Knowledge and the other of action.** (p.627) What is the 'sword of Knowledge'? It is the knowledge that God is our only refuge, our only near and dear one. And the 'sword of action' means that we do all that we are required to do. This is the ideal for those who live in the world.

The Hindu religion does not urge people to give up their duties and take up another way of life. According to the *Gītā*:

Śreyān svadharmo viguṇaḥ paradharmāt svanuṣṭhitāt
Svadharme nidhanaṁ śreyaḥ paradharmo bhayāvahaḥ—

'Better is one's own duty though imperfectly carried out than the duty of another carried out perfectly. Better is death in [the fulfilment of] one's own duty, for to follow another's duty is perilous.'[12] If you are living in the world, do not try to behave like a monk. Don't try to keep your feet in two boats. The *Gītā* describes a true renunciate:

Anāśritaḥ karmaphalaṁ kāryaṁ karma karoti yaḥ
Sa sannyāsī ca yogī ca na niragnirna cākriyaḥ—

'He who does the work which he ought to do without seeking its fruit, he is the sannyasin, he is the yogi, not he who does not light the sacred fire, and performs no rights.'[13] By sitting silent and doing nothing, you don't become a monk or a yogi. You should not neglect your duties.

A man asked Sri Ramakrishna if he should try to increase his income. The Master could not even touch money—a clod of earth and a coin were alike to him. Still, how practical was his advice! **It is permissible to do so to maintain a religious family. You may try to increase your income, but in an honest way.** (p.114)

To Sri Ramakrishna, or to any true monk who depends on God for everything, *samalostāśmakāñcanaḥ*—'a clod, a stone, and a piece of gold are the same.'[14] But I am living in the world and have my family to care for. Many people are dependent on me. I should certainly try to earn money, but in an honest way. It is not right for me to say, 'Money is dirt; dirt is money', as the Master did. On the other hand, I should not become infatuated with money. I should be alert and see that money does not dominate my life. Sri Ramakrishna says: **You see, he alone is a true man who has made money his servant. But those who do not know the use of money are not men even though they have human forms. They may have human bodies, but they behave like animals.** (p.637)

I must spend my money wisely; otherwise it will harm me. In whatever I do, there must be a balance: I will do so much, but no more. It is sometimes difficult to know what the limit is, but my mind will guide me rightly if my goal is God.

Sri Ramakrishna says to those living in the world: **Surely you have duties to perform. You must bring up your children, support your wife, and provide for her in case of your death. If you don't then I shall call you unkind. Sages like Śukadeva had compassion. He who has no compassion is no man.**

Someone asked, **How long should one support one's children?**

Sri Ramakrishna answered: **As long as they have not reached their majority. When the chick becomes a full-grown bird and can look after itself, then the mother bird pecks it and doesn't allow it to come near her.** (p.628)

This is the law of nature. 'Now you are grown, look after yourself.' I make my son self-reliant, and then I have no more duty to him. Now he is independent. Let him do as he wishes, I will not say yes or no. Here is the real test of non-attachment. It sometimes happens that the son is truly self-reliant, but the parents can't accept this. They may not expect money from their son or daughter, but they want to be consulted, they want to give advice. Because of this parents sometimes needlessly suffer. Their attitude should be: 'I will expect nothing from my children. I will wish them well and pray to God for them. If they need money I will give it to them if I am able. But I will not help them unasked, or with the expectation that they will rely on me.' This attitude indicates true non-attachment.

Someone asked Sri Ramakrishna what his duty to his wife should be. He answered, **If she is a chaste wife, you should support her during your lifetime and provide for her livelihood after your death.** (p.628) We call the wife the *sahadharmiṇī*, the partner in the practice of *dharma*. She assists her husband in his religious and moral practices. He has an obligation to her, his life's partner. They protect and inspire each other. This is their duty. What more can they do?

The Master then says: **When you get a respite from your duties, cling to God's Lotus Feet with both hands—live in solitude and meditate on Him and serve Him ceaselessly.** (p.627) **But if you are intoxicated with the Knowledge of God, then you have no more duties to perform. Then God Himself will think about your morrow if you yourself cannot do so. God Himself will think about your family if you are intoxicated with Him. If a landlord dies leaving behind a minor son, then a guardian appointed by the court takes charge of the son.** (p.628)

God takes full responsibility for those who depend on Him completely. The Master illustrated this with a story : The Lord Nārāyaṇa and his consort Lakṣmī were resting in Vaikuṇṭha, their heavenly home. Suddenly Nārāyaṇa got up and hurried off. After a few minutes, he returned. Lakṣmī asked him, 'What happened? Why did you suddenly go and as suddenly return?' Lord Nārāyaṇa answered, 'One of my devotees was in great difficulty. He was walking along chanting my name when he inadvertantly stepped on some clothes a washerman had spread out on the road to dry. The washerman became very angry and started to beat him, so I hurried down to protect him. But then I noticed that he had picked up a stone and was protecting himself. So I came back.' If you give your all to God, God himself protects you in all ways and takes over all your responsibilities. You do not then have to think of protecting yourself.

Śrī Kṛṣṇa says in the *Gītā*,

Teṣāṁ nityābhiyuktānāṁ yogakṣemaṁ vahāmyaham—

'To those who are ever united with me, I bring them what they have not, and protect what they have.'[15]

God has an obligation to those who are ever united with Him, who know nothing but Him. As the *Gītā* says, God has promised to take full responsibility for all such devotees. Sometimes circumstances force a person living in the world to take refuge in God. He reaches the point where he does not know what is right and what is wrong, what he should or should not do. Then he finds there is only one way: to completely surrender himself to God. Sri Ramakrishna says to such a person, **Give God the power of attorney.** (p.628) Sometimes it is written in a legal document, 'From this date, this person will be responsible for conducting all my affairs.' This is called 'giving the power of attorney.'

The Master says: **If a man entrusts his affairs to a good person, will the latter do him any harm? With all the sincerity of your heart resign yourself to God and drive**

all your worries out of your mind. Do whatever duties He has assigned to you. (p.628) A 'good person' means God. If you depend on Him, you need not worry about anything.

To illustrate this point, the Master gives the example of the kitten: **The kitten does not have a calculating mind. It only cries, 'Mew, mew!' It lies in the kitchen contentedly if the mother cat leaves it there, and only calls the mother, crying, 'Mew, mew!' It has the same feeling of contentment when the mother cat puts it on the soft bed of the master of the house. It only cries for its mother.** (p.628)

Sri Ramakrishna says that there are two kinds of devotion, the baby monkey devotion and the kitten devotion. We also find this in the Hindu scriptures, *Pravṛttirdvividhā proktā mārjārī caiva vānarī*—'There are two kinds of propensities: one is like the kitten and the other like the baby monkey.'[16] With its two tiny hands, the baby monkey clings to its mother. When the mother jumps from one tree to another, the baby monkey holds on tightly. It knows that as long as it hangs on to its mother, it need not fear. But if it forgets and loses its grasp, it will be in danger. The kitten, however, does not have this anxiety. Wherever the mother cat puts the kitten, it is contented. It stays wherever the mother puts it. 'Giving God the power of attorney' is the kitten devotion.

Śrī Kṛṣṇa says to Arjuna in the *Gītā*:

Sarvadharmān parityajya mamekaṁ śaraṇaṁ vraja
Ahaṁ tvāṁ sarvapāpebhyo mokṣayiṣyāmi mā śucaḥ—

'Abandoning all duties, come to Me alone for shelter. Be not grieved, for I shall release thee from all evils.'[17] Perhaps Śrī Kṛṣṇa noticed that Arjuna felt inadequate, unable to carry out all his responsibilities, so he said to him 'Only hold on to Me. Do not concern yourself with righteousness and unrighteousness; just remember Me.' Such wonderful words of assurance! Then Śrī Kṛṣṇa promised Arjuna that he would be released from all evils, that he should not grieve. Those who hold fast to God have no worries. In the words of a Bengali song:

In this world he only is happy
Who has realized the ever-blissful Kālī.
He doesn't go on pilgrimages;
He listens only to talk of Kālī.
No rituals does he perform—
He knows only Kālī, Kālī.

Girish Chandra Ghosh, the famous actor and playwright, would sometimes visit the Master. One day he asked him, 'What shall I do now?' He thought that perhaps the Master would tell him to give up the theatre and impart some spiritual instruction. But Sri Ramakrishna said: 'Stay as you are; continue to do as you are doing—only remember God in the morning and in the evening.' Girish thought: 'I don't know where I will be on any particular morning or evening. I won't be able to do as he asked.' The Master understood and said, 'Then remember Him at least at the time of eating and when you go to sleep.' Girish became pensive. He sat silent and was thinking, 'I don't eat at regular times, and when I do sit down to eat I am thinking of how a lawsuit is progressing, how much the lawyer will charge me, or whether the case will be decided in court today, etc. etc. All these thoughts run through my mind when I sit down to eat. How can 1 think of God then?' Girish continued to ruminate: 'Thakur is gracious. He said "Stay as you arc. Do what you are doing." He has made things so easy, but I am so worthless! I can't even do the little he has asked me to do about remembering God.' He was too embarrassed to express his feelings and remained silent. He could not say a word.

Then the Master in a state of ecstasy said, 'Just give me your power of attorney.' (The term he used was *bakalmā*, a Bengali word used when someone signs for another person, such as an illiterate.) Girish was overjoyed. He thought that by giving the power of attorney to the Master, he would have no more responsibilities—no more anxieties or worries. But one day in the Master's presence he said, 'I will do it.' The Master immediately reacted: 'What did you say? "I will do it?" Have you not given me the power of attorney? You should always say, "If it is God's will I will do it." You have no right to say, "I will do it."'

Afterwards Girish said: 'When I gave Thakur the power of attorney, I did not understand there was so much involved. If you perform *japa* and meditation, you do it for a certain length of time every day. But since I have given the power of attorney, I am saying, "Master, Master" all the time. There is no deliverance from it. Every minute I am wondering whether or not I am depending completely on him, or whether I am obeying my own ego. Giving the power of attorney has put me in this condition.' Swami Saradananda made a profound remark about this : 'Girish was afraid to be bound by rules, so he gave Thakur his "power of attorney". At that time he could not understand he had taken on such a great bondage in giving up his own will. It was the bondage of love—the greatest bondage of all.'

Sri Ramakrishna told a story about the seriousness of giving over one's responsibilities. A brahmin worked very hard to make a beautiful flower garden and was extremely proud of it. One day a cow entered the garden and trampled on many of the plants. This made the brahmin angry and he mercilessly beat the cow till it died. At first he felt very guilty and thought: 'I, a brahmin, have been responsible for killing a cow—a great sin.' But he had studied a little philosophy so he began to reason: '*I* did not kill the cow. It was my hand that did it. Indra is the ruler of the hand, so it was really Indra who killed the cow.'

The Hindu scriptures say that there is a ruler for each of the organs.'[18] *Sūrya*, the sun god, is the ruler of the eyes; *Vāyu*, the wind god, is the ruler of the ears, etc. The ruler of the hand is Indra, king of the gods. The brahmin was aware of this, so when the sin of killing the cow tried to enter his body, he blocked its way, saying: 'Where is your authority to enter my body? I did not kill the cow. It was really Indra. My hand killed the cow, but Indra is the ruler of the hand, so the sin is Indra's. Go and enter his body.'

The sin went to Indra and told him the whole story. After hearing it, Indra said, 'Wait a moment, I want to have a few words with that brahmin.' In disguise, Indra entered the brahmin's garden. Walking around, he pretended to be very impressed by the garden's beauty. Then he met the brahmin and started to chat with him.

Indra: 'What a beautiful garden! Who made it? Who does it belong to?'

Brahmin: 'It is my garden.'

Indra: 'Who planted and cared for all these flowers?'

Brahmin: 'It was I who did everything.'

The brahmin was overjoyed. He conducted Indra around the garden, saying, 'Look, look at all I have done!' At last they came to the place where the dead cow was lying. Indra asked,

'And who killed the cow?'

The brahmin could only stand silent. He had been saying, 'I did it,' so often, now how could he say, 'I did not do it'? Then Indra assumed his true form and said: 'You hypocrite! You have been saying "I", "I", so long, and now you are silent. You wanted to blame me for killing the cow, but you yourself will have to suffer the consequences.'

As this story shows, the act of giving over one's responsibilities is not easy. If there is any egotism, it will not work. But if a person gets rid of his 'I', and depends utterly on God, God takes full responsibility for him. That person is fortunate; no suffering can touch him. He has attained the highest bliss and is always happy.

Someone asked the Master if it were possible for a person living in the world to realize God, and if so, what were the signs of such realization. The Master said: **His tears will flow and the hair on his body will stand on end. No sooner does he hear the sweet name of God than the hair of his body stands on end from sheer delight, and tears roll down his cheeks.** (p.629)

Sri Ramakrishna says that such a person's mind is like dry kindling which blazes up as soon as a lighted match touches it. But if the wood is wet, there is no possibility of setting it on fire. This 'wetness' is caused by love for sense objects. In this condition, there is no delight in listening to God's name. Only if the mind is 'dry'—that is, free from desires and unattached—will a person feel great joy and the hair of his body will stand on end when he hears God's name.

We find this same idea in the *Śrīmad Bhāgavatam*:

Evaṁ harau bhagavati pratilabdhabhāvaḥ
bhaktyārdravaddhṛdayaḥ
Utpulakaḥ pramodāt autkaṇṭhyavāṣpakalayā—

'The devotee obtains absorbing love for God. His heart melts in devotion, the hairs of his body stand on end, and tears of surpassing joy almost drown him.'[19]

When these signs are present, we can understand that this person has realized God. There is another sign of God-realization—lack of body-consciousness. Does lack of body-consciousness mean that if someone pinches or cuts us we will not feel pain? It is not that. Lack of body-consciousness means that we do not identify ourself with the body. The feeling 'I am the body' is totally absent. In our present condition we are 'I'-centred, egotistical; we think of ourselves as the body. Sri Ramakrishna says that even while living in the world we can realize God if the consciousness that 'I am the body' disappears. He uses the simile of the dry coconut to explain this.

The sign of a man's having realized God is that he has become like a dry coconut. He has become utterly free from the consciousness that he is the body. He does not feel happy or unhappy with the happiness or unhappiness of the body. He does not seek the comforts of the body. He roams about in the world as a *jīvanmukta*, one liberated in life. (p.629) When we shake a green coconut it does not make any sound, but when it becomes dry it gives off a rattling sound because the kernel is separated from the shell. When a person has realized God, he is like that dry coconut. He is conscious that his Ātman (Self) is separate from his body.

Sri Ramakrishna's nephew Akshay, whom he loved very much, suddenly died. The Master said: 'I saw that his dying was like a sword coming out of its scabbard. The body was the scabbard and the Self was the sword. I noticed that the body remained though the Self came out. Seeing this, I started to laugh.' He could see clearly that the body and the Self were different; the body died, the Self was unchanged.

Another example of God-realization given by Sri Ramakrishna is the discarded leaf-plate. The dry leaf-plate is blown hither and thither by the wind; it has no will of its own. After attaining God, a person lives in the world like this. *Kṣiptaḥ saṁskāravātena ceṣṭate śuṣkaparṇavat*—'Blown by the wind of *saṁskāra*s [past mental impressions], the desireless, independent, free and liberated person moves about like a dry leaf.'[20]

These *saṁskāra*s, or tendencies, are the result of a person's *prārabdha karma*—that is, the actions a person has done previously that are now bearing fruit. Ordinarily a person is swept along by the impressions from three types of *karma*—*prārabdha karma*, *sañcita karma*, and *kriyamāṇa karma*. *Sañcita karma* means actions done previously that have not yet begun to fructify. *Kriyamāṇa karma* means actions being done now that will bear fruit in the future. When a person realizes God, his *sañcita* and *kriyamāṇa karma*s are destroyed, and his body remains only as long as his *prārabdha karma* lasts.

Prārabdha karma has been explained through the example of a wheel. The wheel set in motion continues to roll as long as the force that set it off is not spent. It cannot go further than that. In the same way, after a person realizes God, he acts only through the force of his *prārabdha karma*—his past impressions. When this force is exhausted, he gives up the body; he has no will of his own to start further actions, or even to breathe.

But some Realized Souls keep their bodies to help others. If we had not seen such people, we would say that God-realization is mere imagination, an impossibility. But we have seen persons who live in the world but are not of the world. They are in the body, but not of the body. Swami Brahmananda was such a person. Surrounded by people, he would sit in his room with his eyes half-shut, inattentive. Sometimes he would suddenly open his eyes, and it would seem that he was seeing something new. He could not at first recognize his surroundings.

We saw this also in Swami Shivananda. All night long he would be struggling for breath sitting up on his bed, bent over a pillow. His attendants would speak in whispers, wondering what would happen next. But in the morning when we went to him, he would smile and his face would beam with joy. Someone would ask him, 'Maharaj, how are you?' And he would respond, 'Me? I am very well, child. Through the Master's grace I have understood that I am not the body, I am very well. But if you ask about the body, I will say that it follows its own law. After a few days it will be destroyed.' He was like a dry coconut; his Self was completely separate from his body. When he said 'Through the Master's grace I am in bliss', it was not just a conventional way of speaking. People often speak this way as a formality. But Swami Shivananda's face, his behaviour, that light that shone through him—everything showed that he was really blissful.

Another example can be found in Swami Turiyananda. When he underwent an operation, he had no anesthetic, but remained silent, watching everything. It seemed as if the operation were happening to someone else. He was like the dry coconut. The Master said that such persons know that their Self is separate from the body.

We sometimes dream that we are dead. According to a learned Swami, this kind of dream is very auspicious because it indicates that we are aware that we are not the body. Most of the time my life is centred around the body. But if I know for certain that 'I am different from the body', I understand that death does not affect my real Self, that there is no misery or happiness, no birth or decay for me. Then whatever happens in the world cannot touch my Self. I am free from all anxiety.

We find in the *Kaṭha Upaniṣad*, *Taṁ svāccharīrāt pravṛhenmuñjādivesīkāṁ dhairyeṇa*—'Let a man separate Him (the Self) from his body with steadiness, as one separates the tender stalk from a blade of grass.'[21] The Master says that then he will roam about in the world as a *jīvanmukta*, one liberated in life. **The devotee of Kālī is a *jīvanmukta*, full of Eternal Bliss.** (p.629) He is always blissful. We are always searching for happiness, but we do not find unmixed happiness anywhere in the world. What little joy we get is followed by suffering. In the words of a Bengali saying, 'As much as you laugh, so much will you cry.' But if a person realizes God, he will always be full of joy and afraid of nothing. He will wander about aimlessly. What is there to fear? To whom shall I bow my head? The king? No! My king is living in my heart; I shall not rely on anyone else. I am *ātmatṛpta*—'satisfied in the Self', *paryāptakāmaḥ*—'I have everything' (Having Him, I have nothing more to desire.), *vimṛtyuḥ*—'I have gone beyond birth and death'. (Death is for the body, not for the Self.)

How then do I live in the world? In poetic language Śrī Śaṅkara has said:

Śakunīnāmivākāśe jale vāricarasya ca
Padaṁ yathā na dṛśyeta tathā jñānavatāṁ gatiḥ—

'As the bird soars in the sky effortlessly, as the fish and other aquatic animals swim about in the water freely, leaving no trace, no footprint—so it is with the sage, the knower of

Brahman.'[22] The sage moves about in the world utterly unconcerned, unattached. He does all his worldly duties, but nothing can entangle him.

Sri Ramakrishna says: 'When the mother bird is sitting on her eggs, have you noticed her eyes? They are open, but it is as if they do not see. The bird's whole mind is centred on her eggs. Her eyes are still open, and they still do not see.' They have a bewildered appearance. A *jīvanmukta*, one who is free while living, is like that bird. He does not see the world as we see it. To him it is a dream—another world. In the words of the *Gītā*, *Ātmanyevātmanā tuṣṭaḥ*—'His spirit is content in itself.' *Vītarāgabhaya-krodhaḥ*—'He is one from whom passion, fear, and anger have passed away.'[23] Passion means attachment or attraction to any worldly object or person.

Śrī Śaṅkara says in his *Ātmabodha*:

Tīrtvā mohārṇavaṁ hatvā
Rāgadveṣādirākṣasān
Yogī śāntisamāyukta
Ātmārāmo virājate—

'Having crossed the ocean of delusion and having killed the monsters of attachment and aversion, the yogi becomes united with peace and dwells in the Bliss derived from the realization of the Self alone.' Swamiji used to say, and it is in our scriptures also, that where there is passion, there is hatred; where there is attraction, there is aversion. These are pairs of opposites. The ideal is to rise above both, to be free from duality—to be 'free while living'.

The next verse of the *Ātmabodha* says:

Bāhyānityasukhāsaktiṁ
Hitvātmasukhanirvṛtaḥ

Ghaṭasthadīpavatsvasthaḥ
Svāntareva prakāśate—

'Relinquishing attachment to illusory external happiness, the Self-abiding *jīvanmukta*, satisfied with the Bliss derived from the Ātman, shines inwardly like a lamp placed inside a jar.'[24] This is the way a person who has realized God continues to live in the world.

But how does a person reach this state? I have been told that God is my all, the source of my happiness, and that He is always within me, but how do I become conscious of this? Sri Ramakrishna says, **No sooner does attachment to worldly pleasure dry up than the spark of God flashes forth.** (p.629) How do worldly pleasures dry up? How does one get rid of the attraction to sense objects?

Sri Ramakrishna says, 'Call on the Divine Mother in all earnestness.' He says this is a natural way. You do not have to study the scriptures or perform austerities. Just pray to the Divine Mother and love her. He says that **She is your own mother.** (p.629) We find the same insistence in the words of Sri Sarada Devi. She said, 'I am not your mother only in name, nor simply your guru's wife, nor your godmother. I am your *real* mother.' Again, she said, 'Wherever you go, whatever you do, always remember you have a mother.' She gives us so much assurance.

Referring to the Divine Mother, Sri Ramakrishna says, **She is by no means a godmother. She is your own mother. With a yearning heart persist in your demands on Her. The child holds to the skirt of its mother and begs a penny of her to buy a kite. Perhaps the mother is gossiping with her friends. At first she refuses to give the penny and says to the child: 'No, you can't have it. Your**

daddy has asked me not to give you money. When he comes home I'll ask him about it. You will get into trouble if you play with a kite now.' The child begins to cry and will not give up his demand. Then the mother says to her friends: 'Let me pacify this child.' (p.629)

The child acts in such a way that the mother is compelled to give him the penny. She is compelled—because she is his own mother. The child is stubborn. What can his mother do? **Immediately she unlocks the cash-box with a click and throws the child a penny.** (p.629)

Devotees once gave the Holy Mother some new clothing, which she in turn distributed among her attendants. One attendant, however, refused to accept the cloth saying, 'I have enough, you need not give me one.' A few days later, Holy Mother called the attendant to her and asked him why he had refused the cloth. The attendant said: 'Mother, the devotees give you things for your own use; why should I take them? You don't keep any for yourself.' The Holy Mother scolded him: 'Foolish child! Don't you know anything? Can a mother ever stop giving things to her child? I am telling you today, whenever you need anything, ask me. I'll be happy then.' Saying this, the Mother gave the attendant not one, but three dhotis. Tears came to the attendant's eyes. Then Mother said to him affectionately: 'The child can force his demands on his mother. So my child, when you want anything, ask me for it.'[25]

Sri Ramakrishna says: **You . . . must force your demand on the Divine Mother. She will come to you without fail. I once said the same thing to some Sikhs when they visited the temple at Dakshineswar. We were conversing in front of the Kālī temple. They said, 'God is compassionate.' 'Why compassionate?' I asked. They said, 'Why, revered**

sir, He constantly looks after us, gives us righteousness and wealth, and provides us with our food.' 'Suppose', I said, 'a man has children. Who will look after them and provide them with food—their own father, or a man from another village?' (pp.629-30)

Parents take the responsibility for their child. Who else will do it? Do we say: 'Thank you, father, thank you, mother, for your great kindness'? We never say that. In the same way we know that God is our very own. He is responsible for us; He protects us. Do we need His compassion?

Someone then asked the Master, **Is not God, then compassionate?** He replied, **Why should you think that? I just made a remark. What I mean to say is that God is our very own.** (p.630) He is certainly compassionate, but if I say that God is compassionate and ever gracious, I am thinking of his greatness, his majesty. When I think of God's majesty, I am building a wall between Him and me. A lover of God does not bother himself with His greatness. He likes to think that God is his own. He thinks, 'I love to love. I don't know why, but I love.' Sri Ramakrishna would say, **We can exert force on Him. With one's own people one can even go so far as to say, 'You rascal! Won't you give it to me?'** (p.630) One needs this faith that God is one's very own.

The Master says, **A man thinks of God, no doubt, but he has no faith in Him. Again and again he forgets God and becomes attached to the world. It is like giving the elephant a bath; afterwards he covers his body with mud and dirt again.** (p.632) To further illustrate attachment, Sri Ramakrishna uses the expression 'Casting their anchor, they plied the oars of the boat'. He is referring to the story of some boatmen who one night cast their anchor near the shore. The next morning they wanted to leave, so they started to row the boat. They rowed and rowed, but the boat didn't move an inch because they had forgotten to pull up the anchor. In the same way, our minds are attached to the world; still we are practising *japa* and other disciplines. Although we are going through the motions of *japa*, etc., our minds are elsewhere. We read the scriptures while inwardly we are thinking of money. The mind is everything. If our minds don't go towards God, if we don't remember Him, all spiritual disciplines are useless. This is most evident at the time of death. The Master said; **If they cherish within themselves attachment to the world, it must show up at the hour of death.** (p.631)

He said that sometimes at the hour of death a person will rave irrationally if he is strongly attached to the world. What we think of at the time of death determines our after-life existence. The ancient sage Bharata died when he was thinking of his pet deer, so he was born as a deer. Śrī Kṛṣṇa says in the *Gītā*,

Yaṁ yaṁ vāpi smaran bhāvaṁ tyajatyante kalevaram
Taṁ tamevaiti kaunteya sadā tadbhāvabhāvitaḥ—

Thinking of whatever state (of being) he at the end gives up his body, to that being does he attain, O son of Kuntī, being ever absorbed in the thought thereof.[26]

What you think about at the time of death, you become. At first glance, this seems very easy. All my life I will live happily; then at the hour of death I will think of God and go to Him. But this is not so easy. In order to think of God at the last moment, you must work all your life. The Master said that we must practise and gave an example: If a person can write English well, did he learn this all at once? No, he studied very diligently to accomplish this. The same with a musician who plays the piano without ever looking at the keys, never making a mistake. He had to practise again and again to accomplish this.

In Hindu scriptures we find the term *abhyāsayoga*, meaning the yoga of practice. *Practice* is called a yoga. There are many kinds of yoga, but they all have one thing in common, the yoga of practice. The term is used in the *Gītā*, *Abhyāsayogayuktena cetasā nānyagāminā*—'He who meditates on the Supreme Person with his mind undistracted through constant practice and not wandering after anything else. . .'.[27]

At first the mind does not want to go towards God, but if you continue to practise, you will find that your mind will not go anywhere except to God. Sri Ramakrishna would be displeased if those who visited him would talk about anything but God. *Anyā vāco vimuñcatha*—'Give up all other talk.'[28] Try again and again to turn your mind towards God.

The poet-saint Kabīr said, 'With every breath remember God; there is no other way.'[29] There are some people who are able to do this. They say God's name with every breath. As we do not have to make an effort to breathe, they do not have to try to say God's name. This is called *ajapā*. God's name constantly comes to their mind of its own, naturally. When this state is reached, at the time of death that person will do nothing but chant God's name.

I know of one Swami who on his death-bed was not outwardly conscious, yet his fingers were moving, indicating that inwardly he was repeating the Lord's name. This was the result of practice. You can reach a state in which you cannot think of anything but God, even if you try.

Swami Vivekananda used the expression, 'nervous association'. One great thought dominates your mind in such a way that you can think of nothing else, even in a dream. It is as if someone is preventing you from thinking anything else. Your whole body, mind, and intellect are completely engrossed. Today's psychologists acknowledge this and call it *censorship*. In India it is called *viveka*, discrimination, or *nītibodha*, moral consciousness. These terms mean about the same as censorship. The mind is being admonished, 'Be careful; don't do this; don't go that way.' This comes as a result of practice.

'Habit is second nature' is a common saying. Swamiji said, 'Second nature—no! First nature. It is first nature and the whole of nature of man. Everything that we are is the result of habit.'[30] What we practise, we become. Our character is the product of what we practise. What we have done in this birth or in previous births is impressed on our minds and the sum total of these impressions makes our character. There may be bad impressions in my mind, but from now on, I will start to do only what is good so that good impressions will begin to form. Gradually the bad impressions will disappear—the result of practice.

We practise many things throughout our lives—some good, some bad. We give up old habits and adopt new ones. If we could only practise meditation and remembrance of God! At first we might not like it, but once we begin to practise, we will not even have to try to remember God. Our mind will go of its own accord towards Him. If we forget Him for a minute we will feel pained. Such is the power of practice!

Sri Ramakrishna pointed out the way for those who live in the world: **The way lies through constant practice. If a man practises meditation on God, he will remember God even on the last day of his life.** (p.632)

References

1. *Bhagavad-Gītā*, III.6
2. *Ibid.*, II.3
3. *Ibid.*, IX.27
4. *Mahābhārata, Śāntiparva*, XVII.19
5. *Uttaragītā*, III.2
6. *Garuḍa Purāṇa, Uttara Khaṇḍa*, VII.82
7. *Śrīmad Bhāgavatam*, VI.1.10
8. John Philpot Curran's speech on the Right of Election of the Lord Mayor of Dublin, July 10, 1790
9. *Garuḍa Purāṇa, Uttara Khaṇḍa*, VII.95
10. *Gītā*, V.10
11. *Ibid.*, II.56
12. *Ibid.*, III.35
13. *Ibid.*, VI.1
14. *Ibid.*, VI.8
15. *Ibid.*, IX.22
16. *Sannyāsa Upaniṣad*, II.101
17. *Gītā*, XVIII.66
18. *Muṇḍaka Upaniṣad*, III.2.7
19. *Bhāgavatam*, III.28.34
20. *Aṣṭāvakra Saṁhitā*, XVIII.21
21. *Kaṭha Upaniṣad*, II.3.17
22. *Muṇḍaka Upaniṣad, Śaṅkara Bhāṣya*, III.2.6
23. *Gītā*, II.55-6
24. *Ātmabodha*, 50, 51
25. *Śrī Mā*, Ashutosh Mitra, pp.182-83
26. *Gītā*, VIII.6
27. *Ibid.*, VIII.8
28. *Muṇḍaka Upaniṣad*, II.2.5
29. *Kabīr Panthā*, Swami Bhumananda, 1340, p.17
30. *C.W.*, Vol. I, 1962, p.207

X

Holy Company and the Ideal of Renunciation

It was Sunday morning [April 8, 1883]. The Master, looking like a boy, was seated in his room, and near him was another boy, his beloved disciple Rakhal. M. entered and saluted the Master. Ramlal also was in the room, and Kishori, Manilal Mallick, and several other devotees gathered by and by. Manilal Mallick, a business man, had recently been to Benares, where he owned a bungalow. (pp.200-01)

Benares is a unique city. Thought to be the oldest city in the world, it has always held a great attraction for Hindus. Lord Viśvanātha (Śiva) and Mother Annapūrṇā (the Divine Mother) live there. It is believed that if a person dies there, he is immediately liberated from the cycle of birth and death. When the Master went to Benares, he saw at the cremation ground exactly how this happens. He had a vision of Lord Viśvanātha Himself whispering the name of God in the ear of each *jīva* (embodied soul), and Mother Annapūrṇā untying all the ropes that bind him.

Benares is a great meeting place for holy persons of all the various sects in India. The garb and spiritual practices of these holy men and women vary widely, but these holy people are all regarded as leaders of Hindu society. Hence the Master said to Mani Mallick: **So you have been to Benares. Did you see any holy men there?** (p.201) We would probably ask: 'Was it hot or cold there?' or 'What kind of food did you find there?'

etc. But the Master's question was different. He wanted to know if Mani Mallick had seen any holy men.

We normally visit a holy place to see a particular image of God, and if we don't see the image, our whole pilgrimage is in vain. But there are two kinds of images. One kind is in the temple where the god or goddess is worshipped; it is called the unmoving image. (Of course, in the eye of a highly developed spiritual person, this image is not unmoving, but to the ordinary person, it seems to be unmoving.) The other kind of image is the moving image. The ascetic holy persons, the *sādhus*, are the moving images. We must also see these holy persons when we visit a holy place. They have so much renunciation, so much self-control; they have gone through so much hardship to realize God, that they inspire us also to try to realize Him.

Sri Ramakrishna himself went to visit many holy persons. He went to see Keshab Sen, for example, because he had heard that Keshab talked about God. He also went to see Bhagavan Das Babaji at Kalna and Dayananda Sarasvati in Calcutta. Then when he was in Benares, he went to see Trailangaswami. This holy man was a *maunī*, which means that he had taken a vow of silence. He communicated only with gestures. Sri Ramakrishna said that he was a *paramahaṁsa*, a perfected soul of the highest order.

This belief in the value of *sādhu-darśan*, seeing holy persons, is an ancient Hindu tradition that continues to this day. By observing and listening to these holy person, we begin to understand the meaning of life, the purpose of human birth.

There are in fact two forms of India. One is the outer form; that India is the changeful India. It changes with the passing of time. There is nothing wrong in that. But there is another India, an inner India. Because of this inner form, India is 'India'. This is the eternal India which tells us 'This changeable world, the world perceived by the senses, is not lasting, is not real. There is something beyond this world, which is the only Reality. The goal of life is to realize this Reality, this Truth. You may be far from the goal, but never forget what the goal is. Some day or other you will reach it. It may be only after a long time, but you will certainly reach it some day.' If you can see that ideal exemplified in those who have reached the goal, or who are very near that goal—holy persons—then your faith will grow. Go to them and learn from them.

Sri Ramakrishna said, **This power of assimilation comes from associating with holy men.** (p.737) These holy persons protect the eternal India. Seeing them you are reminded once again of the goal of life and you know that it is possible to reach that goal. Swami Vivekananda said again and again that spirituality is the very basis of life in India. We can believe this when we see how the common people of India are so greatly attracted to these holy persons. Sri Ramakrishna emphasized the importance of holy company. He said that through association with holy persons you become aware that God is the only Reality; all else is unreal. In his words, 'A person has his watch set right through holy company.' To see if my watch is set right, I sometimes compare it with someone else's watch. The company of the holy is that other watch. If I am involved in worldly life, I may become confused and not know just what to do—what is right and what is wrong, but if I visit holy persons they set me straight. They let me know where I am and inspire and encourage me to do what is right.

Holy persons not only solve spiritual problems, they also solve problems relating to worldly life. Because their intellects are pure and their vision clear, they can probe deeply into any problem. They don't tell everyone to renounce the world.

Rather, they give instructions on how to stay on the path of righteousness and proceed towards God while living in the world. They understand that there is a need for earning money if you are living in the world. But if you begin to be greedy and desire much more money than you need, or if you try to earn money by immoral means ignoring all rules of right and wrong, then holy persons will warn you. They will remind you that you are not doing the right thing, that it isn't good to be so attached to money. You will then become more restrained and will try to change your ways.

Sri Ramakrishna advises us to do our duties in the world with one hand holding the feet of the Lord. Holy persons remind us of this teaching. They ask, 'Do you have one hand on God, or have you completely forgotten Him?' The Master says, **Holy company begets yearning for God.** (p.96) **The company of holy men awakens *śraddhā*, faith in God. Then comes *niṣṭhā,* single-minded devotion to the Ideal.** (p.503)

Further, he says that holy company is like the water in which rice has been soaked. This is sometimes given to a person who has drunk too much wine and has become intoxicated. It is supposed to bring him back to his normal state. We are all intoxicated with worldly happiness. Through holy association we regain our natural state; our intoxication with worldly objects and sense pleasures is removed. **One finds peace of mind in the company of holy men.** (p.431)

A verse in the *Kulārṇava Tantra* says, *Satāṁ saṅgo hi bheṣajam*—'Holy company is a medicine.'[1] The disease of worldliness is very difficult to cure. Holy company is the only remedy. Why is worldliness called a disease? It is because, though we listen to many teachings about God, renunciation, etc., and though we endure much suffering and misery in the world, we are still attracted to worldly pleasures and do not want to give them up. This worldliness is a terrible disease that can cause our moral and spiritual death. Though it is such a serious malady, it can be cured through association with holy persons.

The *Garuḍa Purāṇa* says, *Anekajanmajanitaṁ pātakaṁ sādhusaṅgame kṣipraṁ naśyati dharmajña jalānāṁ śarado yathā*—'In the rainy season, the river is muddy, but in the fall, the water becomes clear and pure. In the same way, sins accumulated in many past births are quickly destroyed through association with holy persons.'[2]

Tulasīdāsa has said:

Tāta svarga apavarga sukha dhariya tulā eka aṅga
Tūla na tāhi sakala mili jo sukha lava satasaṅga—

'There is much happiness on earth. If on one side of a scale you put heaven and liberation, and on the other side you put holy company, you will find that holy company far outweighs heaven in blissfulness.'[3]

It was my good fortune to meet M. and have many conversations with him. Many people would come to meet him after having read the *Gospel*, and he would send them to Belur Math to observe the monks there. He used to say that Sri Ramakrishna was a monk, a renouncer of lust and greed, and that in order to understand him, we must see his all-renouncing disciples. He said that the Master's monastic disciples were very good mangoes; his householder disciples were also mangoes, but not of the same quality. When someone would return from the Math, M. would question him: 'Did you see the holy men there? What were they doing? How were they meditating? How were they working?' He wanted everyone to take careful note of these things. I remember him asking me all these questions.

In order to get the benefit of holy company, you must try to understand these holy persons and what they are doing. You must not judge them superficially. When you visit the Math, you might see a monk hurriedly picking flowers. It is late, so he must hurry. The flowers are for God in the temple and it is time for them to be offered. Then in another part of the Math you may see some monks seated together chopping vegetables.

You see all these things going on at the monastery and they seem to be very ordinary. Don't you see the same things happening in your own home? But there is a difference. The monks are doing everything for God. If you understand this, then you will see that all these common, ordinary actions are in reality uncommon, extraordinary—because they are directed to God. And a sense of devotion will be aroused in you.

M. had great reverence for all the monks. When any monk came to see him, M. would say, 'Seeing you inspires me. You remind me of the Master.' But M. is not the only person to be inspired by seeing monks. If anyone comes in contact with a real monk, his life can be changed. A monk's life, his thoughts, are all for the good of others. Whatever he does is for the good of all. Even if a monk scolds a person, he does it only to help him. Sri Ramakrishna used to say that the anger of a holy man is like a mark on water. When you make a mark on water, it doesn't stay. The anger of a holy man is like that; it doesn't last. Holy Mother said about Sri Ramakrishna's monastic disciples, 'One will be benefited if one even touches the place where they have bathed.' Their lives were that pure.

Śrī Śaṅkarācārya has said: *Kṣaṇamapi sajjanasaṅgatirekā, bhavati bhavārṇavataraṇe naukā*—'If one has association with a holy person for even one moment, that will be a raft to carry him across the ocean of the world.'[4] You will be able to tear asunder the bonds of the world. Such is the greatness of holy company!

Someone asked Sri Ramakrishna, **How can one recognize a holy man?** The Master answered, **He who has surrendered his body, mind, and innermost self to God is surely a holy man.** (p.327) That is one important sign of a holy man. He has renounced everything for God. God is his all. Whoever with all his heart and mind has said, 'I want God and nothing else,' is a real holy person.

Sri Ramakrishna continued his discussion of the marks of a holy man. **He who has renounced 'woman and gold' is surely a holy man.** (p.327) 'Woman and gold'—lust and greed—these are two things a monk must renounce. Renouncing lust does not mean despising women. Rather it means looking at women in a pure way. The Master continued: **He is a holy man who does not regard woman with the eyes of a worldly person. He never forgets to look upon a woman as his mother, and to offer her his worship if he happens to be near her.** (p.327)

To a monk, all women are forms of the Divine Mother of the Universe, so they are to be worshipped. But still he keeps his distance from women because his life is dedicated to one ideal. People learn from watching holy men, so a monk must be careful of how he appears to others. The Master said, **Worldly people learn renunciation by seeing the complete renunciation of a monk.** (p.184)

Śrī Caitanya was very strict with his disciples in regard to their relationship with women. One of his monastic disciples, 'the younger Haridāsa', had a loving nature and was very devoted to Śrī Caitanya, yet Śrī Caitanya disowned him because, in spite of his guru's command, he had talked with a woman devotee when he went to her house for alms.

A young devotee named Nityagopal used to visit Sri Ramakrishna. The Master loved him very much and said that he had reached a high state of spirituality, the state of a *paramahaṁsa*. Nityagopal sometimes visited a woman who was devoted to the Master; she was about thirty years old. She loved Nityagopal as she would a son, and she sometimes caressed him like a child when he visited her home. There seemed to be nothing wrong in this, but one day the Master said to Nityagopal, 'Holy man, beware! Don't go too often!'

M. was present when the Master gave that warning to Nityagopal. In the *Gospel* he has written his thoughts about this incident: **The young man has developed the state of a *paramahaṁsa*. . . . Is there still a possibility of his falling into danger in spite of his high spiritual state? What an austere rule is laid down for a *sādhu*!. . . How can an ordinary man expect to attain liberation unless such a high ideal is set by holy men? The woman in question is very devout; but still there is danger. Now I understand why Caitanya punished his disciple, the younger Haridāsa, so severely. . . . He was a *sannyāsi*, therefore Caitanya banished him. What a severe punishment! How hard is the rule for one who has accepted the life of renunciation. . . .**

'Beware, holy man!' These words of the Master echoed in the hearts of the devotees like the distant rumbling of thunder. (p.188)

Once at the Advaita Ashrama at Benares there was a reading of the *Śrīmad Bhāgavatam*. The monks all sat on a large carpet spread out on the floor while they listened to the reading. Swami Premananda and Swami Turiyananda were among those seated there. Also present was Swami Atmananda, Swamiji's disciple, a highly advanced soul. Shortly after the reading had started, a woman devotee came and sat at the end of the carpet, keeping a proper distance from the monks. At this, Swami Atmananda got up and left. Afterwards someone asked him why he had left before the reading was finished. He replied, 'It is not proper for a monk to sit on the same carpet with a woman.' When it was pointed out to him that Swami Premananda and Swami Turiyananda had remained sitting there, Swami Atmananda said: 'Look, they are in a class of their own; you can't judge them by the same yardstick as you would judge others. One slap of theirs can make knowers of Brahman out of a thousand persons like me. Don't compare me with them. I must go by the usual rules.'

The life of a monk is indeed meant for teaching others. Because of that he must be very careful. Holy Mother said, 'Monks are like a white cloth. If a spot appears on a white cloth it is very noticeable.' Monks must live cautiously.

Sri Ramakrishna said: **The holy man constantly thinks of God and does not indulge in any talk except about spiritual things. Furthermore, he serves all beings, knowing that God resides in everybody's heart. These, in general are the signs of a holy man.** (p.327) The most important sign of a holy man is that he is immersed in God. To him, God is the only reality—all else is unreal. He always thinks of God. The Master said that it is nothing to be wondered at if a holy man thinks about God. It would be surprising if he didn't. People would criticize him.

We find all these signs perfectly manifest in Sri Ramakrishna himself. He was an ideal monk. Holy Mother once said that he had one hundred per cent renunciation, that renunciation was his ornament. Swami Vivekananda called him 'the Emperor of

Renunciation'. The following incident is a vivid example of his renunciation: One day Mathur Babu, the temple proprietor, offered him some property so that he wouldn't have to be concerned about his living expenses. What could be more tempting to a poor temple priest than that? But Sri Ramakrishna was furious and almost beat Mathur Babu when he heard his proposal. 'Rascal, do you want to make a worldly man of me?' he said.

On another occasion Mathur Babu said to the Master's old mother, 'Dear Granny, you have never accepted anything from me. Now please accept something or I will think you don't love me.' Hearing this, the old woman was troubled. What could she ask for? She didn't need anything. At last, after thinking it over, she said: 'Yes, I know what you can give me. For several days I have been without dried tobacco leaves for cleaning my teeth. Please bring me two paisa worth of tobacco leaves. That is all I want.' Tears came to Mathur Babu's eyes and he said, 'Only this kind of mother could have given birth to a son like Sri Ramakrishna.'

A wealthy Marwari devotee once offered Sri Ramakrishna ten thousand rupees which he of course refused. But the Master wanted to test Holy Mother, so he told the devotee to offer the money to her. Holy Mother also would not accept the gift. She was the fit companion for the Master. If he was the Emperor of Renunciation, she was the Empress of Renunciation.

Sri Ramakrishna's renunciation was so intense that he could not even touch money. If he did, his hand would become bent and his body would ache. Once Swamiji placed a coin under the Master's mattress when he was out of the room. When Sri Ramakrishna returned and wanted to lie down, he couldn't. He tried, but something prevented him. This seems impossible, but it is not. Our minds influence our bodies. One thought, one feeling, can dominate not only our mind, but also our sense-organs, our nerves, our bodies. It is like a musical instrument that is tuned to one pitch. Sri Ramakrishna was perfectly 'tuned'. He had so much aversion to money that if he came in contact with a coin even unknowingly, he could not bear it.

His attitude toward women was firm and unwavering. He saw the Divine Mother of the Universe in all women and called every woman, even those who were considered immoral by society, 'the Blissful Divine Mother'. He worshipped his own wife as a goddess, and accepted a woman as his guru. No one has ever given so much honour to women as he has. He showed how a monk should regard women.

Name and fame, which most people have such a hankering for, the Master considered as so much rubbish. He prayed to the Divine Mother: 'Mother, I don't want people's respect. I don't want occult powers. I want only pure love for Thee.' One night when Baburam Maharaj (Swami Premananda) was sleeping in Sri Ramakrishna's room at Dakshineswar, he woke up in the middle of the night and saw the Master walking about in the room. He had his wearing cloth under his arm and was only half-conscious of his surroundings. From his mouth came the sound, 'thu, thu!' as if he was spitting. Then Baburam Maharaj heard him say fervently, 'Don't give, Mother, don't give!' It seemed that the Divine Mother was offering the Master name and fame and he was terrified, thus his anguished cries. Milton said, 'Fame is the last infirmity of a noble mind.'[5] Fame is one of the most difficult temptations to overcome, but the Master, through his cries to the Divine Mother, was able to ignore this attraction.

As we have seen, Sri Ramakrishna was the ideal monk. But he differed from most monks in that he did not wear any particular garb of a monk, and did not go into the forest or mountains away from human habitation. Still, he performed the rites of sannyasa according to scriptural injunctions. The Advaitic monk Totapuri initiated him into the monastic life with all the traditional rites.

Monks in India are attached to various communities. Śaṅkarācārya founded ten monastic communities called *daśanāmī*. Their names are *Tīrtha*, *Āśrama*, *Vana*, *Araṇya*, *Giri*, *Parvata*, *Sāgara*, *Sarasvatī*, *Bhāratī*, and *Purī*. The Ramakrishna Order monks are included in this *daśanāmī* and belong to Totapuri's *Purī* sect. Thus, they can add *Purī* to their names if they wish—for example, Swami Vivekananda Puri, or Swami Brahmananda Puri.

Śaṅkara created these ten communities as part of his work in reviving the Vedic religion. They follow the Vedānta philosophy. He established a monastery at each of the four corners of India, and each of the ten communities is connected with one of these monasteries. In this way, Śaṅkara provided for the future protection of the Vedic religion and Hinduism.

There are many monks outside of the *daśanāmī* community. You find various kinds of religious practices and customs among them, and they wear different kinds of religious emblems or marks. Some wear *geruā*, and some don't; some have shaven heads and others have long hair and beards. But the essential characteristic of all true monks is this—they are completely dependent on God and they love Him.

Some monks do not stay long in any one place. They are called *bahūdaka* monks. Then there are monks who stay in one place to practise spiritual disciplines. They are called *kuṭicaka* monks. Sri Ramakrishna said, '*kuṭicaka* after *bahūdaka*', which means that after travelling around and seeing the holy places, a monk should stay in one place and practise spiritual disciplines. He should be like the bird perched on the mast of a ship that was not aware that it had come to the middle of the ocean. When it saw where it was, it flew off—first in one direction, then in another. When it could not find land anywhere, it returned to the ship and stayed perched on the mast. After wandering about, a monk should stay in one place.

Some monks are called *haṁsas*—'swans'. The word *haṁsa* has a deep meaning. A *haṁsa* is capable of drinking only the milk from a mixture of milk and water, leaving only the water. In the same way, this world is a mixture of the real and the unreal, the eternal and the non-eternal. The *haṁsa* monk discriminates between the eternal and the non-eternal and accepts only the eternal. There is a group of monks higher than the *haṁsa*s called *paramahaṁsa*s. They live completely in the Ātman, the inner Divine Self. Through discrimination they have learned to renounce the non-eternal and are always established in the Eternal—the Self.

Sri Ramakrishna was a *paramahaṁsa*. No one knew how to classify him, so if anyone asked what kind of monk he was, people would say that he was a *paramahaṁsa*. A *paramahaṁsa* goes beyond all rules and regulations. Sri Ramakrishna had only one rule—to live completely in God. He did not know anything but God. He was a monk, yet he lived among his relatives and near and dear ones. He lived in the world, but he did not accumulate money or anything else. He regarded his own wife as a manifestation of the Divine Mother of the Universe. Being a householder was no bondage to him. He was beyond all distinctions—beyond all bondage.

An incident in the life of Swami Shivananda is significant. He was then living at Belur Math. He always wore *geruā*-coloured clothes and never white. Once on Sri Ramakrishna's birthday celebration, Swami Brahmananda suddenly said to him :

'Brother Tarak, there are many people here today. Can you wander around this crowd wearing a white silk cloth?' Swami Shivananda immediately agreed. He put on a good white silk cloth and walked around the Math grounds among the crowd with his walking stick. He didn't look at anyone.

The meaning of this incident is that he had reached a state where the monk's garb was unnecessary for him. Ordinary monks need to wear the monk's garb and to abide by the rules, but *paramahaṁsa*s are beyond all rules. They can obey rules or not obey them, that is to say, they are incapable of doing anything wrong.

The *Mahānirvāṇa Tantra* lists these characteristics of a monk : *nistraiguṇyaḥ*, *nirvikalpaḥ*, *nirlobhaḥ*, and *asañcayī*.[6]

Nistraiguṇya means that he is beyond the three *guṇas*: *sattva*, *rajas*, and *tamas*. *Rajas*, activity, is better than *tamas*, sloth; and *sattva*, calmness and purity, is better than *rajas*. But even the *sattva guṇa* is a golden chain. A monk cuts off even this chain and is free from all the *guṇa*s.

Nirvikalpa means that he has no vacillation. He is always unattached; there is no variation from this in his life.

Nirlobha means that he is completely free from greed.

Asañcayī indicates that he never accumulates anything. To practise this, some holy men adopt the *ajagaravṛtti* discipline. They imitate the python which stays in one place, such as the stump of a tree. When an animal comes near, he quickly grabs it in his mouth and swallows it. The holy men practising this discipline do not ask for anything. *Yadṛcchālābhasantuṣṭaḥ*—They are satisfied with whatever comes by chance.[7] If someone gives them something, they will eat; otherwise not. God is the only giver; only if He gives will the holy men eat.

Sri Ramakrishna said that a monk should not accumulate anything. **The *Avadhūta* accepted a bee as another teacher**. [A story in the *Bhāgavatam* tells about an *Avadhūta*, a type of monk, who had among his twenty-four teachers, a bee.] **Bees accumulate their honey by days of hard labour. But they cannot enjoy their honey, for a man soon breaks the comb and takes it away. The *Avadhūta* learnt this lesson from the bees, that one should not lay things up. *Sādhus* should depend one hundred per cent on God. They must not gather for the morrow. . . . Birds and monks do not hoard.** (p.314)

An incident in Swamiji's days as a wandering monk illustrates a monk's complete dependence on God. When he was travelling on a train, a man started to taunt him for being a penniless monk, and then began to eat his lunch. When he had finished he said: 'Look, I have eaten all this. I am a worldly man, so I can eat. It is your fate not to get anything. What do you gain by being a monk?' Swamiji remained silent. What could he say? He was hungry and did not have a thing to eat.

The two men got down at the next station. Swamiji sat down at the foot of a tree while the man attended to some business at the station. Suddenly a sweet-meat seller came up to Swamiji and said to him: 'I was resting after eating, when Rāma appeared to me in a dream and said, "My devotee, a holy man who is sitting at the station, has not eaten. Give him some food." Three times he appeared to me and told me to feed you.' Swamiji said: 'You are mistaken. Rāma must have meant some other holy man.' But the man replied, 'No, I know you are that holy man, because there is no other holy man here but you!' Swamiji then accepted the food. Meanwhile, his fellow traveller had come out of the station and had seen the whole incident. He was astonished. This is an example of the 'python' discipline. When anyone depends completely on God, God, in unexpected ways, takes care of him.

In the *Bhāgavatam* we find,

Sāyantanaṁ śvastanaṁ vā na saṅgṛhṇīta bhikṣitam
Pāṇipātrodarāmātro makṣikeva na saṅgrahī—

'An ascetic should not store the food received as holy alms for the evening or for the next day. His palm should be his receiving plate and the stomach, the preserving vessel. He should not accumulate like the bee.'[8]

Sri Ramakrishna could never accumulate the slightest thing. At one time he needed one bathing dhoti and asked M. to bring one, but M. brought two. The Master kept one and returned the other one to M. He could not keep more than he needed. Another time, when he was leaving a festival at Beni Pal's home, Beni Pal wanted to put some food in the carriage for the Master to take to Ramlal. But the Master said, 'O Beni Pal, I have this fault. I cannot store up anything.'

Sri Ramakrishna once went to the *Nahabat* to get some betel leaves to chew. The Holy Mother gave him some, which he chewed, and then she put a few other leaves in his hand for him to use later. With that trifling thing in his hand, he was in such a state that he could not find the way back to his room. He started staggering towards the Gaṅgā saying, 'Mother, I am drowning! Mother I am drowning!' Holy Mother saw what was happening, but as she never appeared in public, she could not go to his rescue. Just then a man came by, saw what danger the Master was in and summoned Hriday. Hriday came running and took him back to his room. We see here the range of a monk's genuine renunciation.

Another sign of a monk is that he never hurts anyone. In the *Gospel* Thakur says to Ishan, **'Please tell us . . . how the**

heart of the *sādhu* is the greatest of all'. Ishan replies, **'Larger than the earth is the ocean, and larger than the ocean is the sky. But Viṣṇu, the Godhead has covered earth, sky, and the nether world with one of His feet. And that foot of Viṣṇu is enshrined in the *sādhu's* heart. Therefore the heart of the holy man is the greatest of all'.** (p.289) His heart embraces everyone.

Because of this, the holy man never retaliates. He forgives anyone who mistreats him. Sri Ramakrishna demonstrated this trait in one incident at Dakshineswar. A hereditary priest of Mathur Babu's family became jealous of the Master because of Mathur's devotion to him. One day when the Master was in a state of ecstasy, the priest approached him and said, 'O Brahmin, tell me how you have gotten control over Mathur Babu.' Being in a state of ecstasy, Sri Ramakrishna could not say a word. Enraged, the priest violently kicked him. In spite of his bruises, Sri Ramakrishna did not tell anyone about what happened, and forgave the priest. If Mathur Babu had found out about it, he would have had the priest's head chopped off. A monk's *dharma* is to practise forgiveness and non-resistance. The Master said that a householder should hiss, that is, make a show of resistance, but a monk should not resist in any way.

Another example of non-resistance is seen in an incident that occurred during Swamiji's days as a wandering monk. He was riding on a train when two Englishmen entered his compartment. Thinking Swamiji did not know English, they started speaking ill of him in very vulgar language. After the train stopped at the next station, Swamiji, in perfect English, asked the station master for a glass of water. The two Englishmen were surprised. This man knew English! They asked Swamiji, 'Didn't you hear us when we were speaking that way about you?' Swamiji replied, 'Of course I heard you.' They said, 'Then why didn't you say anything to us?' Swamiji answered: 'Should one react to all the words that fools say?' He had not reacted at all to their vilification.

But Swamiji, at other times, undoubtedly reacted. When he was on a ship returning from the West, a missionary was speaking ill of the Hindu religion in his presence. For some time Swamiji was patient, but at last he could endure no more. Getting up from his chair, he grasped the missionary's collar and said, 'If you say one more word against my religion, I will throw you overboard!' The missionary was terrified. From the look on Swamiji's face, it appeared that he really would throw him overboard. The missionary at once asked Swamiji's forgiveness and never behaved like that again in Swamiji's presence.

If a monk is living in the world, he must deal with various kinds of people, and to protect the honour of his ideal, he must sometimes make a show of resistance. But he must always be conscious that he is acting only on behalf of his ideal. He does not react for his own sake, for his own defence. This is the *dharma* of a monk—to silently endure everything.

But forgiveness, non-violence, and non-resistance are not weaknesses in a monk. They are demonstrations of his strength. If he wished he could inflict injury on, or even utterly defeat his tormenter, but still he forgives him. Here is his greatness—he does not rely on anything or anyone in the world and expects no one to defend him. He depends only on God.

He is like a lion, free; he has cut the bonds of the world and wanders about at will. He does not bow down to anyone. He only bows down to his Ideal, to Truth, to God. He may be destitute, but he will not submit to anyone. There is such glory, such nobility in his demeanour that everyone is in awe of him. In Swamiji's days as a wandering monk he endured much privation and completely neglected his body, yet all who saw him were attracted to him. He was an unknown monk, but wherever he went, everyone—ordinary people and prominent officials—were drawn to him.

One day Swami Brahmananda, dressed in very ordinary monk's clothes, was waiting in a railway station. Seeing him, a young boy said to his friend, 'Can you tell me who that man is?' His friend replied, 'I don't know for sure, but I think he must be some kind of king.' He was a monk in every way, yet he appeared to be of royal birth. His bearing and demeanour showed that he was perfectly free—dependent on no one. A true monk cannot be compared to other people. He lives in another world.

The most important characteristic of a monk is his love for all beings. He always works for the welfare of others, unmindful of his own needs. It is my nature to breathe and I breathe unconsciously. A monk's compassion and love for others are like that. They are as natural to him as breathing is to me. Even if someone abuses a monk, he will not stop doing good to that person.

This characteristic of love for all creatures is illustrated in a story about a monk who rescued a scorpion that had fallen into the river. When the monk picked it up, it stung him and fell back into the river. The monk again rescued the scorpion and was again stung. This happened several times. The monk's hand was painfully swollen, yet he continued to rescue the scorpion. A man who had observed all this said to him: 'Why do you keep saving that scorpion? Don't rescue it anymore. Let it drown in the river!' The monk replied: 'It is the scorpion's nature to sting, so it stings. And it is a monk's nature to be compassionate. The scorpion doesn't give up its nature, why should I give up mine?' Saying this, he brought the scorpion out of the water again and this time threw it some distance from the river so it was safe. This is how a real monk behaves.

Another story tells about a monk who was beaten so badly by a ruffian that he lost consciousness. His brother monks carried him back to the monastery. There they gave him some milk to drink after he had regained consciousness. One of his brothers asked him, 'Tell us who it was that beat you.' And the monk replied, 'Brother, the one who beat me is now giving me milk.' To that monk, his beloved Lord was in everyone. He saw no difference between the man who beat him and the man who was lovingly caring for him. He loved all equally.

Buddha said, *Mātā yathā niyaṁ puttaṁ āyusā ekaputtamanurakṣe evam api savvabhūtesu mānasambhāvaye aparimāṇam*—'How will you love people? As a mother loves her son. The mother protects her only son with her own life.'[9] A mother does not make an effort to love her son. Her love for him is spontaneous. A holy man loves all beings like that—he doesn't have to make an effort. Buddha further emphasized this point when he said: 'Who is a monk? He is a monk whose inner, essential nature is love.'

Śrī Śaṅkarācārya also taught unselfish love; He said:

Śāntā mahānto nivasanti santo
vasantavallokahitaṁ carantaḥ
Tīrṇaḥ svayaṁ bhīmabhavārṇavaṁ
janānahetunānyānapi tārayantaḥ—

'There are pure souls who have attained peace and greatness. They bring good to mankind, like the coming of spring. They themselves have crossed the dreadful ocean of this world. Without any selfish motive, they help others to cross.'[10]

These rare souls come to earth only for the welfare of others. The Master used to say, 'Even living on sago I shall do good to others'. Shortly before he died he told Holy Mother that she must also live for others. He said to her: 'Must I do everything alone? Will you do nothing? The people of Calcutta are living like worms. Take care of them.' He wanted to put the burden of these poor souls in the hands of a fit person—Holy Mother. Swami Vivekananda said about the Master, 'The current of his love flows unobstructed, even to the outcaste.' His love flowed freely, like the current of a river, and it was for all—especially the poor and lowly. He wanted Swamiji to have that same all-embracing love and scolded him for asking to remain in *nirvikalpa samādhi*. Swamiji learned his lesson well, and later told a brother monk that his heart had grown very large and he had learned to enter into the sufferings of others. Another of the Master's disciples, Swami Shivananda, said that his blessings were 'always flowing, always flowing' They were on all.

A well-known Sanskrit prayer says:

> *Sarve bhavantu sukhinaḥ sarve santu nirāmayāḥ*
> *Sarve bhadrāṇi paśyantu mā kaścit duḥkhabhāk bhavet*—

'May all be happy! May all be free from disease! May all realize what is good! May none be subject to misery!' It seems that the author of this prayer wanted no one in the world to ever suffer.

Swami Akhandananda used to pray to God saying that his only desire was to relieve people's suffering. He also used to say: 'My Lord is not on a mountain peak or even in heaven. My Lord dwells in all beings. I am giving my life in service to God in the form of all beings, and I don't know how many more lives I will give.'[11]

This attitude is the very basis of the Ramakrishna Math and Mission. When Swamiji established the Ramakrishna Monastic

Order, it was in many ways a new type of monastic organization. He was often criticized. People would say: 'What kind of monk are these? They should be living at the foot of trees, but they build pleasant places to live in. They should live by begging alms, but they don't go out begging.' They seemed to be different from traditional monks, but the basis of their lives was not different. Monks of the Ramakrishna Order also renounce everything for God, though they do not live in mountain caves or forests. They come out of the bonds of one family and take on a vast family. Everyone in the world is a member of their family.

The Ramakrishna Math and Mission has established branches not only in Bengal and India, but all over the world. Still, the basis is renunciation, purity, and utter dependence on God—the time-honoured basis of all monastic life. Their renunciation is not simply an outward display; it comes from the heart. Real renunciation is the renunciation of desires. There are three basic desires: the desire for offspring, the desire for wealth, and the desire for name and fame. Monks of the Ramakrishna Order renounce these three desires. Whatever other desires they have are centred in God; they are not selfish desires.

When Swamiji established the Ramakrishna Math and Mission, he formulated its ideal with this Sanskrit verse: *Ātmano mokṣārthaṁ jagaddhitāya ca*—'For one's own liberation and for the good of the whole world'. He said to one of his disciples, 'Look, if you want your own liberation, you will go to hell, and if you work for the good of others, you will have liberation in the palm of your hand.'

Holy men give their lives for the good of the world, but how do they see the world? They see that it is the temple of God. The beings in the world are not merely *jīva*s—creatures—they are *Śivas*—God. The basic *mantra* of the Ramakrishna Mission is 'Seeing a human being, know him to be God.' Sri Ramakrishna first enunciated this ideal; Swamiji gave it its present form as a *mantra* for the Mission.

We see the image of God in the temple, but the universal form of that image, his more visible form, is living outside the temple. That image wanders around in various forms, with various names, before our eyes. He is in the form of the poor, the sick, in those who long for Him, and in many other forms. I don't know whether or not the image in the temple accepts my worship; on the other hand I can see that the moving image in front of me is accepting my service and is happy, so I am happy.

Swami Vivekananda said: 'Leaving this living god, will you worship a stone image? Sitting on the bank of the Gaṅgā, you want to dig a well?' The Ramakrishna Order monks carry out their activities keeping this in mind. All their work is for the sake of the Omnipresent Divinity, God in the form of man. They run hospitals and do relief work in places of famine or flood; they teach in schools and give lectures—they do everything knowing that in serving man, they are worshipping God. Work for them is not work; it is worship.

Monks who work in the monastery's business office have to keep account of every rupee. Seeing this, you might think that they have the same attachment to money that worldly persons do, but that is not so. To the monk, all work is worship. The money is Thakur's. The monk must see that the money is properly accounted for.

One of our monks once made a mistake in his book-keeping and discovered he was several hundred rupees short. He was very disturbed and started to weep. Where could he get the money? He didn't have a rupee of his own. At last he had to beg from different people for the money to make up the deficiency. Later the mistake was detected—one amount had been entered in the ledger twice. His devotion, his care, his intense concern over the faulty account, had no personal basis. Everything was for God.

This great concern for the Master's work is a form of austerity. Austerity is not only of the body, it is also of the mind. Whatever is done for the Lord is an austerity. In times past, holy men and monks used to go to the jungles and forests and mountain caves to practise austerities. But monks of the Ramakrishna Order perform austerities while living in the midst of society. They can go from office to office doing work for the Order. Sometimes they even go to court. People at times criticize them for this. They say: 'A monk's *dharma* is forgiveness. Should he bring a law suit against his opponents?' But our feeling is that everything belongs to the Master. No one should be allowed to take anything from him wrongfully. We must try to protect his property as far as possible. If after that our court case is lost, we understand that this was the Master's will. We don't suffer from that loss.

I once went to call on a friend from my pre-monastic days in his office. I was carrying a portfolio, so he said, 'You are a holy man. Instead of an ascetic's begging bowl, why are you carrying a portfolio?' I answered him by saying, 'If I had an ascetic's begging bowl, the doorkeeper would not let me enter your office. Besides, the portfolio is my begging bowl. The papers in it are not for myself; they are for the monastery. This portfolio is as pure and as sacred to me as an ascetic's begging bowl.'

To holy persons, all their work is holy because it is all done for God. The bonds of a monk's work are cut through work itself. Sri Ramakrishna said that if a person can cry for God for three days, God will reveal Himself to him. Swami Turiyananda gave this teaching a new orientation when he said, 'If a person is able to serve others for three days, seeing God in them, he will become a *siddha*, a perfected soul.'

Another characteristic of the monks of the Ramakrishna Order is that they do not give much importance to their personal likes and dislikes. The Master's will is the will of the Order. A monk may be the head of a large institution. He may have been there a long time and be greatly loved and revered by all the people of that locality. Suddenly an order comes from the monastery headquarters that he is to be transferred to another centre. So he quietly leaves the large institution where he has been so long, and with only his few personal belongings and some books, goes to his new assignment. The new place may be smaller than his former one, and now he may be only an ordinary worker, where previously he had been the head of the centre. But he is not at all disturbed. His attitude is, 'Wherever the Master wants me to go, I will go. Whatever he wants me to do, I will do.'

The Ramakrishna Order of monks is a new kind of monastic organization. Formerly, holy men and monks would go far away from society. But society was thus deprived of their holy influence. As a result, the highest spiritual conceptions did not spread very widely among the ordinary people. The Ramakrishna monks live in the world and are seen by all and are accessible to all. They practise the Vedānta of the forest while living among people.

After the Master's passing, Holy Mother prayed with tears in her eyes: 'Thakur, you came and left. Is that the end of everything? Then what need was there for you to take so much trouble in coming? It is my wish that all those who follow your teachings will live together, and worldly people coming to them will hear their words and get peace.'

That prayer of Holy Mother was granted in full. An Order was established by Sri Ramakrishna's all-renouncing sons. It was small, but with formidable power. Today that Order stands as a vast tree. Its branches and shoots are spread out all over the world. Thousands of men and women get peace and a new life as they hear the eternal message of India through the words of the Ramakrishna monks and see these living images of renunciation and purity.

References

1. *Kulārṇava Tantra*, I.56
2. *Garuḍa Purāṇa, Uttara Khaṇḍa*, VII.111
3. *Rāmacaritamānasa, Sundarakāṇḍa*, 4
4. *Mohamudgara*, 5
5. *Lycidas*, Milton
6. *Mahānirvāṇa Tantra*, VIII.277
7. *Gītā*, IV.22
8. *Bhāgavata*, XI.8.11
9. *Suttanipāta Uragavagga, Mettāsutta* (Quoted from *Buddhadev*, Rabindranath Tagore, 1363, p.50)
10. *Vivekacūḍāmaṇi*, 37
11. Letter written to Pramadadas Mitra on 10.1.1899 ('*Swami Akhandananda*', Swami Annadananda)

XI
Self-effort and Divine Grace

One day Dr Mahendralal Sarkar and Girish Ghosh had a debate in the presence of Sri Ramakrishna. The Master was then staying in a rented house at Shyampukur, and the two men had gone there to see him. Those who visited Sri Ramakrishna often engaged in such debates, and sometimes the Master himself initiated the discussion of controversial subjects. He enjoyed watching the fun, and at times entered the fray, giving his own conclusion on the matter.

On this particular day, the Master started the discussion by saying that everything happens by the will of God.

Master: Without His will not even a leaf can move.

Doctor: If everything is done by the will of God, then why do you chatter? Why do you talk so much to bring knowledge to others?

Master: He makes me talk; therefore I talk. 'I am the machine and He is the Operator.'

Doctor: You say that you are the machine. That's all right. Or keep quiet, knowing that everything is God.

Girish (to the doctor): Whatever you may think, sir, the truth is that we act because He makes us act. Can anyone take a single step against the Almighty Will?

Doctor: But God has also given us free will. I can think of God, or not, as I like.

Girish: You think of God or do some good work because you like to. Really it is not you who do these things, but your liking of them that makes you do so.

• • •

Doctor: Suppose a child is being burnt. From a sense of duty I rush to save it.

Girish: You feel happy to save the child; therefore you rush into the fire. It is your happiness that drives you to the action. . . .

Master: A man must have some kind of faith before he undertakes a work. Further, he feels joy when he thinks of it. Only then does he set about performing the work. Suppose a jar of gold coins is hidden underground. First of all a man must have faith that the jar of gold coins is there. He feels joy at the thought of the jar. Then he begins to dig. As he removes the earth, he hears a metallic sound. That increases his joy. Next he sees a corner of the jar. That gives him more joy. Thus his joy is ever on the increase. . . .

Doctor: . . . It is not an unadulterated joy that one reaps from the performance of duty. Duty has its painful side too.

M. (to Girish): As the proverb goes: 'If the stomach gets food, then the back can bear a few blows from the host.' There is joy in sorrow also.

• • •

Girish (to the doctor): Duty must be pleasant; or why do you perform it?

Doctor: The mind is inclined that way.

M. (to Girish): That wretched inclination draws the mind. If you speak of the compelling power of inclination, then where is free will? (pp.892-93)

This is the great question: Do we move by our own free will, or is everything God's will? In the *Gītā*, Arjuna said: 'I cannot fight. I could not enjoy gaining a kingdom by killing my own people.' Later Śrī Kṛṣṇa showed Arjuna His Universal Form and said :

Mayaivaite nihatāḥ pūrvameva nimittamātraṁ bhava savyasācin—'By Me alone are they slain already. Be thou merely the instrument, O Savyasācin.'[1]

Here it seems that everything is God's will; the devotee is only His instrument. He learns to say: 'I am nothing; You do everything. Why You do what You do, I do not know. I am the machine; You are the operator of the machine. I am the house; You are the dweller in the house. I am the chariot; You are the charioteer. I move as you make me move.'

Śrī Kṛṣṇa tells Arjuna:

n *Īśvaraḥ sarvabhūtānāṁ hṛddeśe'rjuna tiṣṭhati*
Bhrāmayan sarvabhūtāni yantrārūḍhāni māyayā—

'The Lord dwells in the hearts of all beings. He turns them round and round upon the wheel of His *māyā*'[2]

Rāmaprasāda said, 'O Mother, you are flying kites in the marketplace of the world.' As children fly kites, so does the Divine Mother play with us : we are Her kites. We are held by a cord that She holds in Her hand. We may think that we are free, but in reality we are bound. Rāmaprasāda is telling us that the Divine Mother is the source of all power. We have no power of our own; we are utterly dependent on Her. *Tasya bhāsā sarvamidaṁ vibhāti*—'By His light all this is lighted.'[3]

Vedānta philosophy gives an illustration. Suppose you are cooking rice in a pot, with potato, egg-plant, and other vegetables. After a while the potatoes, egg-plant, rice, and the rest begin to jump about in the pot. They seem to say with pride : 'We are moving! We are moving! We are jumping!' The children see it and think the potatoes, egg-plant, and rice are alive and so they jump

that way. But the elders, who know, explain to the children that the vegetables and the rice are not alive; they jump not of themselves, but because of the fire under the pot; if you remove the burning wood from the hearth, then they will move no more. Likewise the pride of man, that he is the doer, springs from ignorance. Men are powerful because of the power of God. All becomes quiet when that burning wood is taken away. The puppets dance well on the stage when pulled by a wire, but they cannot move when the wire snaps. (p.893)

According to this attitude, God is responsible for everything. Everything happens through His will. But there is another attitude. Some devotees say, 'Mother, it is not anybody else's fault. I myself am responsible for my own suffering. I myself have dug the well that I am drowning in. My bondage is my own fault, and I alone must free myself from my miserable condition. I won't stretch out my hand for help. I am a king. My greatest mistake would be to think that I am a poor beggar. This mistake is the root of all my suffering. I will remember that I am a king!'

These two attitudes are apparently conflicting. According to one way of thinking, everything happens as a result of God's will. The other view holds that we are responsible for our own actions. Can these two approaches be reconciled?

If we accept the idea that everything happens as a result of God's will, then the question naturally arises: 'Is it God's will that we steal and kill and behave unjustly?' If so, then why should we not commit crimes? If God does everything, it is not our responsibility to behave well. When God wills, we will be good. Further, there is no need for spiritual disciplines; when God wills, He will reveal Himself to us. According to this logic, when we do evil, that is His will; when we get His vision, that is also His will.

But we should remember that in all ages and countries, spiritual aspirants have undertaken many spiritual disciplines, rigorous austerities. Sri Ramakrishna used to rub his face on the ground so hard that it bled because he could not see the Divine Mother. What difficult austerities he practised! Yet he said, 'Everything depends on God's will.' Indeed, those who practise the severest austerities and have the greatest renunciation are the ones who insist the most that 'Everything is God's will.' What do they mean by 'God's will'?

Sri Ramakrishna explains this:

[Virtue and sin]... **both exist and do not exist. If God keeps the ego in a man, then He keeps in him the sense of differentiation and also the sense of virtue and sin.** (p.328) **This awareness of distinction is due to God's *māyā;* and it is necessary for the purpose of running His illusory world.** (p.893)

As long as a man has not realized God, he retains the sense of differentiation and the knowledge of good and bad. You may say: 'Virtue and sin are the same to me. I am doing only as God bids me.' But you know in your heart of hearts that those are mere words. No sooner do you commit an evil deed than you feel a palpitation in your heart. (p.328)

A man will cherish the illusion that he is the doer as long as he has not seen God, as long as he has not touched the Philosopher's Stone. So long will he know the distinction between his good and bad actions. (p.893)

Thus, though we can say that everything is the will of God, we can't really believe it until we have realized God. Because of our egotism, we believe that we are the doers; that if we do something good we will receive good in return, and if we do something bad, we will suffer. But we must be honest. We should not be like the brahmin who laid claim to creating a beautiful garden, and then blamed his killing of a cow on Indra. If we claim that we created the garden, we must acknowledge the fact that we killed a cow. In reality God does everything, but as long as the ego sense remains active in us and we believe we are doing everything, we are responsible for our actions.

If a person can truly say, 'Everything is God's will', he will have neither virtue or vice. He will be like a child. A child does not commit sin, and he is not held accountable for his actions. Even in the eyes of the law, a child is not held responsible for his actions. A child may fire a gun while playing and kill someone, but he will not be held legally accountable for his act. A child has no real 'I-consciousness'. This is also true of those great souls who are in the state of a child; the concept of virtue and sin has no meaning for them. They are completely dependent on God.

Sri Ramakrishna did not always follow social customs. For example, though holy men traditionally recite sacred verses from the scriptures before they begin to eat, Sri Ramakrishna would begin eating as soon as the food was placed in front of him. The other holy men would say, 'What is he doing?' But the Master was not concerned about rules and regulations. He was a child. Those who visited him noticed his childlike behaviour. Sri Ramakrishna had only this child's ego; he depended completely on his Divine Mother.

But we do not come to this state until we have realized God. And to realize God, we must try with all our might to remove the darkness from our minds. We must pray to God: 'O Lord be gracious unto me. Make my mind and speech one so that I can truly say, "I am the machine and You are the Operator of the machine." May I also be vigilant; may I always discriminate between the good and the evil.' Then, after illumination, we will be able to say with assurance, 'Everything is His will.' We will understand that God does everything, that everything depends on His will. Before that, we should proceed by our own efforts to reach that state.

The *Gītā* says, *Uddharedātmanātmānam*—'Let a man raise himself by his own self.'[4] If we are sunk in the mire of worldliness, we have to be our own saviour. If we do not lift ourselves, no one else can save us. The guru tells us, 'I am your guide and protector, but you must at least take one step forward.' Once when a man quoted Sri Ramakrishna's dictum, 'If you take one step towards God, He takes ten steps towards you', his companion at once corrected him. 'No', he said, 'if you take one step towards God, God takes a thousand steps towards you.' But whether God takes ten steps or one thousand steps, we must take that first step. Without that first step, we will get nowhere.

Swamiji once said that if you want to learn chemistry and sit in your room and cry, 'O Chemistry! Come to me!', and do not study, will you learn chemistry? You will not learn even a little if you do not study or carry out research in the laboratory. You must sincerely make an effort.

We seek guidance in our search for God, and if we are sincere, God gives us what we need. Spiritual teachers came to Sri Ramakrishna of their own accord. And if we sincerely pursue our spiritual ideal, a teacher will come to us. The Master said that if a pilgrim travels north instead of south while going to Puri, someone or other will tell him that he is going the wrong way and give him the right directions. The guru is like the person who gives us the right directions. He shows us the way, but it is for us to proceed along the path. If, in spite of our best efforts we go off in the wrong direction, the guru will come to help us. But we must always make the effort ourselves.

The verse in the *Gītā* continues, *Nātmānamabasādayet*—'Let a man not degrade himself.'[5] We should never think of ourselves as weak. We must remember that all power is within us. If one person has attained God, it proves that we can also attain Him. The power that was in Buddha is also in me. I must simply become aware of it. No one is really a sinner; people only make mistakes. A man may commit a crime, but he may some day redeem himself. Who can say when that will happen?

Śrī Kṛṣna continues in the *Gītā*: *Ātmaiva hyātmano bandhurātmaiva ripurātmanaḥ*—'The Self alone is the friend of the self and the Self alone is the enemy of the self.'[6] When we think of ourselves as weak and helpless, we become enemies to ourselves. No other person can help us or hurt us. Also when we lack self-control and self-discipline, we become our own enemies. We hurt ourselves by our jealousy, hatred, etc.

There can of course be external enemies. But Śrī Śaṅkarācārya in his commentary on the *Bhagavad-Gītā* states that though the enemy may be an external enemy, I have created that very enemy. My character and habits have produced that enemy. When I was born, I had neither friend nor foe. Later I created both.

Hindu philosophy tells us that we are responsible for the circumstances that we find ourselves in, that we have created our own *karma*. But bad tendencies can be destroyed by the force of self-effort; we ourselves can make the impossible possible. Our destiny lies in our own hands. Hinduism is not 'fatalistic', as it has often been accused of being.

Swamiji said: 'It is the coward and the fool who says, "This is fate.". . . But it is the strong man who stands up and says, "I will make my fate." It is people who are getting old who talk of fate. Young men generally do not come to astrology.'[7] Why do so many people go to astrologers? It is because, when attacked by some physical infirmity or mental turmoil, they become frightened and can't decide what to do. So they go to an astrologer. But those who rely on themselves can overcome any obstacle.

Swamiji did not approve of people taking too much interest in astrology. His opinion of astrologers is reflected in a story he told: Once an astrologer told a king that he would die in six months. The king was very sad, but one of his ministers came to him and consoled him by saying, 'Don't believe what astrologers say. They don't know anything.' Then the minister went to the astrologer and said, 'Look at your palm and tell me how long you yourself will live.' The astrologer replied, 'I already know. I will live at least twelve more years.' At that the minister drew his sword from its scabbard and cut the astrologer's throat. He then returned to the king and said: 'You were unhappy because you trusted the words of an astrologer, but he can't even make a correct prediction about his own life. He said he would live twelve more years. Why is he dead now?'

We do not live under the sway of some incomprehensible power; we are not subject to 'the stars'. We have free will. We sometimes ask, 'Why did God give us so many problems and weaknesses, such as attachment and greed?' We must however remember that though all power comes from God, it is up to us to decide how that power is used. Sri Ramakrishna says that the piece of iron is drawn to the magnet, but the magnet doesn't move. God is the unmoving magnet, beyond good and evil. We are the piece of iron that moves; we are responsible for our good and evil deeds. We can change our character from bad to good, from good to better, but that requires effort on our part. It is not a matter of mere intellectual understanding. Practice is necessary. Self-control comes with the practice of spiritual disciplines, and gradually we are able to overcome our weaknesses. Many give up their long-standing habit of smoking through sheer strength of will.

A seemingly hopelessly wicked person can change and become good. Ratnākar the robber became Vālmīki, the great poet of the Rāmāyaṇa. The same change took place in the life of King Aśoka. He was first known as Aśoka the Terrible, but he changed and later came to be known as Aśoka the Pious. There are many such examples. Because of this it is said: 'No saint without a past: no sinner without a future'. You can change yourself through practice, spiritual discipline and self-effort.

The Master explained the relationship between God's will and human effort through an example: A cow is tethered in a field to a post with a rope forty feet long. Within that forty feet the cow can wander as she chooses—ten feet, thirty feet, or forty feet, but she can never go farther than forty feet. That forty feet is her world. It is the same with our limited self-effort. Outside of that small sphere is a vast field which is God's domain. If the rope is cut, the cow can wander anywhere in the field. When we attain liberation, we can wander around God's domain. God gives us a little power; when we make full use of that power, God's grace descends on us and the rope is cut. Then we have unlimited power; our will and God's will become one.

An Indian fable illustrates this truth.[8] A bird with a nest full of eggs lived happily in a tree near the ocean. One day a storm arose and carried the nest with its eggs into the ocean. At first the bird begged the ocean to return the eggs, but the ocean would not listen. Finally the bird said, 'If the ocean does not give me back my eggs, I will dry it up!' She then began to take water drop by drop into her beak and carry it away. All day long for many days, she continued her task. Other birds tried to reason with her, but she would not listen. She untiringly went about her work. Still, with only the beak of one bird how much water could be removed? The ocean remained as it was.

One day the sage Nārada happened to arrive at the place where the bird was working. He listened to her story and was astounded at her perseverance. He decided to tell Garuḍa, the King of Birds, about her. When Garuḍa heard Nārada's story, he became very angry and flew to the ocean. Violently flapping his huge wings, he created such turmoil in the water that the ocean became frightened and gave up the eggs. The bird at first tried by her own efforts to rescue her eggs. The task was impossible, even absurd, but she persevered. At last help came from God; she received divine grace.

Another story further explains this idea.[9] When a monk who had not eaten for several days came to a house to beg alms, the master of the house said to him, 'Who has brought you here?' The monk replied : 'Kṛṣṇa is within me in the form of acute hunger; He Himself has brought me to you.' The man replied, 'Is that so? I have been searching for him. Let me say a few words to him before you eat. I want to ask Kṛṣṇa something because he is apparently hard of hearing. After you have eaten, you will fall asleep, so let me talk to him first.'

The monk said, 'What will you say to him?' The man replied : 'I want to tell him, "I have come again and again to this world-stage. Now I want to be released from all this coming and going."' The monk said: 'I will teach you a trick. This time Kṛṣṇa will fall into a trap. Tell him: "Eight hundred forty thousand times I have been born and have played my role on this world-stage. You have always come on the stage along with me. If my performances have pleased you, please reward me and grant me liberation. And if you have found that my acting was not good and I have not passed the test, then please free me from this role. Grant me liberation."' The man was pleased and said, 'This is very good advice! If I speak in this way, Śrī Kṛṣṇa will be in great difficulty. He will *have* to grant me liberation!' However, the man didn't speak right then to Śrī Kṛṣṇa, but fed the monk. A few days later, the monk returned and asked, 'Have you spoken with Lord Kṛṣṇa? Have you followed my advice?' The man replied: 'Yes, I spoke with Kṛṣṇa. One night he came to me in a dream and I told him everything that you suggested. But then I also added: "I well understand that you suffer from confinement just as I suffer from being in a body. Your own father and mother were imprisoned by Kaṁsa. Moreover, you are eternally imprisoned in the hearts of all beings. I understand the extent of your power. How can you bless me? You need to be blessed yourself! I shall arrange for your liberation. You are imprisoned in my heart. You may be a lion, but you are caught in a net. I am like a mouse whose power is little, but who still can gnaw at the rope and free a lion from his bonds. I will free you from the prison of my heart. I am not like the *cātak* bird who drinks only rainwater. I will dig the earth with my spade and satisfy my thirst with the water that I find there. I will not depend on you any more for liberation."'

The monk was very pleased with the householder's reply and said: 'Please do not worry. Śrī Kṛṣṇa himself sent me to you in order to guide you on your path. You have the grace of your own self, though you may not realize it. When the tide comes in, ordinary people do not understand the reason for this, but scientists know that the tide is caused by the forces of the sun and the moon. In the same way, those who have received the grace of their own selves can't understand their own condition. But men and women of high spiritual attainment are qualified to judge a person's spiritual progress. By observing a spiritual seeker's speech and demeanour, they can see that he has received the grace of his own self. And because he has received the grace of his own self, he has also received the grace of God. You tell me that you will dig for water with your own spade. From this statement I can see that you have received the grace of your self. Thus you have also received the grace of God.' When a person earnestly practises spiritual disciplines ('digs the earth with his own spade'), God's grace descends on him.

The *Kaṭha Upaniṣad* says, 'The Self can be known only by him who longs for It; verily unto him does the Self reveal its true being.'[10] The Self reveals Itself to those who wish to attain It. To realize that 'I am in reality the Divine Inner-Self' is the goal of all spiritual disciplines, and it is the Self which empowers us to seek for the Self. Wherever there is self-effort, there is the grace of your own self; when the grace of your own self is awakened, you receive the grace of God. 'God helps those who help themselves.'

Sri Ramakrishna said, **By practising spiritual disciplines one sees God, through His grace.** (p.429) You can realize God through His grace, but that grace comes only after you have done spiritual practice. There may be a breeze, but if you do not raise the sails of the boat, what good will the breeze do? Similarly, the breeze of God's grace is always present, but we must raise our sails to catch that breeze. We must make ourselves fit to receive God's grace.

If we lack the fitness to receive something, we cannot keep it. If someone hands us money, it will vanish in a few days if we don't know how to spend it wisely. This applies to spiritual life as well. Sometimes it happens that those who perform *kīrtana* have unusual spiritual moods and experiences for which they are unprepared. They have awakened within themselves a spiritual power which they can't contain. If they haven't regularly practised spiritual disciplines, they may suffer a contrary reaction when the *kīrtana* is over. Their minds, which rose so high during the ecstatic singing and dancing, may fall to a state lower than before. For this reason we must 'raise the sails' and practise spiritual disciplines. Otherwise we will not be prepared to receive God's grace.

When Sri Ramakrishna says, **Nothing can be achieved without his grace;** he means that in reality everything comes from God. But then he adds, **Strive with a longing heart for his grace.**(p.625) Truly we need to strive for discrimination and strength, which cut the bonds of *karma*. Then we will have the grace of our own self, and the grace of God will descend on us. So, first the grace of our own self; the grace of God comes next.

References

1. *Gītā*, XI.33
2. *Ibid.*, XVIII.61
3. *Śvetāśvatara Upaniṣad*, VI.14
4. *Gītā*, VI.5
5. *Ibid.*
6. *Ibid.*
7. *C.W.*, Vol.VIII, 1959, p.184
8. See Madhusūdana Sarasvatī's Commentary on the *Gītā*, VI.23. Swami Premananda also used to tell this story.
9. *Ātmabodha*, see '*Kṛpācatuṣṭaya*' in Introduction.
10. *Kaṭha Upaniṣad*, I.2.23

XII

Bhakti Yoga—The Path of Devotion

Sri Ramakrishna says, **For the *Kaliyuga* the path of devotion described by Nārada is best.** (p.464) He did not condemn the path of Knowledge (*Jñāna Yoga*) or the path of Work (*Karma Yoga*). All paths lead to God; the goal is the same for all—only the paths are different. But the Master says that the path of Devotion is best for most people in the present age.

According to Indian mythology, Nārada is a great lover of God who wanders about the world incessantly singing and praising the name of God. Full of joy, he asks for nothing. Ordinarily we appeal to God when we are in trouble; then when the trouble is gone, we forget Him completely. But Nārada is not like that. He is always singing God's name simply out of love. He has said, 'I, who am devoted to the vow of continence, have been endowed by Mahāviṣṇu's grace with the power to go about unobstructed everywhere within the three worlds, as also beyond it to the transcendental realm. Playing on this *vīṇā* given by the Lord Himself and which possesses the power of automatically playing the various musical notes, I go about the world singing the excellences of the Lord.'[1]

As Sri Ramakrishna says, this kind of devotion to God that Nārada exemplifies is the best path to God in this age.

The Path of Devotion is Easy

The Hindu scriptures, i.e., the Vedas, are divided into two parts: one part deals with work (*karma kāṇḍa*), and the other with knowledge (*jñāna kāṇḍa*). The work portion deals with the meticulous observance of rites and ceremonies and is not suitable for most people. The knowledge portion deals mostly with the attainment of supersensuous knowledge and is found mainly in the Upaniṣads. It also is too difficult for most people to practise.

In Sri Ramakrishna's time, Swami Dayananda, founder of the Ārya Samāj was travelling about proclaiming the value of Vedic rituals and sacrifices. But the Master pointed out that the *karma kāṇḍa* path, with its elaborate rituals, was not suitable for modern man. He said: **Nowadays the decoctions of roots and herbs of the orthodox Hindu physicians cannot be given to fever patients. Therefore only a drastic medicine like the allopathic 'fever mixture' is effective now.** (p.464) The path of Devotion is the allopathic fever mixture; the root and herb decoctions are *karma kāṇḍa*. Sri Ramakrishna warned against following the path of *karma kāṇḍa* with a story.

A man was performing the *śrāddha* ceremony at his house. He was feeding many people. Just then a butcher passed, leading a cow to slaughter. He could not control the animal and became exhausted. He said to himself: 'Let me go into that house and enjoy the feast of the *śrāddha* ceremony and strengthen my body. Then I shall be able to drag the cow along.' So he carried out his intention. But when he killed the cow, the sin of the slaughter fell also on the performer of the *śrāddha*. (p.617)

This can happen when you follow the path of ritualistic worship. That is why the Master said that you should not undertake this practice. Vedic rites are difficult, and if one little mistake is made—for example, a word is mispronounced—there may be disastrous consequences. **That is why I say the path of Devotion is better than the path of action (*karma kāṇḍa*).** (p.617)

Buddha also discouraged the performance of sacrifices. He said: 'You sacrifice animals, but what do you gain? Does your mind become pure? Your problem is in the mind. You are not able to control your mind, and still you want to sacrifice animals!' The Upaniṣads are in agreement with this. They say that liberation comes from Knowledge and not from rites and rituals.

Still, rituals cannot be completely given up. *Japa*, meditation, breath control, etc. are all a type of ritual. But the Master says, **When prescribing rituals, remove the 'head and tail'.** (p.464) He means that we should do only the essentials and not get involved in too many formalities. Simply chanting God's name and loving Him make the easiest and shortest path to God.

The Master also contrasted the path of Knowledge with the path of Devotion. He said: **One cannot obtain *Jñāna* (Knowledge) if one has the least trace of worldliness. . . . This is not the path for the *Kaliyuga.*** (p.150) If you take the path of Knowledge you must discriminate, always thinking '*Neti, neti*'—'Not this, not this'. Eventually you negate the whole world process by coming to realize that everything you see in this world is not lasting. Brahman alone is eternal, real. But you see the world in front of you—your friends and relatives, and so many things going on. Can you say it is all unreal? I can force myself to say it, but can I really believe it?

Speaking of the difficulty of following the path of Knowledge, Sri Ramakrishna says: **How can he have the**

consciousness that Brahman alone is real and the world illusory? In the *Kaliyuga* it is difficult to have the feeling, 'I am not the body, I am not the mind, I am not the twenty-four cosmic principles. I am beyond pleasure and pain, I am above disease and grief, old age and death.' However you may reason and argue, the feeling that the body is identical with the soul will somehow crop up from an unexpected quarter. You may cut a peepal-tree to the ground and think it is dead, but the next morning you will find a new sprout shooting up from the dead stump. One cannot get rid of this identification with the body. (p.172)

Śrī Kṛṣṇa says in the *Gītā*,

Kleśo'dhikatarasteṣāmavyaktāsaktacetasām
Avyaktā hi gatirduḥkhaṁ dehavadbhiravāpyate—

'The difficulty of those whose thoughts are set on the Unmanifested is greater, for the goal of the Unmanifested is hard to reach by the embodied beings.'[2]

Sri Ramakrishna mentions an incident to show how deceptive the path of Knowledge can be. A man by the name of Krishnakishore used to follow strictly the disciplines of Advaita Vedānta. He used to say 'I am like the *ākāśa*—the sky.' He meant that just as a cloud suddenly covers the sky and then quickly disappears, so it is with his real Self. He may be temporarily covered with the body, mind, ego, etc., but he knows that in reality he is the eternal, pure, enlightened, free Ātman. Krishnakishore used to say: 'Although there are many things going on in this world, I am unaffected—the witness. Nothing happens to me; I am like the *ākāśa*.' Accordingly, Sri Ramakrishna sometimes addressed him as '*Kha*', meaning *ākāśa*.

One day the Master went to visit him at his house and found him despondent. Krishnakishore said, 'The tax collector came and, since I had no money, threatened to take away all my pots and pans. The Master jokingly said : 'But you are *Kha*; you are Brahman, the Self. Can you have any pots or pans? Nothing can disturb you.' He teased Krishnakishore this way. He meant: 'You still have body-consciousness; the world is real to you. Still, you engage in Vedāntic reasoning and say "Brahman alone is real; the world is false." How brittle your reasoning is! It gives way as soon as it comes in contact with reality. This shows that you are not yet ready for the Vedāntic standpoint.'

This is the way it is for most of us. When we are faced with life's problems, our Vedāntic reasoning does not help. Sri Ramakrishna says: **The feeling, 'I am He', is not wholesome. A man who entertains such an idea, while looking on his body as the Self, causes himself great harm. He cannot go forward in spiritual life; he drags himself down. He deceives himself as well as others. He cannot understand his own state of mind.** (p.172)

It is difficult for anyone to understand his own mind. It is so agitated that it has been compared to a restless monkey which has been given wine and then stung by a scorpion. In addition to this, he has been possessed by a ghost. Our minds are that disturbed. Arjuna says in the *Gītā*:

Cañcalaṁ hi manaḥ Kṛṣṇa pramāthi balavaddṛḍham
Tasyāhaṁ nigrahaṁ manye vāyoriva suduṣkaram—

'For the mind is very fickle, O Kṛṣṇa, it is impetuous, strong, and obstinate. I think that it is as difficult to control as the wind.'[3]

In the path of Knowledge you must bring your mind under control through much discrimination and reasoning. But the path of Devotion is different; there is not so much reasoning on this path. Your only concern is to love God.

A Bengali song says:

How many waves there are in the ocean of the mind!
Seeing such big waves, I am terribly frightened
And can find no way to cross over this turbulent ocean.
The mind is not an expert helmsman,
And six disobedient sense-organs are the boatmen.
They don't ever listen to me
But only act according to their whims—
They may cause the boat to sink. . . .
But Premik says, 'Keep the raft of God's name within
reach;
Then even if your boat starts to sink in the storm,
O brother, you can cross the ocean on that holy raft.'

Sri Ramakrishna has explained the difference between the path of Knowledge and the path of Devotion with an illustration: 'When the fields are flooded with water, you can go from one village to another by rowing across the fields in a boat. At other times, you have to go around them on the dirt ridges; the path of Knowledge is like this. You debate and reason; then at last you reach the goal. But the path of Devotion is like taking a boat and going swiftly across the water-covered fields. You can't even see the ridges. All questions and reasoning are drowned in a flood of devotion. You go directly to your goal.'

Sri Ramakrishna liked this song:

O Mother, make me mad with Thy love
What need have I of knowledge or reason?
Make me drunk with Thy love's Wine;
O Thou who stealest Thy *bhaktas'* hearts,
Drown me deep in the Sea of Thy Love! (p.399)

A devotee of the Divine Mother used to sing this song:

> I don't know Tantra or sādhanā,
> I have the name of Kālī on my lips.
> I repeat my Mother's name,
> And my house becomes a place of pilgrimage.
> Sitting in my room,
> I am visiting a holy place.

The lover of God depends on Him completely. He does not reason about Him. As he proceeds towards God, he becomes less involved in worldly concerns. The more he loves God, the less he desires other things. Many of his problems are solved as he draws near to God; his own mind becomes his friend and guide.

We are all searching for happiness. For this we eat candy, go to the movies and many other things. But the greatest happiness, the happiness from which all other happiness comes is the happiness of God-realization—*Brahmānanda*, the bliss of Brahman. Compared to that bliss, worldly happiness is trifling. Sri Ramakrishna used to say that if you taste sugar candy, you can no longer enjoy molasses.

The *Śrīmad Bhāgavatam* uses another simile:

Yasya bhaktirbhagavati harau niḥśreyaseśvare
Vikrīḍito'mṛtāmbhodhau kiṁ kṣudraiḥ khātakodakaiḥ—

'What use is there for the dirty water of a muddy pit for one who sports in the limitless ocean of Bliss, as a result of his having cultivated deep devotion for Vāsudeva, the Lord of all and the bestower of liberation?'[4]

Whoever has unswerving devotion to God does not glance in any other direction. He has arrived at the Ocean of Nectar, why should he look at ditch water? When he is attracted by a big magnet, can he be attracted by a small magnet? If once you get the joy of remembering God and chanting His name, your attraction for other things vanishes.

A verse in a minor Upaniṣad says,

Bhaktavatsalaḥ svayameva sarvebhyo
mokṣavighnebhyo
Bhaktiniṣṭhān sarvān paripālayati
Sarvābhīṣṭān prayacchati mokṣaṁ dāpayati—

'The Lord loves his devotees. He Himself comes to remove all their obstacles to liberation. He looks after them and fulfils all their desires. And He even gives the greatest boon— liberation.'[5] God Himself removes all impurities from the mind, and all inner and outer obstacles that prevent one from going to Him.

Can I get rid of lust and greed through reasoning? Only if I turn these God-ward will they disappear. The Master says, 'Change your direction.' If I love God, all my desires will be centred in Him so they will no longer be a source of bondage or sorrow. They will be sweet.

The Master gives another simile: Suppose a room has been shut up and left in darkness for a thousand years. It might seem that the darkness will never disappear. What do you do? Do you reason about how the room got in this condition, who made it that way, etc.? No, you bring a light, and the darkness disappears in an instant. In the same way, impurities won't stay in your mind forever. Call on God. Then when you learn to love Him, He enters your life and draws you to Himself, and you see that all darkness has disappeared from your mind and many good qualities have appeared. You have become a new person.

Why is the path of Devotion easy? Because on this path there is no forced renunciation. **The Master says: The inner**

organs are brought under control naturally through the path of devotion. . . . It is rather easily accomplished this way. (p.203) If you love God, renunciation naturally follows. In the path of Knowledge, there is much reasoning, restraint of the senses, etc. But, **Through love one acquires renunciation and discrimination naturally.** (p.123) **When one has such love and attachment for God, one doesn't feel the attraction of *māyā* to wife, children, relatives, and friends. One retains only compassion for them. To such a man the world appears a strange land, a place where he has merely to perform his duties. It is like a man's having his real home in the country, but coming to Calcutta for work; he has to rent a house in Calcutta for the sake of his duties.** (p.173)

Devotees live in the world unattached. They perform all their duties, but they are not entangled in them. Through devotion this non-attachment comes about spontaneously.

The Master said to one of his devotees: **Yours is the path of *bhakti*. That is very good; it is an easy path. . . . Having attained this rare human birth, my supreme need is to develop love for the Lotus Feet of God.** (p.150)

The Importance of a Devotional Mood

Sri Ramakrishna says, **He is grasped through ecstasy of love.** (p.107) True religion, *dharma*, means this ecstatic love. Intensity of feeling is the main thing. The more intense is one's devotion, the nearer one is to God. But to have this intense devotion, this ecstatic love, one must cultivate a particular mood, called in Sanskrit *bhāva*. There are many different moods or relationships one may adopt. At first the mood may be artificial and imaginary, but later it becomes real.

Sri Ramakrishna says, **But in order to realize God, one**

must assume one of these attitudes: *śānta*, *dāsya*, *sakhya*, *vātsalya*, or *madhura*. (p.115) If a person is able to establish a particular relationship with God, spiritual life becomes easy. What do Hindus do? In the morning we wake up our deities and decorate them with flowers, sandal paste, and clothing, and then we feed them. In the afternoon we put them to bed for a rest. We believe that God is a person like ourselves. He stays in our homes; He is not far away. He is one of the family, so there is a sweetness in our relationship with Him.

The Hindu scriptures give the five principal ways of thinking about God mentioned by the Master: the peaceful attitude (*śānta*), as well as regarding God as the master (*dāsya*), friend (*sakhya*), child (*vātsalya*) or the beloved (*madhura*).

Sri Ramakrishna describes these relationships: ***Śānta*, the serene attitude. The Rishis of olden times had this attitude toward God. They did not desire any worldly enjoyment.** (p.115) In the serene mood, there is only dependence on God. There is no consciousness of love or attachment. The poet Vidyāpati has expressed this mood in a poem:

> O Lord, You are the saviour of the world,
> Ever gracious to the distressed and afflicted,
> My trust is in you.
> I also am a person in this world,
> So you will be gracious to me.
> I am no longer afraid of death
> Because I have taken refuge in you.
> O Lord, You are the source of all;
> You are my saviour.[6]

The sign of the peaceful mood is firm faith (*niṣṭhā*). Sri Ramakrishna said, **It is like the single-minded devotion of a wife to her husband.** (p.115)

Sri Ramakrishna then described the servant attitude: ***Dāsya*, the attitude of a servant toward his master. Hanumān had this attitude toward Rāma. He felt the strength of a lion when he worked for Rāma. A wife feels this mood also. She serves her husband with all her heart and soul. A mother also has a little of this attitude, as Yaśodā had toward Kṛṣṇa.** (p.115) This servant attitude has been expressed in a Bengali poem:

Lord, when will that day come
When my eyes will be filled only with you?
I will touch your feet and serve you.
How shall I serve you?
I will put camphor in your betal leaves to make your lips red![7]

This is the *dāsya* attitude, the master-servant relationship; God is the master, and the devotee is the servant.

Next, the Master described the attitude of friendship. ***Sakhya*, the attitude of friendship. Friends say to one another, 'Come here and sit near me.' Śrīdāma and other friends sometimes fed Kṛṣṇa with fruit, part of which they had already eaten, and sometimes climbed on His shoulders.** (p.115) Śrīdāma and Sudāma were cowherd boys of Vṛndāvana. They are examples of those who practise the attitude of friendship with God. They used to tend the cows with Śrī Kṛṣṇa and play with Him. They regarded Him as their dearest friend. In the devotional scriptures we find a description of how the cowherd boys played with Śrī Kṛṣṇa:

One of the cowherd boys steals the horn,
Another throws it away,
But laughing, brings it back.
The boys run away from Kṛṣṇa,
And then rush back to meet and touch him.[8]

This is an example of seeing God as a friend, the *sakhya* attitude.

Sri Ramakrishna continued his description of the five attitudes towards God with a discussion of the *vātsalya* mood. ***Vātsalya*, the attitude of a mother toward her child. This was Yaśodā's attitude toward Kṛṣṇa. The wife, too, has a little of this. She feeds her husband with her very life-blood, as it were. The mother feels happy only when the child has eaten to his heart's content. Yaśodā would roam about with butter in her hand, in order to feed Kṛṣṇa.** (p.115)

The sign of this parental attitude is affectionate cherishing. It is as if the devotee is caring for God as a mother would her own child. An example of this is given in the *Caitanya Caritāmṛta* where Kṛṣṇa says: 'Mother holds me as she would her son. She caresses and nurtures me who am utterly helpless.'[9] The devotee completely forgets that God is the Ruler of the world, and cares for Him as she would a helpless child.

Fifth and last, the Master described the *madhura* attitude. ***Madhura*, the attitude of a woman toward her paramour. Rādhā had this attitude toward Kṛṣṇa. The wife also feels it for her husband. This attitude includes all the other four.** (p.115) The *madhura* attitude is the deepest of all. Kṛṣṇadāsa Kavirāja has said, 'That love is not of this world.'[10] The *madhura bhāva* is not for everyone. As long as one has body-consciousness, one should not try to practise it. There is a danger of it being corrupted.

When any one of these five moods becomes intense, when you acquire real love, then you are liberated. Because of this, you must be very careful of what you think and how you regard yourself. If you think of yourself as a child of God, how can you believe that you are a sinner? The mind is everything. 'What you think, you become.' The Master used to say, 'If a person thinks himself to be a sinner, he becomes a sinner. Instead, he should think: "I have chanted God's name. How can I be a sinner?"' In the path of devotion, one establishes a definite relationship with God. The idea is to keep reminding yourself 'I am His child,' or 'I am His friend,' or 'I am His beloved.' Whatever mood you adopt, if you continue to regard yourself in that way, you will become transformed. Your whole life will gradually change. All your habits and actions will show that you belong to God, and no one will be able to think of you in any other way. The *Yogavāśiṣtha Rāmāyana* says : *Dṛḍhabhāvanayā ceto yad yathā bhāvayatyalaṁ tat tat phalaṁ tadākāraṁ tāvat kālaṁ prapaśyati*—'He who adopts one attitude firmly, gets the result of that mood in course of time.'[11]

Sri Ramakrishna used to sing this song by Rāmaprasāda:

How are you trying, O my mind, to know the nature of God?
You are groping like a madman locked in a dark room.
He is grasped through ecstatic love;
How can you fathom Him without it? (p.107)

All paths of devotion are founded on this feeling of love. Most religions emphasize this. I once met two Moslem gentlemen, both reputed scholars. One of them said in course of conversation: 'I don't go regularly to any mosque. I don't recite the traditional prayers, but in my mind I chant "Allah! Allah!" again and again. I think that is best for me.' The other gentleman said: 'No, that is not right. You should go regularly to the mosque. According to our religion, one should repeat the *namāz* [the special prayer of the Moslems] at certain times every day. Those who pray this way are doing the right thing. I myself observe all these rules.'

Then I said: 'Look, if you think of the *namāz* as only a physical exercise—bowing down and getting up—you gain nothing but physical exercise. It has no other meaning. But if you do it with faith and devotion, it is certainly meaningful and beneficial. The feeling is all-important. Without feeling, the performance of religious rites is worthless.'

A Bengali song says, 'What is the use of my ceremonial vessels and the lifeless rituals?' Without real feeling, traditional observances done machinelike produce no results. They are like 'an insincere smile'—lifeless. But if there is genuine feeling, that is a different thing. God does not see the ritualistic observance. He sees the heart, the feeling. As it is said in the *Nārada Pañcarātra*:

> *Mūrkho vadati viṣṇāya budho vadati viṣṇave*
> *Nama ityevamarthañca dvayoreva samaṁ phalam*
> *Yasmai dattañca yajjñānaṁ jñānadātā hariḥ svayam*
> *Jñānena tena sa stauti bhāvagrāhī janārddanaḥ*—

'One person does not know Sanskrit, so he says *Viṣṇāya* when he should say *Viṣṇave*. Another person is a scholar and says *Viṣṇave namaḥ* (Salutations to Viṣṇu) correctly. But both people mean the same thing. The result is the same. God has given one man intellectual knowledge, so he can praise Him using correct words. But God does not notice all this; He sees only the inner feeling.'[12]

A man once asked me, 'If in reading the *Gītā* my pronunciation is not exactly right, will I incur sin?' The answer comes from the Master: 'Little children are not able to say "Father" or "Mother." They only utter some sounds. But the father and mother understand that the child is speaking to them, and they are happy hearing his childish speech.' It is the same with God. If I love Him, then in whatever way I call on Him, in whatever language, by whatever name I call Him, He understands and listens to me.

In reality, with what language can we call on God? Can we win His heart with our language? He comes to whoever sincerely loves Him. So it is said, 'If you have real love, you can attract God just as a magnet attracts a piece of iron.'

Swami Vivekananda sometimes performed the worship at Belur Math, but it was without any ritual. He would take a handful of flowers to the shrine and place them at the Master's feet, not uttering any *mantras*. At Dakshineswar, the Master would do the same kind of worship, without any rituals. Rites, ceremonies, and *mantra*s all seemed trifling to them. They were taking part in a game being played by God and His devotee. Sri Sarada Devi also performed this kind of worship. Looking at the picture of Sri Ramakrishna, she would say : 'The cooking is done. Now come and eat.' It was as if she were taking the Master to his seat.

Swami Ramakrishnananda would worship in a very natural way. Anyone who saw his worship would feel that the Master was actually present. One night he was unable to sleep because it was so hot. Suddenly he thought that the Master must also be suffering, so he spent the rest of the night in the shrine fanning the Master's picture. Once the ceiling of the shrine developed a crack and when it rained, drops started falling on the Master's picture. So the Swami sat holding an umbrella over the picture until the rain stopped. We see only a picture, but these holy people see that God is actually present, and they devotedly serve Him.

Devotion means this play of love. Meditation, *japa*, and devotional singing without this feeling mean nothing. This is expressed in a verse from the *Kaulāvalī Tantra*:

Bahujāpāttathā homāt kāyakleśāttu vistaraiḥ
Na bhāvena vinā caiva tantramantrāḥ phalapradāḥ[13]

Japa, sacrificial fires, rites, and ceremonies are worthless if there is no feeling of love. Without feeling, worship is not worship, *japa* is not *japa*.

Don't be like a parrot in its cage that mindlessly utters God's name. When you chant His name, you should feel blissful, and your eyes should be filled with tears. Meditating on Him you should think: 'He is looking at me and smiling at me. He is very near me, the only one in the world who is mine.'

Before visiting holy places, your mind should be prepared; otherwise you will gain nothing. There is a story about an old woman who went to Puri to get the blessings of Lord Jagannātha. She went humbly on foot, but there was no end to her worries as she made her way along the road. She had planted a new gourd plant at home and she wondered if her daughter-in-law was looking after it. Was she allowing the cows and goats to eat it? Was she watering it properly, etc., etc.? When the old woman at last reached Puri and went to see the Lord, she could not see Him. In place of Jagannātha, all she could see was a gourd plant!

What is the purpose of going to a holy place? It is to remind us of God, to kindle our minds and inspire us. Those whose minds are prepared have their minds easily enkindled, but those whose minds are unprepared do not gain anything. Sri Ramakrishna's mind was always prepared. Whatever he saw aroused his feeling for God. When he saw a prostitute, he was reminded of the Divine Mother of the Universe. An English boy with his body bent in three places reminded him of Śrī Kṛṣṇa, who is often pictured in that pose. The Master once saw a lion at the zoo and was reminded of the Goddess Durgā, who is pictured riding on a lion.

Swami Brahmananda once went to East Bengal with Swami Premananda. Sitting by the side of the pond at the home of the Master's disciple Nag Mahashay, he said: 'Ah! How full of Divine Consciousness this place is! How full of Divinity!' He saw Brahman manifested everywhere. If the mind is prepared, if it is tied to God, it is easily enkindled. Because of this it is said:

Mantre tīrthe dvije deve daivajñe bheṣaje gurau
Yādṛśī bhāvanā yasya siddhirbhavati tādṛśī—

'*Mantras*, holy places, brahminical rites, divinity, knowledge of God, medicine, and the words of the guru—whatever one takes up one gets the result.'[14] If a person has faith in medicine, he gets the result if he takes it. The same is true of the *mantra*, the words of the guru, etc. If you follow faithfully whatever you believe in, you will get the results. 'As is one's feeling, so is one's gain.'

Again, it is said in the *Aṣṭāvakra Saṁhitā*, *Yā matiḥ sā gatiḥ*—'As one thinks, so one becomes.'[15] Another verse, from the *Kāmadhenu Tantra* says:

Na devo vidyate kāṣṭhe na pāṣāṇe ca pārvati
Bhāveṣu vidyate devo bhāvo mokṣasvarūpakaḥ—

'God is not in wood or in stone. He is in ecstatic love. Liberation comes from that love. Love is all.'[16]

One should not see God's Majesty

A speciality of Hinduism is that we make God our own; we do not keep our distance. Members of the Brāhmo Samāj used to give lectures in which they would emphasize God's majesty. They would say: 'O God, you have made such beautiful flowers, the sky, the stars, the ocean. What a wonderful creation! and so on.' But Sri Ramakrishna would say to them: 'Why do you talk so much of God's splendours? When you describe His majesty, you keep yourself far from Him.' Is God your father only because He is rich or majestic? Do you respect Him only for his wealth? If He had no splendour would you not honour Him or love Him or call Him *Father*? Father is father. Whatever he is or has, he is your father.

The Master said: **Shall I tell you the truth? Man loves his own riches, and so he thinks that God loves His, too. He thinks that God will be pleased if we glorify His riches. . . .**

Once a thief broke into the temple of Viṣṇu and robbed the image of its jewels. Mathur Babu and I went to the temple to see what was the matter. Addressing the image, Mathur said bitterly: 'What a shame, Lord! You are so worthless! The thief took all the ornaments from Your body, and You couldn't do a thing about it.' Thereupon I said to Mathur: 'Shame on you! How improper your words are! To God, the jewels you talk so much about are only lumps of clay. Lakṣmi, the Goddess of Fortune, is His Consort. Do you mean to say that He should spend sleepless nights because a thief has taken your few rupees? You mustn't say such things.'

Can one ever bring God under control through wealth? . . . He wants from His devotees love, devotion, feeling, discrimination, and renunciation. (pp.321-22) The *Caitanya Caritāmṛta* says: 'If you are engrossed in God's wealth, your love for Him is small. He wants your love; you must love Him, and Him alone.'[17] The devotee does not want to know about God's wealth or splendour; he only loves Him and forgets all His splendour. You must think of Him as your very own.

Sri Ramakrishna says much the same thing when talking about the Divine Mother: **She is by no means a godmother. She is your own mother.** (p.629) **A son can force his demand on his mother.**(p.634) **Once cartloads of money were coming from the estate of Trailokya's mother. They were guarded by many red-turbaned stalwarts armed with big sticks. Trailokya, who had been waiting on the road with his men, pounced upon the money and took it away by force. A son has a very strong claim on his mother's wealth. People say that a mother cannot very well sue her son in a court of law.** (p.634)

If any other person had done this, there would have been a lawsuit. But the son took the money so there could be no legal action against him. Sometimes the mother says to her child, 'No, you can't have any pennies.' She keeps the coins in her fist. Then she relents and says, 'Well, I'll give you one penny, but no more.' But the child does not listen. He forcefully opens his mother's fist and takes all the coins, and the mother smiles.

The Divine Mother has infinite wealth and splendour—our rightful possession. What does Her splendour consist of? It consists of love, devotion, discrimination, dispassion, etc. She must give them all to me. If She doesn't, I'll take them by force—even if She holds them tightly in Her fist.

Sri Ramakrishna said to the Divine Mother Kālī: 'If you don't give me your vision, I'll cut my throat!' The Mother was helpless; what could she do? She was forced to appear before him. He was like a little child who threatens his mother: 'If you don't give me what I want, I'll run away from home.' The mother at once says, 'Don't go. I'll give you what you want.' Sri Aurobindo said that Sri Ramakrishna was 'taking, as it were, the Kingdom of Heaven by violence.'[18]

Sri Ramakrishna said, **People say that the mother's attachment to the child is stronger than the father's.** (p.634) You may be very old, but if you are unhappy or in distress, your first thought is of your mother. We can't think of anyone closer to us than our mother. Because of this, the practice of calling on God as Mother was developed in Bengal. Some scholars believe that this discipline developed under the influence of Tāntric teachings, but whatever the cause, it is true that many famous worshippers of the Divine Mother come from Bengal. Rāmaprasāda is one of them. In one of his songs, he tries to frighten Śiva.

> This time you will see what I will do!
> I have discovered your great offence,
> You are the husband—
> How dare you keep your wife's feet on your chest?*
> I'm her child and I'll keep her feet on my chest.
> If you don't let go of my mother's feet
> I'll tell everyone how bad you are.
> If even then you don't let go,
> I'll force you to give them to me.
> Those feet belong to me,
> I have a claim on them—
> Not only now, but in many previous births.

The devotee is not afraid of God and does not show Him any respect; he even threatens Him. God is his very own. There is no diffidence, nothing hidden. When devotion is deep you feel very close to God.

---

*In Kālī images, She stands on Śiva's body.

When the new son-in-law first comes to the house, he is given a cordial reception and much special attention. But gradually he becomes the old son-in-law; he is one of the family. Then the mother-in-law says to him, 'Son, will you bring something from the market?' And the son-in-law brings it with a smile on his face. Now he is not the son-in-law, but the son of the family. It is a natural relationship. We must establish this natural relationship with God.

Swami Brahmananda used to say, 'Establish a common, ordinary relationship with God.' We have ordinary, everyday clothes—clothes that are not special, but worn for our work and play. We have to have this 'ordinary, everyday' relationship with God. We must think, 'He is always with me; there is no one nearer than He. There is no difference between Him and me.'

In the *Caṇḍī* there are many hymns to the Divine Mother and much praise of Her great power and glory. She subdues the wicked and protects the good. But in Bengal at the time of the Durgā Pūjā, the same Goddess, as Umā, becomes the daughter. She is not a goddess then, but the daughter of the family, the Bengali daughter. In mythology she is the daughter of Himalaya and his wife Menakā, but Bengalis believe that Umā belongs to them; she is their own daughter who has come back to her father's home after a year's absence. All Bengal is filled with joy. In songs we hear the Umā has come home and told her mother Menakā that her husband, Śiva, lives in the cremation grounds. Menakā asks, 'Is it not very troublesome, living with Śiva?'

Is it not astonishing that She who is the Ruler of the World, its Creator, Preserver and Destroyer, comes to us as a young girl? She has ten arms, but even so, She is our daughter. The

Divine Mother in the form of the Bengali daughter is irresistible. The whole year we have waited for Umā to come. Although we worship her in an image (often life-sized and beautifully decorated with a silk sari, flowers, etc.), she is not an image to us. She is our own daughter.

Once Rāmaprasāda was making a fence and the Divine Mother in the form of a little girl came to help him. Perhaps God is happy to leave aside his wonderful powers and come to his devotees in such a simple, natural way. Our power is limited, so He comes to us with limited power. If He came to us with all His majesty and glory, we could not accept Him. In the *Gītā* Kṛṣṇa shows Arjuna his Universal form, but Arjuna is overwhelmed. 'How can this be?' he thinks. 'Can Kṛṣna be everything? Yes, creation, preservation, and destruction are all in Him. The past, the present and the future—all are His manifestations.'

Yathā nadīnāṁ bahavo'mbuvegāḥ
Samudramevābhimukhā dravanti
Tathā tavāmī naralokavīrā
Viśanti vaktrāṇyabhivijvalanti—
Yathā pradīptaṁ jvalanaṁ pataṅgā
Viśanti nāśāya samṛddhavegāḥ
Tathaiva nāśāya viśanti lokāḥ
Tavāpi vaktrāṇi samṛddhavegāḥ

'As the many rushing torrents of rivers race towards the ocean, so do these heroes of the world of men rush into Thy flaming mouths. As moths rush swiftly into a blazing fire to perish there, so do these men rush into Thy mouths with great speed to their own destruction.'[19]

Ākhyāhi me ko bhavānugrarūpo
Namo'stu te devavara prasīda—

'Tell me who Thou art with form so terrible. Salutations to Thee, O Thou great Godhead, have mercy.'[20]

Then Arjuna becomes ashamed of having treated Kṛṣṇa so familiarly.

Sakheti matvā prasabhaṁ yaduktaṁ
He Kṛṣṇa he Yādava he sakheti
Adṛṣṭapūrvaṁ hṛṣito'smi dṛṣṭvā
Bhayena ca pravyathitaṁ mano me
Tadeva me darśaya deva rūpaṁ
Prasīda deveśa jagannivāsa—

'I called you "friend", "Kṛṣṇa", "Yādava" in rashness. I have seen what was never seen before and I rejoice, but my heart is shaken with fear. Show me that other form of Thine, O God and be gracious, O Lord of the gods and Refuge of the Universe!'[21, 22]

Arjuna had known Kṛṣṇa as his friend, as his charioteer, as his near and dear one, but now it seemed that Kṛṣṇa was not even a human being! So Arjuna begged him to assume his human form again. Kṛṣṇa withdrew his Universal Form and Arjuna was consoled.

When Śrī Kṛṣṇa was a child, his mother Yaśodā used to say to him : 'When you take the cows to graze, don't walk in front of them or they may butt you with their heads. And don't go very far. Wherever you go, sometimes play on your flute. I want to be able to hear you while I am doing my housework.'[23] Yaśodā tells Him, who is God Himself, the Saviour from all dangers, to be careful! This may seem strange to people from other traditions, but Hindus find that if they establish an intimate relationship with God, they can easily love Him.

In one of our devotional scriptures Śrī Kṛṣṇa says, 'I am under the control of that person who regards himself as greater than me.'[24] We like to think that we are greater than God because we love Him. We like to think of the object of our love as small and helpless. Yaśodā used to think, 'If I don't watch over Kṛṣṇa, who will?' The *gopīs* stood guard with sticks lest Kṛṣṇa should be seized by a tiger.[25]

The devotees are eager to protect God, who is the Protector of all. And He is happy playing this role. He is not angry, nor does He feel Himself demeaned. When I think of God as small, I forget His majesty; I see only the person and love Him. God says, 'I regard that person as my own who loves me. I am his slave and am bound by his love.'

Brother Lawrence in his book *The Practice of the Presence of God* describes his spiritual disciplines. He would always think that God was with him. He spoke with Him, was sometimes angry with Him and concealed nothing from Him. If he would make a mistake while working and someone would criticize him, he would feel hurt and say to God : 'Why didn't you warn me before? Then I would not have to bear this censure.' God was his very own. All his feelings—his anger, sorrow, joy—centred around God.

Once Holy Mother was walking with other people from Calcutta to Jayrambati. Along the way they stopped to cook their meal. After the rice was cooked, the pot broke and the rice was scattered on the ground. What could they do? Holy Mother took a little from the top of the heap and offered it to Thakur saying: 'Thakur, today it is your fate to eat this rice. Please accept it.' Holy Mother's mother, Shyamasundari Devi had the same intimate relationship with God. On the last day of the Jagaddhātrī Pūjā at Jayrambati, she whispered in the ear of the image of the goddess, 'Mother Jagāi, come again!' She felt as if her daughter were going away. When we feel that God is our very own, we act that way.

Rāmaprasāda said: 'When I lie down, I am making my obeisance to Mother; sleeping, I am meditating on Her. When I eat I am feeding Mother. All the time, under all conditions, in all work, I am remembering Her.'

I once visited Assam where Christian missionaries have converted many people to Christianity. They have taught the people that Sunday is 'God's Day'. They tell them: 'You can keep six days for yourselves, but keep at least one day a week for God—Sunday.' On that day people are not supposed to work. I wanted to buy some tea at a tea-shop. The owner, who was a Christian, was poor and wanted to sell me the tea, though the price was only two paisa; but it was Sunday and he was not supposed to work. So he said, 'Do one thing—take a packet of tea from the shelf and then give me the price marked on the box.' That way he could make the sale and still not be guilty of working on Sunday.

To Hindus, God's day is not just one day; every day is God's day. Every moment is God's moment, and all work is God's work. Swami Vivekananda used the expression 'Sunday hat'. Some people's religion is like a 'Sunday hat'. It is reserved for Sundays only. My relationship with God can't be like that. I am related to Him every moment.

Sometimes people ask me, 'When I do *japa*, must I bathe and change my clothes? Should I sit on a bed or on a special mat, etc.?' Sri Ramakrishna, Holy Mother, and Swami Vivekananda all give the same advice: 'Know God to be your own. Why do you reason so much about calling on Him? Call on Him wherever you are.' Are there any rules for a child to talk with his mother? He chats with her while he is lying on his bed or while he is eating. If I should decide that I must change my clothes or sprinkle my body and mat with Gaṅgā water before talking with my mother, people would certainly say I am mad; and they would be right. The Divine Mother is my real mother. I will talk to Her however I wish—after bathing or without bathing, sitting on a mat or not sitting on a mat. I can talk to Her any time, any way.

At Belur Math we used to watch Swami Shantananda, a disciple of Holy Mother. Everyone revered him highly. He used to do *japa* much of the time. He would walk around the Math grounds, speak with people, then return to his room, sit on his bed, and do *japa*. He was always close to God through *japa*.

Someone asked Holy Mother, 'What should we do? You said we should chant the name of God early in the morning, but we are in the habit of drinking tea when we get up.' Holy Mother replied, 'Why not do *japa* after drinking tea?' In her view, one's relationship with God is one of love; it is an intimate relationship. There are no hard and fast rules and regulations in that relationship.

I once asked my guru, Swami Shivananda, 'Can I do *japa* while walking down the street?' He answered, 'Certainly you can, my child, but be careful that you are not run over by a car.' You can call on God at all times and places.

The Grace of God and Intense Longing

But even though we perform *japa* and meditation, there is no certainty we will by this realize God. We realize Him through His grace. Holy Mother said, 'If one does *japa* and meditation, the sense-organs are brought under control, but one cannot realize God without His grace.' Sri Ramakrishna says the same thing: **It is not that God can be realized by this work and not by that. The vision of God depends on His grace.** (p.646)

God sometimes seems to be as whimsical as a child. We can't predict whom He will shower His grace on. A story, *Our Lady's Juggler*, by Anatole France illustrates this.

Many years ago there was a man who made his living as a juggler; but at heart he was a sincere lover of God and was especially devoted to the Virgin Mary. He lived near a monastery and in time came to know its abbot. Gradually he began to associate with the monks, and at last decided to renounce the world and live at the monastery.

All the monks there worshipped the Virgin Mary. They had various kinds of talents. Some wrote religious books, some copied out old manuscripts, some painted religious pictures, some composed hymns, and some sang songs for Mary. Everything was done as worship of Mary; whatever they did was for Her. Seeing their beautiful way of living, the juggler became very sad. He thought: 'I can't write books or paint pictures or compose hymns—I don't know anything. I have no way of serving Mary. Alas, how unfortunate I am!'

Then suddenly a thought came to him: 'I can perform my juggling act and in that way make Mother Mary happy.' From then on, he waited for a time when no one was in the church, then he would go there and perform his juggling in front of Mary's image. Every day he performed for her. Slowly his sadness left him, and a great joy could be seen on his face. Yet, he could not hide forever what he was doing. Soon a murmur rose in the monastery; the monks wanted to know what was going on every day in the church so the abbot sent two old monks to find out.

When they came to the church they saw that the juggler was entertaining Mother Mary by standing on his head and then juggling knives and balls. It was the act he used to perform before he became a monk. The old monks thought that the man must be out of his mind. Does anyone act like this in a church? This was a terrible infringement of the rules. But before they could say anything, they saw Mother Mary coming down from the altar. She walked straight to the juggler, who was exhausted and sweating profusely, and wiped the sweat from his brow with a corner of her mantle.

The monks were wonderstruck. They had prayed so much, they had worked so hard for Mary, yet she had never come to them. But this juggler, who had never done anything, had been touched by Her. How could that happen?

Sri Ramakrishna also told a story to illustrate how unpredictable God's grace seems to be. A man was going to perform a difficult religious rite in the forest. With great effort he procured the necessary ingredients—a corpse and many other things. But just as he sat down to meditate, a tiger appeared, dragged him away, and killed him. Another man who was passing through the forest and, in fear of the tiger, had climbed a tree, came down, sat where the other man had been sitting and started to meditate. At once the Divine Mother appeared before him. The Master was pointing out through this story how difficult it is to understand God's ways, and that we shouldn't think that by doing so much *japa*, etc. we can realize God. We realize Him through His grace.

Does this mean that we should not perform our spiritual practice—that we should just fold our arms, sit quiet and do nothing? The real question is, 'What do we want?' If we want God intensely, we will carry out the disciplines and receive His grace. The Master said: **Still a man must work a little with longing for God in his heart. If he has longing he will receive the grace of God.** (p. 646) Sri Ramakrishna said that if a person has a strong desire to go to Puri, he will get there somehow or other. He may start walking towards the north, but if he is really anxious to get to Puri, someone will tell him that he must go south. He may wander about for a while, but at last he will reach Puri because he had an intense desire to go there. We need that intense desire to see God. Then we will get the right directions from some holy person, do what he says, and reach the goal. The Master told a story to explain this further.

In a certain family a man lay seriously ill. He was at the point of death. Someone said 'Here is a remedy: First it must rain when the star *Svāti* is in the ascendant; then some of that rain-water must collect in a human skull; then a frog must come there and a snake must chase it; and as the frog is about to be bitten by the snake, it must jump away and the poison of the snake must drop into the skull. You must prepare a medicine from this poison and give it to the patient. Then he will live.' The head of the family consulted the almanac about the star and set out at the right moment. With great longing of heart he began to search for the different ingredients. He prayed to God, 'O Lord, I shall succeed only if You bring together all the ingredients.' As he was roaming about he actually saw a skull lying on the ground. Presently there came a shower of rain. Then the man exclaimed: 'O Gracious Lord, I have got the rain-water under *Svāti*, and the skull too. What is more, some of the rain has fallen into the skull. Now be kind enough to bring together the other ingredients.'

He was reflecting with a yearning heart when he saw a poisonous snake approaching, His joy knew no bounds. He became so excited that he could feel the thumping of his own heart. 'O God', he prayed, 'now the snake has

come too. I have procured most of the ingredients. Please be gracious and give me the remaining ones.' No sooner did he pray thus than a frog hopped up. The snake pursued it. As they came near the skull and the snake was about to bite the frog, the frog jumped over the skull and the snake's poison fell into it. The man began to dance, clapping his hands for joy.— So I say that one gets everything through yearning. (p. 647)

Sometimes a question arises in our mind. We are eager to find the answer but no one even understands our question.

Then we happen to go somewhere and find that someone who knows is talking about the exact question that was on our mind. Unsought, we get our answer—because we were so eagerly seeking it.

Jesus Christ said, 'Knock, and it shall be opened unto you.'[26] If you knock the door will open; yet it sometimes happens that the door opens of itself, if you have that intense yearning. If you have longing, everything becomes favourable. A difficult obstacle that you could not cross over suddenly vanishes. The impossible becomes possible. God holds your hand and takes you forward. If you sincerely want God, He makes everything favourable for you to realize Him.

At the time of Sri Ramakrishna's fatal illness, he had a desire to eat an *āmalakī* fruit, but it was not the season for *āmalakī*s. No one could find one anywhere. When his disciple Nag Mahashay heard of this, he set out to find an *āmalakī*. He wandered about for three days and nights and at last found some. Such was his deep longing to serve his Master that he could not but be successful.

We ourselves sometimes feel a longing to serve God. But we must keep in mind that even though we have great longing, we need as much perseverance in our spiritual practice. If we do not persist in our practice, our longing will be in vain. To realize God, we need both—intense longing and perseverance in practice. Nag Mahashay had great longing to serve his beloved Master, but he was equally persistant in his efforts to serve him—and he succeeded against all odds.

The Master says: **God reveals Himself to a devotee who feels drawn to Him by the combined force of these three attractions: the attraction of worldly possessions for the worldly man, the child's attraction for its mother, and the husband's attraction for the chaste wife. If one feels drawn to Him by the combined force of these three attractions, then through it one can attain Him.** (p.83)

He tells us that we must cry:

> **Cry to your Mother Śyāmā with a real cry,**
> **O mind!**
> **And how can She hold Herself from you?**
> **How can Śyāmā stay away?**
> **How can your Mother Kālī hold Herself away?**
> (p.83)

In age after age, those who cried intensely for God were able to realize Him. They cried with a 'real cry'.

Sri Ramakrishna used to say that a person's mind is like a pair of scales. It either goes down to the side of the world or to God. Mīrābāī, the medieval saint, was a great lover of God. The scales of her mind always went in one direction—towards God. Her mind never went towards wealth, fame, position or any other thing. She often used to sing songs to God. In one of them she says:

> Come, my love, show me yourself.
> I cannot live in your absence.
> As the lotus cannot survive without water,

the night without the moon,
I cannot live without you.
I spend restless nights
suffering this separation.
All day I cannot eat,
at night I cannot sleep.
Who can describe my agony?
Who will listen to me?
Come, my love,
Cool this fire that rages within me.
Your presence alone can heal me.
Why do you keep me waiting?
I know you are everywhere.
Through countless births Mira has loved you.
She loves you still.[27]

Mīrābāī is only one in a long succession of great devotees in India. Among the others are:

The poet Vidyāpati who said: 'You are to me as wings to a bird. Without wings the bird is helpless; without You, I am also helpless. If you take the fish from the water it struggles restlessly. It can't live. I also can't live without you. You are the life of my life.'[28]

Another devotee, Lālana, who said: 'The *cātak* bird will not drink any water but rainwater, such is its steadfast determination. And Hanumān did not know anything but Rāma. He always meditated on Him and saw nothing but Him.

Rāmadāsa was a shoemaker by caste, yet because of his intense longing, Mother Gaṅgā came to his cottage.'[29] If you have intense feeling, anything is possible.

Sri Ramakrishna emphasized the need for intense longing. He said that if someone holds your head under water, you feel that you are suffocating. You know that you will die if you can't get some air. You must feel the same desperation if you can't see God—you must have such intense yearning that you feel you can't live a moment more if you don't see Him. 'What will be will be'—this attitude will get you nowhere. The Master did not like this way of thinking. A Hindi song says that taking the name of God one can gradually get everything. Sri Ramakrishna did not like this word 'gradually.' He would say, 'I must see God this very moment, in this very birth.' We need this kind of stubborn resolve.

He used to tell about two farmers. Their fields needed water, and there was a canal nearby from which a duct had to be dug to bring the water to the fields. One farmer started to dig his duct, but when his wife came to call him for his meal, the farmer lay down his tools and said, 'Yes, I'll come and eat. Tomorrow there will be enough time for digging.'

The other farmer also started to dig his duct, but when his wife called him for his meal, he threatened to beat her. As long as the duct was not made and water brought to the field, he refused to stop working. At last, when he had finished making the duct and the water was running into the field, he returned home and said: 'Now prepare my pipe, I want to smoke; and give me some oil, I want to take a bath.' His mind was at ease; he had finished his work. Sri Ramakrishna liked this kind of resoluteness. He loved Swamiji for this trait. Swamiji was very obstinate and would not give up till he had accomplished what he started out to do.

Although Sri Ramakrishna emphasized the necessity for intense longing, he also said that this longing can't be forced. As long as we have worldly desires, this longing for God will not come. Still, we can move ahead by repeated efforts. We must cry to Him and chant His name. A man once asked Sri Ramakrishna why he didn't get any joy from taking God's name, why he had no urge to cry for Him or any desire to practise *japa*. The Master said: **Pray to God with a yearning heart that you may take delight in His name.** (p.203) God is a 'storekeeper'. You can get what you want from Him, so pray to Him fervently for devotion, faith, discrimination, and dispassion. And if you pray for intense longing, He will give you that, too.

If someone would say to the Master, 'I can't meditate or do *japa* well,' he would say: 'Pray to the Mother. She will give you what you need.' If you take the path of Devotion, there is one essential teaching, 'Pray to God with intense longing.' God will give you everything—more than you asked for, perhaps more than you deserve, because there are no laws in the domain of His grace. If there were laws, they would be His laws, and He could break them. If God notices your intense longing, He may break the law.

Like the dark room that becomes lighted in an instant when a lamp is brought in, the darkness and impurities of your mind vanish in an instant through God's grace. There is nothing impossible in the domain of religion. The robber Ratnākar was transformed into the great sage Vālmīki. Vilvamaṅgal had gone astray, but he became a great devotee. St. Francis of Assisi at first lived a very undisciplined life, then there came a great change and he was transformed into a saint. Through God's grace, the impossible becomes possible—man becomes divine.

But we must be restless for God. Sri Ramakrishna says: **An intense restlessness is needed. Through it the whole mind goes to God. A man had a daughter who became a widow when she was very young. She had never known**

her husband. She noticed the husbands of other girls and said one day to her father, 'Where is my husband?' The father replied: 'Govinda (Kṛṣṇa) is your husband. He will come to you if you call Him.' At these words the girl went to her room, closed the door, and cried to Govinda, saying: 'O Govinda, come to me! Show Yourself to me! Why don't You come?' God could not resist the girl's piteous cry and appeared before her.

One must have childlike faith—and the intense yearning that a child feels to see its mother. That yearning is like the red sky in the east at dawn. After such a sky the sun must rise. Immediately after that yearning one sees God. (pp.337-38)

The Master told a story about a little boy who had to pass through a forest on the way to school. He would be frightened so his mother said to him: 'Your elder brother lives in the forest; his name is Madhusūdana [a name of Kṛṣṇa]. When you are frightened, call him and He'll come to you.' The next day when the little boy entered the forest and became frightened, he cried out: 'Where are you, Madhusūdana? I'm very scared.' Seeing his tears, God could not stay away from him. He appeared to the boy and accompanied him till he was out of the forest and on the road to school. Then he said, 'Whenever you need me, call, and I'll come to you.'

Another of Sri Ramakrishna's stories is also about a little boy with faith. The boy's father had to go somewhere, but before he left he said to his little son, 'Since I won't be here today, you must offer food to God in the shrine.' The boy took his bath and then placed the food before the image saying, 'Lord, please eat this food.' He thought God would really eat what was offered to Him. Time passed, but God did not eat the food. Then the little boy started to cry. He said, 'Lord, eat right now; it's getting late and I can't wait any longer!' Seeing his tears, the Lord could not stay away. He came out of the image and ate the offered food. Sri Ramakrishna says, **One must have this faith of a child, this yearning.** (p.338)

A person also needs favourable circumstances. The Master says: **To attain God a man must have certain favourable conditions : the company of holy men, discrimination, and the blessings of a real teacher. Perhaps his elder brother takes the responsibility for the family.** (p.646) If there is intense longing, everything becomes favourable. It seems that God collects everything and places it in your hands.

A man who lived in Calcutta had to move to Bombay for his work. When he first went there he said to himself, 'Where have I come? I was in Calcutta, the city of Kālī, with Dakshineswar and Belur Math close by. My friends and relatives and I used to get together and talk about God, sing *bhajans*, etc.' But if there is intense yearning, one finds that God's grace is always there. The man made new friends who were also devotees. They became more near and dear to him than his friends and relatives in Calcutta. Through God's grace, a new world opened up for him and he was very happy.

If you have intense yearning, all obstacles gradually disappear. What seemed impossible actually happens.

Four Kinds of Devotees

Those who adopt the path of devotion are not all the same. Among them are differences, distinctions, various modes of being. Sri Ramakrishna says: **As worldly people are endowed with *sattva*, *rajas*, and *tamas*, so also is *bhakti* characterized by the three *guṇas*.** (p.146) He explains the differences among these three types of devotees:

First, ***sattva*****. A devotee who possesses it meditates on God in absolute secret, perhaps inside his mosquito net. Others think he is asleep. . . . His love for the body goes only as far as appeasing his hunger, and that only by means of rice and simple greens. There is no elaborate arrangement about his meals, no luxury in clothes, and no display of furniture. Besides, such a devotee never flatters anybody for money.** (p.146)

I have sold my head to one Person, to God. Can I bend my head to anyone else? We find this *sāttvika* devotion in the Bible where God says, 'I, the Lord thy God, am a jealous God.'[30] One must seek only Him. And Jesus said, 'No one can serve two masters,. . . You cannot serve God and mammon'.[31] This single-minded devotion is found in *sāttvika* devotees.

Second, ***rajas*****. An aspirant possessed of *rājasika bhakti* puts a *tilak* on his forehead and a necklace of holy *rudrākṣa* beads, interspersed with gold ones, around his neck. At worship he wears a silk cloth.** (p.147) He likes outer pomp and display. He seems to say to people, 'See what a great devotee I am!'

Third, ***tamas*****. A man endowed with *tāmasika bhakti* has burning faith. Such a devotee literally extorts boons from God, even as a robber falls upon a man and plunders his money. 'Bind! Beat! Kill!'—that is his way, the way of the dacoits.** (p.147)

Sri Ramakrishna used to say that the *tamas* of devotion is a very good thing. Rāmaprasāda followed this *tāmasika*, dacoit way. He tried to frighten the Divine Mother saying, 'Mother, if you don't appear to me, I'll sue you in court— then you'll have to give me your vision.' There is this quarrel between mother and son. Girish Ghosh had this *tāmasika* devotion, this burning faith. The Master said that he had one hundred and twenty-five per cent faith. He would say to the Master, 'You must be gracious to me; otherwise how can you be called an *Avatāra*?'

This is the dacoit way—no tears, no humble begging—only force, only coercion. The Divine Mother is our very own, so we can use force. A person who has this *tāmasika* devotion does not worry about sin. He says: **'What? I have chanted the Mother's name. How can I be a sinner any more?'** (p.147) I may have committed many sins, but when I uttered Her name, all my sins were completely destroyed. With great force he says, **'I am Her child, heir to Her powers and glories.'** (p.147)

The Master liked this attitude. He said, **Assume the *tāmasika* aspect of *bhakti*. Say with force: 'What? I have uttered the names of Rāma and Kālī. How can I be in bondage any more? How can I be affected by the law of *karma*?'** (p.252)

The fourth class of devotees consists of those few who have gone beyond the three *guṇas*. The Master said: **There is also another class of devotees, those who are beyond the three *guṇas*. They have the nature of a child. Their worship consists in chanting God's name—just His name.** (p.322)

Formal Devotion, Ecstatic Devotion, and Knowledge Mixed with Devotion

Sri Ramakrishna used to speak of two kinds of devotion. One kind is *vaidhī bhakti*, formal devotion—devotion according to rules and regulations. The other kind is *premā bhakti*, ecstatic devotion. In formal devotion you must do so much *japa*, fast, go on pilgrimages, perform special types of worship, make sacrificial offerings, etc. This kind of devotion is easy, but is not lasting. You can't realize God through formal devotion. For that you need ecstatic devotion.

Sri Ramakrishna says: **One can see God through *bhakti* alone. But it must be 'ripe' *bhakti*, *premā-bhakti* and *rāga-bhakti*.** (p.173) Then it is not formal devotion. When the northwest wind comes, everything is blown away. In the same way, when the wind of ecstatic devotion comes, all formal rites and ceremonies are blown away. There are then no rules, no shame, and no social conventions. The devotee loves God; worldly life seems trifling to him. This is ecstatic devotion, *premā-bhakti*.

When one has that *bhakti*, one loves God even as the mother loves the child, the child the mother, or the wife the husband.., If the devotee but once feels this attachment and ecstatic love for God, this mature devotion and longing, then he sees God in both His aspects, with form and without form. (p.173)

The *gopīs* had ecstatic love, unswerving and single-minded devotion to one ideal. (p.228) There is no reasoning in this steadfast devotion—only love, unalloyed love, pure love.

The Master said: **Do you know the meaning of devotion that is not loyal to one ideal? It is devotion tinged with intellectual knowledge. It makes one feel: 'Kṛṣṇa has become all these. He alone is the Supreme Brahman. He is Rāma, Śiva, and Śakti.' But this element of knowledge is not present in ecstatic love of God. Once Hanumān came to Dvārakā and wanted to see Sītā and Rāma. Kṛṣṇa said to Rukmiṇī, His queen, 'You had better assume the form of Sītā; otherwise there will be no escape from the hands of Hanumān.'**

Once the Pāṇḍava brothers performed the Rājasūya sacrifice. All the kings placed Yudhiṣṭhira on the royal

throne and bowed low before him in homage. But Vibhīṣaṇa, the King of Ceylon, said, 'I bow down to Nārāyaṇa and to none else.' At these words the Lord Kṛṣṇa bowed down to Yudhiṣṭhira. Only then did Vibhīṣaṇa prostrate himself, crown and all, before him. (pp.228-29) (Kṛṣṇa is a form of Nārāyaṇa)

Sri Ramakrishna gave another example of steadfast devotion: **Do you know what devotion to one ideal is like? It is like the attitude of a daughter-in-law in the family. She serves all the members of the family—her brother-in-law, father-in-law, husband, and so forth—, bringing them water to wash their feet, fetching their towels, arranging their seats, and the like; but with her husband she has a special relationship.** (p.229) The devotee has an intimate relationship with his Chosen Ideal. 'I honour all the deities, but I love only one, my own Chosen Ideal.'

There are two elements in this ecstatic love: 'I-ness' and 'my-ness'. (p.229) Here, 'I' and 'my' are not given up. The devotee thinks that he is serving God, 'God is my own. If I do not care for Him, who will?' This is the way of Yaśodā. **She did not look on Kṛṣṇa as God . . . . Uddhava said to Yaśodā: 'Mother, your Kṛṣṇa is God Himself. He is the Lord of the Universe and not a common human being.' 'Oh!' exclaimed Yaśodā, 'I am not asking you about your Lord of the Universe . . . but my Gopāla.'** (p.229)

Gopal-Ma was an extraordinary devotee of Sri Ramakrishna. Her real name was Aghoramani Devi, but as she worshipped God as Gopāla, the child Kṛṣṇa, everyone called her Gopal-Ma. A poor brahmin child-widow, from a very early age she spent her days and nights meditating on God. Her life was extremely austere.

Someone told her about a holy man who lived at Dakshineswar, and she decided to visit him. When she first saw Sri Ramakrishna, she felt a strong attraction for him; she realized that he was not an ordinary man. The second time she went to see him, he said to her, 'Please give me what you have brought.' With much diffidence she took out a piece of dry *sandeś* from the corner of her sari and gave it to him. The Master liked it very much but he said, 'Why did you buy *sandeś* for me? You can make *nāḍu* yourself and bring it to me. I would rather have something you cooked yourself. You could also make some curried vegetables for me.'

Gopal-Ma said to herself : 'What kind of holy man have I come to see! He doesn't talk of religion, but only "I want to eat this, I want to eat that." I won't come here anymore.' Yet such was the attraction of the Master that several days later she came again bringing some vegetables she had cooked. After Sri Ramakrishna had eaten them he said, '*Sudhā*!' meaning 'nectar'. The vegetables had been cooked with devotion so they were as sweet as nectar to him.

As time passed, Gopal-Ma had many kinds of spiritual experiences. She had the vision of Gopāla; then she saw that Sri Ramakrishna himself was Gopāla. When she came to visit the Master, he would be overwhelmed with emotion and assume the gestures and appearance of Gopāla.

God is eager to make His devotees happy, so He comes to them in the form they love best. He who is the Ruler of the Universe came to Gopal-Ma as a little boy. He seemed to be helpless and completely dependent on her. She never thought of him as all-powerful. She thought, 'He has no one but me, and I have no one but him.'

The milkmaids of Vṛndāvana, the gopīs, had this steadfast love for Śrī Kṛṣṇa. Sri Ramakrishna said: **How faithful to**

Kṛṣṇa the *gopīs* were! After many entreaties to the door-keeper the *gopīs* entered the royal court in Mathurā, where Kṛṣṇa was seated as king. The door-keeper took them to Him; but at the sight of King Kṛṣṇa wearing the royal turban, the *gopīs* bent down their heads and said among themselves: 'Who is this man with a turban on his head? Should we violate our chaste love for Kṛṣṇa by talking to him? Where is our beloved Kṛṣṇa with the yellow robe and the bewitching crest with the peacock feather?' (p.229)

The love of the *gopīs* for Śrī Kṛṣṇa is discussed in the chapter on Madhura Bhāva. The *gopīs* are frequently cited as persons who most perfectly personify ecstatic love for God. Sri Ramakrishna says, **The ideal of Vṛndāvana is unique.** (p.229)

Someone then asked, **'Which is better, ecstatic love or love mixed with knowledge?'** (p.229). The Master replied : **It is not possible to develop ecstatic love of God unless you love Him very deeply and regard Him as your very own.**

Listen to a story. Once three friends were going through a forest, when a tiger suddenly appeared before them. 'Brothers,' one of them exclaimed, 'we are lost!' 'Why should you say that?' said the second friend. 'Why should we be lost? Come let us pray to God.' The third friend said: 'No, why should we trouble God about it? Come, let us climb this tree.'

The friend who said, 'We are lost!' did not know that there is a God who is our Protector. The friend who asked the others to pray to God was a *jñānī*. He was aware that God is the Creator, Preserver, and Destroyer of the world. The third friend, who didn't want to trouble God

with prayers and suggested climbing the tree, had ecstatic love of God. It is the very nature of such love that it makes a man think himself stronger than his Beloved. He is always alert lest his Beloved should suffer. The one desire of his life is to keep his Beloved from even being pricked in the foot by a thorn. (p.229)

Nārada at one time developed a terrible conceit; he thought that there was no devotee in the whole world as great as he. To rid him of this egotism, Śrī Kṛṣṇa took him to meet a poor brahmin who was very devoted to Lord Viṣṇu. The brahmin did not believe in killing any living being, so he ate only dry dead grass, still, he always had a sword hanging around his neck. Śrī Kṛṣṇa said to him, 'You don't kill any living being, so why do you wander around with a sword around your neck?'

The brahmin answered: 'I carry the sword because I want to kill three people: First Nārada who is always calling out the Lord's name and singing. This disturbs my Lord and makes Him unhappy, so I will kill Nārada first. Next, I will kill Arjuna. Why did he make my Lord Kṛṣṇa drive his chariot? And the third person I will kill is Draupadī. She had the audacity to feed my Lord with impure food. I wander about with this sword so that I can kill these three persons.' The brahmin thought he had to protect his Lord.

Sri Ramakrishna says, **The devotee regards himself as a higher, and God as a lower being.** (p.471) This kind of devotee has an enormous ego. He thinks God is smaller and weaker than he himself, so He must be protected and comforted.

Swami Vivekananda once went to Kṣīra-Bhavāni, an old temple of the Divine Mother in northern India. Moslems had long ago desecrated it. Feeling very sad, Swamiji said to the Divine Mother: 'Mother, if I had been here, I would not have permitted them to desecrate Your temple. I would have protected it with my life.' At once Swamiji heard a divine voice saying, 'My child, do you protect me? Don't you know that it is I who am always protecting you? You don't protect me. This all happened through my will. If I so desire, I can build a great temple here in an instant.' Swamiji's intense love for the Divine Mother had made him forget Her greatness.

The devotee has a vast ego and is afraid lest a thorn might prick his Lord's foot. Once Kṛṣṇa was walking barefoot along a country path. One of the *gopīs* said, 'His feet are so soft; walking on that hard ground must be painful for Him. Let us lie on the ground and let him walk over our bodies.'

Rūpa, a disciple of Śrī Caitanya, was fasting and Śrī Kṛṣṇa, disguised as a village boy, brought him some milk. When Rūpa's brother Sanātana heard about this, he became very angry and said to Rūpa: 'You were fasting, and Kṛṣṇa could not bear to see it. He had to come bringing food for you. Why did you trouble him this way?'[32]

When you have ecstatic devotion, *prema*, you think of yourself as big and your Lord as small. Your only desire is that your Lord, your Beloved, should not suffer in the slightest.

'The purpose of this love is the complete realization of Śrī Kṛṣṇa; Kṛṣṇa is under the control of this love—so says the *Bhāgavatam*'.[33]

With what name, with what language shall we call on Him? Our language is inadequate, the mind is powerless. Can we grasp Him with them? He can be attained only through love.

Many saints and sages have spoken about love:

Śrī Kṛṣṇa says in the *Bhāgavatam*, 'The holy men who have deep-rooted affection for Me and respect My presence in all alike, win Me over as a faithful wife does a dutiful husband.'[34] He also says, 'I am under the control of my devotee. It is as if I am not free.'[35] He who is the ever-free, independent Lord says, 'I am not free—I am tied to my devotee.'

Rāmaprasāda said, 'God, the enjoyer of sweetness; lives happily in the city.' 'In the city' means 'in the heart'. God dwells in the devotee's heart and enjoys the sweetness of love.

Śrī Kṛṣṇa says in the *Gītā*:

Teṣām satatayuktānām bhajatām prītipūrvakam
Dadāmi buddhiyogam tam yena māmupayānti te—

'To these who are constantly devoted and worship Me with love, I grant the concentration of understanding by which they come unto Me.'[36]

Nārada in his *Bhakti Sūtra*s states, 'Devotion is intense love for God.'[37] God has a weakness for love. When there is ecstatic devotion and deep affection, God is attracted. Ordinarily God attracts the devotees to Himself, but sometimes the devotees attract *Him*. Sri Ramakrishna points this out: **Sometimes God acts as the magnet and the devotee as the needle. God attracts the devotee to Himself. Again, sometimes the devotee acts as the magnet and God as the needle. Such is the attraction of the devotee that God comes to him, unable to resist his love.** (p.471) Further, the Master said that the heart of the devotee is God's drawing room; he carries God in his heart.

Meister Eckhart, the German monk and mystic, says that 'Love is like a fisherman's hook.'[38] With that hook one catches God. Sri Ramakrishna says something similar: ***Prema* is like a cord: by *prema* God is bound to the devotee; He can no longer run away.** (p.680) The devotee keeps God bound with the cord of love.

Someone asked Sri Ramakrishna, **'What is *ekāngī prema*?'** The Master replied: **It means one-sided love. For instance, the water does not seek the duck, but the duck loves water. There are other kinds of love : *sādhāraṇī*, *samañjasā*, and *samarthā*. In the first, which is ordinary love, the lover seeks his own happiness; he doesn't care whether the other person is happy or not. That was Candrāvali's attitude toward Kṛṣṇa. In the second, which is a compromise, both seek each other's happiness. This is a noble kind of love. But the third is the highest of all. Such a lover says to his beloved, 'Be happy yourself, whatever may happen to me.' Rādhā had this highest love. She was happy in Kṛṣṇa's happiness. The *gopīs*, too, had attained this exalted state.** (p.766) In this last kind of love, the devotee loves God for no reason, with no expectation. 'I love because I love. I don't know why I love.' This is 'love for the sake of love', which is discussed in the next section.

Love for the Sake of Love

The best devotion of all is 'motiveless love', or 'love for the sake of love'. The *Gītā* says, *Bhaktyā labhyastu ananyayā*—'He can be attained by unswerving devotion to Him alone'.[39]

Unswerving devotion means, 'I don't want anything but God.' Sri Ramakrishna used to pray, 'I don't want people's praise or anything else. I want only pure love.' The Bengali poet D.L. Ray spoke of this pure, motiveless love in a song: 'I don't know whether You love me or not, and I don't want to know. I only know that I love You.'

People may criticize us and say our love is blind, but love is always blind. We love blindly, for no reason. If we ask ourselves why we love, we can't give an answer. We don't say,

'He has this kind of nose, that kind of eyes, etc.' No one reasons this way about the person he loves. If you reason this way, it is not real love. Real love is always blind. 'I love because I love. I don't know why I love.'

The *Caitanya Caritāmṛta* says, 'He who calls upon the Lord with love attains Him.'[40] Here love means motiveless love. There is no expectation behind this love. Someone once asked Swamiji the definition of real love. He answered, 'It is love without desire.' Sri Ramakrishna referred to real love as 'pure love'.

If there is even a trace of self-interest, that love is not 'pure'. 'Give me wealth, give me honour, give me health—I will love you as long as you give me all those.' This is not the way of love. Swamiji called it *shopkeeping*. Real love is desireless; it has no motive. Any other kind of love is not real love. 'I love Him for no reason at all. I suffer because of that love, still I love. If I feel well or don't feel well, if He looks at me or if He doesn't look at me, if He is kind or if He is cruel, I can never think anything but good of Him.' This desireless, motiveless love is real love.

A popular Hindi verse says: 'I don't understand Brahman, I don't understand *māyā*. I also don't understand human beings, and I don't understand all this talk of Vedānta. I don't understand time. I don't even understand myself or whether or not I exist. I have only Krsna—I know only Him.'

Hindu devotional scriptures place much emphasis on disinterested, motiveless love. In the *Bhāgavatam* the Lord says: 'Apart from Me, neither the position of an emperor nor the lordship of *Rasatala*, neither the state of Brahma nor the attainment of all yogic powers—why for that matter not even liberation from the cycle of births and deaths—is desired by a devotee who has completely resigned himself to Me.'[41]

Sri Ramakrishna said, **Prahlāda loved God for the sake of love.**(p.866) Prahlāda said to God: 'One who seeks favours and boons from Thee is not a true servant, a true devotee. He is only a trader masquerading as a devotee.'[42] Swamiji said that devotion is unpaid service. You receive no wages. You are not even a servant; you are less than that. You don't want anything from God, and you don't complain to Him. This is pure, unmotivated love—love for the sake of love.

Sri Ramakrishna says, **While praying to God, ask only for love for His Lotus Feet.** (p.902) According to the *Nārada Pañcarātra*, 'The devotee does not want anything but love for Kṛṣṇa. He has no other desire.'[43] Another Hindu scripture says, 'Those who are inferior devotees with small intellects practise yoga to get occult powers.'[44] A real devotee wants nothing but love. The Holy Mother said: 'Ask nothing from God. If you must ask for something, ask for desirelessness.' She also said: 'You can ask Him for devotion. The desire for love cannot be counted as a desire.'

Sri Ramakrishna mentioned Ahalyā as an example of pure love. He said, **When Rāma redeemed Ahalyā from the curse, He said to her, 'Ask a boon of Me.' Ahalyā said, 'O Rāma, if You deign to grant me a boon, then please fulfil my desire that I may always meditate on Your Lotus Feet, even though I may be born in a pig's body.'** (p.902) Ahalyā was turned into stone for committing a transgression. Her transgression would not have been regarded as serious for anyone else, but her husband was the great sage Gautama and he could not tolerate even the appearance of a fault. When he cursed her he said, 'After you have spent several thousand years in this condition, Śrī Rāma, the son of Daśaratha, along with his brother Lakṣmaṇa will be coming to this place. When he places his feet on the rock with which you will now gain identity by my curse, you will be freed from sin.'

What happened when Rāma arrived to redeem Ahalyā by stepping on the rock is described in the *Adhyātma Rāmāyaṇa*:

'Rāma . . . saluted Ahalyā. . . . Seeing Rāma, . . . Ahalyā shed tears of joy. She remembered the words of Gautama and recognized Rāma to be Nārāyaṇa Himself. That holy lady, with her eyes brimming with tears, worshipped Rāma in due form. . . . Then falling before him in full prostration and getting up, she saw the lotus-eyed Rāma once again, and with horripilations all over her body, and voice choking with emotion, began to praise him with a hymn:

'O Thou Indweller of the whole universe!
Blessed am I with the contact I have had
with the particles of dust adhering to Thy Lotus-feet—
The feet which form only an object of quest
for Brahmā and Śaṅkara with yearning hearts,
But which I have now been fortunate
to contact even with my physical body. . . .
O Lord! Wherever I might be and at all times,
May I have unobstructed devotion to Thy Lotus feet!'[45]

There are many illustrations of this motiveless, pure love in the Hindu scriptures:

Sri Ramakrishna gives Nārada as one example. He said: **Nārada went to Ayodhyā to remind Rāma that He was to kill Rāvaṇa. At the sight of Rāma and Sītā, he began to sing their glories. Gratified at Nārada's devotion, Rāma said: 'Nārada, I am pleased with your prayer. Ask a boon.' Nārada replied, 'O Rāma, if Thou must give me a boon, then grant that I may have pure love for Thy Lotus Feet and that I may not be deluded by Thy world-**

bewitching *māyā*.' Rāma said, 'Ask something more.' 'No, Rāma' answered Nārada. 'I do not want anything else. I want only pure love for Thy Lotus Feet, a love that seeks no return.' (p.894)

Śrī Caitanya prayed: 'O God, I do not want wealth, family, a beautiful wife, or scholarship. May I have only desireless love for you in birth after birth. I don't even want liberation. If I must be born again and again, I don't mind. But may I always have desireless love for Thee!'[46]

In the *Brahmavaivarta Purāṇa*, Rādhā says to Yaśodā: 'Śrī Kṛṣṇa is Consciousness, and I am his Śakti [power]. Ask me for whatever you wish. I will give you what even the sages cannot get.' Yaśodā said: 'Do you know what I want? I want unwavering devotion to God, and to be His servant. That is all I want.'[47]

Tulasīdāsa said: 'I don't want happiness in heaven after death. I don't want learning, and I do not even want to be a great scholar. I don't want wealth, or miraculous powers or great honour. I only desire pure love for the feet of Rāma, and that love will increase day by day.'[48]

In the *Nārada Bhakti Sūtras* it is said that pure love is the only thing to be desired. 'If you get that love, you want nothing more. You should pray only for this.'[49]

Sri Ramakrishna and his disciples are the greatest of all exemplars of this pure love. Swami Vivekananda demonstrated this love when he endured uncomplainingly the Master's utter indifference to him for weeks on end. The Master refused to look at him or talk with him when he came to see him. He was testing Swamiji. At last, when the Master asked him why he continued to come when he received no love or attention, Swamiji said, 'I come because I love you.' He had nothing but pure love for the Master. It was this Swamiji whose pillow would be soaked with tears every night after the Master passed away—he had so much love for him.

Sri Ramakrishna often talked about this pure love. He used the expression, 'Leaping from a palm tree without grasping at anything.' He meant: 'I don't know whether or not I will realize God. I'm not concerned with this world or the next, but still, such is God's attraction that even if I don't reach Him, I must run after Him.'

The Master used the example of the hereditary farmer to further explain pure love. The hereditary farmer never stops farming whether there is rain or not. The real devotee keeps calling on God whether God listens or not. He likes to chant His name, so he chants His name. The joy of chanting God's name completely fills his heart. God may or may not give him something; he does not have time to think of that. This is pure, unmotivated love.

Sri Ramakrishna said: **I prayed to the Divine Mother only for love. I offered flowers at her Lotus Feet and said with folded hands: 'O Mother, here is Thy ignorance and here is Thy knowledge; take them both and give me only pure love for Thee. Here is Thy holiness and here is Thy unholiness; take them both and give me only pure love for Thee. Here is Thy virtue and here is Thy sin; here is Thy good and here is Thy evil; take them all and give me only pure love for Thee. Here is Thy *dharma* and here is Thy *adharma*; take them both and give me only pure love for Thee.** (p.902)

The Master used to say that devotion is more difficult to attain than Knowledge, that is, knowledge of the Self—another name for liberation. Holy Mother said, 'Liberation is easy to get, but God does not readily give devotion.' Śrī Kṛṣṇa says the same thing in a song that Sri Ramakrishna liked to sing:

> **Though I am never loath to grant salvation,**
> **I hesitate indeed to grant pure love.**
> **Whoever wins pure love surpasses all;**
> **He is adored by men;**
> **He triumphs over the three worlds.** (p.228)

We find an example of this pure love in how the two disciples of Sri Ramakrishna, Latu Maharaj and Sarat Maharaj, behaved on the famous Kalpataru Day, the first January of 1886. The Master had unexpectedly left his sick bed and gone downstairs and out into the garden at the Cossipore country house where he was staying. There, in response to a remark Girish Ghosh made, he went into an ecstatic mood and started showering blessings on all those present. This created a big uproar. Everybody was rushing to Sri Ramakrishna for his blessings.

While all this was going on below, Latu Maharaj and Sarat Maharaj were using the opportunity to air the Master's bedding and clean his room. They could hear the noise below but they did not go down leaving their work. Later someone asked Sarat Maharaj why they had not gone down and received the Master's special blessings. He replied, 'We were busy airing his bedding and cleaning his room quickly, before he came back up. Besides, the thought of getting something from him never entered our minds. He was our own!'

This is pure love, 'He was our own.' He will give us what we need. Why would we ask him for anything? We are his servants; we want nothing from him. We are happy with whatever he gives, and when he gives it. And if he gives nothing, we are also happy.

We find another example of this pure love in the behaviour of one attendant-monk of Mahapurush Maharaj. Mahapurushji was then president of the Order. He was very sick, his eating and drinking being strictly regulated by the doctors. He was told to take only a thin broth. One day he said, 'Bring me everything that has been offered to Thakur in the temple. I want to eat today.' Everyone was aghast. Breaking his dietary regime would be sure to make his condition worse, but no one said a word except the attendant who said, 'Maharaj, though it may be a sin, I will not give you any of that to eat.'

It is as if he were saying, 'I am your servant and I will do what is good for you. You want me to give you something to eat that the doctor has forbidden and which will make you even sicker. I can't do that. You may be angry; you may curse me—still I will not give you something that will harm you.' This is real love. A devoted attendant, a real devotee should be like that.

Swami Brahmananda used to say: 'Do you know what real love is? The beloved does not know that he is loved, and the lover does not realize that he loves.' Loving and serving the beloved are kept secret. The more love is hidden, the sweeter it is.

Swamiji said in a poem: 'Give, Give away—whoever asks return, His ocean dwindles down to a mere drop.' Give everything you have, but never barter. Take no account of what you give. Be like the tree which only gives and goes on giving, and receives nothing.

In India there are many stories about devoted service to the guru. Sometimes the guru torments his disciple and puts him through many hard tests, yet the disciple endures everything with a smiling face. He continues without respite to serve the guru. Swamiji used to say, 'Stay like a dog near the guru.' Some days the dog is given something to eat; some days it is beaten with a stick—still the dog stays with his master. Love God like that. Don't desire anything. 'I don't know why I love, I just go on loving.' That is real love.

The Devotee and his Relationship with God

The devotee plays with God in many ways. God tests the devotee, but the devotee also tests Him, The devotee wants to find out whether or not God really exists, whether or not He hears his prayers—so he tests God.

He finds that God sometimes fulfils his childish, whimsical demands, yet sometimes God seems to be merciless. When He is cruel, the devotee thinks that God is testing him. He may feel as if he were dying, but God watches unconcerned. Still the devotee knows that he is being tested so he doesn't desert God. 'You may give me suffering and hardship, but I will still cling to you. In good times and in bad times, in happiness and misery, in victory and defeat—under all circumstances, I am devoted to You.' One song Sri Ramakrishna liked expresses this idea: 'You may want to leave me, but Mother, I will not leave You. I will always stay at Your holy feet. I will be the bells that make a tinkling sound on Your anklets.'

God and His devotee sometimes play hide-and-seek. There is much beauty and sweetness in this conception. In this play there is suffering, but that suffering is sweet. Sometimes the devotee laughs, sometimes he cries. If I don't see God, there are tears, but after that, when God comes, there is great joy. Tears are the price we pay for smiles. If there are only smiles, then they aren't worth much.

Bhakti Yoga, the Path of Devotion, is full of variety. The Master says that it is like music in which many instruments are playing together. There are many melodies, many themes—

enchanting variations. It is the path of adventure. You never know what will happen next.

Our devotional scriptures contribute to this fascinating aspect of Indian culture. They are a vast treasury of myths and legends, hymns and songs. They often describe in detail different forms in which God has been experienced by devotees. From a countless number of images, we cite a few examples:

—*Śiva*. He is like a silvery mountain; the crescent moon is his ornament. In one of his four hands is a hatchet, in another a deer. With the third hand he bestows boons, and with the fourth he grants liberation. Sitting in the lotus-posture on a tiger skin, he is ever-content. All the gods praise him. He existed at the beginning of the world; he himself is the root-cause of the world. With his three eyes and five faces, he removes the fears of all.

—*Rāma*. Tulasīdāsa says that Rāma's two eyes are like full-blown lotuses. His face and hands and feet are also like lotuses, and the bottoms of his feet are red like a lotus. His body is the colour of a dark blue cloud.

—*Śrī Kṛṣṇa*. He is the most popular of all Indian deities. He is pictured in many different ways—as Gopāla, the playful little boy, as the beloved companion of the cowherds, and the lover of the *gopīs*. Then as the revered teacher, Śrī Kṛṣṇa delivers the wonderful message of the *Bhagavad Gītā*. The poet Govindadāsa in one of his poems says, 'Śrī Kṛṣṇa's charm has spread all over the world; the whole world is entranced. The sweet smile on his face makes everyone swoon.'[50] (We also see this 'sweet smile' on the face of Sri Ramakrishna. It is not an ordinary smile. Devotees can see this smile on the faces of their Chosen Ideals, but ordinary people can't see it.)

—*Kālī*. The image of Kālī is a startling one. We ordinarily like to think of God as being very beautiful and sweet. But in India we sometimes worship God in a dreadful form, such as Śiva in his destructive aspect or the form of Mother Kālī. **The Mother . . . stands on the prostrate body of Her Divine Consort, Śiva. . . . She wears a golden garland of human heads, and a girdle of human arms. . . . She has four arms. The lower left hand holds a severed human head and the upper grips a blood-stained sabre. One right hand offers boons to Her children; the other allays their fear. . . . She deals out death, as She creates and preserves.** (p.9)

God is sweet, God is beautiful. This same God is also harsh, merciless and destructive. God is all these. There are not two powers, but two aspects of the one God. In the world there is creation and destruction, happiness and misery, smiles and tears. 'I love God in whatever way he comes to me. I love because it is my nature to love.'

Swamiji had this kind of love. In his poem 'Kālī the Mother' he says:

Who dares misery love
And hug the form of death,
Dance in destruction's dance
To him the Mother comes.[51]

Sister Nivedita was also devoted to Kālī. When the lightning flashed she cried, 'Kālī, Kālī, Kālī!' She saw the Divine Mother in the terrible aspect of nature. Kālī is terrible and also beautiful. She is music, She is the moon, She is poetry, She is a flower, She is sad, She is smiling, She is weeping, She is pain, She is death, She is frightful, She is terrible—still She is my Mother, my very own.

Once Holy Mother's cat annoyed her and she picked up a stick to frighten it, but the cat lay down at her feet, as if to seek refuge. We are like that cat. Mother comes to us in a frightening form, but what can we do? We have no one besides Her. We place our head at Her feet.

Rāmaprasāda was a great devotee of Kālī. He describes Her in one of his songs:

Who is the Woman yonder who lights the field of battle?
Darker Her body gleams even than the darkest storm-cloud,
And from Her teeth there flash the lightning's blinding flames!
Dishevelled Her hair is flying behind as She rushes about,
Undaunted in this war between the gods and the demons.
Laughing Her terrible laugh, She slays the fleeing *asuras*,
And with Her dazzling flashes She bares the horror of war. (pp. 619-20)

In another song Rāmaprasāda says:

Taking the name of Kālī, dive deep down, O mind,
Into the heart's fathomless depths,
Where many a precious gem lies hid.
But never believe the bed of the ocean bare of gems
If in the first few dives you fail;
With firm resolve and self-control
Dive deep and make your way to Mother's realm.

(p.124)

In still another song, Rāmaprasāda is a plaintive child complaining to his mother:

I will not call you Mother anymore,
O Mother, you give me so much pain!
I was a householder; you made me a monk,
Now I go from door to door with my begging bowl
and will not return to you.
Again and again I have called you,
But you are deaf and blind.
Your child is suffering so much when his mother is alive,
She might as well be dead!

Besides these gods and goddesses in the Indian tradition, there are countless remarkable devotees. Many stories have been told about them. One fascinating incident concerns Sanātana, one of Caitanya's dearest companions.

When Sanātana lived in Vṛndāvana, he used to go to the house of a brahmin widow for alms. The widow worshipped an image of Śrī Kṛṣṇa. Sanātana fell in love with this image and longed to be near it and serve it, but he could say nothing. Whenever he looked at the image, it seemed that Kṛṣṇa was also looking at him. Kṛṣṇa seemed to be calling to him, so he went every day to see him.

The widow had a son named Sadan. Sanātana noticed that the widow saw Śrī Kṛṣṇa in that son. She seemed to have two sons, Kṛṣṇa (in the image) and Sadan. Kṛṣṇa was Sadan's elder brother; what she gave Kṛṣṇa to eat, she also gave to Sadan. One day Sanātana said to the widow, 'Mother, you see Śrī Kṛṣṇa in the form of your son; that is not right. It is a hindrance to his worship. It would be better to worship Kṛṣṇa in the proper way.' The widow agreed and decided to worship and serve Kṛṣṇa only in the image. After she had done this for some time, Śrī Kṛṣṇa appeared to her in a dream and said: 'What are you doing? I can't eat anything. You don't take care of me properly. We were two brothers, Sadan and I. We used to eat together. Do as you used to do; feed us together.' So the widow again began to worship as she had before, seeing God in her son as well as in the image. Sanātana understood his error and did not protest.

As days passed by Sanātana became more and more eager to serve Kṛṣṇa. Kṛṣṇa seemed to understand his longing and he said to the widow, 'I want to go to live with that holy man.' Sanātana was very happy, but he was worried because he was so poor. He said to Śrī Kṛṣṇa: 'What will I give you to eat? The widow feeds you with so many good things. I can't give you all that.' Śrī Kṛṣṇa said: 'Whatever you eat, I will also eat. Every day you eat a ball of coarse meal. Give me the same, only roast it.' This was done. Every day Kṛṣṇa ate the ball of roasted coarse meal—there was not even any salt. The diet was very monotonous.

At last Kṛṣṇa could stand it no longer. He told Sanātana: 'I can't stand this. Day in day out, this ball of meal. Sometimes give me something good to eat.' Sanātana said: 'I told you before that I have no money to buy good food. You yourself will have to arrange for something better.' And Śrī Kṛṣṇa did just that.

Shortly afterwards a merchant ship was forced to stop there because of an obstruction in the river. The owner of the ship came and said to Sanātana: 'I am in great danger, please save me. I am carrying a very valuable cargo. If you help me, I'll give you money.' The obstruction miraculously disappeared and the ship was released. The merchant then gave Sanātana the money he had promised, and a temple for Śrī Kṛṣṇa was built. Every day there was worship, and delicious food was served. But Śrī Kṛṣṇa could not rid Himself of the habit of taking the ball of coarse meal; and to this day, every day that ball of meal is included in the offered food at that temple.

God and His devotee sometimes play together this way. There is much variety in the path of Devotion—various colours, various notes, various moods—no monotony. Sri Ramakrishna said: **His feeling does not flow in only one direction. He feels both the ebb-tide and the flood-tide of divine emotion. He laughs and weeps and dances and sings in the ecstasy of God. The lover of God likes to sport with Him. In the Ocean of God-Consciousness he sometimes swims, sometimes goes down, and sometimes rises to the surface—like pieces of ice in the water.** (p.277)

The World in the Eyes of the Devotee

The special characteristic of the follower of the path of Devotion is that he does not deny the world. Sri Ramakrishna says, 'The best devotee accepts both the *nitya* and the *līlā*, the Absolute and its manifestation.' The *jñānī*, the follower of the path of Knowledge, accepts only the Absolute. To him, the world is a dream; Brahman alone is real. But the devotee accepts the *līlā*, the world. God is everything. The devotee does not have any mood, any emotion, any thought that is not centred in God. His whole life, all his activities, are God-centred. To him life is a drama and God Himself is the central character. Nothing is insignificant because everything is related to Him.

A prayer in the *Śrīmad Bhāgavatam* stresses God's presence in everything: 'May our words be devoted to the narration of excellences! May our ears be always hearing accounts of Thy deeds! May our hands be ever engaged in Thy work! May our minds ever rest in constant remembrance of Thy feet! May our heads always remain bowed in reverence before Thy habitation, the whole universe! And may our eyes be ever engaged in seeing Thy devotees who are really Thy embodiments!'[52] With his body, mind, and intellect—with all his being—the devotee wants to enjoy God's play.

Sri Ramakrishna says that devotees enjoy their play with God. They don't want liberation. *Mukti nirādara bhagati lobhāne*—'I don't want liberation, I want love.'[53] The devotee says: 'I don't want to be sugar; I want to eat sugar. I don't want to become one with God; I want to be different from Him and play with Him.' The *jñānī* says that he does not want to be born again because this world is unreal to him. But the devotee wants to come back again and again; he wants to enjoy the divine play of God.

Sri Ramakrishna used to tell the story of Nikaṣā, Rāvaṇa's mother. When Rāma entered Laṅkā he saw Nikaṣā running away. Lakṣmaṇa said to Rāma, 'Look, all of Nikaṣā's sons have been killed, yet she is still attached to life and wants to live.' Nikaṣā overheard him and said: 'That is not so, Lakṣmaṇa. I am not fleeing because I am afraid of death but because I have not satisfied my desire to see Rāma's divine play. If I am alive, I will be able to see more of His divine play; that is why I was running away. I am no doubt attached to life, but this attachment is for Rāma, to see his divine play.'

Rabindranath Tagore has said, 'I don't want to die in this beautiful world.' To the devotee this world is beautiful; God's beauty is manifested in everything. To him, *saṁsāra*, the world, is 'a mansion of mirth'. He doesn't want to leave it. His love for the world is intense and intimate because he does not see the world, he sees only God, his dearest one, who is in all things and all beings. Whatever he sees is God's image. 'His image is in the temple, but with my eyes closed I see that image within my heart. Then when I open my eyes, I see that same image, his moving image which is everywhere with various names and forms. I can't turn my back on anyone or criticize anyone. I love everyone and can't help loving them.' This is the way of the devotee.

Tukārām, a sixteenth-century saint, was a great devotee of Śrī Kṛṣṇa. His father had been a prosperous farmer, but Tukārām's mind was torn between God and the world. He tried to farm, but he was completely ruined. He had two wives, one of whom died, and the other abused Tukārām so much that at last he was obliged to leave home. After that he wandered about singing God's name and glories and serving people. His mind was completely given to God. Sometimes he was able to eat, and sometimes not. If he could gather together some rice, he would give it to the first hungry person he saw. He served people as much as he could, always uttering the name of Kṛṣṇa.

Everywhere there are people who think, 'Holy persons should think only of God. Why should they be concerned about others? The world is ephemeral, people are also ephemeral. Why should anyone worry about them?' These people said to Tukārām: 'Tukārām, you say that you have surrendered yourself at the feet of Śrī Kṛṣṇa, that you do not know anything but Kṛṣṇa—then why are you wandering about loving and caring for men and women?'

Tukārām answered: 'Śrī Kṛṣṇa is my husband; I am His wife. My love for Kṛṣṇa completely fills my heart. Since I am His wife, I am always taking care of my mother-in-law, father-in-law, sister-in-law, brother-in-law—all Kṛṣṇa's and my relatives. I serve them because Śrī Kṛṣṇa loves them. The whole world is His. All men and women and children are His near and dear ones. They are dear to Śrī Kṛṣṇa, so they are also dear to me. By serving them, I am serving Him. If Śrī Kṛṣṇa is happy, I am happy, because I am His wife and maidservant.' Like Tukārām, all real devotees see the world this way.

When the monks of the Ramakrishna Order started to serve the sick in northern India, other monks criticized them. They called our monks, *bhāṅgī sādhus*—'scavenger monks'. They noticed that the Ramakrishna monks even cleaned the excrement of sick people. This was work for scavengers, hence the name, 'scavenger monks'. Later the Ramakrishna monks came to be respected and revered by the other monks in the area.

Swamiji has said, 'Serving living beings is worshipping God.' A human being is more than a mere man or woman—he is God Himself. The Sanskrit term used is *nara-nārāyaṇa*—man is God. Sri Ramakrishna uttered this truth; and Swami Vivekananda proclaimed it to the whole world. In a poem, 'To a Friend', Swamiji has written:

From the highest Brahman to yonder worm,
And to the very minutest atom,
Everywhere the same God, the All-love;
Friend, offer mind, soul, body, at their feet.
These are His manifold forms before thee,
Rejecting them, where seekest thou for God?
Who loves all beings without distinction
He indeed is worshipping best his God.

This is not a new truth. There are well-known Sanskrit verses that say the same thing, for example: *Sarvaṁ khalvidaṁ brahma*—'All this is indeed Brahman,' *Brahmamayaṁ jagat*—'The world is Brahman,' *Jīvo brahmaiva nāparaḥ*—'The individual soul is not different from the Supreme Soul [Brahman].' But Sri Ramakrishna and Swami Vivekananda have given us a new understanding of these words. They say that religion does not mean aversion to the world, it means acceptance of the world after understanding it to be God's manifestation. When you see the world in this way, you can work for the welfare of all. If your mind has become stainless, if your self-centredness has been rooted out through the practice of spiritual disciplines, then whatever you do is for the welfare of others.

Swami Brahmananda has said: 'People say, "I will work for the welfare of the country." This is an indigestion of English education. No one can work for the good of the country without first building up his own character. If anyone gives his mind to God and worships Him, his thoughts and work will be for the good of others.' The *Bhāgavatam* emphasizes this teaching. It says that just as when you water the root of a tree, you water the whole tree— its trunk, branches, leaves, etc.; similarly, when you worship God, all beings get the benefit and rejoice, because God is in every creature. The ordinary conversation, glances, laughter, even the scoldings, of those holy persons who are always worshipping God are for the good of all. Such persons transform the lives of many by their mere presence. They may live far from human society, but by their lives and thoughts they benefit the world.

Some people believe that holy persons are a burden to society. What do they give to the world? They sit silent; they depend on others for their food and clothing. But in reality, they are the real treasure of society. In any country, in any age, they are the true aristocrats. People can't recognize them, so they may neglect them. But love, purity, discrimination, dispassion, etc.—the qualities for which a man can truly be called a *man*—are found to perfection in them. Unobserved by most, in age after age they preserve those treasures of heart and mind. Culture and civilization exist because of them. Society is eternally indebted to them. They are not burden—they are our most precious possession.

One such holy man was Pavhari Baba. When a snake bit him he said, 'This is a messenger from my Beloved.' The snake was not a snake to him—it was God Himself who had come to show His love. In another incident, a tiger was about to seize a holy man and he said, 'My Beloved has sent a messenger to accompany me.' This is the way a holy person sees things. He knows that even death comes from God, so he welcomes it with a smile.

Not just holy persons, all real devotees see God in everything and in all circumstances. Rabindranath Tagore said, 'I do not pray to be saved from danger; I pray to be fearless in danger.' Blows may come, afflictions may come; I won't ask God not to give them to me. I will pray: 'May I be able to accept these blows, and give me even more of these troubles, Lord! Can You give me anything more? Happiness and misery are the same to me. You give suffering, so it is sweet to me. Happiness is sweet, and suffering is also sweet—because they both come from You.'

A frog was a great devotee of Rāma. One day Rāma accidentally mortally wounded it. The frog didn't say a word. Rāma was puzzled and said, 'Why didn't you tell me you were hurt?' The frog replied: 'Before when I was hurt, I would call out, "Rāma, Rāma!" But now that You Yourself have wounded me, who can I call on? That is why I am silent.' When the devotee sees that God is doing everything, he accepts even death as a gift from Him.

Sri Ramakrishna says, **However much a *bhakta* may experience physical joy and sorrow, he always has knowledge and the treasure of divine love. This treasure never leaves him.** (p.276) What is this treasure? It is the realization that, 'In happiness and in misery, God is my own; He is all that I possess. I will never forget Him. I accept both happiness and misery as gifts from God.' This is our ideal— the tranquility that comes from the awareness that both happiness and misery are good; they both come from God.

Sri Ramakrishna said: **Take the Pāṇḍava brothers for instance. Though they suffered so many calamities, they did not lose their God-Consciousness even once. Where can you find men like them endowed with so much knowledge and devotion?** (p.276)

A man I know had only one son. This son died just after completing his medical course. When the neighbours came to console the father, he said to them: 'Don't pity me. The son was God's. He gave him to me, and now He has taken him away. I am not sad.'

Another man I know reacted in an altogether different way when he lost one of his sons. I went to see him some years later and noticed that he had become, broken. He asked me, 'Can you tell me how long I will live?' I asked him how old his son had been when he died. He answered, 'So many years, so many months, so many days.' He had counted up every day of his son's life; he couldn't forget anything about him. And in fact he did not live much longer—shortly after I saw him he died. The first man was at peace because he depended on God; he accepted both happiness and misery alike. And the second man found every moment painful; to him life was a curse.

The devotee has enormous strength. No accident or event in the world can disturb him. The ordinary person is shattered, but not the lover of God. He has great faith in himself. Steady, firm, unmoving, resolute—he is like an emperor. He may be outwardly poor, but he is inwardly an emperor because he does not expect anything from the world and he is not afraid of anyone. He is not arrogant, but when he fights for his ideal, he does not rely on anyone. He is carefree. 'My Mother is Empress of the Universe, so why should I fear anyone? She is my Protector, who can frighten me? I have nothing to fear from any quarter.'

Sri Ramakrishna and the Path of Devotion

What does Sri Ramakrishna say about the path of Devotion? He says again and again that the most essential element in devotion is intense yearning for God. But it isn't so much what he says—his life is his message. We find this intense yearning for God in his own life.

He once described how intense that yearning was: 'I felt as if someone were wringing a towel in my chest, I suffered so much because I couldn't see the Divine Mother.' He would sob broken-heartedly and people would gather around him. He had so little consciousness of the external world that they seemed to him like shadows. Sometimes he would rub his face on the ground so hard that it bled. Some people thought he had colic pain and others thought his mother had just died.

This intense yearning has been called 'the mad quest on uncharted seas.' A boat without anchor drifts away; no one knows what will happen to it. It might reach the shore, or it might sink—nothing is certain. Still it drifts on and can't stop.

Sri Ramakrishna advanced this way to God. As he passed through the storm of his 'mad quest', his only thought was : 'Where am I going? How can I reach the Divine Mother? I have no support in the whole world; I have turned my face from it and am looking towards God. Can I find the Divine Mother? Does She want to turn Her face to me? What if she doesn't want to reveal Herself to me? Can I keep on living like this?' This was the Master's condition.

He would cry to the Divine Mother: 'Mother, You revealed Yourself to Rāmaprasāda, why don't you reveal Yourself to me?' When the bells rang for the evening worship, he would burst into tears and cry bitterly : 'Mother, another day has passed and I have not seen You—one more day has been in vain.' Then one day he thought : 'I call on Mother so much and still She does not answer. Will I never see Her? What good is this life without Her? I don't want to live this miserable life.' He grabbed a sword that was hanging on the wall of the Mother's temple and was about to cut his throat when suddenly something tremendous happened. Sri Ramakrishna later described it:

The buildings with their different parts, the temple and everything else vanished from my sight, leaving no trace whatsoever, and in their stead I saw a limitless, infinite, effulgent Ocean of Consciousness. As far as the eye could see, the shining billows were madly rushing at me from all sides with a terrific noise, to swallow me up. I was panting for breath. I was caught in the rush and collapsed, unconscious. What was happening in the outside world I did not know : but within me there was a steady flow of undiluted bliss, altogether new, and I felt the presence of the Divine Mother. (p.14)

This was the Master's first vision of Mother Kālī. After that, what a wonderful play took place between Mother and son! He performed the worship, but there were no formalities in it, no rules, no *mantras*. He talked with the Mother and sometimes caressed her chin. Putting rice to Her mouth, he would say, 'Eat, Mother, eat!' On some days he would say: 'Shall I eat first? All right, if you want me to, I'll eat.' After feeding himself, he would hold some food to Mother's mouth—as a little boy would to his mother. Sometimes the child would thrust food into the mother's mouth and then see a look of satisfaction on her face—a look that he could not describe.

One day a cat entered the temple when he was about to make the food offering. He said to it, 'Shall I feed you, Mother?' Then he fed the cat some of the food meant for an offering to Mother Kālī. He was seeing God in all beings, even in the cat. Some people noticed this and thought he was breaking all scriptural rules. They reported the incident to Mathur Babu, the temple proprietor. He came shortly after to observe the worship for himself. Wealthy and worldly wise, Mathur Babu was also a great devotee of Kālī. He could understand that he was seeing a wonderful spectacle—the divine *līlā* of Mother and son, and felt fortunate to be able to observe it. He told the temple workers not to interfere in any way with the Master's worship.

As days passed, Mother Kālī became more and more real to Sri Ramakrishna. He once put his hand under Her nostrils and found that she was actually breathing. She talked with him and played with him. Sometimes he saw Her as a young girl running along the upper floor of the temple; he could even hear the tinkle of the anklets on Her feet. Again he would see Her standing on the embankment of the Gaṅgā with Her dishevelled hair flying.

But it was not only as Mother that Sri Ramakrishna saw God. He was related to God in many ways—with the peaceful attitude, as a servant, as a friend, as a parent, as a beloved. He experienced all the traditional ways of seeing God.

Our scriptures say, *Na ca prasādāt tapaso vāpyaliṅgāt*—'One does not realize God by spiritual endeavour without assuming some particular attitude.'[54] Whatever attitude Sri Ramakrishna assumed, he became wholeheartedly absorbed in that. When he was in the mood of a servant, he thought of himself as Hanumān, the devoted monkey who was Rāma's servant. He behaved exactly like a monkey during that period, walking on his hands and feet, and sometimes sitting on a tree. From time to time he would cry 'Rāma! Rāma!'

When he was in the mood of a parent, he thought of himself as the mother of the child Rāma. A holy man showed him his image of the child Rāma, called Rāmalālā, and one day Rāmalālā said to the holy man, 'I want to stay with this holy man.' So Sri Ramakrishna accepted the image and soon became absorbed in the thought of Rāmalālā. He began to see him as a living boy and bathed him and fed him. Rāmalālā always wandered around with the Master. When the Master went to take his bath in the Gaṅgā, Rāmalālā would go along and playfully splash water on him, One day, annoyed with his pranks, Sri Ramakrishna gave Rāmalālā a slap, then he began to cry. With tears in his eyes he said, 'I have hurt my beloved child!' Sri Ramakrishna's experiences with Rāmalālā are amazing. They seem to us to be imaginary, but to Sri Ramakrishna they were real.

When Sri Ramakrishna practised the Vaiṣṇava discipline, he put on all the Vaiṣṇavas' marks, wore a plain white cloth and a white rosary, etc. When he performed the *Śakti* (Tāntric) discipline, he wore a red cloth and put vermillion on his forehead in the traditional manner. Then when he practised the *madhura* discipline, he dressed and behaved exactly like a woman. He thought of himself as Rādhā, Kṛṣṇa's beloved. In all his movements and habits, even in the shape of his body, he became the image of a woman.

He said, 'Whether you eat a piece of cake straight or sideways, it tastes sweet.' However you see God, you get bliss. Sri Ramakrishna experienced God in every possible way—omitting none.

All through his life, he was constantly thinking of God. His whole life was one long prayer—everything else was secondary. He was almost always either chanting the name of God or talking about Him with the devotees. At night when everyone else was sleeping, he did not sleep—he chanted the name of God. For him there was prayer in the morning, prayer in the evening, prayer during the day, prayer at night. He was always talking with his Divine Mother.

We have discussed two kinds of devotion, monkey devotion and kitten devotion. Sri Ramakrishna practised the kitten devotion. He said: 'I don't know anything, I only eat and drink merrily and chant Mother's name.' He accepted whatever Mother did, whatever Mother said. When the monk Totapuri came to teach him Vedānta, Sri Ramakrishna said to him: 'I must first ask my Mother; if she gives her approval I'll learn Vedānta from you.' In little things and in big things, he depended on Mother. Mother was his very life. Happiness and misery, good and bad, blame and praise—all were the same to him. He didn't desire anything except the company of the devotees.

The Master didn't want to be sugar, he wanted to taste sugar. He prayed to the Mother, 'I don't want to be dry, I want to be truly human and enjoy divine bliss.' He was not a dry holy man. He loved to be with the devotees. Whenever he saw a devotee he would eagerly approach him. He didn't expect anything, he just wanted to talk about God with him. That was his only desire.

How captivating his personality was! The leading members of society who came to see him were charmed. He did not flatter anyone, but he respected people's good qualities. He sometimes spoke very frankly, for example to Saurindra Mohan Tagore to whom he said: 'Everyone calls you ***king***; I can't call you that. How can I tell a lie? You are not a real king.' He criticized Bankim Chandra Chatterjee, the famous writer, in front of everyone because Bankim had given a flippant answer to the Master's question, 'What is the purpose in life ?' The Master told him, 'I see you are a big cheat!'

What manliness we see in him! Again, what love! He gives refuge to those who are afflicted and distressed. How much sympathy he has for them! He gives them fearlessness and self-confidence and leads them along the path to the highest good. We notice especially his perception of the divinity in all beings. He saw God even in the thief and the hypocrite whom he referred to as the 'thief-god' and the 'hypocrite-god'. He saw in an English boy the manifestation of Śrī Kṛṣṇa and in a prostitute, the Divine Mother. He says, 'I see everyone is Rāma; I see everything is God.' He had such an abundance of purity, kindness, devotion, renunciation and power that he was truly, the living embodiment of Divine Love.

Sri Rarnakrishna used to say that a *bhakta* never loses 'the treasure of divine love.' We find an inexhaustible store of that treasure in him.

References

1. *Śrīmad Bhāgavatam*, I.6.32-3
2. *Bhagavad Gītā*, XII.5
3. *Ibid.*, VI.34
4. *Bhāgavatam*, VI.12.22
5. *Tripādavibhūti Mahānārāyaṇa Upaniṣad*, 8th Chapter
6. *Vaiṣṇava Padāvalī* (*Cayana*), Khagendranath Mitra et al., 8th Edition pp.105-06
7. *Ibid.*, p.107
8. *Vaiṣṇava Padāvalī* : *Pada O Padakāra*, Dhirendranath Saha, 1975, p.9
9. *Caitanya Caritāmṛta*, *Adilīlā*, 4th Chapter
10. *Ibid.*, *Madhyalīlā*, 2nd Chapter
11. *Yogavāśiṣṭha Rāmāyaṇa*, *Sthitiprakaraṇa*, XXI.56-7
12. *Nārada Pañcarātra*, I.12.39-40
13. *Kaulāvalī Tantra*, 11th Chapter
14. *Pañcatantra*, *Aparīkṣita Kāraka*, 90
15. *Aṣṭāvakra Saṁhitā*, I.11
16. *Kāmadhenu Tantra*, 15th Chapter
17. *Caitanya Caritāmṛta*, *Madhyalīlā*, 19th Chapter
18. *The Synthesis of Yoga*, Sri Aurobindo, Centenary Edition, 1972, p.36
19. *Gītā*, XI.28-9
20. *Ibid.*, XI.31
21. *Ibid.*, X1.41
22. *Ibid.*, XI.45
23. *Vaiṣṇava Padāvalī* (*Cayana*), p.17
24. *Caitanya Caritāmṛta, Adilīlā*, 4th Chapter
25. *Bhaktamāla*, 3rd *Mālā*
26. *New Testament*, St. Luke, XI.9
27. *Songs of Meera* : *Lyrics in Ecstasy*, 1977, p.113

28. *Vaiṣṇava Padāvalī* (*Cayana*), p.40
29. *Bāṅglār Bāul O Bāulgān*, U. Bhattacharya, pp.581-82
30. *Old Testament*, Exodus, XX.5
31. *New Testament*, St. Matthew, VI.24
32. *Bhaktamāla*, 2nd *Mālā*
33. *Caitanya Caritāmṛta*, *Madhyalīlā*, 8th Chapter
34. *Bhāgavatam*, IX.4.66
35. *Ibid.*
36. *Gītā*, X.10
37. *Nārada's Bhakti Sūtras*, 2
38. Meister *Eckhart*, *A Modern Translation*, Raymond B. Blakney, 1941, p.123
39. *Gītā*, VIII.22
40. *Caitanya Caritāmṛta*, *Madhyalīlā*, 8th Chapter
41. *Bhāgavatam*, XI.14.14
42. *Ibid.*, VII.10.4
43. *Nārada Pañcarātra*, II.8.5
44. *Yogatattva Upaniṣad*, 22
45. *Adhyatma Rāmāyaṇa*, *Adikāṇḍa*, 5th Chapter, *Ślokas* : 37, 38, 41-3, 58
46. *Śikṣāṣṭakam*, 4
47. *Brahmavaivarta Purāṇa* (*Kṛṣṇajanma Khaṇḍa*), 111.65
48. *Vinaya Patrikā*, Tulasīdāsa, 103
49. *Nārada's Bhakti Sūtras*, 5
50. *Vaiṣṇava Padāvalī* (*Cayana*), p.30
51. *In Search of God and Other Poems*, p.25
52. *Bhāgavatam*, X.10.38
53. *Rāmacaritamānasa*, *Uttarakāṇḍa*, Tulasīdāsa, *Dohā* 205
54. *Muṇḍaka Upaniṣad*, III.2.4

XIII

The *Madhura Bhāva*

Sunday, June 15, 1884. Sri Ramakrishna arrived in the morning at the garden house of Surendra, one of his beloved householder disciples, in the village of Kānkurgāchi near Calcutta. Surendra had invited him and a large number of devotees to a religious festival. Occasions like this were a source of great happiness and rejoicing to the Master's devotees. . . .

The devotees stood in rows inside the big hall of the garden house to hear the music sung by the professional singers. The floor of the room was covered with a carpet over which was spread a white sheet; a few bolsters, pillows, and cushions lay here and there. (p.444) As was the custom, the musicians first sang about Gaurāṅga (Śrī Caitanya) and his ecstatic love for Śrī Kṛṣṇa. Then they **sang of the episodes in the life of Śrī Kṛṣṇa especially associated with His divine love for the *gopīs* of Vṛndāvana. This was a theme which always appealed to the Master and would throw him into ecstatic moods.** (p.444)

Next the musician sang about the anguish of Rādhā at her separation from Kṛṣṇa. When Sri Ramakrishna heard the song he suddenly stood up. Assuming the mood of Rādhā, he sang in a voice laden with sorrow, improvising the words : 'O friend, either bring my beloved Kṛṣṇa here or take me to Him.' Thus singing, he

completely lost himself in Rādhā and could not continue the song. He became speechless, his body motionless, his eyes half closed, his mind totally unconscious of the outer world. He was in deep *samādhi*.

After a long time he regained normal consciousness and said in the same heart-rending voice : 'O friend, take me to my beloved Kṛṣṇa and make me your bondslave. I shall be your handmaid for ever. O friend, it was you who taught me how to love Kṛṣṇa. O Kṛṣṇa! O Beloved of my soul!' (p.445)

Sri Ramakrishna often improvised lines in songs. For most people this would be difficult to do, but his improvisations came spontaneously; they were very beautiful and moving. In this song the Master identified himself with Rādhā and was crying bitterly for Krsna.

Rādhā is a lover of God, and Śrī Kṛṣṇa is God Himself. Rādhā is the *jīvātman*, the individual soul, and Śrī Kṛṣṇa is the *paramātman*, the Supreme Soul. The name *Rādhā* is derived from *rā*, which means 'to acquire', and *dhā* which means 'running towards'— that is, one hurries to get God or liberation. Rādhā symbolizes the intense feeling, the intense longing, of anyone who is desperate for God-realization. Rādhā and the other *gopīs* say : 'We have renounced shame, hatred, and fear. On one side is God, on the other, all worldly attractions. We have chosen God—Kṛṣṇa is our all-in-all. We know nothing but Him.'

And who is Kṛṣṇa? He is one who attracts. The word Kṛṣṇa comes from the root *kṛṣ*, which means 'to attract'. Śrī Kṛṣṇa attracts everyone. He is the magnet, and the lovers of God are pieces of iron. Can the iron ignore the attraction of the magnet? Can the river flow away from the ocean? Can the devotees keep themselves from Kṛṣṇa? No, Kṛṣṇa draws them to himself. The music of his flute is the call of the Infinite. It beckons us, 'Come! Come to me!' Unable to resist him, we run to Him. People may criticize us and call us crazy, but we know nothing but Kṛṣṇa. Like the *gopīs*, we find worldly life to be nothing. Kṛṣṇadāsa Kavirāja has said of the *madhura bhāva*, 'That love is not of this world.'[1]

The *madhura bhāva* was manifest in Śrī Caitanya. In the latter part of his life he was completely absorbed in the feeling that he was Rādhā and spent his days crying bitterly for Kṛṣṇa. All those who try to realize God through the *madhura bhāva* try to be like Rādhā; she is their model. Sri Ramakrishna also practised the *madhura bhāva* and felt he was Rādhā. Though he experienced the other moods—the peaceful mood, the attitude of a servant, of a friend, of a mother, of a child—his practice of the *madhura bhāva* included and carried to perfection all these other ways of approaching God.

The great woman saint Mīrābāī practised the *madhura bhāva*. At one time she visited Vṛndāvana and wanted to see Rūpa Goswāmī, who was living there; but Rūpa Goswāmī did not want to meet her because she was a woman. He sent a message : 'I live in the groves and do not speak to women.' At that Mīrābāī replied : 'You do not know anything. As long as you think of yourself as a man, you will never understand the Vṛndāvana *līlā*. Śrī Kṛṣṇa is the only man here.' In the discipline of the *madhura bhāva*, we are all women; Śrī Kṛṣṇa is the only man.

The *madhura bhāva* is also found in Christianity. When Catholic nuns take their final vows, they are married to Jesus Christ. As Dr R. Panikkar says, 'It is an essential feature of the Carmelite spirituality to consider Christ as the bridegroom of the soul and to find in that loving union (spiritual marriage) the most perfect transformation into God. . . .'[2]

Another writer says : 'The veil of a Christian nun symbolizes continence in flesh and spirit, holiness to the Lord. It signifies an espousal (marriage), not that harmonious union of two unlike human beings on which conjugal happiness depends, but a far more perfect union of two unlikes— viz. of the human soul and Christ, effected by means of prayer, obedience, and the sacraments.'[3] St. Teresa of Avila, a great nun of the sixteenth-century, used to say, 'I am the bride of Jesus Christ.'

We also find this *madhura bhāva* attitude in certain Muslim lovers of God, chief among them being the Sufi ascetic Fardosi, and the Sufi poets Abu Sayed and Omar Khayyam. Though in some of their poems we find mention of wine, ordinary wine is not meant, but ecstatic love of God. One of the verses of Omar Khayyam's famous poem, *The Rubaiyat*, says :

And, as the Cock crew, those who stood before
The Tavern shouted—'Open then the Door!
You know how little while we have to stay,
And, once departed, may return no more.'[4]

Open the door of your heart, God is calling you. He has sent his messenger; do not delay. If he goes away, he will not come again. Open the door! Don't wait even a moment. 'And, once departed, he may return no more.' The lover must be united with the beloved—the *bhakta* with God.

As the *kīrtana* at Surendra's garden house continues, Rādhā says, **'O friend, I shall not go again to the Jamunā**

to draw water. Once I beheld my beloved Friend under the *kadamba* tree. Whenever I pass it I am overwhelmed.' (The Master again became abstracted. Heaving a deep sigh he said, 'Ah me! Ah me!') The song went on. Rādhā says :

'Even the desire for Kṛṣṇa's presence
Has cooled and refreshed my feverish body.'

Now and then the musicians improvised lines to the music, continuing in the attitude of Rādhā : 'O friends, you can wait. Show me Kṛṣṇa, my Beloved.' Again : 'Do not bother about my ornaments. I have lost my most precious Ornament.' And again : 'Alas! I have fallen on evil days. My happy days are over.' And finally : 'This unhappy time lingers so long!'

Sri Ramakrishna improvised a line himself : 'Are not better times yet in sight for me?' The musicians then improvised : 'Such a long time has passed! Are not better times yet in sight for me?'

The musicians sang Rādhā's words to a friend :

O friend, I am dying! Surely I die.
The anguish of being kept apart
From Kṛṣṇa is more than I can bear.
Alas! to whom then shall I leave
My priceless Treasure? When I am dead,
I beg you, do not burn my body;
Do not cast it into the river.
See that it is not given to the flames;
Do not cast it into the water.
In this body I played with Kṛṣṇa.

Bind my lifeless form, I beg you,
To the black *tamāla's* branches;

Tie it to the *tamāla* tree.
Touching *tamāla* it touches black.
Kṛṣṇa is black, and black is *tamāla*;
Black is the colour that I love.
From earliest childhood I have loved it.
To the black Kṛṣṇa my body belongs;
Let it not lie apart from black!

Rādhā reaches her last extremity. She faints away. (pp.445-46)

By continuously chanting God's name, one experiences ecstatic love of God. There are different stages of spiritual disciplines : hearing about God, singing His praises, remembering Him, worshipping Him, serving Him, regarding yourself as His servant or friend, self-surrender to Him, and perfect fulfilment. Rādhā experienced all these stages, culminating in perfect fulfilment—*samādhi*. (*Samādhi* is not only for *Jñānīs* and yogis; *bhakta*s also experience it.)

Rādhā has fallen to the ground;
She lies there lost to outward sense,
Repeating her precious Kṛṣṇa's name,
And straightway closes both her eyes.
Ah, has the drama reached its end?
What ails you, O delight of Kṛṣṇa?
Only a moment ago you spoke.

Her friends, anointing Rādhā's form
With cool and soothing sandal-paste,
Attempt to bring her back to earth.
Some of them weep in bitter grief;
They cannot bear to see her die.

Some sprinkle water on her face;
Perhaps she will revive again!
But, oh, can water give back life
To one who dies of Kṛṣṇa's love? (pp.446-47)

Seeing Rādha in a state of *samādhi*, her friends chant the name of Kṛṣṇa. When her consciousness returns she sees the *tamāla* tree and thinks it is Kṛṣṇa, because he is the same dark colour as the tree.

The musicians continue to sing :

Kṛṣṇa's name restores her life;
Once more her two eyes gaze around,
But Kṛṣṇa's face she cannot see.
Alas, how bitterly she weeps! (p.447)

Rādhā cries out loudly. She is looking in every direction for Kṛṣṇa but can't find him. At last she turns to Kṛṣṇa's friend, Śrīdāma and cries :

'Where is my Kṛṣṇa? Where is He
Whose name you chanted in my ears?
Bring Him but once before me here!'
Seeing the black *tamāla* tree,
She stares at it and cries aloud :
'There is His crest! I see it clearly!
There is my Kṛṣṇa's lovely crest!'
But only a peacock did she see,
Whose glistening feathers she mistook
For the gay feather on Kṛṣṇa's crest. (p.447)

This intensity of Rādhā's love for God is the beauty of the Rādhā-Kṛṣṇa episode. In India there are many songs and stories about Rādhā. What a wealth of intense feeling we find in our *bhakti śāstras*! Here is a different world. Maybe we can't enter it now, but if we could enter it but once, we would never wish to leave it. We would have no more attachment for this world where there is so much hardship, so much monotony, so much cruelty. We would want to stay in the world of Rādhā.

Caṇḍīdāsa has described Rādhā's condition when she is separated from Krsna :

> What is the matter with Rādhā?
> Sitting all alone,
> Not hearing anyone,
> Her eyes fixed on the clouds,
> Refusing to eat—
> She is dressed in the garb of a nun.

As the verse of Caṇḍīdāsa continues, we find that Rādhā's hair is decorated with flowers. But then she thinks that the flowers are hiding her black hair. At once she uncovers her hair in order to see the black colour—the colour of Kṛṣṇa. She cries, 'My hair is the colour of Kṛṣṇa. I do like to see it because it reminds me of my most beloved, Śrī Kṛṣṇa.' Looking at the clouds, she sees his smiling face and reaches forth with her hand to touch him. The clouds are black and remind her of Kṛṣṇa, so she talks to them.

The blue neck of the peacock is the colour of Śrī Kṛṣṇa— black but tinged with blue, so it seems beautiful. Since she loves Kṛṣṇa, she loves anything connected with him—black hair, black cloud, the neck of the peacock—she loves them all. Kṛṣṇa is in her heart, so she sees him everywhere outside.

Rādhā seems to be meeting Śrī Kṛṣṇa for the first time. To lovers, the Beloved is always new. No matter how many times they see Him, their desire for Him is never satisfied.

Every vision of Him produces the same sweetness. It is for this vision that we say *mantras*, sip holy water, sing hymns, etc. God is never old—He is always new to His lovers.

Rādhā says, 'Who has chanted the name of Kṛṣṇa in my ear? I can't tell you how sweet that name is. I have become mad hearing it and I can't give it up. I try, but my mouth keeps moving, uttering the name of Kṛṣṇa, and my body has become lifeless. Tell me, how can I get Kṛṣṇa?'

The year before, at another *kīrtana* at Surendra's house, Sri Ramakrishna had spontaneously improvised these lines, taking the part of Rādhā, mad with love for Kṛṣṇa : **Whose fault is it, my mind's or His beauty's? . . . In the three worlds I see nothing but my beloved Kṛṣṇa.** (p.212)

What a wonderful state Rādhā was in! She is the best of the lovers of God, and as we have said, those who practise the *madhura bhāva* try to become like her, to have that same intense feeling. Mīrābāī, for example, left behind the royal palace in her search for God. 'Without Kṛṣṇa I am nothing,' she said. Shame, hatred, fear, the attractions of life in the palace—all were as nothing to her.

In the *Caitanya Bhāgavatam* there are fascinating stories about Śrī Caitanya's guru's guru, Mādhavendra. Just seeing a cloud he would lose outer-consciousness—the cloud was dark like the colour of Kṛṣṇa.[5] His heart was full of Kṛṣṇa. His mind was always fixed on him. He was like Rādhā who said, **My eyes are blinded. My ears are deaf. I have lost the power of smell. All my senses are paralysed. But alas, why am I left alone?** (p.212) Śrī Kṛṣṇa has left Rādhā, but has taken her eyes, which only see him, her ears, which only hear him—all her sense-organs. Only she herself is far from him. She wonders why she did not go with him.

Rādhā says : 'My mind does not listen to me. I keep saying to it, "Mind, forget about Kṛṣṇa," but it won't listen. It hurries to him. I don't want to say his name, but my tongue is disobedient; it keeps saying "Kṛṣṇa! Kṛṣṇa!" I close my nose, but still it gets the fragrance of Kṛṣṇa. I don't want to listen to Kṛṣṇa's words, but my ears hear them anyway. All my sense-organs are against me. They are always going towards Kṛṣṇa.'[6] Such is Rādhā's condition that everything reminds her of Kṛṣṇa.

We return to the scene at Surendra's garden-house where the *kīrtana* is in progress. Rādhā is extremely agitated because she can't see Śrī Kṛṣṇa. Seeing her great anxiety, her friends conspire to send a messenger to Mathurā to tell Śrī Kṛṣṇa about Rādhā's condition, and to bring him back to Vṛndāvana. The messenger arrives at Mathurā. **She meets a woman of that city of her own age, who asks her where she comes from. Rādhā's friend says, 'I don't have to call Kṛṣṇa. He Himself will come to me.'** (p.447)

This relationship between God and His devotees is mysterious. Sri Ramakrishna says : 'As the magnet attracts the pieces of iron, God attracts His devotees. Again, sometimes the devotee is the magnet and attracts God to himself. God cannot resist the powerful attraction of the devotee.' The Master also says that if you take one step toward God, He takes ten steps toward you. Again, 'The devotee is the lotus, God is the bee. God flies to the sweet fragrance of his devotee.'

But then sometimes the devotee says, 'I am the machine, You are the operator of the machine. I am the house, You are the dweller in the house. I am the chariot, You are the charioteer.' This is the sport, the *līlā* of God and those who love him. It goes on forever. The devotee doesn't want it to end, and God Himself doesn't want it to end.

Sri Ramakrishna says, 'This is the play of Rādhā and Kṛṣṇa. Rādhā and Kṛṣṇa are one, but this "one" divides itself in two to taste its own sweetness.' We find the same idea in the *Caitanya Caritāmṛta* where it says that Rādhā and Kṛṣṇa are one soul having two bodies. They enjoy together the sweet flavour of love.[7]

Devotees in Bengal sometimes sing this song :

As the fish swims in the water,
  we are day and night floating in the ocean of Kṛṣṇa.
The moon in the sky shines brightly, encircled by the stars;
when morning comes, the moon disappears, along with the stars.
We are like the stars, Kṛṣṇa like the moon;
  as long as Kṛṣṇa is there, we are also there.
When he disappears, we also disappear.
The lightning flashes, lighting up the clouds;
  we become bright when we are near God.
As long as He is with us,
  we are free from suffering.

Śrī Kṛṣṇa says, 'Holy men are verily My heart, and I verily am the heart of holy men. They do not know anything but Me and I, of anything but them.'[8] The devotees are mad for God, and He is also mad for them. Kṛṣṇa also says : 'It is as if I am not free, subject as I am to My devotees. Being fond of my devotees, My heart is under their sway.'[9]

At Surendra's garden-house, the *kīrtana* continues. The messenger from Vṛndāvana, Rādhā's friend, has said, 'I don't have to call Kṛṣṇa. He Himself will come to me.' By what power could she say that? It was the power of love. Love is a rope. The lover binds God with the rope of love.

Hearing the words of the simple messenger, a woman of Mathurā laughs and taunts her. Śrī Kṛṣṇa is a king, and she only a common village girl. Is it possible he will come to her without being called?

In scorn says the woman of Mathurā :
'Oh, you are only a simple milkmaid!
How can you go to see our King,
Our Kṛṣṇa, in your beggar's rags?' (p.447)

The messenger is a milkmaid who knows little of the ways of the world, so in begger's dress she wants to enter the king's palace. She doesn't know that one must wear ceremonial dress. The woman of Mathurā continues to upbraid her :

'Behind seven doors His chamber stands.
You cannot enter. How can you go?
I die of shame to see your boldness.
Tell me, how will you manage to enter?'

But the messenger is not embarrassed. She walks along the road loudly crying.

Says the *gopī* : 'Kṛṣṇa! Beloved!
Soul of the *gopī*'s! Oh, where are You?
Come to me here and save my life.
Where are You, adorable Soul of the *gopī*'s?
Come to me, Lord of Mathurā!
And save the life of Your sorrowing handmaid.
Ah, where are You, Beloved of Rādhā?
Lord of our hearts and Friend of our souls!

O Hari, Destroyer of our shame!
O priceless Treasure of the *gopīs*!
Come to Your handmaid and save her honour.'
(pp.447-48)

Thus the messenger weeps and cries out for Kṛṣṇa. When the musicians sang, 'Where are You adorable Soul of the *gopīs*?' the Master went into *samādhi*. As the music neared its end the musicians sang louder. Sri Ramakrishna was on his feet, again in deep *samādhi*. Regaining partial consciousness, he said in a half articulate voice, 'Kitna! Kitna!' He was too much overwhelmed to utter Kṛṣṇa's name distinctly.

The *kīrtana* was coming to a close. At the reunion of Rādhā and Kṛṣṇa the Master sang with the musicians, composing the lines himself :

Behold, there Rādhā stands by Kṛṣṇa;
On His bosom she reclines.
Behold her standing at His left,
Like a golden creeper twining
Round a black *tamāla* tree! (p.448)

Rādhā and Kṛṣṇa are joined at last in the Nidhu Grove of Vṛndāvana
Incomparable their beauty, and limitless their love!
The one half shines like yellow gold, the other like bluest sapphire;
Round the neck, on one side, a wild-flower garland hangs,
And, on the other, there swings a necklace of precious gems.
A ring of gold adorns one ear, a ring of shell the other;

Half of the brow is bright as the blazing midday sun,
The other softly gleams with the glow of the rising moon.
Upon one half of the head a graceful peacock feather stands,
And, from the other half, there hangs a braid of hair. (p.212)

As the music came to a close the Master led the chorus. All chanted together to the accompaniment of drums and cymbals : 'Victory to Rādhā and Kṛṣṇa! Hallowed be the names of Rādhā and Kṛṣṇa!' The devotees felt a surge of divine emotion and danced around the Master. He too danced in an ecstasy of joy. The names of God echoed and re-echoed in the house and garden. (p.448)

Sri Ramakrishna was an artist. Whatever he did was beautiful and very disciplined. His thinking was not uncontrolled, his conduct was never disorderly, and his words never lacked coherence. His dancing was unique—not like any others. When he danced, everyone would gaze at him in wonder. They would forget the place, the time, the circumstances. They would feel that they had gone to another world. All this is described in *The Gospel* and in *The Great Master*.

There was also an article about this in the Brāhmo periodical, *Dharmatattva*, in its November 1, 1879 issue. (It is surprising that a Brāhmo periodical would write in this way, since the Brāhmos were not in agreement with Thakur on many points.)

From the 25th to the 30th of June, the Brāhmos were gathered at their Belgharia hermitage. [It was called a hermitage because they would meet there for worship and meditation.] Revered Ramakrishna Paramahaṁsa Mahashay made an auspicious appearance there. Seeing his great love of God and divine intoxication, everyone was fascinated. They had never before seen such a state of divine bliss. In the *Śrīmad Bhāgavatam* the signs of divine intoxication are enumerated : 'The devotees, with their minds immersed in God, cried, laughed, engaged in divine conversation, danced, sang, chanted the name of God and His glories, and shed tears.'

In the Paramahaṁsa Mahashay, all of these signs are found. That day, he spoke of the vision of God and the yoga of love, very profoundly. He sang again and again in a state of impassioned love. He was often absorbed in *samādhi*, immobile as an idol, often laughing, crying, dancing, behaving like a drunkard or like a child. He astonished everyone with his profound, spiritual utterances. His divine moods infused all with spiritual ardour; the evil of the evil-doer, the atheism of the atheist were dispelled.

On Sunday the 6th, at the home of Acharaya Mahashay [perhaps Keshab Sen] Paramahaṁsa Mahashay [Sri Ramakrishna] was present. On that day he fully manifested his supreme devotion; only his ecstatic dancing was missing.[10]

There was everything—'only his ecstatic dancing was missing.' From this we can imagine what kind of attraction his dancing had for those who were privileged to see it. But everything about him was attractive because of the intense feeling behind all his actions—his talking, his singing, his dancing.

The dance is successful and people respond to it when the dancer is able to manifest his intense inner feeling. Thakur was the emperor of feeling. Because of this people loved his words; they were entranced by his songs, and speechless seeing him dance. It was a heavenly sight—unlike any other. In *Sri Ramakrishna, the Great Master*, there is a description of Thakur's dancing at the festival at Panihati which is held every year in May or June.

The Master went to this festival with some of his disciples in May or June of 1885. The sore in his throat, which later developed into cancer, had just started to trouble him. His disciples were afraid that he would join in the *kīrtana* which was going on in various places in Panihati, and that it might aggravate the pain in his throat. Among those present was a Goswami, elaborately dressed, who was dancing with much posturing, feigning ecstasy, but managing nevertheless to keep the coins people gave him tied up in his wearing cloth. As Thakur and his disciples were watching the Goswami dance, he said, 'Mark the hypocrisy!'

> But the next moment, before the devotees had any idea of the 'how' or 'when' of the matter, the Master, in the twinkling of an eye, came down in one bound to the middle of the *kīrtana* party and passed into ecstasy, losing all consciousness. The devotees then hurried down . . . and stood around him. He sometimes gained partial normal consciousness and danced with the stride of a lion, and sometimes lost outward awareness and stood still. Dancing under the influence of the spiritual emotions, he was now proceeding, now receding with a rapid step to the timing of the music. He seemed like a fish swimming about in great delight in a sea of bliss. Each movement of his limbs clearly indicated it. . . . When his body, overflowing with the intense joy of divine feeling, swayed to and fro with quick steps, one

seriously wondered whether it was made of any solid, physical substance at all. One felt as if waves, mountain high, rose in a sea of bliss, and were going forward carrying everything before them and merging that very moment in the sea, liquid in liquid, only to vanish out of sight. . . .

We have witnessed many beautiful dances full of gesture by both male and female dancers, but never did we have a glimpse of that happy synthesis of power and beauty as we did in the unrestrained and yet perfectly balanced dance of the Master, when he lost himself in the divine moods of spiritual emotions.[11]

To return to the *kīrtana* at Surendra's garden house : The *kīrtana* has come to an end. **The Master went to an adjoining room and began to talk with some devotees there. He said : 'How wonderful was the yearning of the *gopīs* for Kṛṣṇa! They were seized with divine madness at the very sight of the black *tamāla* tree.'**(p.449)

When Śrī Kṛṣṇa went to Mathurā, the *gopīs* wept piteously for him. Uddhava, Kṛṣṇa's friend, came to Vṛndāvana to console them. 'Why do you long so intensely to see Śrī Kṛṣṇa?' he asked. 'Kṛṣṇa is all-pervading. Through meditation and worship you can see him within your own minds.' But the *gopīs* replied, 'Udho, we do not have many minds. We have only one mind, and that mind has gone away with Kṛṣṇa. Without a mind, how can we meditate? We are ignorant women; we do not understand the all-pervading Kṛṣṇa. We only know that he is Rākhāl of Vraja and that he is very dear to us.'[12] (They called *Uddhava Udho*.) 'We can't practise yoga and meditation—these things are not for us. You tell us to close our eyes, but with these eyes we are always seeing Kṛṣṇa. Can't you understand?'[13]

The *gopīs* then became very angry and said to Uddhava, 'You are deceitful. Your words are very sweet, but you are a hypocrite. We will not listen to you any more. Like yogis we will pierce our ears and wear matted hair? We can't endure such hardship! Do we need to smear our bodies with ashes? We are burning day and night from separation from our Kṛṣṇa; ashes come from that fire—why would we need other ashes?

'Look, Udho, yogis practise meditation to attain Him. We already have him. He is very dear to us. Not for one moment is he separated from our minds. What do you know about this? Like the body and its shadow, Kṛṣṇa and we are never separated.'

That is the *gopīs*' feeling—pure love, only love. 'Kṛṣṇa is our all. The whole world is full of Kṛṣṇa.' The Master explains this : 'The *gopīs* were thinking of Kṛṣṇa so intensely that they actually saw him in all beings. They even thought that they themselves were Kṛṣṇa. It seemed to them that the whole world was meditating on Kṛṣṇa—eager for his touch.'

They said, 'This grass growing on the earth—do you know what it is? It is nothing but the earth's hair standing on end. The earth shivers in ecstasy at the touch of Śrī Kṛṣṇa, and grass is its hair standing on end in bliss.' Seeing the trees they said, 'Do you know why they are standing so fixedly? They are engrossed in the thought of Śrī Kṛṣṇa.' Because of this marvellous imagery, Sri Ramakrishna used to say, 'The mood of Vṛndāvana is unique—unlike anything else. Nowhere else can this kind of giving one's all for God, forgetful of one's own self, be found.'

He said, **Separation from Kṛṣṇa created such a fire of anguish in Rādhā's heart that it dried up even the tears in her eyes! Her tears would disappear in steam.** (p.449)

All the other *gopīs* cried because of their separation from Kṛṣṇa, but Rādhā did not cry. She said to them, 'You cry so much for Kṛṣṇa but look at me. How hard my heart is! Not one tear comes from my eyes.' Then Vṛndā said to her, 'Rādhā, you have no tears because as soon as tears come to your eyes, the intense heat of the fire of separation dries them up.' No tears fell from Rādhā's eyes though she suffered more intensely than the other *gopīs*.

A poem, 'Home They Brought Her Warrior Dead', describes a similar scene. When the wife saw the dead body of her warrior husband, she could not cry. Her eyes had a bewildered gaze. She was so grief-stricken that she could not weep; she had become like a stone. Her friends said, 'This is not right—she should cry.' Then they picked up her little child and placed it on her lap. At once she broke into tears; her dammed-up grief burst its bounds.

When one feels very deeply there is no outer expression. The agony of separation was so intense in Rādhā that she could not express it. The poet Vidyāpati writes about her : 'Not a drop of water fell from her eyes; her tears dried up in the fire of her separation from Kṛṣṇa. Unblinking, she could only stare.'[14]

Śrī Caitanya's ecstatic grief is described in the *Caitanya Caritāmṛta* : 'He takes the forest for Vṛndāvana. When he sees a hill, he thinks it is Govardhana.'[15] Again, seeing the ocean, he thinks it is the Jamunā. '"Where is Śrī Kṛṣṇa? Where is Śrī Kṛṣṇa?" Śrī Caitanya is crying. In great agony he wanders about in search of Kṛṣṇa. Suddenly he sees from the garden the ocean, its water sparkling in the moonlight. He thinks it must be the water of the Jamunā and plunges into it.'[16] This is intense devotion—the madness of love.

Sri Ramakrishna says, Y**ou talk glibly about *prema.* But is it such a commonplace thing. Caitanya had this ecstatic love.** (p.202) If you want to understand *prema*, study Caitanya's life.

The Master says, **There are two characteristics of *prema.* First, it makes one forget the world.** (p.202) 'The world' means 'I-ness', 'my-ness'—egotism. 'This is my family, this is my society, this is my world.' We want to put the 'I' everywhere; everything we do revolves around this 'I'. Wealth, friends, social position—they are all for this 'I'. This is what is meant by 'the world'.

But if we have *prema*, we forget the world. It no longer exists for us. The 'I' disappears, and in its place is God. Then whatever we do is unworldly. Ordinary people cannot understand this, so we don't mix with them; our values are different.

One devotee has said : 'This intense love pervades my mind—can I see anything else? My eyes see no one but Kṛṣṇa. Everywhere I see only Kṛṣṇa.'[17] Kabīr has exquisitely expressed this : 'Shall I put collyrium in my eyes? There is no place there for putting anything; Kṛṣṇa completely fills my eyes. Can there be room for anything else?'[18]

The second sign of *prema* is that **one has no feeling of 'my-ness' toward the body, which is so dear to man. One wholly gets rid of the feeling that the body is the soul.** (p.202) The body seems to be only a dream.

We find these two signs of *prema* in Caitanya—forgetfulness of the world and lack of body-consciousness.

He himself has described how he felt : 'Will the day never end? One moment seems like a year. Tears flow from my eyes. Without Govinda, the whole world is empty. The agony of separation burns within—an unquenchable fire! I would like to die—the fire is burning me every moment—but I do not die.'[19]

Narahari Sarkar described Caitanya's condition : 'The golden colour of his body has become pale. He shivers as if he were very cold, then his body becomes wet with perspiration. The next moment he is silent as a painting and as motionless. After a long time he suddenly takes a deep breath and tears flow from his eyes in streams, like the Gaṅgā flowing from heaven. Sometimes he cries, sometimes he sings, sometimes he babbles incoherently.'[20] All for the love of Kṛṣṇa.

Śrī Caitanya revived the Vṛndāvana *līlā*. Before he came, people thought that the Rādhā-Kṛṣṇa *līlā* was a superstition—something imaginary. But seeing how Śrī Caitanya became absorbed in the mood of Rādhā, they had to admit the reality of the *madhura bhāva*. Moreover, some could understand that Caitanya's extreme eagerness for Kṛṣṇa is symbolic of man's deep longing for union with the Supreme Soul, and that Caitanya attained the goal of Advaita Vedānta, oneness with Brahman, when he became united with Śrī Kṛṣṇa. Sri Ramakrishna said, 'Inwardly, Śrī Caitanya was an Advaitin; outwardly he was a devotee who practised the *madhura bhāva*.' It is also said of him that in one body he contained both Rādhā and Kṛṣṇa; inwardly he was Kṛṣṇa and outwardly he appeared as Rādhā. He practised the *madhura bhāva* for the good of the devotees, but how great his renunciation was! How austere his life!

One incident in his life shows how dedicated he was to renunciation.

One of his very dear *sannyāsī* disciples disobeyed him and went for alms to a woman devotee. For this Śrī Caitanya banished him. He was so strict with his *sannyāsī* disciples because he wanted to establish an ideal for the good of the world. Renunciation is of utmost importance because real renunciation culminates in love. He who is able to renounce unconditionally is able to love unconditionally. How much love he had for everyone, how much compassion! Going from door to door, he gave the name of God to all—especially to the sinners, the afflicted, the low-born.

A poem about him says:

If Caitanya had not come,
we would not have understood
the glory or the love of Rādhā
He taught us how to taste
the sweetness of Vṛndāvana.
He came like the *gopī*s of Vṛndāvana
to teach us how to love.[21]

All the aspects of Rādhā's agony of separation from Kṛṣṇa described in the Hindu devotional scriptures are found in Caitanya's life. One example :

In the absence of Kṛṣṇa, day and night he is
trembling;
His incoherent babble shows him to be mad.
Like Rādhā at the sight of Uddhava, he becomes
distraught—
Day and night he raves dementedly.[22]

When Uddhava came to Vṛndāvana, he found Rādhā in a frenzy because of her separation from Kṛṣṇa. Śrī Caitanya had the same madness. And Sri Ramakrishna experienced the same intense grief when during the *kīrtana* he thought of himself as Rādhā.

Today we know where Vṛndāvana is; it was rediscovered by Śrī Caitanya. People had forgotten where it was. Caitanya's discovery of this ancient village is described in *Mahāprabhu Gaurāṅgasundara* by Sudha Sen :[23]

> Travelling around the country, Caitanya arrives in Vṛndāvana. Everyone and everything there recognize him—the people, the trees, the creepers, the animals. They say, 'This is the person who performed so many *līlā*s here. We remember him! Today he has come with a different form. This is a new trick of that deceitful God Kṛṣṇa, the master of beguilement. He played so many tricks on us—no doubt this coming in a new form is another of his tricks.' They say to him, 'Where are you hiding your black colour? We know that the colour of your body is black, but you are now a golden colour—like Rādhā. Inside you are Kṛṣṇa, outwardly you are Rādhā, with "Kṛṣṇa, Kṛṣṇa!" always on your tongue. That's the only sign of Kṛṣṇa.'

For the welfare of all, and to enjoy the sport of the divine *līlā*, Rādhā and Kṛṣṇa took birth in the body of Śrī Caitanya. The description continues :

> All the trees and creepers place their pure flowers and fruit at the feet of their beloved Caitanya, as if they are giving tokens of love to a friend. And Śrī Caitanya lovingly embraces them. Wandering here and there in Vṛndāvana, he comes to a place where two parrots are talking. He can understand their language. The male parrot says,

'Śrī Kṛṣṇa played on his flute and enchanted all the women in the world.' [Here the word *women* means *bhakta*s, devotees. Śrī Kṛṣṇa is the only man in the world ; everyone else is a woman.] 'Kṛṣṇa's flute keeps calling to all the lovers of God. God brings bliss to them all. Glory be to Kṛṣṇa!'

The female parrot replies :

'You say, "Glory to Kṛṣṇa!" Have you forgotten Rādhā? Only if Rādhā is by his side can Kṛṣṇa captivate everyone. If she is not present, he can't attract anyone. And even if he captivates the whole world, he himself has become captivated!'

One must accept both because Rādhā and Kṛṣṇa are not different. They are like Brahman and *māyā*, *puruṣa* and *prakṛti*, *Śiva* and *Śakti*. Śrī Caitanya listens to the parrots' words of wisdom and understands, 'Yes, this must be Vṛndāvana. Where else can the birds speak like this?'

This is how Caitanya discovered Vṛndāvana. All this could be only his imagination, but even if it was only his imagination—what an imagination! Many times imagination brings a sweetness to our lives—how can we call it false? To the lovers of God, the Rādhā-Kṛṣṇa *līlā* is not imaginary; it is real. Still, many have doubts about it.

They ask, 'Is the Rādhā-Kṛṣṇa episode really true?' They want to know if it is historically verifiable. No, there are no historical facts concerning the Vṛndāvana *līlā*. No one can prove that 'it actually occurred. But, for the sake of argument, let us say that there was no Rādhā or Kṛṣṇa no *gopī*s, no cowherd boys, no Śrīdāma or Uddhava—that these were all imaginary characters—what does it matter? If I am a lover of God, it doesn't matter to me. Vṛndāvana is in my heart; Rādhā and Kṛṣṇa are always playing there.

Hearing stories of the outer Vṛndāvana and the Lord's divine *līlā* which was enacted there inspires me to search for the Vṛndāvana within my heart. Sri Ramakrishna used to sing, 'Go seek, go seek, Vṛndāvana in your heart.' The Rādhā-Kṛṣṇa *līlā* may or may not be historically true—that is not the point. The intense longing of Rādhā for Śrī Kṛṣṇa—the longing of man for God—is what is essential. That is what we must try to achieve.

Śrī Caitanya discovered the actual, physical Vṛndāvana, but more importantly, he demonstrated in his life the intense longing of Rādhā for Kṛṣṇa. That longing embodied itself in him. Seeing him people understood that this intense longing for God is nothing fanciful or impossible to achieve. The Master said, **Ah, if anyone has but a particle of such *prema*! What yearning! What love! Rādhā possessed not only one hundred per cent of divine love, but one hundred and twenty five per cent. This is what it means to be intoxicated with ecstatic love of God.** (p.449)

In the modern age we find in Sri Ramakrishna that same ecstatic love of God. Seeing him we understand that the *madhura bhāva* is not mere imagination. For six months he practised that discipline, playing the role of a woman. He wore a sari, ornaments, and everything else that a woman wears. He wanted long hair, but there was no way of growing his own hair long in such a short time, so he wore a wig.

Mathur Babu provided all these necessities. As noted in the previous chapter, he became like a woman in body, mind and speech. His limbs and bodily traits took on all the characteristics of a woman. His nephew Hriday used to see him every day, yet when the Master was seated with several women at Mathur Babu's home, he was unable to recognize him.

One day Mathur Babu himself could not recognize him. *Ārati* was being performed at his house at the time of the *Durgā Pūjā*. The Master, in his woman's disguise, was waving the *cāmara* in front of the image. Afterwards Mathur asked his wife who that woman was. His wife replied, 'Didn't you recognize *Bābā*?' (They called the Master *Bābā*, father.) Many think that this is an impossibility, but it is not impossible. Whatever we see, whatever we think, whatever we desire—it all becomes outwardly manifest. If we have good thoughts, they will be manifested; if we have bad thoughts, they will also be manifested.

When Sri Ramakrishna practised a particular spiritual discipline, his appearance and demeanour would change in accordance with that discipline. This is also seen in Christian devotees. When Jesus was crucified, nails pierced his hands and feet. We can see the many wounds on his body in pictures. Christian devotees sometimes meditate on Jesus thinking : 'It is not Christ, but I who am being crucified. On my body are mortal wounds, and blood is flowing from them.' Some devotees meditate this way so deeply that the wounds, called *stigmata*, actually appear on their bodies. This happened to St. Francis of Assisi and to St. Catherine of Sienna. Several years ago when an old Italian holy man died, on his body were found all the wounds of Christ's crucifixion. So it is not unreasonable to believe that the Master's body could also undergo extraordinary transformations.

When Sri Ramakrishna was practising the *madhura bhāva*, he suffered so much because of his separation from

Kṛṣṇa that he completely forgot about sleeping and eating. Sometimes blood would ooze from his pores; sometimes he would lose outer consciousness. His agony of separation from Kṛṣṇa was exactly like that of Rādhā and Śrī Caitanya as depicted in our devotional scriptures.

He was in this state when he had his first vision of Rādhā. He saw that she was as pure as she was beautiful. After some time she entered into his body. Later he had the vision of Śrī Kṛṣṇa, who also entered his body. He then saw Kṛṣṇa everywhere and could see nothing but Kṛṣṇa. He even thought that he himself was Kṛṣṇa. Rādhā also used to think so intensely of Śrī Kṛṣṇa that she thought herself to be Kṛṣṇa. And she also, like the Master, had the vision of Kṛṣṇa.

One day at Dakshineswar while listening to a reading of the *Bhāgavatam*, Sri Ramakrishna became overwhelmed with ecstasy and saw the figure of Śrī Kṛṣṇa, full of light. From this figure one ray of light emerged and touched the *Bhāgavatam* and his own body. The Master understood from this that the words of God (the *Bhāgavatam*), the lover of God (himself), and God (Śrī Kṛṣṇa) are not different. They are one and the same.

As we have seen, hundreds of years ago Śrī Caitanya revived the *madhura bhāva*. After that, it fell into the hands of unfit persons and became greatly corrupted. Cultured, educated people distrusted it. The Master removed that distrust and once again established the *madhura bhāva*, making it acceptable to sincere religious aspirants. He realized that the *madhura bhāva* is also one way to God, though a very difficult path to follow. It is not for the weak. It demands perfect self-restraint, perfect renunciation, perfect control over body, mind and sense-organs. Without these one should not attempt to follow this path. Sri Ramakrishna says that the *madhura bhāva* should not be taught to those without the proper qualifications. Swamiji is more vehement. He told Asvini Datta, 'Whenever you hear the Rādhā-Kṛṣṇa *kīrtana*, lash the performers!'

It is not that we should despise the genuine Rādhā-Kṛṣṇa *līlā* of the *madhura bhāva*. But the corrupted *madhura bhāva* where there is so much immorality should be condemned.

Sri Ramakrishna says, **Whether you accept Rādhā and Kṛṣṇa, or not, please do accept their attraction for each other. Try to create that same yearning in your heart for God. Yearning is all you need in order to realize Him.**(p.140) **The sum and substance of the whole matter is that a man must love God, must be restless for Him.** (p.449) What kind of restlessness? The kind of restlessness that we see in the lives of Rādhā, Śrī Caitanya, and in Sri Ramakrishna's own life. Like them, we must yearn for God intensely; they are our model.

They are embodiments of yearning. We advance along the path to God keeping the example of their lives before our eyes. They renounced everything for God. Praise, blame, social position, honour, fear—all were as nothing to them. We also can renounce everything. They were mad for God; we also can try to have that kind of madness. We can't exactly be like them, because they were *avatāras*. Ordinary people can't do what they could do. Sri Ramakrishna said, 'I have done sixteen parts; now you do one part.' We must do our one part—going forward inspired by the ideal their lives personify.

We are all mad—some for name and fame, some for money, and some for other things. Why not try once being mad for God? The Master says : **If you must be mad, why should you be mad for the things of the world? If you must be mad, be mad for God alone.** (p.449)

References

1. *Caitanya Caritāmṛta, Madhyalīlā*, Chapter II
2. *The Sanctity of St. John of the Cross and of St. Teresa*, Prabuddha Bharata, June, 1957, Dr R. Panikker
3. *A Catholic Dictionary*, W.E. Addis and T. Arnold, 1955, London, p.592
4. *Rubaiyat of Omar Khayyam*, translated by E. Fitzgerald, Verse III
5. *Caitanya Bhāgavatam,* Vṛndāvana Dāsa, *Ādikhaṇḍa*, Chapter 8
6. *Caṇḍīdāsa Padāvalī*, Biman Bihari Majumdar, 1367, p.148
7. *Caitanya Caritāmṛta, Ādilīlā*, Chapter IV
8. *Bhāgavatam*, IX.4.68
9. *Ibid*., IX.4.63
10. From *Samasāmayik Dṛṣṭite Śrī Ramakṛṣṇa*, pp.12-3
11. *Sri Ramakrishna The Great Master*, 5th Edition, p.947
12. *Bhramaragītā Sāra*, Suradāsa, 1st Edition, p.433
13. *Sur-Granthāvalī* (Suradāsa), Chapter IV
14. From *Padāvalī Sāhitya*, Kalidas Ray, p.215
15. *Caitanya Caritāmṛta, Madhyalīlā*, 17th Chapter
16. *Ibid., Antyalīlā*, 18th Chapter
17. *Suradāsa*, ed. Rajesvara Prasad Chaturvedi, 1st Edition, p.183
18. *Kabīr Granthāvalī*, ed. Savitri Sukla and Rajesvara Prasad Chaturvedi, 1968, p.141

19. *Caitanya Caritāmṛta*, *Antyalīlā*, 20th Chapter
20. From *Pāncśata Batsarer Padāvalī*, Biman Bihari Majumdar, 1367, pp.57-8
21. *Vaiṣṇava Padaratnāvalī*, Sati Ghosh, p.31
22. From *Śrī Śrī Caitanyadeva*, Swami Saradeshananda, 1384, p.311
23. From *Mahāprabhu Gaurāṅgasundara*, pp.144-45

XIV

Jñāna Yoga—The Path of Knowledge

Sri Ramakrishna says, **To know many things is ignorance . . . . The unwavering conviction that God alone dwells in all beings is *jñāna*, knowledge.** (p.899)

The central theme of the Upaniṣads is the Ātman, the pure, non-dual, luminous Self. The Ātman is the God that 'dwells in all beings' which the Master refers to. It is identical with Brahman, the Soul of the Universe. In India, even uneducated Hindus are aware of this truth.

To explain the Ātman, we cited (in Chapter III) a Sanskrit verse :

Eka eva hi bhūtātmā bhūte bhūte vyavasthitaḥ
Ekadhā bahudhā caiva dṛśyate jalacandravat—

'The one Ātman is present in all beings. Though one, It is seen as many, like the moon which is reflected in the water.'[1] There is one Ātman, one Brahman existing in various names and forms. It seems to be many, but in reality it is one. The 'seeming to be many' is a mistake.

Those who take the path of Knowledge must correct this mistake. If they don't see many, but see only the one, they do not even see two. The followers of the path of Devotion see two—God and His devotee. But the followers of the path of Knowledge, the *jñānī*s, call this ignorance. They don't accept the existence of two. There is one Ātman, one Brahman, one indivisible Saccidānanda—nothing else. A favourite verse of *jñānī*s comes from the *Śvetāśvatara Upaniṣad*; it says,

Eko devaḥ sarvabhūteṣu gūḍhaḥ
Sarvavyāpī sarvabhūtāntarātmā—

'The non-dual and resplendent Lord is hidden in all beings.

All pervading, He is the inmost Self of all creatures.'[2]

Still, in everyday life we see the many. There are many kinds of human beings—fat and thin, beautiful and ugly, intelligent and stupid, etc. And there are many different kinds of animals, plants and material objects. The special qualities that differentiate one creature or one object from all others are called *upādhi*s. Brahman has no *upādhi*s, qualities, but they are ascribed to Him. Because of this error, we see the many.

It is *māyā* that causes this error. It is *māyā* that makes us see only the *upādhi*s and not the One. Because of *māyā* we can't understand that we ourselves are Brahman. *Māyā* is difficult to define. It has been called *anirvacanīya*—indescribable, and *aghaṭanaghaṭanapaṭīyasī*—expert in making the impossible possible. It can't be explained. We don't know why *māyā* exists. That it exists we admit, but that is all we can say.

The followers of the path of Devotion acknowledge *māyā* and humbly pray to God, 'O Lord, *māyā* belongs to you, so be gracious and protect us from its spell!' But those who follow the path of Knowledge always try to cut through the net of *māyā* through their own exertions. From the very beginning they have a militant attitude. With the sword of discrimination in their hands, they want to cut asunder the knot of *māyā*. They constantly meditate on one verse : 'Brahman is the only Reality. The world is illusory.'

How can they say that the world is illusory? We see it clearly in front of our eyes. By 'illusory', the *jñānī*s mean 'changeful'. The Sanskrit word for *world* is *jagat* which comes from the verbal root *gam* meaning to move. The Sanskrit word for the world process is *saṁsāra*. *Saṁsāra* comes from *sṛ* meaning to *flow*. This world moves and flows; it is constantly changing—that is why it can never be absolutely real and is called illusory.

We call something real when it is always the same. We say that our dreams, for example, are not real because they cease to exist when we wake up. We can say the same thing about our bodies. They did not exist one hundred years ago and after a few years they will again cease to exist, so our bodies are not real. The same applies to the Taj Mahal. It was built hundreds of years ago, but before it was built it did not exist, and it will not endure forever, so it is not real.

Reasoning this way, we come to the conclusion that nothing in the world is real. We think of it as real, as we indicated above, because of *māyā*, ignorance. Our scriptures say that the world is *rajjusarpavat*—like a rope which in the dim light we mistake for a snake. Or it is *rajataśuktivat*—like the shining mother-of-pearl in an oyster shell which we take for silver. Due to *māyā*, we make this kind of mistake about the world; we do not see it as it really is.

Māyā has two powers, the power of concealment and the power of projection. Truly speaking the world is nothing; Brahman is the only existence, but the true nature of Brahman is covered over by *māyā*. In the darkness we can't see that the rope is a rope or that the mother-of-pearl is mother-of-pearl. This is *māyā*'s power of concealment.

We saw a snake where there was no snake; we saw silver where there was no silver—this is *māyā*'s power of projection. It causes us to see the constantly changing world, though there is nothing but Brahman. Still, whatever false thing we saw had behind it something real. We could see the rope, though we mistook it for a snake; we could see the mother-of-pearl, though we thought it was silver. We are seeing Brahman, but we think it is the world.

But even though we see the world, it is the real substance behind it that gives it its reality. Behind the world that we see is one *adhiṣṭhān*—one Eternal Substance. We call that Eternal Substance Brahman, or Ātman, or *Saccidānanda*, or sometimes only *tat*, meaning *that*.

Many want liberation, but there is no liberation without Knowledge. Śaṅkarācārya said, 'People go to the holy Gaṅgā-sāgar, they make many vows, give gifts and meditate for long hours. Doing all these things they become very pious, but if they do not have Knowledge, they will not attain liberation, even after a hundred births.'[3]

What is liberation? Now I am in bondage because I am ignorant; I have forgotten that I am Brahman, so I continue to perform various actions, good and bad, impelled by desire. To reap the consequences of these actions, I must be born again and again; I must revolve on the wheel of birth and death. Liberation, *mukti*, means getting off of this wheel. Only Knowledge can bring liberation, because only Knowledge is able to destroy the seed of action, *karma*, which comes from ignorance of my true nature, Brahman.

Sri Ramakrishna gives this illustration : **The potter puts his pots in the sun to dry. Haven't you noticed that among them there are both baked and unbaked ones? When a cow happens to walk over them, some of the pots get broken to pieces. The broken pots that are already baked, the potter throws away, since they are of no more**

use to him. But the soft ones, though broken, he gathers up. He makes them into a lump and out of this forms new pots. (p.416)

The *unbaked* pot is a person who has not attained Knowledge; the *baked* pot is a person who has attained Knowledge. As long as we have not attained Knowledge, we will have to return again and again to 'the potter's hands'. We will have to be born again. **But after attaining Knowledge he will not have to come back to this earth or to any other place of existence,** the Master explained. **What is the use of sowing a boiled paddy grain? It will never bring forth a shoot. Likewise, if a man is boiled in the fire of Knowledge, he will not be used for a new creation. He is liberated.** (p.416)

We find a similar example in the *Pañcadaśī* : 'When a seed is fried, it can no longer produce a shoot. In the same way, when a person's desires are destroyed, he no longer experiences the results of his actions.'[4] The *Gītā* also expresses this truth :

Yathaidhāṁsi samiddho'gnirbhasmasāt kurute'rjuna
Jñānāgniḥ sarvakarmāṇi bhasmasāt kurute tathā—

'As the fire which is kindled turns its fuel to ashes, O Arjuna, even so does the fire of wisdom turn to ashes all work'[5] Only the *Prārabdha karma**, action which has already begun to produce its results, continues its course, but the person who has attained Knowledge is unaffected by it.

The force of *Prārabdha karma* maintains the body of that person. As long as that force is not spent, he is a

---

* The three kinds of *karma, prārabdha, sañcita*, and *kriyamāṇa*, have been explained in Chapter IX.

jīvanmukta— one who is liberated while still living in the body.

Sri Ramakrishna says many things about the path of Knowledge. One example: **The *jñānī*, sticking to the path of Knowledge, always reasons about the Reality, saying, 'Not this, not this'. Brahman is neither 'this' nor 'that'; It is neither the universe nor its living beings.** (p.133)

Those who follow the path of Knowledge must always discriminate between the eternal and the transitory. In the world the eternal and the transitory are mixed together; it is difficult to separate them. According to the *Śiva Purāṇa*, when milk and water are mixed together, the swan can separate the two and drink only the milk, leaving the water.[6] Those who follow the path of Knowledge are like the swan, they always take the eternal and reject the transitory objects. The world is full of variety, but in the midst of all this there is one Reality which never changes—it is eternal. We must hold to that eternal substance, Brahman, and reject everything else as a hindrance.

Many things in the world attract us. We hurry toward something and find it does not satisfy us—either we tire of it, or it disgusts us—and then we try something or someone else, and that also fails us. We go on repeating this process and at last find that nothing in the world satisfies us—gives us lasting happiness. This process is called *neti, neti*—'not this, not this'. This is not eternal, that is not eternal—nothing lasts forever. At last we reject everything in the world: only one thing remains. We call that Brahman or the Self.

Sri Ramakrishna gives an illustration: The master is sleeping in a dark room and someone wants to find him. He enters the dark room and gropes about searching for him. He touches the couch and says, 'This isn't the master.' He touches the chair and says, 'This isn't the master.' He touches one thing after another and finds none of them are the master. At last he touches the master; then he doesn't say a word. He has found what he was searching for.

Our scriptures say that the *nitya*, the eternal that you are seeking for, is not outside; it is within you. *Tattvamasi*—You are That. This is the special message of India to the world. 'Look within your innermost Self', our sages say. 'You yourself are that all-pervading Substance; you yourself are Brahman.' You must discover Him within yourself. How do you do this? Through *śravaṇa*, *manana*, and *nididhyāsana*—hearing, reasoning, and meditation.

First, *śravaṇa*—hearing. You must first hear about spiritual knowledge from a teacher. He will explain the Ātman to you, perhaps quoting for you verses from the *Gītā*, such as :

> *Nainaṁ chindanti śastrāṇi nainaṁ dahati pāvakaḥ*
> *Na cainaṁ kledayantyāpo na śoṣayati mārutaḥ*—
>
> 'Weapons do not cleave this Self, fire does not burn Him. Waters do not make Him wet; nor does the wind make Him dry.'[7]
>
> Or, *Avyakto'yamacintyo'yamavikāryo'yamucyate*—
> 'He is said to be unmanifest, unthinkable and unchanging.'[8]
>
> Again, *Na hanyate hanyamāne śarīre*—
> 'He is not slain when the body is slain.'[9]

After thus describing the Self, the teacher will tell you, *Tattvamasi*!—'You yourself are that Self, the Ātman!' This is *śravaṇa*, hearing.

The second step is *manana*, reasoning. You must now reflect on the teacher's words and try to grasp their meaning. You first examine the outer world, and find that it is not lasting—so you reject it. Then you turn to your inner world. You look for the Self within your self. Your tool is *neti, neti*—not this, not this. You discover that you are not the body, nor the mind, nor the intellect. You are none of these because they are all changeable; they grow old and die. Sri Ramakrishna says that it is like removing the skins of an onion one after another. You gradually reject everything till you come to the unchanging, immortal Self.

We find this reasoning process in Śaṅkarācārya's *Six Stanzas on Nirvāṇa* :

I am neither the mind, nor the intellect,
nor the ego, nor the mind-stuff;
I am neither the body, nor the changes of the body;
I am neither the sense of hearing, taste, smell or sight,
Nor am I the ether, the earth, the fire, the air;
I am Existence Absolute, Knowledge Absolute, Bliss Absolute—
I am He, I am He. (*Śivo'ham, Śivo'ham*)
I am neither the *Prāṇa*, nor the five vital airs;
I am neither the materials of the body, nor the five sheaths;
Neither am I the organs of action, nor the object of the senses;
I am Existence Absolute, Knowledge Absolute, Bliss Absolute—
I am He, I am He. (*Śivo'ham, Śivo'ham*)
I have neither aversion nor attachment, neither greed nor delusion;
Neither egotism nor envy, neither *Dharma* nor *Mokṣa*;

I am neither desire nor objects of desire;
I am Existence Absolute, Knowledge Absolute, Bliss
Absolute—
I am He, I am He. (*Śivo'ham, Śivo'ham*)

I am neither sin nor virtue, neither pleasure nor pain;
Nor temple nor worship, nor pilgrimage nor scripture,
Neither the act of enjoying, the enjoyable nor the enjoyer;
I am Existence Absolute, Knowledge Absolute, Bliss
Absolute—
I am He, I am He. (*Śivo'ham, Śivo'ham*)
I have neither death nor fear of death, nor caste;
Nor was I ever born, nor had I parents, friends, and relations;
I have neither Guru, nor disciple;
I am Existence Absolute, Knowledge Absolute, Bliss
Absolute—
I am He, I am He. (*Śivo'ham, Śivo'ham*)
I am untouched by the senses, I am neither *Mukti* nor
knowable;
I am without form, without limit, beyond space, beyond time;
I am in everything; I am the basis of the universe;
everywhere am I.
I am Existence Absolute, Knowledge Absolute, Bliss
Absolute—
I am He, I am He. (*Śivo'ham, Śivo'ham*)[10]

Saccidānanda—Existence Absolute, Knowledge Absolute, Bliss Absolute—is your true nature. All other things are superimposed on that *I*. This is how you practise *manana*— reasoning. In the last stanza of this poem, Śaṅkara says, 'I am neither *mukti* nor knowable.' He can't say *mukti*, liberation, is attained because liberation implies bondage. And where there is only One, how can there be bondage? Truly speaking there is no liberation. You are always Existence Absolute, Consciousness Absolute, Bliss Absolute.

Reasoning in this way, you come to understand, at least intellectually, who you really are; but now you must actually experience this truth. For this, you must take the third step, *nididhyāsana*—meditation. You must meditate deeply on the truth about your Self, that you are Brahman. When your meditation deepens, your mind and intellect cease to function. Meditation, the meditator and the object of meditation become one. Your 'I' no longer exists. Like the salt doll when it enters the ocean, you no longer have an existence apart from Brahman.

Sri Ramakrishna says, **True knowledge is impossible without *samādhi*.** (p.767) He was referring to *nirvikalpa samādhi*, the final stage on the path of Knowledge. **In *samādhi* man becomes one with God. Then he can have no egotism.** (p.767) **He directly perceives Brahman.** (p.151) All reasoning comes to an end. Sri Ramakrishna uses a simile to describe this state : **When the empty pitcher has been filled with water, when the water inside the pitcher becomes one with the water of the lake outside, no more sound is heard. Sound comes from the pitcher as long as the pitcher is not filled with water.** (p.148)

He also gives the illustration of guests at a feast. They make much noise while they eat, but are silent after their stomachs are full. In the same way, **As long as his self-analysis is not complete, man argues with much ado. But he becomes silent when he completes it.** (p.148) Before attaining Knowledge we reason a great deal. When Knowledge is attained, when there is *samādhi*, all reasoning comes to a stop. The individual soul and Brahman have become one. 'There is not the slightest difference from Brahman—not even a shadow remains. The river of Bliss is flowing; there is no break in that joy,' says the *Vedānta Sāra*.[11]

Worldly happiness comes to an end, but the bliss of Brahman is endless. You can't explain that bliss; you can only experience it in silence. Sri Ramakrishna says : 'How can you explain the taste of ghee to someone who has never tasted it? At most you can say, "Ghee tastes like ghee".' The bliss of Brahman is like that. It is indefinable. Whatever is revealed through language must be limited. We can only say that the bliss of Brahman is beyond compare; it can't be compared to worldly happiness. Those who experience Brahman become absorbed in that bliss. Sri Ramakrishna says, **What He is cannot be described,** (p.148) because no one is able to express Him through words.

Sri Ramakrishna warns us that the path of Knowledge is not an easy one. **The path of Knowledge is extremely difficult.** (p.150) **You can easily say, 'I am the embodiment of Existence-Knowledge-Bliss Absolute; I am beyond pain and pleasure; I am not under the control of the sense-organs', but it is very hard to assimilate these ideas and practise them. Suppose I see my hand cut by a thorn and blood gushing out; then it is not right for me to say : 'Why, my hand is not cut by the thorn! I am all right.' In order to be able to say that, I must first of all burn the thorn itself in the fire of Knowledge.** (pp.862-63)

Because of this, the path of Knowledge is not for everyone. The path of Devotion is better for most people. Yes, there are desires and impurities in my mind, but by directing my mind towards God, gradually all these impurities will be removed. They can't be forcibly removed, but as I move towards God, the mind gradually becomes disciplined and I become pure.

The followers of the path of Knowledge do not agree with this approach. **The *jñānīs* say that an aspirant must first of all purify his heart. First he needs spiritual exercises; then he will attain Knowledge.** (p.862) Why must he 'Purify his heart'? Because it is full of impurities—especially of egotism. Egotism does not mean pride. Egotism is the 'I' concept—the 'I' which says, 'I am separate from Brahman.' The Master calls this the 'unripe I', or the 'little I', or the 'I of ignorance'. It is the 'I' covered over with ignorance. Knowledge is self-manifest, like the sun. When the sun is covered by a cloud, it can't be seen. The 'sun of Knowledge' is always shining within our hearts, but some kind of cloudiness or impurity such as egotism has covered it and we are unaware of its presence. Through spiritual disciplines our minds become less clouded. Referring to a *jñānī* monk, Sri Ramakrishna said, **Do you understand the view of teachers like him? According to them, one must first practise spiritual disciplines : self-restraint, self-control, forbearance, and the like.** (p.266)

Our teachers say that you must be prepared in order to practise the path of Knowledge. Śaṅkarācārya in his commentary on the first aphorism of the *Brahma Sūtras* lists four requirements for anyone wishing to study Vedānta, by which he means the path of Knowledge.

First, you must have *nityānityavastuviveka*—you must be able to distinguish between the eternal and the non-eternal. Sri Ramakrishna says that from a mixture of sand

and sugar, an ant will take only the sugar. In the same way, you must take only the eternal from the world, which is a mixture of the eternal and the non-eternal. You must reject the non-eternal.

Second, *ihāmutraphalabhogavirāgaḥ*—you must destroy all desire for enjoyment in this world or in the next. You must have intense dispassion and have no desire except the desire to realize God.

Third, *ṣaṭsampada*—you must acquire the six treasures : restraint of the mind, restraint of the external sense-organs, renunciation of desires, forbearance, attentiveness, and faith. Faith is particularly emphasized—faith in the words of the teacher and faith in yourself.

Fourth, *mumukṣutva*—you must have an intense longing for liberation, the kind of longing you would have if your head were on fire. You would rush to the river. In the same way, you would hurry to your guru if you had that intense desire for liberation.

In addition to these four qualifications, you must be endowed with great inner strength and intelligence.

After undergoing the disciplines of the path of Knowledge, you may wonder if you have attained your goal, if you have realized God. The truth is, this doubt does not arise in the mind of a person who has realized God. If you have any doubts about it, you can be sure you haven't arrived at the state of perfect Knowledge. If you say, 'Perhaps I have attained God-knowledge,' it is certain you haven't attained it. If everyone in the world tells a knower of Brahman that he has not reached the goal, he will not believe them; he knows what he has experienced and has no doubt whatsoever about it. He is one who can say, *Vedāhametam*—'I have known That.'

Someone asked Sri Ramakrishna, **'How can we know that we have Knowledge?'** He answered, **When one has Knowledge one does not see God any more at a distance. One does not think of Him any more as 'He'. He becomes 'This'. Then he is seen in one's own heart.** (p.627) You see Him in yourself.

The *Kaṭha Upaniṣad* states, *Aṅguṣṭhamātraḥ puruṣo madhya ātmani tiṣṭhati*—'The Puruṣa [Supreme Self] of the size of a thumb dwells in the body,'[12] and, *Tamātmasthaṁ ye'nupaśyanti dhīrāsteṣāṁ śāntiḥ śāśvatī netareṣām*—'Eternal peace belongs to the wise who perceive Him within themselves—not to others.'[13]

I see God as my very Self; how can I doubt my own existence? As long as He was different from me, I doubted. I wondered, 'Is the Reality this? Is the Reality that?' But when that Reality completely possessed me there was not more room for doubt. The scriptures say this state is *karāmalakavat*—'like holding a fruit in your hand'. Before I had the fruit, I had to reason about it: 'How big is it? What does it look like? etc.' But now that I am holding the fruit in the palm of my hand I have no more questions. I *know* I have it, and I know what it is like. In the same way, the man who has attained Knowledge has no doubt he has attained it. *Bhidyate hṛdayagranthiśchidyante sarvasaṁśayāḥ*—'The fetters of the heart are broken, all doubts are resolved.'[14]

If a man has attained God, Brahman, he knows beyond a shadow of doubt that he has attained Him, and others will also understand that he has become a different person. Though the realization of God is a very personal experience and can't be explained to others, still from that man's behaviour and speech we can see that he is not an ordinary person. He is completely free from egotism.

Sri Ramakrishna says, **Do you know what it is like? Just at noon the sun is directly overhead. If you look around then, you do not see your shadow. Likewise, you will not find the 'shadow' of ego after attaining Knowledge, *samādhi*.**

But if you see in anyone a trace of 'I-consciousness' after the attainment of true Knowledge, then know that it is either the 'ego of Knowledge' or the 'ego of Devotion' or the 'servant ego'. It is not the 'ego of ignorance'. (p.767) The 'unripe I' has been destroyed.

Suppose a person is said to be a Realized Soul, a Knower of Brahman; still, observing him closely, I find that he is very egotistical. Egotism indicates ignorance; the attainment of Knowledge means the annihilation of ignorance. In the presence of Knowledge, there can be no ignorance; light and dark can't exist together. So I have to conclude that the man is not in reality a Knower of Brahman.

It is true that as long as the body exists there must be some egotism, but the ego of a Realized Soul is not the 'unripe I', the 'I of ignorance'. It is the 'I of Knowledge'. That 'I' can't hurt anyone. Sri Ramakrishna gives the example of a burnt rope. The burnt rope retains its form, but it can't be used to tie anything. Similarly, those who have attained Knowledge keep a semblance of their individuality, their sense of 'I', but it is not like our 'I'. It is like a burnt rope; it is no longer a cause of bondage.

Shame, hatred, fear, and so on, are all bondages, but the illumined Soul is free from them. Sri Ramakrishna used to say that he who is in bondage is *jīva* and He who is free is Śiva, God. This is the difference between them. In their innermost nature they are the same pure consciousness. '*Jīva* is Śiva.'

As individual souls we are all bound. But the person who has realized God is free from all bondages. His way of thinking and behaving is not like ours. Sri Ramakrishna was free from all bondages. He had no shame or fear. Sometimes he took off his wearing cloth and wandered around carrying it under his arm, as a small boy might do. He would not feel the least embarrassed even if many people were present. If a small child wanders about naked, are we disturbed? People felt that way about the Master. He always seemed to be like a little boy.

One day the renowned writer, Asvini Dutta, came to see him. Sri Ramakrishna at first tried to keep his cloth on, but at last began to pace back and forth completely naked. After some time he became aware of his appearance. 'Do you think I am uncivilized?' he asked. Asvini replied, 'No, no, why should I think you are uncivilized? You are very civilized.'

At the time of practising one of his spiritual disciplines, Sri Ramakrishna would sit for meditation at night under a tree, completely naked. His nephew Hriday found him like this and scolded him : 'This is another queer kind of meditation of yours. You have even removed your sacred thread which the son of a Brahmin should always wear.' Sri Ramakrishna replied, 'All fetters must be removed.'

The Master once said, **Shame, hatred, fear, caste, pride, secretiveness and the like are so many bonds.** (p.315) Pride of high birth is a bondage. Another bondage is 'culture'— 'Everyone regards me as cultured.' There are many other bonds, some of which the Master mentioned. **Man is free when he is liberated from all these.**(p.315) He is a Knower of Brahman, free from all bondages. *Kevala*, One—he sees that he is the only one in the universe. If there are two, there can be shame, hatred, fear, and other bondages. When there is only one, my Self, Brahman, these do not exist. Who is there to hate or to be afraid of?

He is *āptakāmaḥ*—he has obtained the most desired thing, the greatest of all objects, God-realization. Compared to that, everything else is as nothing. *Ātmaratiḥ*—he is immersed in his inner bliss. And he becomes *śānto nirindhana ivānalaḥ*—calm like the flame when its fuel is consumed.[15] As long as the wood is not burnt, there is fire; when it is burnt, no more fire. As long as I have desires and passions, I burn in their flame. When I attain Knowledge of God, of my Self, my desires are destroyed and I am at peace. All my fretful activities are at an end.

Tathā' dvayānandarasānubhūtau na vāsti vandho na ca duḥkhagandhaḥ—'On realization of the Bliss Absolute, there is no bondage or the slightest trace of suffering.'[16] I discover within myself a festival of joy and am always immersed in that. That bliss is not dependent on anything or any person in the world.

This is the sign of a liberated soul. Such a person lives in the world like an emperor. He may be destitute, but in his bearing and demeanour he is like a king. He is truly the Emperor of the world. We are all under the control of our worldly desires— even the ruling monarch and the richest man in the world are caught in the net of desire. But the Knower of Brahman is more than the ruler of the world, he is *nirgacchati jagajjālāt piñjarādiva keśarī*—'Like a lion freed from its cage, he has cut through the trap of the world.' *Abhīḥ*—He fears nothing.

The Greek king, Alexander, having conquered half the world, came at last to India and conquered part of our country. He became acquainted with a monk who was very poor but a Knower of Brahman, and wanted to take him back to Greece. The monk refused to go. At first Alexander tried to tempt him with various gifts, but when the monk still refused to go, Alexander threatened him : 'If you don't come with me, I'll kill you.' At this the monk was convulsed with laughter, 'You have never told such a big lie in your whole life', he said to Alexander. 'You think you can kill me? You may be the Emperor of the physical world, but I am not anything physical. I am pure Consciousness and you have no dominion over that. You may kill this body; you can't kill me.'

How does the Realized Soul see the world? His vision is completely free from *māyā*. We are enchanted by *māyā*, but he is free from its beguilements, *māyānirmukta*. Sri Ramakrishna said, 'That is our Hari.' Seeing someone in disguise, we don't know who it is and become frightened. But at last we recognize him and shout, 'That's only our Hari!' Though he is still in disguise, we are no longer afraid because we recognize him. In the same way, one who has realized God knows the real nature of *māyā*, so *māyā* can no longer frighten or confuse him. The world can no longer bind him because he clearly sees its true nature.

The Lord says in the *Gītā* :

Duḥkheṣvanudvignamanāḥ sukheṣu vigataspṛhaḥ
Vītarāgabhayakrodhaḥ sthitadhīrmunirucyate—

'He whose mind is untroubled in the midst of sorrow and is free from eager desire amid pleasure, he from whom passion, fear and rage have passed away is called a man of Knowledge.'[17] In the words of Sri Ramakrishna, 'Both the *māyā* of Knowledge and the *māyā* of Ignorance have been destroyed in him.' We find in the Upanisads : *puṇyapāpe vidhūya nirañjanah paramaṁ sāmyamupaiti*—'He, the wise seer, shaking off good and evil, becomes stainless and reaches the supreme unity.'[18]

All duality has disappeared for the man of Realization. Good and evil, virtue and vice, purity and impurity—he does not notice these differences. Then, does it mean that he can do any evil also? No. Sri Ramakrishna says : **A *jñānī* cannot injure anybody. He becomes like a child. If a steel sword touches the philosopher's stone, it is transformed into gold. Gold can never cut. It may seem from the outside that a *jñānī* also has anger or egotism, but in reality he has no such thing. (p.417)**

Those who have attained Knowledge cannot do anything wrong, even by mistake. Everything they do and think is for the welfare of others. They are called 'free from duality' because they look upon all things in an impartial manner. They see the Self in all. A verse in the *Īśa Upaniṣad* says :

Yastu sarvāṇi bhūtānyātmanyevānupaśyati
Sarvabhūteṣu cātmānaṁ tato na vijugupsate—

'The illumined soul who sees all beings in the Self, and the Self in all beings, hates none.'[19] And the *Gītā* says:

Vidyāvinayasampanne brāhmaṇe gavi hastini
Śuni caiva śvapāke ca paṇḍitāḥ samadarśinaḥ—

'Sages see with an equal eye, a learned and humble Brahmin, a cow, an elephant, or even a dog or an outcaste.'[20]

Sri Ramakrishna told about a holy man who once came to Dakshineswar. He seemed to be mad—his clothes were filthy and he ate sitting with the dogs. Still, standing in front of the Kālī temple, he recited hymns with such fervour that the whole temple resounded. It seemed that the Divine Mother Herself was joyfully listening. When the Master told Hriday that the holy man was not mad but a man of God-realization, Hriday ran after him just as he was leaving the temple. He called to the man, 'Please tell me how to obtain Knowledge.' The holy man did not respond but hurried on his way with Hriday in pursuit. After some time he turned to Hriday and said, 'When the water in the Gaṅgā and the water in this ditch are the same to you, you will have obtained Knowledge.' He meant that one must have same-sightedness; one must see the non-dual Self in all things and beings.

Rāmaprasāda had the same perception. He said, 'When will I lie in that divine house with purity and impurity on my both sides?' 'That divine house' is a state of mind beyond all duality. There you can see even completely opposite things as *One*. Living in that 'divine house', you are a man of God-realization. There are no rules and regulations for you.

Once when Sri Ramakrishna was eating with some *sādhus*, he started to eat as soon as the food was placed in front of him. Ordinarily, when *sādhus* eat together they say some *mantras* before eating, so the *sādhus* were shocked at Thakur's behaviour. They wondered what kind of man the Master was. Didn't he know anything? But a man of Knowledge does not observe any rules. Sri Ramakrishna did not even observe the conventions of holy men. He did as he wished; he was not under the power of any external authority. Rather, the rules were under him—he was beyond everything.

There are rules about food in the Hindu tradition. First, it must not harm the body or be excessively stimulating. Second, it must be free from impurities. Third, the person who serves the food must be pure. If these rules are not followed it is believed that our spiritual life will suffer. But after we attain God-Knowledge, this kind of reasoning isn't needed. Sri Ramakrishna says, **No food can harm a *jñānī*.** (p.564)

Although it is true that the Master, because of his high spiritual state was beyond all rules, he ordinarily followed social customs and conventions—probably so as not to startle people any more than necessary—but sometimes he would act against the rules. He said, 'I went to Keshab Sen's to see *The New Vṛndāvana*. There I ate *lucis* and curried vegetables. I didn't discriminate about the food, but ate everything.'

On another day, he went to another man's house. Narendra was also present. The head of the house brought water for the Master to drink, but he couldn't touch it. Later, Narendra discovered that the man was immoral; that is why Sri Ramakrishna could not drink the water he offered him. The reason for this difference in behaviour is that when Sri Ramakrishna was in the mood of a devotee, he maintained a sense of discrimination and made distinctions. But when he was in the mood of a *jñānī*, a non-dualist, he went beyond reasoning and discrimination. These were no longer operative and he could eat anything and do whatever he liked.

Why doesn't a person who has realized God need discrimination in regard to his eating and drinking? It is because the person does not think that he himself is eating. Sri Ramakrishna says, **According to the *Gītā*, the *jñānī* himself does not eat; his eating is an offering to the *Kuṇḍalinī*.** (p.564)

A woman devotee, Golap-Ma actually saw this happen. One day at Dakshineswar when she was watching the Master eat, it seemed to her that each time he took food to his mouth, a snake came out of his mouth and grabbed it. After some time the Master said, 'Tell me, who is eating?' Golap-Ma told him what she was seeing. He was pleased and said, smiling, 'You are right; you have understood.' What she saw was the *'Kuṇḍalinī* snake'. Thakur had summoned it and Golap-Ma had seen it. This is the way of a *jñānī* : when he eats he thinks, 'I am not eating, the snake is eating.' In other words, 'It is the physical body that is eating. I am Brahman; I eat nothing. I do nothing and I have no hunger or thirst.'

When the Master's young disciples took their meals at Dakshineswar, he would keep a sharp eye on what they ate and would not let them eat anything and everything. But Narendra was an exception. He could eat whatever he liked. The Master said, 'The fire of Knowledge is burning within him. Whatever he eats will be burned to ashes.'

Sometimes someone asks : 'When we take the path of Knowledge, we renounce the world, saying "The world is unreal—like a dream", but when we realize God, how will the world appear to us? Will we still say that it is unreal?' No, the world is then real to you because you see the world as it is—as Brahman. When you saw the world as the world, it was unreal, but now that you see that it is a form of Brahman, it is real to you.

Sri Ramakrishna uses the word *vijñāna*. He says that after *jñāna* comes *vijñāna*. The *jñānī's* perception is : The world is illusory; Brahman alone is real. (The word *jñānī* here refers to a person who has adopted the path of

Knowledge. In other passages the word *jñānī* has meant a Realized Soul.) The *vijñānī* has understood that 'the world is pervaded by Brahman'.

Sri Ramakrishna says, **One must discriminate at first, saying 'Not this, not this', and reach the roof.** (p.271) When I am climbing to the roof, the roof is all-important to me : I hardly notice the stairs. But after I reach the roof I realize **that the steps are made of the same materials as the roof, namely brick, lime, and brick-dust. The devotee realizes that it is Brahman alone that has become all these—the living beings, the universe, and so on.** (p.271)

Then the world the *jñānī* had previously rejected as illusory, he embraces in love. He has become a *vijñānī*, a man of wisdom. He can't hate anyone because he sees everyone in himself and himself in everyone. Can I hate my own self? Do I ever knowingly hurt myself? I see that I am in all beings—even in the most contemptible criminal. I am even in him who hurts me, so I love him.

This love is spontaneous; I don't reason about it. Before attaining perfect wisdom, my love was partial; I was not able to love all indiscriminately, though I knew I should love all. Now that I have attained Knowledge, I see myself in all beings. Nothing can obstruct the current of that love.

It is sometimes thought that those who follow the path of Knowledge are dry. That is not true. Knowledge culminates in love. We have noticed that some monks of the Ramakrishna Order are at first very stern and don't like to mingle with devotees. Later on, as their Knowledge ripens, they become very loving. People coming to them get peace and joy.

Śaṅkara is known as a non-dualist, an Advaitin. Everyone speaks of his great intellect; few mention his great heart. But he once offered his life to fulfil the desires of a Tāntric worshipper, just as Buddha had offered to give his life to save a goat. Śaṅkara's whole life was spent in working for the good of all by re-establishing the Vedic *dharma*. He did nothing for himself; he was full of love for all.

On the other hand, Śrī Caitanya is known to us as an apostle of love. He taught people to take the name of God, *Hari nām*, and gave shelter to all, the high and the low. But within he was a *jñānī*—a man of Knowledge. He, like Śaṅkara, was an Advaitin, though outwardly he was a lover of God.

Sri Ramakrishna said of one of his disciples, Baburam, that he would have Knowledge, not ecstasy. He thus indicated that Baburam would follow the path of Knowledge. Still, later we find that Baburam, as Swami Premananda, captivated people wherever he went by his incomparable love. When he went to preach in East Bengal, he attracted everyone. When he came to leave, even the Muslims cried. They said, 'O! Our *pīr* (Muslim saint) is going away! Our *pīr* is going away!'

Through his Master's grace, Swamiji experienced *nirvikalpa samādhi*, the highest non-dual state. Still, what love we find in Swamiji! He said he was willing to be born again and again for the good of all. One day Swami Turiyananda went to see him at Balaram Bose's house and found him alone on the veranda. Swamiji was pacing back and forth while singing a song, 'He who has suffered alone knows the pain of suffering.' Tears rolled down his cheeks.[21] Swami Turiyananda could only watch in silence. It seemed that Swamiji's heart was burning with the misery of the whole world. His heart was like an enormous cauldron in which he was trying to produce a balm which would heal the sufferings of everyone.

Girish Ghosh was present on another day when Swamiji again gave expression to his great love. He was talking to his disciple, Saratchandra Chakravarti, about Vedānta and was deeply engrossed in his subject. Suddenly Girish said, 'I don't understand all your Vedānta. In such and such a place, people are starving to death; in another place many atrocities are being committed. What does your Vedānta say about that?' When Swamiji heard this, he stopped speaking; tears came to his eyes, and to conceal his weeping, he hurriedly left the room. Then Girish Ghosh said to Saratchandra, 'Did you see how vast Swamiji's heart is? This is why I love your Vivekananda.'[22]

Where did Swamiji get his love? Thakur said that he was one of the seven sages, one who was perfected in meditation before he was born. Then, why did he have so much love for people in this ephemeral world? He had his love because he saw one God in all beings. We find evidence of his belief in Oneness in the following incident.

In Lahore, a mathematics teacher named Tirtharam became Swamiji's friend. When Swamiji was about to leave, Tirtharam gave him a watch. Swamiji put the watch in Tirtharam's pocket and said, 'I shall wear it here in this pocket. You and I are not different. When you wear it, I will also be wearing it.' Then Tirtharam said, 'Swamiji, give me a message.' Swamiji took the watch from Tirtharam's pocket and saw that it was exactly one o'clock. He said, 'That's the message.' The *one* was Swamiji's message. One existence is everywhere; try to see that one in every being. Later

Tirtharam became a monk and took the name Swami Ramatirtha. When he went to preach Vedānta in the West, he would begin his speeches with these words : 'My own self in the form of ladies and gentlemen, I am in you all, so I am going to address myself.'[23] He gave to all that message of Swamiji—the oneness of creation.

This awareness of oneness is the last step on the path of Knowledge. When an aspirant has reached this goal, as a Realized Soul he is full of love for God, and especially for God as He manifests Himself in everyone and everything.

Sometimes someone asks, 'Was Sri Ramakrishna a *bhakta* or a *jñānī*—a devotee or a man of Knowledge? Many think that he was a *bhakta* because in the *Gospel* he most often speaks about devotion. Some even say that his disciples wanted to make him appear great, so they called him a *jñānī*. Max Müller made that mistake. He said, 'Ramakrishna was primarily a *bhakta*, and not a *jñānī*'.[24] But that is not true.

One incident involving both Holy Mother and Swamiji sheds light on this question. When Swamiji returned from the West, he established a monastery high in the Himalayas. It was known as Mayavati. He wanted it to be strictly Advaitic, with no images, rituals, etc. He felt that at least one monastery of the Ramakrishna Order should be free from all dualistic ideas. But after the monastery was established, some monks who were posted there set up a shrine and installed Sri Ramakrishna's picture in it. They thought that Swamiji would not be angry because Sri Ramakrishna was his All-in-All. Moreover, shouldn't Sri Ramakrishna's picture be in his own monastic centre?

To their surprise, when Swamiji visited the monastery and his eyes fell on the shrine, he became very angry. 'What is this?' he thundered. 'Why have you built a shrine to Thakur in an Advaitic monastery?' The monks who had made the shrine were not convinced that they had done wrong. They wrote to Holy Mother telling her the whole story. They were always ready to accept her word on any matter as final. She wrote to them, 'What Naren has said is exactly right. Thakur himself was an Advaitin; you are also Advaitins.'

Though Sri Ramakrishna often spoke in praise of Devotion, he was an Advaitin. He emphasized the value of the path of Devotion for ordinary people because it is an easier path than the path of Knowledge. Though at heart he was an Advaitin, he did not set Advaita in opposition to *Dvaita* (Dualism), or *Viśiṣṭādvaita*, Qualified Non-dualism. They were like steps of a staircase. The last step of all is Advaita. Dualism and Qualified Non-dualism lead up to Advaita.

This is Sri Ramakrishna's distinctive speciality. In him is the harmony of all paths, all doctrines. After he had practised the disciplines of Devotion, he practised *Jñāna Yoga*, the path of Knowledge—Advaita Vedānta. After one guru had left, another would come. When the time came for the Master to take up the path of Knowledge, the monk Totapuri came to Dakshineswar. He did not know the Master and did not come with the idea of teaching him. He had roamed around from holy place to holy place, and had at last arrived at the Kālī Temple. It was his rule to stay no more than three days at any one place, but he made an exception at Dakshineswar where he stayed for eleven months.

When he first saw Thakur at the temple ghat, he was dumbfounded. Here was a very good receptacle for his teaching! He had found a man fit to practise the Advaitic disciplines. When Totapuri asked Sri Ramakrishna if he would practise these disciplines, he answered, 'I don't know; my Mother knows everything. I'll ask her and if she agrees, I'll learn from you.' 'Mother' of course meant Kālī, the Mother of the Universe. When the Master asked her about this practice she told him, 'Yes, learn from him. He has come here to teach you.'

Totapuri set a day for the performance of the rites of sannyasa, to be done with the *homa* fire and all the other traditional requisites. On that day the Master was formally initiated into sannyasa and thus became a monk. After the rites had been performed, Totapuri started to teach the Master how to experience the truths of Advaita Vedānta. He said to him : 'With your mind absorbed in the Infinite, go beyond name and form.' But an obstruction arose. Every time the Master tried to meditate on the Formless One, his Mother Kālī came and stood before him. This went on for three days. On the third day, Totapuri pierced his forehead between his two eyebrows with a piece of broken glass and commanded, 'Concentrate your mind on this point!' Sri Ramakrishna did as instructed; he then banished the form of the Divine Mother from his mind, cleaving Her in two with the 'sword of Knowledge'. Nothing remained in his mind. He went beyond the limits of name and form and became absorbed in *nirvikalpa samādhi*.

It had taken Totapuri forty long years of hard spiritual struggle to reach the plane of *nirvikalpa*. Sri Ramakrishna reached that state in three days and remained in that state for another three days. At last Totapuri uttered a *mantra* in Sri Ramakrishna's ear and brought his mind down to the normal plane. After this, the Master's mind again soared to the *nirvikalpa* plane, and he remained in *nirvikalpa samādhi* for six months. The Divine Mother then told him to remain in *bhāvamukha* and gradually his mind came down from the *nirvikalpa* plane.

In *Sri Ramakrishna The Great Master*, Swami Saradananda discusses in detail the meaning of *bhāvamukha*. *Bhāvamukha* is the boundary line between the plane of non-duality and the plane of duality. When Sri Ramakrishna was in the plane of *nirvikalpa*, his 'I' disappeared; the world and its living beings no longer existed for him. But when he remained in *bhāvamukha*, he retained the 'I'. However, it was the 'vast I', and he saw that he himself was the world and its living beings—he was the All. He called this state *vijñāna*.

The Master would say, 'After tying the Knowledge of Oneness in the end of your cloth, do what you wish.' He himself had done just that. This expression means that we should practise non-duality under our everyday, ordinary circumstances, and that is what the Master did. He proved that the principles of Advaita Vedānta can be applied in our daily life. There is no need to give up the world. We can learn to see and accept the world as a manifestation of Brahman. When Swami Vivekananda said that he wanted to bring the Vedānta of the forest into the home, he was simply echoing what he had seen and heard from his Master.

Sri Ramakrishna regarded himself as one with all creatures, and even with the grass, as is seen in one incident at Dakshineswar. When someone there walked across the grass, the Master felt as if someone were walking on his chest, causing him intense pain. On another occasion, when a man in a boat in the middle of the Gaṅgā struck his fellow boatman, red marks appeared on the Master's back, as if someone had given him a hard slap.

During Sri Ramakrishna's last illness, he stayed at Cossipore, a suburb of Calcutta. There he endured the unbearable pain of throat cancer; still his face beamed with joy. It seemed that the disease had no connection with him. He said, **Do you know what I see now? I see my body as a frame made of bamboo strips and covered with a cloth. The frame moves. And it moves because someone dwells inside it.** (p.969) A little later he said, **Now I perceive only this: the Indivisible *Saccidānanda* is covered with skin, and this sore is on one side of it.** (p.969)

He saw clearly that he was separate from the body. The body suffered, but not he himself. He was not the body—he was the Indivisible Existence-Knowledge-Bliss Absolute. **The Indivisible *Saccidānanda*—I see It both inside and outside. It has merely assumed this sheath** [meaning his body] **for a support and exists both inside and outside.** (p.969) Then Narendra said to Sri Ramakrishna, 'The Divine Mother listens to you. Tell her for our sake to relieve your illness so that you can eat a little.' The Master forced himself to say those words to Kālī, but she replied, 'Why, are you not eating through many mouths? Must you also eat through your mouth?' Sri Ramakrishna told his disciples, 'When I heard those words of Mother, I could not open my mouth for shame.'

The Upanisads say, *Sarvato'ksiśiromukham*—'The Brahman has His eyes, heads and faces everywhere.'[25] And, *Brahma veda brahmaiva bhavati*—'He who knows the Supreme Brahman verily becomes Brahman.'[26] He then sees that all eyes are his eyes, all faces his faces. He encompasses everything.

We find this in Sri Ramakrishna. He felt the misery of the whole world so he went on talking about God even in the midst of the unbearable pain in his throat. He couldn't give up the body until he had finished what he wanted to do. Before leaving the world, he wanted to prepare his beloved disciple, Narendra, for his great task of working for the good of the world. And he also wanted Holy Mother to give her life as a sacrifice for others. He told her, 'This is not only my work, it is yours also.' He passed on to her his work of relieving everyone's suffering.

He said, 'I am not free. I will have to come to earth again.' Why did he have so much love for the world? It was because he saw himself in all beings—their suffering was his suffering.

He was the greatest of those who follow the path of Knowledge, *jñānīs*, so he was the greatest of the lovers of God, *bhaktas*.

References

1. *Amṛtabindu Upaniṣad*, 12
2. *Śvetāśvatara Upaniṣad*, VI.11
3. *Carpaṭapañjarikāstotra*, Verse 17
4. *Pañcadaśī*, VII. 164
5. *Gītā*, IV.37
6. *Śiva Purāṇa, jñānasaṁhitā*, 5th Chapter, 7
7. *Gītā*, II.23
8. *Ibid.*, II.25
9. *Ibid.*, II.20
10. *In Search of God and Other Poems*, Advaita Ashrama, 1981, pp.78-9 (Swami Vivekananda)
11. *Vedānta Sāra*, 119

12. *Kaṭha Upaniṣad*, II.1.12
13. *Ibid*., II.2.13
14. *Muṇḍaka Upaniṣad*, II.2.8
15. *Vivekacūḍāmaṇi*, 33
16. *Ibid*., 319
17. *Gītā*, II.56
18. *Muṇḍaka Upaniṣad*, III.1.3
19. *Īśa Upaniṣad*, 6
20. *Gītā*, V.18
21. *Yuganāyaka Vivekānanda*, 1st part, 1384, pp.421-22
22. *Bāṇī O Racanā*, 9th Part, 1384, p.39
23. *Prabuddha Bharata*, 1975, April and May, pp.171, 214
24. *Ramakrishna : His Life and Sayings*, F. Max Müller, 1978, p.69
25. *Śvetāśvatara Upaniṣad*, III.16
26. *Muṇḍaka Upaniṣad*, III.2.9

XV

Karma Yoga—The Path of Selfless Action

A man once asked Sri Ramakrishna, **Must we give up our activities until we realize God?** (p.142) This is a pertinent question for Hindus. Our ideal is liberation—freedom from the bondage of birth and death, yet our actions force us to take repeated births in order to reap the results of those very actions. Thus we revolve on a seemingly endless wheel of birth and death. We want to realize God and thereby get off of that painful wheel.

Like that man, we wonder if we should not give up all actions since actions keep us on the wheel of birth and death. Are we not creating new bondages by continuing to perform actions? Moreover, if we work, we may become deeply engrossed in the world. Our teachers tell us to think only of God and forget the world. So we become cowards, afraid to do anything. We feel that we should withdraw from the battle of life.

But Sri Ramakrishna says, **No. Why should you? You must engage in such activities as contemplation, singing His praises, and other daily devotions.** (p.142) As for ordinary worldly activities, he says, **Yes, you can perform them too, but only as much as you need for your livelihood.** (p.142)

Sri Ramakrishna also points out the impossibility of giving up work. He says, **Your very nature will lead you to it whether you like it or not.** (p.452) Work means not only bodily action, but the activities of the mind as well. We are always at work. The Master says, **Even to chant the name and glories of God is work, as is the meditation of the non-dualist on 'I am He'. Breathing is also an activity. There is no way of renouncing work altogether.** (pp.113-14)

As Śrī Kṛṣṇa says in the *Gītā* :

Na hi kaścit kṣaṇamapi jātu tiṣṭhatyakarmakṛt
Kāryate hyavaśaḥ karma sarvaḥ prakṛtijairguṇaiḥ—

'For no one can remain even for a moment without doing work; everyone is made to act helplessly by the impulses born of nature.'[1]

Although we are impelled to work, Śrī Krṣṇa stresses the importance of doing the work suited to our nature. *Sahajaṁ karma kaunteya sadoṣamapi na tyajet*—'One should not give up the work suited to one's nature, O Son of Kuntī.'[2] We should follow our own natural bent. If we want to do physical work, we should do that as well as possible. There are many different kinds of work for different kinds of people. All work will have some defects in it, but we should nevertheless try to work as well as possible.

Our attitude to our work is what is important. There are two ways of working. One way is to work in the ordinary way, to fulfil our selfish desires. That kind of work will bind us; it will cause us to be reborn again and again. The other way of working will give us liberation; it will not bind us, but free us. It is called Karma yoga, the way of unselfish action. Sri Ramakrishna says, **To work in a spirit of detachment is known as Karmayoga.** (p.452) Śrī Krṣṇa tells Arjuna to work in this spirit of detachment :

Tasmādasaktaḥ satataṁ kāryaṁ karma samācara
Asakto hyācaran karma param āpnoti puruṣaḥ—

'Therefore, without attachment, perform always the work that has to be done, for man attains to the highest by doing work without attachment.'[3]

Sri Ramakrishna says : **The scriptures ask you to work in a detached spirit, that is to say, not to crave the work's results.** (p.452) This is the central message of the *Gītā*—Work, but without any selfish motive. Śrī Kṛṣṇa says : *Karmaṇyevādhikāraste mā phaleṣu kadācana*—'To action alone hast thou a right and never at all to its fruits.'[4]

Two terms, *karma* and *akarma*, meaning action and inaction, are mentioned in the fourth chapter of the *Gītā*. Śrī Kṛṣṇa says that it is difficult to understand the difference between the two. A man may sit silent, not moving his hands or feet, still this does not mean that he is not engaged in action. If his mind is busy with such thoughts as, 'I did this, I will do that', he is performing action because activity is going on in his mind. This activity, which springs from desire, binds him. But if he is conscious that he is not the doer, that the Lord alone does everything through him, then even though he may be doing many things, he is a true *Karma yogī*, because he is not doing anything with a selfish motive.

Whatever we do with the desire for the results, that is, for our own selfish benefit, binds us. If we do good work, we get good results, but even that is a cause of bondage. Swamiji said, 'Fetters though of gold are not less strong to bind.'[5] As a result of your good deeds, you may go to heaven, but you will not be able to stay there forever. Eventually the merit acquired through those good deeds will come to an end. It may be after five years or it may be after five million years—still you will have to take birth again. Because of this our scriptures tell us, 'Do not desire that which is transitory.' Any actions that we perform which are impelled by selfish desires can never give us lasting satisfaction, because the results, no matter how pleasing, are always transitory.

The Master says, **A lover of God prays to the Divine Mother : 'O Mother, I am very much afraid of selfish actions. Such actions have desires behind them, and if I perform them I shall have to reap their fruit.'** (pp.468-69) Karma yoga helps us to rid ourselves of these selfish actions.

There are two ways of practising it : the way of the *jñānī*, the man of Knowledge, and the way of the *bhakta*, the devotee.

How does the man of Knowledge regard action? Śrī Kṛṣṇa answers this in the *Gītā* :

Tyaktvā karmaphalāsaṅgaṁ nityatṛpto nirāśrayaḥ
Karmaṇyabhipravṛtto'pi naiva kiñcit karoti saḥ—

'Having abandoned attachment to the fruit of works, ever content, without any kind of dependence, he does nothing though he is ever engaged in work.'[6] He knows that he is in reality the Ātman, the Divine Self, actionless, indifferent—the Observer. The world is full of incessant activity, due to *māyā*. The man of Knowledge also does many things and seems to be engrossed in his work, still, he is not working at all. Only the body and mind are at work. He is simply the Observer of everything.

This concept is emphasized in the *Gītā* where Śrī Kṛṣṇa says to Arjuna :

Yasya nāhaṁkṛto bhāvo buddhiryasya na lipyate
Hatvāpi sa imāṁllokānna hanti na nibadhyate—

'He who is free from self-sense, whose understanding is not sullied, though he slay these people, he slays not nor is he bound (by his actions).'[7] The man of Knowledge does not have the ego that 'I am the doer'; there is not this 'I' sense. If he kills all people on earth, he does not kill anyone, for he is not prompted by egotistical desires. Egotism is at the bottom of all evil. Sri Ramakrishna says, 'When the "I" disappears, all rubbish is done away with.'

The Master told a story about Vyāsa to explain action as the *jñānī* sees it. The *gopīs* were once unable to cross the Yamunā river which was in full-flood. They were wondering what to do when Vyāsa happened to wander by. They said to him, 'Please show us how to cross the Yamunā.' Vyāsa said, 'First give me something to eat.' The *gopīs* fed him with milk, bread and sweets. After wiping his mouth Vyāsa said to the Yamunā, 'If I have not eaten anything today, please make a path for the *gopīs*.' The Yamunā divided itself into two parts making a path in the middle. The *gopīs* were astonished. They said, 'He ate right in front of us, still he said, "If I have not eaten anything today . . ." and the Yamunā obeyed him!' Vyāsa had this power because he was firmly convinced that he was the Ātman, and the Ātman does nothing. It was his body that ate—not he himself. This is the way of the *jñānī*, the man of Knowledge.

But how does the *bhakta* practise Karma yoga? The devotee thinks, 'All work belongs to the Lord, my Chosen Ideal.' He tries to work without desiring anything for himself. He does everything for his Lord. But can you work without any selfish purpose? Can you study for an examination if you don't care to pass? Shouldn't you have the desire to pass? Of course you will try to pass, but the devotee learns to say, 'I will study, and I'll also try my best to pass, but I am doing this for the Lord. I dedicate all my actions to Him, and I dedicate the results of all my actions to Him. I want nothing for myself.'

Sri Ramakrishna explains Karma yoga as a devotee sees it: **Do you know the meaning of Karmayoga? It is to surrender to God the fruit of all action.**(p.849) **So do your work, but surrender the result to God**. (p.114) He seems to be echoing Śrī Śaṅkarācārya who says in his commentary on the *Gītā* that working without attachment (Karma yoga) means working for the sake of the Lord.[8] In another verse he says, 'To me Vāsudeva, the Supreme Lord, the Omniscient, the Self of all, surrender all actions, with the wise thought the "I, the agent, do this for the Īśvara's sake, as his liege."'[9]

If we work for the sake of the Lord, we are working without attachment. The devotee wants to offer everything he does to God. Śrī Kṛṣṇa says :

Yat karoṣi yadaśnāsi yajjuhoṣi dadāsi yat
Yat tapasyasi kaunteya tat kuruṣva madarpaṇam—

'Whatever thou doest, whatever thou eatest, whatever thou offerest, whatever thou givest away, whatever austerities thou dost practise—do that O Son of Kuntī, as an offering to Me.'[10]

If we offer all our actions to the Lord, we will be free from the bondage of work.

In our formal worship—*homa*, *ārati*, etc., we offer everything to the Lord saying :

Om, itaḥpūrvaṁ prāṇabuddhidehadharmādhikārato jāgratsvapnasuṣuptyavasthāsu manasā vācā karmaṇā hastābhyāṁ padbhyāmudareṇa . . . yatkṛtaṁ yaduktaṁ yatsmṛtam tatsarvaṁ brahmārpaṇaṁ bhavatu svāhā.

This prayer makes an offering to the Lord of all actions done at any time or under any circumstances. Actions include all mental activities as well as physical actions. Everything is offered to Brahman; nothing is kept back. Even the result of the worship and the worshipper himself are offered to God.[11] This is one way the devotee practises Karma yoga.

Important as it is, Karma yoga is a path and not the goal. Sri Ramakrishna says, **The aim of life is the attainment of God. Work is only a preliminary step; it can never be the end. Even unselfish work is only a means; it is not the end.** (p.453) **The goal of life is the attainment of God.** (p.453)

We purify the mind by doing unselfish work. Now our minds are cloudy, impure, because we have the consciousness of 'I' and 'mine'—egotism. By working to fulfil our selfish desires, our minds have become like that. All work either helps or hinders our spiritual life. If we work selfishly we go further away from God. But if we work without selfish motives, the impurities of the mind are removed and we see God—acquire perfect Knowledge.

Our scriptures say that in acquiring Knowledge or God-realization you get nothing from outside yourself. God, the Ātman, is always within you, but the cloud of ignorance has covered It. Through unselfish action, the cloudiness is removed and immediately you are able to recognize your true nature. You 'see God'. The Master says, **Through such action one develops love and devotion to God and ultimately realize Him.** (p.108)

The practice of unselfish action is not easy. Our ego so often deceives us. We think we are working without selfish desires, but these desires spring up in spite of our best efforts. We begin to work with the best intentions, then we forget our ideals. We lose our concern for others. Because of this the *Gītā* says, *Gahanā karmaṇo gatiḥ*—'Hard to understand is the way of work.'[12]

Speaking of trying to work in a detached manner, Sri Ramakrishna says: **But it is very difficult. . . . You may think you are working in a detached spirit, but attachment creeps into the mind from nobody knows where. You may worship in the temple or arrange a grand religious festival or feed many poor and starving people. You may think you have done all this without hankering after the results. But unknown to yourself the desire for name and fame has somehow crept into your mind. Complete detachment from the results of action is possible only for one who has seen God.** (p.452)

But until I have realized God, should I not work? If people ask me for help, should I not do what I can for them? Certainly you'll help them. No one can exist without working. You must work to the best of your ability and try to serve others. Still, always be alert. Ask yourself, 'Am I doing this work in an unselfish manner? Am I working for God, or only for myself?' Pray, 'O Lord, make me never forget that I am the machine, You are the Operator of the machine. You are doing everything through me. I offer all the results of my work to you.' As the Master said, **The goal of life is the attainment of God.** (p.453) Always try to remember that and don't get too involved in your work.

The Master also says that you should not give up work forcibly. At the proper time, work falls off of itself, as a flower falls from the tree when the fruit appears, or as a scab falls from a sore when it is healed. We must work till the time is ripe to renounce it.

In the meantime, Sri Ramakrishna says, 'Hold fast to the pillar as you whirl around it.' The pillar is God. As long as you are in the field of work, hold fast to God. He is your support; don't forget Him. This attitude does not come in a day. Many times you will forget Him; instead of working for Him, you work for yourself. But through repeated practice, you become aware that everything is His. 'Whatever I do, Lord, is all Your work.' You are ashamed to say 'I', 'I' all the time. Your work becomes a blessing; your mind becomes purified. Step by step you are going towards God.

The question sometimes arises : 'Will I take as much pains with my work for God as I do when I work for my own benefit? May not carelessness unknowingly creep into my work?' No, this will not happen if you truly love God. 'He is my All-in-All, my most beloved. How could I be careless doing His work?' you will say. If it were for yourself, you might be careless, but if there is even a trifling defect in the work you do for Him, you will feel very bad. So you take more pains with His work than you would with your own.

I have seen Swami Visuddhananda adding up long columns of figures. He worked very rapidly, but he never checked his work and he never made a mistake. He was not doing arithmetic; he was meditating—doing God's work.

Swami Brahmananda used to say, 'if a person is able to meditate well, he will be able to work well.' One day he went to the kitchen at Belur Math where the monks were peeling potatoes and said, 'Bring all your potato peelings to me and I will tell you who is meditating well.' The monks brought their peelings to him in separate baskets. Swami Brahmananda examined them carefully. Then he pointed to one basket and said, 'Whoever placed his peelings in this basket is the best meditator.' That monk was Swami Suddhananda, Swamiji's disciple. Later he became General Secretary and then President of the Order. He was highly esteemed by his fellow monks and is remembered even now with great reverence.

By observing the noble examples of these monks, we see that work and worship are not opposed to each other. Sometimes we think that if we meditate on God our work will suffer, or that if we work, we will not be able to meditate well. But we can do both. Karma yoga teaches us that we should work and that our work should be flawless and beautiful in all respects. We should not neglect work or be indifferent to it. Through Karma yoga work is no longer work; it has become worship of our Chosen Ideal.

There are many stories about monks at our monasteries who try to put this teaching into practice. One of them concerns a swami who had been a brilliant scholar before he joined the Order. His father, a Deputy Magistrate, had wanted his son to go into a prestigious branch of the government service. When the boy insisted on joining our Order, the father became irate and filed a suit against the Ramakrishna Mission. But the boy told the court, 'I am of age and have become a monk of my own free will.' The father lost his case and felt insulted. He came to the monastery one day carrying a revolver : he would shoot his son if he did not come back. He was taken to the place where his son was seated with other monks cutting up pumpkin. Seeing his brilliant son engaged in this menial work, he exclaimed, 'I don't know whether to laugh or cry! I am a Deputy Magistrate, and I find my son who I expected would have a brilliant career is cutting up pumpkin!' The young monk bowed down to his father and said, 'Father, I am not cutting up pumpkin; I am worshipping God. I feel that everything I do is His worship.'

I myself played a role in a small incident related to work. I had just joined the Order and was teaching at our school in Deoghar. On a short visit to Belur Math, I happened to see an old Swami who had on his table a stack of letters ready for mailing. He called me to him and asked me to put stamps on the letters. I hurriedly moistened the stamps and put them on the letters haphazardly, in a slipshod fashion. Later that day, the Swami again called me to him. I was thinking, 'Heavens! Am I going to put more stamps on letters?' Going nearer, I noticed that the Swami was carefully removing the stamps from the letters and placing them on the envelops neatly. He said to me, 'I am correcting your work! Looking at your work, I can understand what kind of teaching you are giving your students!'

I became very embarrassed and said, 'Give me the letters; I will stamp them more neatly.' But he said, 'No, I now know your abilities! You need not do this work for me any more.'

He did not think of this work as only pasting on stamps, and that the letters would reach their destination no matter how they are stamped. He thought, 'This work is worship—worship of Sri Ramakrishna.' That is why he was so particular even about this small task.

When Swami Suddhananda was editor of *Udbodhan*, he worked very hard to bring out the books. Sometimes he would stay awake all night long proof-reading. But he would say, 'I am not just proof-reading. I am worshipping God. I get the same joy doing this work as I do staying awake all night for the Kālī Puja.'

Seeing our ashrams so neat and clean, people are amazed and sometimes ask, 'Do the monks do or supervise all this cleaning.' We tell them that the monks either do the work or supervise it, but they do everything as worship. Those who work with them, salaried or volunteer workers, also have this attitude. The Lord is present not only in the temples, but in hospitals and schools as well. All our work is worship, and all beings are images of God. We serve the sick, we come to the aid of victims of famine and flood. This is not for love of man; it is love of God. We serve all creatures knowing them to be God.

Swamiji said, 'My God the afflicted, my God the ignorant, my God the poor.' This is the *mantra* for the new age : 'Not man, but God'. Those who are not monastics, who live in the world, should also work with this attitude. Whatever they do, they should think they are serving God through that medium. In his poem 'To A Friend' Swamiji says,

> These are His manifold forms before thee,
> Rejecting them, where seekest thou for God?
> Who loves all beings, without distinction,
> He indeed is worshipping best his God.

When I teach, the student is my God. When I care for the sick person, he is my God. He has come to me in these forms so that I may serve Him. I am blessed to have this privilege. Swamiji said, 'Do not throw a few coins at a beggar with disdain. Give them to him with love knowing that God has come to you in this form so that you can purify your mind by serving Him. You benefit yourself by serving Him.' God's image in the temple is His unmoving image. And surrounding us everywhere is His moving image. Worship God in that moving image.

We often hear about the 'dignity of labour' and that we should respect all work. Swamiji said, 'Each is great in his own place. The scavenger in the street is quite as great and glorious as the king on his throne.'[13] If each does his own work diligently, there is no difference between them as to their character. No one is to be judged by what kind of work he does, but by the spirit in which he does it. Not everyone is fit for the same kind of work—difference is the law of nature. This will never change; but we can change our way of seeing things and our attitude towards our work.

If I do my work wholeheartedly, knowing it to be the worship of God, I will be worthy of honour. But if I am given a high position and don't honestly fulfil my obligations; if I am dominated by my own self-interest, then I won't be worthy of anyone's respect.

The English poet Alexander Pope has said much the same thing in one of his poems :

> Honour and shame from no condition rise
> Act well your part, there all the honour lies.[14]

A story about the power which comes from the faithful performance of one's own duties is found in our scriptures. A young monk had acquired supernatural powers as a result of his meditation. One day as he was seated beneath a tree, he was disturbed by some leaves falling on his head, the result of an altercation between a crow and a crane. Very irate at this distraction, he used his newly acquired powers to burn both birds to a crisp with a mere glance at them.

Not long after that he went to a nearby house to beg for alms. When he called out the customary request for alms, a voice from within the house responded, 'Father, please wait a moment; I will come soon.' When no one came after a few minutes, the monk became angry and thought to himself,

'Why are you ignoring me? Don't you know my power?' As soon as this thought crossed his mind, the voice from inside the house said, 'Father, do not be so proud. I am not a crane or a crow that you can burn with a curse. I am now serving my husband and can't leave him.' The monk was astonished. This was no ordinary housewife!

When at last the woman came and gave him some food, the monk bowed down to her and asked, 'Mother, how could you read my mind?' The woman replied, 'I do not know how to worship and meditate; I only serve my husband with all my heart.' She then told him to go to a certain hunter.

After talking with this hunter, the monk understood that he was also an unusual person, a perfected man of Knowledge. He asked the man, 'How did you obtain such knowledge and spiritual realization?' The hunter said, 'I sell meat in an honest way, and I devotedly serve my parents. I do not know yoga, and I have not renounced the world. I do what I must do without attachment, unselfishly. That is how I became a man of Knowledge.'

This devotion to duty, or faithfully carrying out one's work knowing it to be worship of God, is natural, easy. I love God, and I spend my whole life doing His work. At first sight, my work may seem to be very ordinary, but to me it is not ordinary because I am having the privilege of serving my Beloved. If we all have this outlook, our lives will be changed—the whole human race will be transformed. No work will be secular; if the goal is God-realization, all work is sacred.

Sister Nivedita said: 'No distinction, henceforth, between sacred and secular. To labour is to pray. Life is itself religion. To him [Swami Vivekananda], the workshop, the study, the farmyard, and the field are as true and fit scenes for the meeting of God with man as the cell of the monk or the door of the temple.'[15]

No matter where I am, no matter what I am doing—it is all His work. Everything I say is His *mantra*; everything I hear is His voice. With body, mind and speech, I am always worshipping Him. Work has become worship.

References

1. *Bhagavad Gītā*, III.5
2. *Ibid*., XVIII.48
3. *Ibid*., III.19
4. *Ibid*., II.47
5. *C.W*., Vol. IV, 1962, p.393
6. *Gītā*, IV. 20
7. *Ibid*., XVIII.17
8. *Śaṅkara Bhāṣya*, *Gītā*, III.19
9. *Ibid*., III.30
10. *Gītā*, IX.27
11. *Sri Ramakrishna Pūjāpaddhati*, Udbodhan, 1390, p.52
12. *Gītā*, IV. 17
13. *C.W*., Vol. I. 1962, p.42
14. *The Poetical* Works *of Alexander Pope*, 1956. 'An Essay on Man'. Epistle IV
15. *C.W*., Introduction, Vol. I., 1962. p.XV

XVI

Samādhi

Sri Ramakrishna was often seen in *samādhi*. But what is *samādhi*? It is something remarkable, an experience you have to have to understand. It is like losing your identity in God, like a lump of salt melting in water. Union with God through this ecstatic state is the ultimate goal of all spiritual disciplines. It can be attained through the practice of concentration, meditation and the constant repetition of the Lord's name, *japa*. If you experience *samādhi*, you lose consciousness of the body and of the outside world.

It is an astonishing fact that Sri Ramakrishna would be merged in *samādhi* frequently. Like a dry match that blazes into flame with one strike, the Master's mind could rise in a moment to the highest spiritual plane. The most insignificant incident or sight could prompt him to go into *samādhi*.

M. describes the Master's *samādhi* in the *Gospel*. **As his soul soared into the realm of Divine Consciousness, his body became motionless, his eyes were fixed on the tip of his nose, and his breathing almost ceased.** (p.195)

Sri Ramakrishna was as motionless as a figure in a painting. Once Dr Mahendralal Sarkar tested him when he was in that state by touching his eyeballs, but Sri Ramakrishna did not blink or react in any way. Further, Dr Sarkar could not feel any pulse. All the signs of death were present, but he was not dead. His body remained in this world.

In a village near Kamarpukur it was rumoured that the Master was an amazing person who had died seven times and miraculously came back to life each time. How could they understand his *samādhi*? Some people used to say that he had epilepsy, and some thought he was mentally deranged.

Even Keshab Sen, a very learned and spiritually advanced man, couldn't fathom the Master's *samādhi*. When Sri Ramakrishna went into *samādhi* on hearing the song, 'Who is there that can understand what Mother Kālī is?', Keshab was puzzled. 'What is all this?' he said. Shivanath Shastri, after seeing his *samādhi* said, 'There must be something wrong with the Paramahaṁsa's head.' When the Master heard about this remark he said, 'Shivanath thinks it is all right to keep his mind on worldly matters day and night, and I have become deranged thinking about Pure Consciousness? How can that be?' But who can understand the Master? As he himself used to say, 'Can an eggplant seller ever understand the value of a diamond?'

Among the few who could understand the value of the Master's *samādhi* was a British teacher, William Hastie. A Christian missionary, he held the position of principal at the General Assembly Institution where Swami Vivekananda was a student. One day while discussing William Wordsworth's poem, 'The Excursion', he said that Wordsworth, on seeing the beauty of nature, had gone into a state beyond the ordinary sense plane. Mr Hastie then said, 'I know one person who has also experienced this kind of *samādhi*, Ramakrishna Paramahaṁsa of Dakshineswar. You should go to see him some time.' It is surprising that, at a time when many spoke of Sri Ramakrishna's *samādhi* as a derangement of the brain or a disease, a Christian missionary was able to understand what the Master's *samādhi* was.

When a devotee asked Sri Ramakrishna how he felt in *samādhi* he replied, **You may have heard that the cockroach, by intently meditating on the *bhramara*, is transformed into a *bhramara*. Do you know how I feel then? I feel like a fish released from a pot into the water of the Ganges.** (p.196)

The black bee sits on the neck of the cockroach and frightens it. The cockroach is so stunned by its fear of the bee that its mind is completely focused on it. This intense meditation brings about the transformation of the cockroach into a black bee. This was a popularly held belief at one time. A similar concept is found in the *Śrīmad Bhāgavatam* :

> The worm, placed in a hole by a wasp
> and continually frightened by its buzzing sound,
> turns into the shape of the wasp—
> Even without giving up its former body.[1]

Whatever we think of, we become. The cockroach is transformed into the black bee, the worm takes the shape of a wasp. The spiritual aspirant becomes one with God. As a river flows into the sea and no longer has a separate existence, as a drop of water falls into the ocean and becomes part of it, in the same way, when you think deeply and repeatedly of Brahman, you become Brahman. You attain the state of *samādhi* and go beyond the body, the world, and all limitations. The finite becomes infinite.

In his *Yoga Aphorisms*, Patañjali explains the eight steps leading to and ending in *samādhi* :

Yama—non-violence, truthfulness, non-covetousness and self-restraint. Self-restraint, or continence, leads to the purification of the mind, an indispensable requisite for meditation.

Niyama—Austerity, study of the scriptures, contentment, purity, and meditation on God.

Āsana—sitting in a steady and comfortable position at the time of meditation.

Prāṇāyāma—inhaling and exhaling in a regulated and rhythmic manner. This gives calmness to body and mind.

Dhāraṇā—fixing the mind on *Paramātman*, the Self, the object of meditation.

Dhyāna—deep meditation on an object, uninterrupted by any other thought. Difficult to begin with, by constant effort the mind can be held to one thought, the thought of the Self. As we find in the *Vedānta Sāra*, *Tatrādvitīyavastuni vicchidya vicchidyāntarindriyavṛttipravāho dhyānam*—'*Dhyāna* is fixing the mind on Brahman, one without a second, for a longer period of time. There may be breaks in this meditation, but the mind is brought back to Brahman.'[2]

Samādhi—a state of deep meditation in which one *vṛtti* remains in the mind, the Brahman *vṛtti.* There are two kinds of *samādhi*: *savikalpa* (*samprajñāta*), in which you are conscious only of the object of your meditation and nothing else; and *nirvikalpa* (*asamprajñāta*), in which you, the object of your meditation, and meditation itself merge together. You are not conscious of anything. *Nirvikalpa samādhi* is the highest state of consciousness. *Savikalpa samādhi* is one step below the *nirvikalpa* state.

There are four kinds of obstacles on the path to *nirvikalpa samādhi* :

First, *laya*—At the time of meditation you become tired and fall asleep.

Second, *vikṣepa*—There is no thought of Brahman, but only of worldly objects.

Third, *kaṣāya*—Either in this birth or in a previous birth, you experienced some enjoyment which left an impression on your mind. This impression, *saṁskāra*, which was buried deep in your mind, suddenly comes to the surface during meditation and draws your mind away from the thought of the Supreme Self.

Fourth, *rasāsvāda*—this is a subtle obstacle in which the mind does not like to leave the bliss of *savikalpa samādhi*. This obstacle rose in the mind of Sri Ramakrishna at the time of his initiation into *Advaita Vedānta* by Totapuri. He tried repeatedly to rise to the state of *nirvikalpa*, but the Divine Mother stood before him in the form of the essence of Pure Consciousness and his mind could not go beyond this. At last, after repeated efforts, he was able to leave the Divine Mother. He said, 'With the sword of Knowledge, I clove Her in two.' His mind then soared to the realm of *nirvikalpa samādhi*. Vedānta scriptures say that enjoyment is an obstacle, because our goal is *nirvikalpa samādhi*. If we stay in the *savikalpa* state we will not advance. We must go beyond this state for perfect fulfilment.

After gradually overcoming these obstacles, we come to the realm of *nirvikalpa*. The *Vedānta Sāra* says,

> *Nirvikalpakastu jñātṛjñānādivikalpalayā-*
> *pekṣayādvitīyavastuni tadākārākāritāyā-*
> *ścittavṛtteratitarāmekībhāvenāvasthānam*—

'Absorption without self-consciousness [*nirvikalpa samādhi*] is the total mergence in Brahman, the One without a second, of the mental state which has assumed Its form, the distinction of the knower, knowledge and the object of knowledge being obliterated.'[3]

What happens then is explained in the next verse of the *Vedānta Sāra.*

Tadā tu jalākārākāritalavaṇānavabhāsena
Jalamātrāvabhāsavadadvitīyavastvākārākarita
Cittavṛttyanavabhāsenādvitīyavastumātramavabhāsate—

'Then, just as when salt has been dissolved in water it is no longer perceived separately, and the water alone remains, similarly the mental state that has assumed the form of Brahman, the One without a second, is no longer perceived, and only the Self remains.[4]

Brahma veda brahmaiva bhavati—'He who knows Brahman verily becomes Brahman.' Sri Ramakrishna explains this with the metaphor of a salt doll. **A salt doll went to measure the depth of the ocean, but before it had gone far into the water it melted away. It became entirely one with the water of the ocean. Then who was to come back and tell the ocean's depth?** (p.197) In that state, how can you tell of your experience? *Mūkāsvādana*—He only experiences in silence.

Sri Ramakrishna says that there are many kinds of *samādhi*. **My own spiritual experiences tally with the words I heard from a *sādhu* of Hṛṣīkeśa. Sometimes I feel the rising of the spiritual current inside me, as though it were the creeping of an ant. Sometimes it feels like the movement of a monkey jumping from one branch to another. Again, sometimes it feels like a fish swimming in water.** (p.237)

The Master also compared the rising of the *kuṇḍalinī* to the movements of a snake, a frog, and a bird. (*Sri*

Ramakrishna The Great Master, by Swami Saradananda) Hindu scriptures describe these very experiences. The words of the scriptures are verified in the life and experiences of the Master.

Hindu teachers say that there is a path from the brain to the base of the spine called the *suṣumnā*. At the base of the spine the *kuṇḍalinī* power lies sleeping. It is compared to a snake which is sleeping with its head turned downward. Whether we take the path of Devotion, the path of Knowledge, or the path of Yoga (Meditation), knowingly or unknowingly we must arouse the *kuṇḍalinī* from its sleep so that it can rise through the *suṣumnā* to the brain. The *suṣumnā* has six way-stations, so to speak. They are called *cakras* or lotuses.

The *cakra* at the base of the spine is called the *mūlādhāra*. Above that is the *svādhiṣṭhāna*. The third *cakra*, the *maṇipura*, is located near the navel. The fourth, near the heart, is the *anāhata*. The fifth, at the throat, is the *viśuddha*. Above that, between the eyebrows, is the sixth *cakra*, called the *ājñā*. At the uppermost end of the *suṣumnā* is the *sahasrāra*, which is located at the top of the head. Another name for the *sahasrāra* is God, or the *Supreme Self*.

The *kuṇḍalinī* in most people lies sleeping in the *mūlādhāra cakra*. The Supreme Self, God, high up at the top of the *suṣumnā*, is always attracting the *kuṇḍalinī*, but that power remains sleeping so it can't feel this attraction. Thus man, overwhelmed by desire for sense objects, forgets God. But when a person comes to the spiritual path, the *kuṇḍalinī*'s sleep is eventually broken, and it gradually rises up through the *suṣumnā*. As it reaches each *cakra*, the aspirant may have different kinds of unusual experiences. He may see light, or hear the sound of *Om*, for example.

Sri Ramakrishna gives a remarkably clear and detailed description of the rise of the *kuṇḍalinī*. He says, **The *Kuṇḍalinī*, when awakened, passes through the lower centres and comes to the *Anāhata*, which is at the heart. It stays there. At that time the mind of the aspirant is withdrawn from the three lower centres. He feels the awakening of Divine Consciousness and sees Light. In mute wonder he sees that radiance and cries out : 'What is this? What is this?'. . .**

According to the Vedas these centres are called '*bhūmi*', 'planes'. . . . The centre at the heart corresponds to the fourth plane of the Vedas. According to the Tantra there is in this centre a lotus called *Anāhata*, with twelve petals. The centre known as *Viśuddha* is the fifth plane. This centre is at the throat and has a lotus with sixteen petals. When the *Kuṇḍalinī* reaches this plane, the devotee longs to talk and hear only about God. Conversation on worldly subjects, on 'woman and gold', causes him great pain. He leaves a place where people talk of these matters.

Then comes the sixth plane, corresponding to the centre known as *Ājñā*. This centre is located between the eyebrows and it has a lotus of two petals. When the *Kuṇḍalinī* reaches it, the aspirant sees the form of God. (pp.499-500)

But even then a little trace of ego remains. At the sight of that incomparable beauty of God's form, one becomes intoxicated and rushes forth to touch and embrace it. But one doesn't succeed. It is like the light inside a lantern. One feels as if one could touch the light, but one cannot on account of the pane of glass. (p.151)

And last of all is the seventh plane, which, according to Tantra, is the centre of the thousand-petalled lotus. When the *Kuṇḍalinī* arrives there, the aspirant goes into *samādhi*. In that lotus dwells *Saccidānanda* Śiva, the Absolute. There *Kuṇḍalinī*, the awakened, Power, unites with Śiva. This is known as the union of Śiva and *Śakti*. (p.500) What the Tantra scriptures call the union of Śiva and *Śakti* is called the union of the individual soul with the Supreme Soul in Vedānta Philosophy.

When the *Kuṇḍalinī* rises to the *Sahasrāra* and the mind goes into *samādhi*, the aspirant loses all consciousness of the outer world. He can no longer retain his physical body. If milk is poured into his mouth, it runs out again. In that state the life-breath lingers for twenty-one days and then passes out. Entering the 'black waters' of the ocean, the ship never comes back. (p.500)

Sri Ramakrishna would sometimes try to tell about his experiences of *samādhi*, but he couldn't. He would say, 'At the time of *samādhi*'—and before he could say another word, he would again be in *samādhi*. The Upaniṣads say, *Yato vāco nivartante aprāpya manasā saha*—'Whence words together with the mind turn away, unable to reach it .' How can that state be expressed in words?

Sri Ramakrishna says, **Only he who experiences it knows what it is like. In *samādhi* one forgets the world. When the mind comes down a little, I say to the Divine Mother: 'Mother, please cure me of this. I want to talk to people.'** (p.237)

If an ordinary aspirant experiences *nirvikalpa samādhi*, he will give up the body after twenty one days because the body exists only if there are some desires. The person who experiences *samādhi* has no desires, so he cannot continue his earthly existence. His body falls off of itself. But *Avatāras* and *Īśvarakoṭis* are an exception to this.

The Master says, **But the *Īśvarakoṭis*, such as the Incarnations of God, can come down from this state of *samādhi*. They can descend from this exalted state because they like to live in the company of devotees and enjoy the love of God. God retains in them the 'ego of Knowledge' or the 'ego of Devotion' so that they may teach men. Their minds move between the sixth and seventh planes.** (p.500)

Their minds fluctuate between these two planes and never descend to lower planes. For six months Sri Ramakrishna remained in the state of *samādhi* which brings about the death of ordinary aspirants after twenty one days. His body became almost inert. Flies would enter his nose and mouth, but he was not aware of it. His hair became matted and tangled. He was not conscious of the passing of days and nights. At that time a holy man came there and was able to understand that the Master's life was only for the good of the world, and that his body should be preserved. The holy man would beat him with a stick to bring his mind down to his body. Then Thakur would get a little external consciousness and the holy man would feed him something. Again he would enter into *samādhi*.

After six months of this almost continuous *samādhi*, the Master heard the Divine Mother saying, 'Remain in *bhāva-mukha*, and teach people.' After that he suffered from terrible abdominal pain caused by blood-dysentery. It is said that the Divine Mother brought about this illness so that his mind would stay on a lower plane.

Someone once asked the Master if he had any ego at all when he was in the state of *samādhi*. He answered, **Yes, a**

little of it remains. (p.196) The ego that remains is the 'I' of the devotee or of the man of Knowledge, or of the *Avatāra*. The *Avatāra* keeps his ego, his 'I', for the good of the world. Without any ego, he can't do anything. The Master says that without the ego, the game can't continue; that is why the *Avatāra* keeps a little ego, even when he is in *samādhi*.

He says, **In *samādhi* I lose outer consciousness completely; but God generally keeps a little trace of ego in me for the enjoyment of divine communion. Enjoyment is possible only when 'I' and 'you' remain.** (p.196) If there aren't two, there is no enjoyment. God is the object of enjoyment, and the devotee is the enjoyer. 'There are You and I, O Lord, so I am full of bliss.'

Then the Master continued, **Again, sometimes God effaces even that trace of 'I'. Then one experiences *jaḍa samādhi* or *nirvikalpa samādhi*. That experience cannot be described.** (p.197) Like the salt doll which dissolved in the ocean when it tried to measure its depth, the person who enters *nirvikalpa samādhi* loses his personal identity. When he returns to a lower state, he can't describe his experience. He is *mūkāsvādanavat*—like a mute person enjoying something. He is unable to explain his experience to anyone. Only he understands it.

In the *Mahābhārata* we find a description of *samādhi*.[6] After the Kurukṣetra War had come to an end, Yudhiṣṭhira found Śrī Kṛṣṇa seated in a state of *samādhi*. He was motionless and impassive, yet full of light like a blue cloud. Yudhiṣṭhira asked him, 'Are you really Mādhava (Kṛṣṇa)? Why are you sitting like this? Not even a hair on your body is moving. Your mind and intellect are inert. You seem to be like a wall, or like a stone. You do not even seem to breathe, but remain indifferent, inactive, motionless. Lord you are like a flame of light in a windless place, an unflickering lamp. I can't understand you.'

In the devotional scriptures, Rādhā is also found in a state of *samādhi*, referred to there as *mahābhāva*, ecstasy. Because Śrī Kṛṣṇa had gone away, she was distraught. In her agony, she lost all consciousness of the outer world, and even her own body. Her friends thought she was dead, but when they chanted the name of Kṛṣṇa in her ear, she showed signs of life.

Śrī Caitanya also experienced *samādhi*. Sri Ramakrishna said, **Caitanya experienced three states of mind. First, the conscious state, when his mind dwelt on the gross and the subtle. Second, the semi-conscious state, when his mind entered the causal body and was absorbed in the bliss of divine intoxication. Third, the inmost state, when his mind was merged in the Great Cause.**

This agrees very well with the five *koṣas*, or 'sheaths', described in the Vedānta. The gross body corresponds to the *annamayakoṣa*, the subtle body to the *manomayakoṣa* and the *vijñānamayakoṣa*, and the causal body to the *ānandamayakoṣa*. The *Mahākāraṇa*, the Great Cause, is beyond the five sheaths. When Caitanya's mind merged in That, he would go into *samādhi*. This is called the *nirvikalpa* or *jaḍa samādhi*. (p.330)

The *Caitanya Caritāmṛta* describes Śrī Caitanya's *samādhi* : '[He] remains in his inmost self—in *samādhi*, not revealing himself. No outward life can be seen. Sometimes immersed in ecstasy, sometimes half-conscious of the outer world,. . . he is always in one of these three states.'[7]

Sri Ramakrishna said that when Caitanya had consciousness of the outer world, he chanted and sang the names of God; when he had only partial consciousness of the world, he danced with the devotees. When he had no external consciousness, he was utterly absorbed in Divine Consciousness. Inert and motionless, he was in *nirvikalpa samādhi*—his mind had become one with Brahman.

Sri Ramakrishna's *samādhi* was similar to that of Caitanya. It has been described in the *Gospel*. **Now and then he went into *samādhi*, standing still as a statue. While he was in one of these states of divine unconsciousness, the devotees put thick garlands of jasmine around his neck. The enchanting form of the Master reminded the devotees of Caitanya. . . . The Master passed alternately through three moods of divine consciousness : the inmost, when he completely lost all knowledge of the outer world; the semi-conscious, when he danced with the devotees in an ecstasy of love; and the conscious, when he joined them in loud singing.** (pp.289-90)

Holy Mother also experienced *samādhi*, though few knew about her ecstatic states. Swami Premananda said, 'We did not see anyone but Thakur in this state. He could not suppress it. In the twinkling of an eye he could enter into *samādhi*. But no one knew about Holy Mother's ecstasy and *samādhi*.' On several occasions, however, she was discovered in that state. Once when Yogin Maharaj (Swami Yogananda) was staying at Dakshineswar, in the middle of a moon-lit night he noticed Holy Mother sitting by the door of her room completely motionless, absorbed in *samādhi*. She also went into *samādhi* on hearing a flute while she was staying at Nilambar Babu's house at Belur.

Swami Vivekananda was a *dhyānasiddha*, an adept in meditation. Once Girish Ghosh sat for meditation with him but was unable to concentrate because of the mosquitoes.

He then looked at Swamiji and found him deeply absorbed in meditation though completely covered with a dark blanket of mosquitoes. Motionless as stone, Swamiji's mind had gone far beyond the body.

He had a similar experience at Thousand Island Park when he was in America. He was seated for meditation with two disciples in an open field when a fierce thunderstorm arose. One disciple held an umbrella over his head to protect him. Nothing could disturb his absorption. After some time he regained normal consciousness. He had been in *samādhi*.

Swamiji was perfect in meditation from the time he was a child and could easily slip into a meditative state. In the picture of him seated in meditation, we see him in a state of *samādhi*. The photographer was about to take his picture and asked him to assume his meditation pose. As soon as Swamiji seated himself in that pose and closed his eyes, he went into the state of *samādhi*.

On another occasion, when he was staying as a guest at the country estate of his friend Francis Leggett, he entered *samādhi* while meditating beside a lake on the estate. Some of the other guests found him in that state and tried to arouse him by shouting in his ear and pushing his body, but Swamiji did not respond. He seemed to be dead as he was completely motionless and apparently not breathing. Everyone in the house was alerted and hurried to him. They were in a state of shock over what they regarded as his death. But after a long time, Swamiji drew in a few deep breaths and slowly regained body-consciousness. He had been in deep *samādhi*.

In his Bengali poem, 'A Song on *Samādhi*', Swamiji describes what he has experienced in *samādhi*.

> Lo! the sun is not, nor the comely moon,
> All light extinct; in the great void of space

Floats shadow-like the image-universe.
In the void of mind involute, there floats
The fleeting universe, rises and floats,
Sinks again ceaseless, in the current 'I'.
Slowly, slowly, the shadow-multitude
Entered the primal womb, and flowed ceaseless,
The only current, the 'I am', 'I am'.
Lo! 'Tis stopped, ev'n that current flows no more,
Void merged into void—beyond speech and mind!
Whose heart understands, he verily does.[8]

Swamiji had *samādhi* in his grasp, but through the Master's will, he came down from *samādhi* to a lower state so that he could work for the welfare of the world.

Swami Brahmananda was often in a state of *samādhi*. He used to say that real spiritual life begins after the attainment of *nirvikalpa samādhi*. We can understand from this how advanced his spiritual state was. Swami Sivananda is also known to have experienced *samādhi*. He wrote to Romain Rolland, 'I myself had the privilege of attaining this high spiritual consciousness three times through his touch and by his will. I still live to bear direct witness to his tremendous spiritual power.'[9]

The world of religion is so pervasive, so variegated that people cannot easily comprehend it. There are many rooms in the world of religion—outer rooms and inner rooms, for example. Some of us are not able to go even to the outer rooms, but can only see them from afar. Some are able to enter a little into the inner rooms. Those who are fortunate, enter deeply into the inner rooms.

In Shakespeare's *Hamlet*, Hamlet says to Horatio, 'There are more things in heaven and earth, than are dreamt of in your philosophy.'[10] This is especially true in the world of religion. It is hard for us to believe what we are told about this world. Still, we can't deny that in age after age great souls whose lives are superhuman have come to earth. They are called *superhuman* because their renunciation, purity, and austerity are far beyond the reach of ordinary human beings. Śrī Caitanya was this kind of person, as was Sri Ramakrishna. Holy Mother and the monastic disciples of Sri Ramakrishna were also superhuman individuals.

Seeing their lives we are compelled to believe that ecstasy and *samādhi* are not imaginary. A person can have these and other spiritual experiences at different stages in his spiritual life. These experiences are not restricted to any one religion, country, class or age. They are always possible, and possible for everyone. We see these experiences in Christians and Buddhists and those belonging to other religions. Mohammed experienced ecstasy and *samādhi*.

Jesus Christ also experienced *samādhi*. Besides experiencing it during his recorded life, he is thought by some to have experienced *samādhi* while he was on the cross, at the time of his crucifixion. These people believe that he was in a state of *samādhi* when he was placed in his tomb, and that after his *samādhi* was broken, he left the tomb. That is why Mary Magdelene and Mary the mother of James found that the tomb was empty when they went there the following day. However, Christians believe that he 'rose from the dead', and call this event the 'resurrection'.

It is also thought by some that he travelled to Kashmir in India where even today you can see a place called *Īśā* meaning the grave of Jesus Christ. In my student days, I heard this theory in a speech by a Christian minister. He said that Jesus Christ came to India and visited Puri, where he met and talked with holy men.

The American psychologist, William James, sometimes called the father of modern psychology, was well-acquainted with Swamiji and read his *Rāja yoga* with deep interests. In his book *Varieties of Religious Experience*, he describes the spiritual experiences of aspirants from different religions. His description of what one experiences in meditation agrees with the Hindu conception of *samādhi*. '. . . the mystical feeling of enlargement, union, and emancipation has no specific intellectual content whatever of its own.'[11]

The same kind of description is found in the poem, 'The Prisoner' by Emily Bronte. '. . . first, a hush of peace, a soundless calm descends. The struggle of distress, and fierce impatience ends. Mute music soothes my breast, unuttered harmony, that I could never dream, till Earth was lost to me.'[12] This beautiful poem is one person's description of *samādhi*.

The *Gītā* describes *samādhi* as *brāhmī sthiti*—'the state of Brahman.'[13] The *Vedānta Sāra* uses these words, *Cittaṁ nivātadīpavat acalaṁ sadakhandacaitanyamātramavatisthate*—'Like the flame of a lamp sheltered from the wind. There is no movement. There is only undivided consciousness, only the consciousness of Brahman, nothing besides this.'[14]

I am not conscious that I exist and God exists. I do not know anything but God. There is no consciousness of difference, no duality. I and God are one. There is no form. This is the state of *nirvikalpa samāsddhi*. No words can adequately describe it.

Though *samādhi* is very difficult to attain, Sri Ramakrishna easily attained it. Not only that, he found it difficult to come down from that state. It is desires that keep our minds on the earthly plane, but he had no ordinary desires. So, to preserve his body, he created a few trifling desires, such as 'I want to drink water', or 'I want to smoke.' With the help of these desires he would bring his mind from *samādhi* down to a lower plane.

Sri Ramakrishna experienced *samādhi* even in his boyhood days. Once he entered into *samādhi* when he saw a flock of white cranes flying across a dark sky.

It took his guru in *Advaita Vedānta*, Totapuri, forty years of hard discipline to reach the plane of *nirvikalpa samādhi*. Sri Ramakrishna, under his instruction, reached that state in three days. Totapuri was astonished. He said, 'What a divine *māyā*?' Is it in truth *samādhi*? Is it the *nirvikalpa samādhi*, the ultimate result attained through the path of knowledge spoken of in the Vedānta? Ah! How very strange is the *Māyā* of the Divine![15]

It was truly Divine *Māyā*. There is no explanation for *māyā*. There is no explanation for Thakur's spiritual experiences. He himself could not explain them, though he tried.

It is the nature of our minds to drift towards sense objects. It was the nature of the Master's mind to go upward—to the plane of *nirvikalpa*. A description of this is given in the Gospel. One day Narendranath, Dr Sarkar, M. and others were seated near Sri Ramakrishna, who was just then beginning to suffer from the sore in his throat which eventually became cancerous and brought about his death. Narendra sang the song beginning, 'This universe, wondrous and infinite, O Lord, is Thy handiwork.' Then he sang the song beginning, 'In dense darkness O Mother, Thy formless beauty sparkles.' The song inspired everyone.

Dr Sarkar said to M., **'This song is dangerous for him.' Sri Ramakrishna asked M. what the doctor had said. M. replied, 'The doctor is afraid that this song may throw your mind into *samādhi.*'**

In the mean time the Master had partially lost consciousness of the outer world. Looking at the physician, he said with folded hands : 'No, no. Why should I go into *samādhi*?' It was as if he were trying not to go into *samādhi.*

Hardly had he spoken these words when he went into a deep ecstasy. His body became motionless, his eyes fixed, his tongue speechless. He sat there like a statue cut in stone, completely unconscious of the outer world. Turned inward were his mind, ego, and all the other organs of perception. He seemed an altogether different person. (p.898)

One time he had become embarrassed by his *samādhi.* He had said, **Something happens to me in that state of intoxication. Now I feel ashamed of myself. In that state I feel as if I were possessed by a ghost. I cease to be my own self.** (p.882) He seemed to have no control over himself. Sometimes when he was in *samādhi* he would say, 'There it comes! There it comes!' A great flood seemed to engulf him—a flood of light. Though he tried, he could not keep himself in a normal state. He felt as if he were possessed by a ghost.

It is possible for a person to be possessed by a ghost. The spirit of a dead person may enter him and he will then act like that person. Sri Ramakrishna behaved like a different person when he was under the influence of divine ecstasy, so he said, 'I cease to be my own self.' Further, **While coming down from that state I cannot count correctly. Trying to count, I say, 'One, seven, eight', or some such thing.**(p.882) M. remarked, 'Amazing arithmetic! Truly astonishing!'

But then everything about Sri Ramakrishna is truly astonishing. In writing about him biographers sometimes refer to him as a 'Man-God' and sometimes as a 'God-Man'. Who can say which is right? No language, no name can truly describe him.

Today his picture, taken when he was in the state of *samādhi*, is found in many, many homes. We have meditation poses of Buddha and Śrī Caitanya, but they come from the imagination of the artist. Sri Ramakrishna's is the first photograph of a great soul in *samādhi*.

Those who saw him have described his state of *samādhi* as something utterly unique. One person described it as 'an embodiment of love, an embodiment of bliss'. His niece Lakshmi used to say that when he was in *samādhi*, you would think that there was no more beautiful person on earth than he. An unearthly beauty would be seen emanating from his whole body. His eyes were half-open, and on his lips was a beatific smile. A glimpse of that smile is found also in some of his photographs.

If he had not come, we would never have believed there could be ecstasy, *samādhi*, and many other spiritual experiences. Yet in him we see one person living in our age who achieved all these, so we can no longer doubt.

Sri Ramakrishna is the embodiment of the Vedas, the embodiment of *dharma*, of true religion. Having drawn all the many treasures in the world of religion to himself, he has become a veritable treasure-house where all the many different kinds of spiritual experiences are collected. We find in him the essence of all scriptures. Even so, his spiritual experiences go beyond the scriptures. The scriptures could not describe the state of *samādhi* in which he lived. Can one describe the indescribable?

We can only say that Sri Ramakrishna's life is like a room inlaid with precious gems, the door of which has opened a little before us. Peeping through that door we see all the precious jewels that have risen from the churning of the scriptures and have been beautifully arranged there, one upon another—in the life of one incomparable individual.

References

1. *Śrīmad Bhāgavatam*, XI.9.23
2. *Vedānta Sāra*, 207
3. *Ibid.*, 197
4. *Ibid.*, 198
5. *Taittirīya Upaniṣad*, II.9
6. *Mahābhārata*, *Śānti Parva*, 45.25.6
7. *Caitanya Caritāmṛta, Antyalīlā*, 25th Chapter
8. *C.W.*, Vol. IV, p.498
9. *The Life of Ramakrishna* by Romain Rolland, 1970, p.216, f.n.
10. *Hamlet*, Act I, Scene V
11. *The Varieties of Religious Experience*, William James, 1936, pp.416-17
12. *Poems of Emily Bronte*, 1906, p. 19, 'The Prisoner'
13. *Gītā*, II.72
14. *Vedānta Sāra*, 214
15. *Sri Ramakrishna The Great Master*, p.252

XVII

Yata Mat Tata Path

The Many Religions Are So Many Ways To God

Sri Ramakrishna used to tell a story about a fanatical devotee of Śiva who worshipped only Śiva and refused to honour any other deity. Śiva told him again and again, 'My child, you should not behave this way; you should also respect other gods and goddesses.' But the man continued to honour only Śiva. He especially hated Viṣṇu, even though Śiva had told him, 'I am also Viṣṇu.'

One day as the man sat for worship, he saw that the image he was worshipping was half-Śiva and half-Viṣṇu, so he turned his face towards Śiva and tried not to look at Viṣṇu. When he burned the incense, he realized that Viṣṇu would also be inhaling its sweet fragrance, so he plugged up Viṣṇu's nose. People also came to know that he didn't like Viṣṇu at all. So when he wandered in the streets, people would tease him by chanting the name of Viṣṇu. This made him furious, and he threatened them with a stick, but this did not stop them from chanting Viṣṇu's name. So he tied a bell to each of his ears so that when he heard Viṣṇu's name he could shake his head and make the bells drown out that hated name. Because of this the people called him *Ghaṇṭākarṇa*—'Bell-eared'.

The Master was pointing out with this story the ludicrous lengths to which some people will go in their fanaticism. He would tell everyone, **'Don't be dogmatic.'** (p.634) 'My religion is the only true religion, my God is the only God. If you don't accept my religion, you will go to hell.' This is the way of dogmatism.

Sri Ramakrishna came at a time when bigotry abounded. Even now this attitude can be found. A Christian priest once said to me, 'If a Moslem goes to heaven, he goes by mistake.' But Sri Ramakrishna says that we should never think that our religion alone is true and the other religions false. 'Don't be dogmatic,' is one of his fundamental teachings.

He says, **There are innumerable pathways leading to the Ocean of Immortality.** (p.467) How can we limit Him to one path who is beyond all limits? If we limit Him, He can't be the Unlimited; still we try to limit Him to our narrow conceptions. The Master used to say, *Yata mat tata path*—'The many religions are so many ways to God.' He could say this so emphatically because he himself experienced all ways of approaching God.

First he had a vision of Mother Kālī, seeing her as his Divine Mother. After that he practised the discipline of *dāsya*, viewing himself as Hanumān, the monkey who was Rāma's servant. The Master would sit on the limb of a tree and cry 'Rāma! Rāma!', and at last he had the vision of Rāma. Then he practised the Tāntric disciplines under the supervision of the Bhairavi Brahmani and attained perfection in all sixty-four branches of that discipline.

After that he underwent the discipline of *madhura bhāva*, thinking of himself as a woman yearning for Śrī Kṛṣṇa. He spent six months dressing and behaving in all ways like a woman. All the signs of ecstatic *samādhi* found in our devotional scriptures appeared in his body, and he had the vision of Kṛṣṇa. He thus proved that the *madhura bhāva*, which had fallen into disrepute, could also lead one to God.

Then he practised the discipline of *vātsalya,* regarding himself as a parent of God. A *sādhu* gave him an image of the child Rāma, called *Rāmalālā,* with which the Master carried out this discipline. He was like a mother, full of love for her little son. (This has been discussed in chapter XII, in the section, 'Sri Ramakrishna and the Path of Devotion'). He felt that the child Rāma, God himself, was truly his son. At last he saw Rāmalālā everywhere—not only in the image—thus achieving the height of perfection in this discipline.

But this was not the end of his spiritual journey. He now practised the disciplines of Advaita Vedānta. The monk Totapuri was his guru at this time. Totapuri after forty years of hard practice had experienced the ultimate goal of all spiritual disciplines—*nirvikalpa samādhi.* Sri Ramakrishna reached this state in three days. (This is described in detail in chapter XIV.)

Later, he practised the disciplines of Islam, behaving and dressing exactly like a Muslim—repeating the *namāz* five times a day. He lived like this for three days, never entering the temple of Kālī. He completely forgot the Divine Mother without whom he thought he could do nothing, and achieved God realization as a devout Muslim.

Next he had the vision of Jesus Christ. It happened like this: One day when he visited Jadu Mallick's garden house, his eyes fell on a picture of the child Jesus seated on the Virgin Mary's lap. As Sri Ramakrishna gazed intently at the picture, a ray of light suddenly emanated from it and entered his body. At once all his Hindu ways and mental impressions disappeared, and he became a devotee of Christ. He saw in a vision Christian devotees praying to Jesus Christ in a church. For three days, Sri Ramakrishna felt himself to be a devotee of Christ. Then, on the third day, while walking in the Pañcavaṭī at Dakshineswar, a God-man of fair complexion wearing an unusual garment, came walking towards him. It was Jesus Christ. He came near and entered into the Master, who then went into deep *samādhi*.

Long after that, when Swami Vivekananda and Swami Saradananda and others started coming to Dakshineswar, Sri Ramakrishna talked to them one day about his vision of Christ. The disciples remarked that they had heard that Jesus Christ was very tall and had a pointed nose. But Sri Ramakrishna disagreed. He said, 'I saw him, and his nose was flattened at the tip.' Ordinarily a Jew's nose is pointed, but Sri Ramakrishna saw that Jesus's nose was flattened. After the Master's passing, the young disciples found a description of Christ's appearance which proved the truth of Sri Ramakrishna's description.

Sri Ramakrishna's whole life was truly one vast *Centre for Religious Research.* He took many different paths to God, and had many conceptions of Him—this was all part of his research. As a result of this research he could say with certainty, 'There are innumerable ways to God.'

He says, **There are the paths of *jñāna*, of karma and of *bhakti*. If you are sincere, you will attain God in the end, whichever path you follow. Roughly speaking, there are three kinds of yoga : *jñānayoga*, karmayoga, and *bhaktiyoga*.** (p.467) (He does not mention Rāja yoga here.)

He goes on to discuss the different yogas—the different ways to God. **What is *jñānayoga*? The *jñānī* seeks to realize Brahman.**(p.467) If a person knows Brahman, he knows everything, because Brahman is manifest in the world. Further, knowing Brahman, he becomes Brahman. *Brahma veda brahmaiva bhavati*—'He who knows the Supreme Brahman verily becomes Brahman.'[1] It is like the river entering the ocean; it is no longer the river but has become the ocean. *Tadākārākārita*—'The self has become absorbed in Divine Consciousness.'

The *jñānī* discriminates, saying, 'Brahman is real and the universe illusory.' (p.467) Śrī Śaṅkarācārya often expresses this truth. He says, *Brahma satyaṁ jaganmithyā*—'Brahman alone is real, the world illusory.'[2] And, *Ayaṁ prapañco mithyaiva*—'This phenomenal world is illusory.'[3] The only reality is Brahman. Sri Ramakrishna says that it is like peeling the skins from an onion, one by one, and at last finding there is nothing—*neti, neti*. God is the only Reality, and *Ahaṁ brahmāsmi*—'I myself am that Reality.'[4]

Sri Ramakrishna says, **As he [the *jñānī*] comes to the end of discrimination, he goes into *samādhi* and attains the Knowledge of Brahman.** (p.467) The Master means *nirvikalpa samādhi* in which Knowledge, the known and the knower become one. There is no consciousness of two—only the consciousness that 'I am Brahman, I am indeed All'. No one has been able to adequately describe this state.

Sri Ramakrishna says that the path of Knowledge, *Jñāna Yoga*, is very difficult and not suited for most people, as pointed out in chapter XIV. People are dependent on food, their life-span is short and they can't rid themselves of body-consciousness. Because of this they can't realize that 'I am Brahman, the world illusory.' If a thorn pricks my hand and the blood oozes out, can I say, 'I feel nothing?'

You may say it, but would you be speaking the truth? Very few are able to go beyond body-consciousness and attain perfection by following the path of Knowledge. The path of Devotion is better for most.

The Master next discusses Karma Yoga. **What is karmayoga? Its aim is to fix one's mind on God by means of work. . . . If a householder performs his duties in the world in a spirit of detachment, surrendering the results to God and with devotion to God in his heart, he too may be said to practise karmayoga.** (pp.467-68)

Sri Ramakrishna gives the illustration of smearing your hands with oil before cutting open the jack-fruit so that they don't become soiled with the fruit's sticky milk. Prepare yourself for living in the world by developing the conviction that the world is the Lord's and everything in it belongs to Him; you are only His agent, His machine. Then you can do your work, but as you don't desire the work's results, you will not be bound by it. The Master continues : **Further, if a person performs worship, *japa*, and other forms of devotion, surrendering the results to God, he may be said to practise karmayoga. Attainment of God alone is the aim of karmayoga.** (p.468)

Cittasya śuddhaye karma—'Right action purifies the heart.'[5] If you don't desire the results of your work, if you work for others unselfishly, your heart becomes purified. And with a pure heart, you see God. Even so, the Master says, **It is extremely difficult to perform one's duties in a spirit of detachment, without craving the results. One cannot work in such a spirit without first having realized God. Attachment to the result somehow enters the mind, though you may not be aware of it.** (p.468)

That is why Sri Ramakrishna says that we must pray to God in this way : **May my actions be fewer every day till I attain Thee. May I perform, without attachment to the results, only what action is absolutely necessary for me. . . . May I not entangle myself in new work so long as I do not realize Thee. But I shall perform it if I receive Thy command. Otherwise not.** (p.469)

After discussing Karma Yoga, the Master took up the subject of *Bhakti Yoga*. He said : **What is *bhaktiyoga*? It is to keep the mind on God by chanting His name and glories. For the *Kaliyuga* the path of devotion is easiest.** (p.468)

In our devotional scriptures the Lord says, 'O sage! It is as if I am not free, subject as I am to my devotees. Being fond of my *devotees*, my heart is under their sway.'[6] These scriptures sometimes call love a rope; the devotee ties God to himself with that rope. And God likes to be bound this way. He longs for love. God wants to be close to his devotee. Jesus Christ says, 'I stand at the door and knock : if any man hear my voice, and open the door, I will come in to him, and will sup with him, and he with me.'[7] And the devotee longs to be with God. Rabindranath Tagore said, 'If my heart's door is shut, open the door and enter my life. Do not go away O Lord!'

As the devotee's relationship with God deepens, he feels more and more intimate with Him. This is what *Bhakti Yoga* is. Sri Ramakrishna says that it is the easiest of all paths to God. ***Bhaktiyoga* is indeed the path for this age.** (p.468)

The fourth path is called Rāja Yoga. Ordinarily when we use the term yoga, we mean Rāja Yoga, and the person who practises it is called a yogi. The Master says, **The yogi seeks**

to realize the *Paramātman*, the Supreme Soul. . . . He withdraws his mind from sense-objects and tries to concentrate it on the *Paramātman*. (p.134)

Our minds are like water in a pond in which different waves are constantly rising. These mental waves are called *vṛttis*. Some *vṛttis* are good and some bad. The yogi doesn't want either the good or bad *vṛttis* to rise. Patañjali has said, *Yogaścittavṛttinirodhaḥ* —'Yoga is the cessation of all the waves of the mind.'[8]

Sri Ramakrishna says, **The yogi's ideal is the union of the embodied soul and the Supreme Soul.**(p.134) He says that as at noon both hands of the clock are together, the embodied soul and the Supreme Soul come together as one if you practise Rāja Yoga. But if you aren't able to lead a very pure life while practising this discipline, there is every fear of falling to a low state. So the Master does not recommend this path for most people.

As we see, Sri Ramakrishna does not reject any path, still he says : ***Bhaktiyoga* is the religion for this age. But that does not mean that the lover of God will reach one goal, and the philosopher and worker another.** (p.468) All aspirants are trying to reach the same goal. **He who is called Brahman by the *jñānīs* is known as Ātman by the yogis and as *Bhagavān* by the *bhaktas*. The same Brahmin is called priest, when worshipping in the temple, and cook, when preparing a meal in the kitchen.** (p.133) There is one God, but He has different aspects and is called by different names.

Sometimes one path leads into another. The Master says : **If a person seeks the Knowledge of Brahman he can attain It by following the path of *bhakti*, too. God,**

who loves His devotee, can give him the Knowledge of Brahman if He so desires. (p.468) It was generally thought that a person must follow the path of Knowledge, *Jñāna Yoga*, to attain the non-dual Brahman, but Sri Ramakrishna teaches that *Bhakti Yoga*, the path of Devotion can also lead to Brahman. He says, **By realizing the Divine Mother of the universe, you will get Knowledge as well as Devotion. You will get both.** (p.468)

The reverse is also true. We can acquire devotion by following the path of Knowledge. Devotion and Knowledge are not opposed to each other. We call Śaṅkara a Vedantist, a *jñānī*, but what a great heart he had! How hard he worked to revive Hinduism for the good of all! As previously noted, he composed hymns to gods and goddesses, erected temples, and established monasteries. We see in him the very embodiment of love, proving that the follower of the path of Knowledge can also be a great devotee.

The Master says further. **In *bhāva samādhi* you will see the form of God, and in *nirvikalpa samādhi* you will realize Brahman, the Absolute Existence-Knowledge-Bliss.** (p.468) He had realized both kinds of *samādhi* so he knew this from experience. But, as we have seen, he says that the path of Devotion (leading to *bhāva samādhi*) can also lead one to *nirvikalpa samādhi*. When we come to this state, there is Brahman and nothing else. *Brahmamayaṁ jagat. Jīvo brahmaiva nāparaḥ*—'The individual soul and the world are Brahman. There is nothing but Brahman.'[9] The *jñānī* and the *bhakta* both have this experience of oneness as a culmination of their spiritual disciplines.

Still, the devotee has an approach to this highest state that is different from the path of Knowledge that the *jñānī* follows. The devotee experiences this Oneness through the state of *sāyujya*—complete Oneness with God. In repeatedly thinking of God, the devotee sometimes becomes so absorbed in Him that he forgets his own separate existence. There is only God, and no one else. The devotee himself has ceased to exist; he is God. This experience is described in stories about Rādhā and Kṛṣṇa. Rādhā meditated so deeply on Kṛṣṇa that she thought she *was* Kṛṣṇa. This is the state of Oneness.

Sri Ramakrishna gives the illustration of the cockroach thinking so intensely on the black bee that it is transformed into the black bee. The devotee's 'I' melts into God. He sees that 'He is I, and I am He.'

We find an example of this in the life of Sri Ramakrishna. When he was to offer food to the Divine Mother Kālī, he would sometimes eat some of it first, and then offer the rest to Kālī saying, 'Now you eat.' Sometimes he would place the flowers for worship at his own feet before offering them to the feet of the Mother. To him, there was no difference between Her and himself.

Gopal Ma, Gopal's mother, had this same attitude. The story of how she saw Gopal, the child Kṛṣṇa as her own living son, has been related elsewhere. After that, she saw that Sri Ramakrishna was not different from her own child Kṛṣṇa. It is recorded in *The Great Master* that at the end of her life, Gopal Ma saw her child Kṛṣṇa in everyone, and she also thought that she herself was Gopal. She would never say, 'I will eat', or 'I will sleep.' She would say, 'Gopal will eat,' or 'Gopal will sleep.' She attained that complete oneness with God. All differences had disappeared. God and his devotee were one soul.

Thus, whether we take the path of Devotion or the path of Knowledge, we reach the same destination. The final experience of both is the same. Sri Ramakrishna says, **Pure Knowledge and Pure Love are one and the same thing. Both lead the aspirants to the same goal.** (p.278) Those who follow the path of Knowledge say, *Ahaṁ brahmāsmi*—'I am Brahman,' and *Sarvaṁ khalvidaṁ brahman*—'All this is Brahman.'[10] But the devotee sees that *Sarvabhūtamayaṁ harim*—'Hari (Kṛṣṇa) is in all beings.'[11] He realizes that, *Harireva jagat jagadeva hariḥ / Harito jagato nahi bhinnatanuḥ*—'Kṛṣṇa is the world, the world is Kṛṣṇa; Kṛṣṇa and the world are not different.'[12] And, *Yānhā-yānhā netra paḍe tānhā kṛṣṇa sphure*—'Whatever he sees, he is seeing Kṛṣṇa.'[13] He can't see anything but Kṛṣṇa.

Swamiji in his poem, 'To A Friend' says, 'These are His manifold forms before thee. Rejecting them where seekest thou for God?' God is standing before me. He is in my friend and He is also in my enemy. Who can I hate? Who can I reject? *Vasudhaiva kuṭumvakam*—'Everyone in the world is my near and dear one,' because I see my God in everyone. When a snake bit Pavhari Baba, he said, 'This is a messenger from my most beloved.' This is the way the devotee has the realization of Oneness. He sees God in everyone and everything.

Even so, the Master says that **the *bhakta* wants to realize the Personal God endowed with form and talk to Him. He seldom seeks the Knowledge of Brahman.** (p.468) Further, he says, **Do you know what the truth is? God has made different religions to suit different aspirants, times and countries. All doctrines are only so many paths; but a path is by no means God Himself.**

Indeed, one can reach God if one follows any of the paths with whole-hearted devotion. (p.559)

This whole-heartedness is the essential thing. The Master says, **Be firm in one ideal—either in God with form or in the formless God. . . .With firm and unwavering belief the followers of God with form will realize Him, as will those who speak of Him as formless. You may eat a cake with icing either straight or widewise; it will taste sweet either way.** (p.624) Be firm in whatever path you choose and you will reach God. If you make a mistake, all is not lost. God is within you. He knows you want to come to Him. He will take you by the hand and lead you along the right path.

Suppose there are errors in the religion that one has accepted; if one is sincere and earnest, then God Himself will correct those errors. Suppose a man has set out with a sincere desire to visit Jagannātha at Puri and by mistake has gone north instead of south; then certainly someone meeting him on the way will tell him : 'My good fellow, don't go that way. Go to the south.' And the man will reach Jagannātha sooner or later. (p.559)

'Religion is one, religions are many.' All religions lead to God, so in one sense, all religions are the same. But there are differences in the way we go to Him, so in another sense, the various religions are different. Because of these differences, there is a need for the many religions in the world.

Sri Ramakrishna says : **I see people who talk about religion constantly quarrelling with one another. Hindus, Mussalmāns, Brāhmos, Śāktas, Vaiṣṇavas, Śaivas, all quarrel with one another. They haven't the intelligence to understand that He who is called Kṛṣṇa is also Śiva, and**

the Primal *Śakti*, and that it is He, again, who is called Jesus and Allah. 'There is only one Rāma and He has a thousand names.'. . . That which is called *Saccidānanda* Brahman in the Vedas is called *Saccidānanda* Śiva in the Tantra. Again it is He alone who is called *Saccidānanda* Kṛṣṇa in the *Purāṇas*. (p.423)

The Master explains this further with a metaphor. He says that there are several ghats on a lake. At one ghat the Hindus take water in their waterpots and call it *jal*. At another ghat Muslims take water and call it *pāni*. Christians take water from still another ghat and call it *water*. It is the same water, though it has different names. If someone were to say, 'That is not *jal*, it is *pāni*;' or 'That is not *pāni*, it is water,' people would certainly think him foolish.

Sri Ramakrishna says that as long as you involve yourself in the outer part of religion, you will argue and disagree. But if you once enter the inner essence, you will understand that through all religions you can realize God. *Yata mat tata path*—'The many religions are so many ways to God.' **If one is able somehow to reach Calcutta, one can see the *Maidan* and the museum and other places too. The thing is how to reach Calcutta.** (p.468)

The Master tells a story about this. As a man was walking through the jungle, he noticed a beautiful animal on a tree. When he arrived in his village he told his friend, 'Brother, I just saw a red animal on a certain tree in the jungle.' His friend said, 'I also have seen it, but why do you say it is red? It is green.' Another person who was listening to the conversation said, 'No, it is not green or red, it is yellow.' The three men started to quarrel. At last they decided to find out for themselves the truth of the matter.

When they went into the jungle, they found a man sitting under the tree. They told him about their disagreement. He said, 'I know that animal very well. You are all correct. The animal is a chameleon. Sometimes it is red, sometimes blue and sometimes other colours. And sometimes it has no colour at all.' God appears in different ways to different people, and sometimes He is without any form at all.

Sri Ramakrishna says, **These things do not become clear until one has realized God. He assumes different forms and reveals Himself in different ways for the sake of His devotees. . . . Only the man who lives under the tree knows that the chameleon can assume various colours and that sometimes it remains colourless. Others, not knowing the whole truth, quarrel among themselves and suffer.** (pp.858-59) We must somehow realize God; then we will have no need to quarrel.

But I say that we are all calling on the same God. Jealousy and malice need not be. . . .I say, let one man meditate on God with form if he believes in form, and let another meditate on the formless Deity if he does not believe in form. What I mean is that dogmatism is not good. It is not good to feel that my religion alone is true and other religions are false. The correct attitude is this : My religion is right, but I do not know whether other religions are right or wrong, true or false. (p.558)

Whether God is with form or if He is formless has been an endless source of disagreement among scholars and philosophers. Sri Ramakrishna gives a unique solution to the problem. He says that the coolness of devotion causes water to freeze into ice, meaning that God manifests Himself in the form the devotee loves most. Then the sun of Knowledge melts the ice, and he becomes one with God. God's form has melted away.

In the *Caitanya Caritāmṛta* we find:

Yei yei-rūpe jāne, sei tāhā kahe
Sakala sambhave Kṛṣṇe, kichu mithyā nahe—

'People see God in various forms; they are all true. He is revealed in many ways.'[14] All images of God are not beautiful. For example, the images of Ganeśa and Kālī do not seem beautiful to everyone. Still, many love to think of God in those forms. God comes to the devotee in the form he loves most, so he may even come to the house begging for alms, or crawling as Gopāla, the baby Kṛṣṇa. In Bengal we have many wonderful images of God. One for example is called Haṁseśvarī Devi and is unusual. A devotee living in the Hooghly district saw God in a particular form in a vision. He had an image made in that form and worshipped it. The image is still there today.

These forms are not imaginary. All forms are His forms; all names are His names. *Sādhakānāṁ hitārthāya brahmaṇo rūpakalpanā*—'Brahman assumes a form for the good of the devotees.'[15]

But it is important to remember our supreme goal. Swamiji said, 'Each soul is potentially divine. The goal is to manifest this Divinity within, by controlling nature, external and internal. Do this either by work, or worship, or psychic control, or philosophy—by one or more all of these—and be free.'[16] We need Knowledge, Selfless Work, Devotion and Meditation. Swamiji said that if one is neglected, the aspirant's character will not be formed in the model of Sri Ramakrishna. His ideal is the harmony of all paths, all religions.

Swamiji further said that you can't show disrespect for any part of religion. It may not be necessary for you, but it may be the right way for others. In India there are many spiritual aspirants; they all seek God in their own way. The *Gospel* tells of a man who used to gaze at the sky and loudly chant the name of Gaṇeśa, so he was called *Gaṇeśagarjī*. He gazed at the sky because he didn't want to see any kind of worldliness; he wanted to think only of his Chosen Ideal, Gaṇeśa. Even in such unusual ways people can realize God.

Some people practise the *sahaja sādhanā*—'the easy discipline'. It is called easy, but how difficult it is! It involves spiritual practices in the presence of members of the opposite sex and other kinds of objects of enjoyment. One must resist the attraction of all these. Swamiji and other young disciples were one day criticizing these practices in the presence of the Master, but Sri Ramakrishna told them that they should not criticize even these things, for some people have realized God following this method also. But he warned them, 'This path is dangerous. There are two entrances to a house, the front door and the rear door where the scavengers enter to remove the garbage, etc. This path is like the rear door, but even by this door people enter the house. However, this path is not pure; it is not for you.'

We must judge a tree by its fruits. Later, Swamiji was to echo these words, saying : If by worshipping an idol our lives would become like Ramakrishna's, I would say that idol worship is certainly good. If we see in any discipline that a person practising it has become God-like, we will understand that that discipline is undoubtedly a valid one.[17] All world religions have produced great souls—all religions are true.

We need a religion for the worship of God with form, as well as a religion for the worship of God without form. It is not possible for most of us to think of God without form; we need some kind of form especially at the beginning of our spiritual journey. Members of the Brāhmo Samāj worship God without form but with attributes. Still, many find they cannot dispense with some kind of form or image altogether. One of their members once said to me, 'When I think of God as compassionate and forgiving, the face of my grandfather comes to my mind—his white beard and smiling face. He used to forgive my many childish offences, so I can't help but think of him when I think of the compassionate God.'

Another member of the Brāhmo Samāj, a cultured woman, tried all her life to worship the formless deity, but towards the end of her life she said to her husband, 'I find this kind of worship lifeless—worshipping God without form. I love to have a deity in my shrine whom I can bathe and feed and dress.' Her husband was very liberal in his views. He took the woman to Belur Math to meet Swami Virajananda who was then President of the Ramakrishna Order. Later, the woman received initiation from him and was able to worship God as she wished.

Sri Ramakrishna says : **Can all comprehend the Indivisible *Saccidānanda*? . . . People have different tastes. Besides, all have not the same fitness for spiritual life. . . . Don't you know what difference in taste is? Some enjoy fish curry; some, fried fish; some, pickled fish; and again, some, the rich dish of fish pilau.** (p.910)

The *Śivamahimnaḥ Stotra* says,

Rucīnāṁ vaicitryādṛjukuṭilanānāpathajuṣāṁ
Nṛṇāmeko gamyastvamasi payasāmarṇava iva—

'People have different tastes, so they choose different paths. But all arrive at the same place—they reach God, the way all rivers reach one ocean.'[18] There are various tastes, various languages, various beliefs, but there is one destination—God.

The Master says further: **Then too, there is difference in fitness. I ask people to learn to shoot at a banana tree first, then at the wick of a lamp, and then at a flying bird.** (pp.910-11) We proceed from step to step. In the words of Swamiji, we go 'from a lower truth to a higher truth.'

As long as you have body-consciousness you will think of God as having a body, a form. As long as you think of yourself as a person, you will think of God as a person. There is one God, one Brahman. Depending on the state of our minds, we think of God as with form or without form; with qualities or without qualities. Sometimes we think we are separate from Him and sometimes we think we are one with Him.

Hanumān said to Rāma, 'O Lord, while I identify myself with the body, I am Thy servant. When I consider myself as an individual soul, I am Thy part. And when I look upon myself as the Self, I am one with Thee—this is my firm conviction.'[19] Sri Ramakrishna says the same thing : **I have come to the final realization that God is the whole and I am a part of Him, that God is the Master and I am His servant. Furthermore, I think every now and then that He is I and I am He.** (p.572) Swamiji said that from deep in a cave we see the sun in one way. Another person who is on the ground level sees the sun in a different way. Some see the sun through the fog, and some from a mountain top. All people see the same sun, though in differing ways.

We think of God as with form, through a particular image. Gradually our outlook widens and we see that all forms are His form, all thoughts are His thoughts, all names are His name. We then no longer see any form; we see only Him. As we go towards God, our thoughts are changing, becoming more pure. Still, it is always the same God we are trying to reach.

Swamiji once said about the Christian religion, 'You have one coat for everyone. All people—little or big, man or woman—must wear this same coat.' But Hindus are very accommodating. In Hinduism there are different kinds of coats for different kinds of people. There are various paths in Hinduism, but they all lead to one goal—God.

Swamiji said, 'In all religions the superconscious state is identical. Hindus, Christians, Mohammedans, Buddhists and even those of no creed, all have the very same experience when they transcend the body.'[20] The highest state, the Absolute Truth, is always One. But our minds and intellects are limited; we cannot grasp the whole truth, and we accept a partial truth, the relative truth. Each person has his own mental make-up. That is why truth is different to different people. But the final experience of the highest stage is the same for everyone.

Swamiji said, 'This is like the different photographs of the same sun taken from various distances. Each of them seems to represent a different sun. The diverse relative truths have the same kind of relation with the absolute truth. Each religion is thus true, just because it is a mode of presentation of the absolute religion.'[21]

In the words of Sri Ramakrishna, **Hindus, Mussalmāns, Christians, Śāktas, Śaivas, Vaiṣṇavas, the Brahmajñānīs of the time of the rishis, and you, the Brahmajñānīs of**

modern times [he meant Brāhmos], all seek the same object. A mother prepares dishes to suit the stomachs of her children. Suppose a mother has five children and a fish is brought to the family. She doesn't cook pilau or *kāliyā* for all of them. All have not the same power of digestion; so she prepares a simple stew for some. (p.559) There is a difference in tastes and in the abilities of different aspirants. **But she loves all her children equally.** (p.559)

We also acknowledge differences in aptitude in worldly affairs. In the field of education, for example, some study Science, some study the Humanities, and some study Commerce. Each individual studies what he is most interested in.

From ancient times, Hindus have accepted variety in the field of spirituality because they believe that differences cannot be denied. The many religions and ways to God in Hinduism make it a universal religion. Its speciality is its all-embracing vastness. Swamiji said : To many it is disturbing that there are so many religious beliefs in the world. But I am glad of that, because many people thus have an opportunity to approach God. I would be even happier if there were as many religious sects on earth as there are people—each person following his own religion according to his own mental tendencies.[22]

Someone said that the Hindu religion is a kind of jungle—'a trackless forest'. If you once enter this jungle you can't find your way; there is no footpath. A missionary who made many speeches attacking Swamiji wrote this : 'What is Hinduism? Imagine you are going somewhere on the ocean when a storm comes up and dark clouds appear in the sky. You can't see anything and can't find your way to the shore. This is Hinduism.'

Once a Christian said to me, 'Hindus themselves can't say what Hinduism is.' I replied, 'This is not a weakness in Hinduism; it is its special characteristic; it is a sign of its strength. It is so vast that we can't tell where it ends. It devours everything.' It includes in its fold the basic tenets of all religions. At first sight it seems to be a 'trackless forest', but if your goal is God-realization, you will understand that it is not a jungle. Here you will find a path that is designed only for you.

Sri Ramakrishna says, 'In the home many people sit eating together, and the wife serves them all—her husband, her brother-in-laws, her father-in-law, and others. Although she serves everyone, she has a special relationship with her husband, and she gets more joy from serving him. In the same way, you have a particular relationship with your own Chosen Ideal who dwells in your heart. Still, you respect others' beliefs and serve them when necessary.' Accept everyone and respect all beliefs, but stay devoted to your own ideal.

Sri Ramakrishna says, **When you mix with people outside your Samāj, love them all. When in their company be one of them. Don't harbour malice toward them. Don't turn up your nose in hatred and say : 'Oh, this man believes in God with form and not in the formless God. That man believes in the formless God and not in God with form. This man is a Christian. This man is a Hindu. And this man is a Mussalmān.' It is God alone who makes people see things in different ways. Know that people have different natures. Realize this and mix**

with them as much as you can. And love all. But enter your own inner chamber to enjoy peace and bliss. (p.637)

Then the Master gives an example : **The cowherds take the cows to graze in the pasture. There the cattle mix. They all form one herd. But on returning to their sheds in the evening they are separated. Then each stays by itself in its own stall. Therefore I say, dwell by yourself in your own chamber.** (p.637)

Since Sri Ramakrishna's advent, we find many people saying, 'All religions are true.' Of course some bigoted persons don't accept this ideal, but most people now believe that we should respect all religions. It is as if Sri Ramakrishna came to start a revolution in the world of religion. That revolution has gradually spread everywhere.

Some time ago, a German gentleman came to visit the Ramakrishna Mission Institute of Culture. He was head of a religious institution in Germany which was soon to celebrate the seventy-seventh year of its founding. He invited us to attend. The purpose of his Institution was to find the essence at the base of all religions. They wanted to build a bridge between the various religions. The man informed me that many books published in the German language contain teachings of Sri Ramakrishna and Swami Vivekananda. He also told me that many small groups interested in Indian spiritual ideals were springing up in Germany and other European countries. People were eager to learn about Sri Ramakrishna and Swamiji. When I told him some of the ideas of Sri Ramakrishna and Swamiji, he jokingly said, 'Have you read my speeches? You are saying exactly what I say. Either you are quoting me, or I have quoted you!'

Two of Swamiji's ideas that came to my mind in this discussion were :

—If you sit quietly in one place—it may even be in an impenetrable cave—and concentrate deeply on one great thought, that thought will spread to the outer world. Many minds will vibrate with that thought.

—Truth is eternal, for everyone, for all times. It is not limited to one person, one caste, to one particular time. But in each age we find one principal aspect of Truth predominating.

In one of Swamiji's speeches at Chicago he said, 'Help and not Fight', 'Assimilation and not Destruction', 'Harmony and Peace and not Dissension'.[23] And at the close of his first speech there he declared, 'I fervently hope that the bell that tolled this morning . . . may be the death-knell of all fanaticism, of all persecutions with the sword or with the pen, and of all uncharitable feelings between persons wending their way to the same goal.'[24]

This message, the words of harmony and reconciliation which Swamiji addressed to the world in Chicago, he received from Sri Ramakrishna. The wave of that message is floating around us even today. That thought-wave is spreading everywhere. It seems to be looking for a good place to embody itself. If it finds a favourable place, such as a fit individual, that thought-wave takes form, the way a sound-wave takes form in a radio-receiver.

The thought-current of Sri Ramakrishna-Vivekananda is something superhuman. It is not limited to any one society or person. Its essence will spread by its own power, and will pervade everything. Gradually it will vibrate in the minds of all. Whether we wish it or not, whether we understand it or not, this great event will take place.

Were Sri Ramakrishna's words about the harmony of religions anything new? No, Hindus had often heard the famous verse from their ancient scriptures, *Ekaṁ sadviprā bahudhā vadanti*—'Truth is One, wise men speak of it in various ways.'[25] But it had not been practised by most people. Sri Ramakrishna, by his superhuman spiritual disciplines, revived this truth and placed it clearly before us.

Swami Vivekananda, in his hymn to Sri Ramakrishna says : *Sthāpakāya ca dharmasya*—'Thou art the founder of *dharma*, true religion.' It was not any particular religion that he founded, but the essence of all religions. All religions, all moods and spiritual paths are in him. When Vaisnavas went to see him, they viewed him as one of themselves. The worshippers of the Divine Mother looked on him as their leader. The non-dualists claimed him as the greatest Advaitist. All religions, all paths are found in him.

Someone has called him 'A Federation of Religions'. Swamiji said that he is 'A Parliament of Religions', Romain Rolland felt that he was a 'Symphony of India', meaning that he is the common chord of all religions. In a beautiful poem to Sri Ramakrishna, Rabindranath Tagore has said, 'Diverse courses of worship from varied springs of fulfilment have mingled in your meditation.'

It seems that Sri Ramakrishna with both arms outstretched is saying to us : 'I accept all of you, whatever path you may follow on your way to God. I reject no one.' He draws everyone to him in an embrace of pure love.

References

1. *Muṇḍaka Upaniṣad*, III.2.9
2. *Brahmajñānāvalīmālā*, Śaṅkarācārya, 21
3. *Brahmānucintana*, Śaṅkarācārya, 26
4. *Ibid*., 5
5. *Vivekacūḍāmaṇi*, 11
6. *Bhāgavatam*, IX.4.46
7. *Revelation of St. John*, New Testament, III.20
8. *Yoga Sūtras,* Patañjali, I.2
9. *Brahmajñānāvalīmālā*, 21
10. *Chāndogya Upaniṣad*, III.14.1
11. *Viṣṇu Purāṇa*, I.19.9
12. *Gurugītā and Stotramālā*, Haridvar Bholananda Sannyāsāśrama, publisher, Compiler : Ramakumar De
13. *Caitanya Caritāmṛta*, *Ādilīlā*, 4th Chapter
14. *Ibid*., 5th Chapter
15. *Kulārṇava Tantra*, VI.73
16. *C.W*., Vol. I, 1984, p.257
17. *C.W*., Vol. III, 1989, p.218
18. *Śivamahimnaḥ Stotra*, 7
19. *Universal Prayers*, Swami Yatiswarananda, 1954, Verse 309
20. *C.W*., Vol. VII, 1964, p.43
21. *Reminiscences of Swami Vivekananda* by His Eastern and Western Admirers, 1983, pp.26-7
22. *Bāṇī O Racanā*, Vol. III, pp. 178-79, 1980
23. *Chicago Addresses*, Advaita Ashrama, Calcutta, p.46
24. *Ibid*., p.4
25. *Ṛig Veda*, I.164.46

XVIII

Avatāravariṣṭha

The Greatest of Avatars

I remember seeing a drama in which the Mother of the World is crying. Someone asks her, 'Mother, why are you crying?' She answers, 'There are so many injustices in the world. My children have lost their way and are attracted to evil ways, so I am crying to God and telling him, "Lord, come! If you don't show the way, the whole world will be lost."'

Hindus believe that God comes to earth again and again for the need of the age.* He moves about as we do; He endures grief and pain as we do. At first sight He seems to be in every way like an ordinary person. Still, in every way He is extraordinary. Though He is human, He is also superhuman.

Why does God come to earth? Why does He behave like an ordinary human being? It is to enable us to come to Him, to

---

* The *expression* 'need of the age' is very meaningful here. As we understand it, God assumes different bodies according to the need of the time. Hindus believe that a fish was the first avatar; it lived in the water. The turtle was next; it lived on land and water both. After that came the boar avatar, which lived only on land. The next avatar was Nṛsimha, half-man, half-lion.

After that He came as a man, but in the form of a dwarf. Then came Paraśurāma, Rāma, and others who were fully men. Scientists can find the theory of evolution in this Hindu conception of the gradual transformation of lower into higher beings.

become like Him. 'God becomes man so that man can become God.' Sri Ramakrishna says, **It is just like the sun at dawn. You can easily look at that sun. It doesn't dazzle the eyes; rather it satisfies them. God becomes tender for the sake of His devotees. He appears before them, setting aside His powers.** (p. 282)

We find avatars in most religions, though the conceptions vary. Hindus say that God Himself takes on a body. Other religions have other views. For example, Christians believe that God sent his Son, and Moslems believe that He sent His Messenger.

The *Bhāgavatam* says :

Avatārā hyasaṁkhyeyā Hareḥ sattvanidherdvijāḥ
Yathāvidāsinah kulyāḥ sarasaḥ syuḥ sahasraśaḥ—

'Innumerable are the descents of Kṛṣṇa, who is absolutely pure in His essence. They are as numerous as waterways streaming out of a perennial lake.'[1] The *avatar* is always God, but the stream of His compassion flows through different bodies, at different times.

Christians, however, do not accept the idea of many avatars. They say that Jesus Christ is God's 'only begotten Son'. They believe that other great souls such as Buddha, Mohammed and Caitanya, were good, but no one is equal to Christ. Moslems also do not accept anyone but Mohammed. They say Mohammed is the last prophet, the last and most perfect.

But when does the avatar make his appearance on earth? The Lord answers that question in the *Gītā* :

Yadā yadā hi dharmasya glānirbhavati Bhārata
Abhyutthānamadharmasya tadātmānaṁ sṛjāmyaham

Paritrāṇāya sādhūnāṁ vināśāya ca duṣkṛtām
Dharmasaṁsthāpanārthāya sambhavāmi yuge yuge—

'Whenever there is a decline of righteousness and rise of unrighteousness, O Bhārata, then I send forth Myself. For the protection of the good, for the destruction of the wicked and for the establishment of righteousness, I come into being from age to age.'[2]

Some time ago, representatives of various Christian sects, most of whom were clergymen, visited the Ramakrishna Mission Institute of Culture to have an exchange of ideas with us as representatives of Hinduism. At first one of the Christians gave a brief account of the life of Sri Ramakrishna. In his view, Sri Ramakrishna was not only a Hindu; he practised other religions as well, including Islam and Christianity.

One of the group then asked how long Sri Ramakrishna had practised Christianity. A Hindu who was present replied that it was only for a few days. This brought forth a spirited response from a member of the Christian group, a professor of Philosophy, who said in a very agitated manner, 'He could not be a Christian that way. One must have a lifelong commitment. If I am a Christian, I must worship Christ and no one else. If I am a Christian for only one day, or seven days, or six months, I can't be called a Christian.' After that many questions arose. At last one of the Christians, a woman from the Netherlands, gave a short talk on Sri Ramakrishna which astonished us. It seemed that the Master was speaking that day not through us, but through that woman.

Towards the end of the discussion, the mood changed; the Christians became more friendly. Later, when we were having tea, we asked the philosophy professor what he meant by the phrase 'lifelong commitment to Christ'. Was this Christ a particular person, or the symbol of an ideal? The professor made the mistake here. He said, 'A person. Not an ideal or idea or philosophy—a person!' I said, 'But Hindus worship Kṛṣṇa because He says in the *Gītā*, "On Me fix thy mind; to Me be devoted; worship Me; revere Me. . . ."' But the professor retorted, 'That's all said in mythology!' He meant that Kṛṣṇa lived in prehistoric times, so I said to him, 'Did Mohammed live before or after Jesus Christ?' The Professor answered, 'After.' Then I said, 'Mohammed has also asked us to follow him. If we must follow some person, we should follow him. Then we will have to reject all those who came before him, the way you reject Śrī Kṛṣṇa. Your Jesus Christ will also have to be rejected then.'

The man did not know how to answer. I tried to explain to him our point of view, 'Look,' I said, 'commitment, certainly—but not to any person or image—to one ideal. That ideal is in my religion, in your religion, in all religions. That ideal takes a whole life to achieve.' Hindus believe that that ideal is manifest in many different Incarnations of God, called avatars.

In Binodesvar Das Gupta's Bengali song, he names the various avatars in their order of appearance, but before the fish-avatar, he puts the word *Vedoddhāraṇa*, meaning 'the saviour of the Vedas.' The Vedas were not written by any person; no one created them. The word *Veda* comes from the root *vid*— to know. The Vedas are accumulated knowledge and eternally true. In age after age, this truth is made manifest by the sages. So it is first essential that these Vedas be saved.

Moses received a message from God. At another time Mohammed received a message. They both experienced the Eternal Truth, and practised It, which we call Veda. They preached this Truth according to the need of their age, relieving the people of their burdens. Because God relieves our burdens, He is called *Hari* in India. *Hari* comes from *hara*, meaning 'to steal'. God steals away our suffering and the burden of worldly life. He comes in different forms, from a fish to the highest human being, according to the need of the time.

Though Hindus accept Buddha as an avatar, he did not teach from the Vedas because he thought that too much reasoning about the scriptures was useless, and that it was a waste of time to argue about their meaning. The goal of life, which was the attainment of liberation, or what he called *nirvāṇa*, could not be attained by scriptural knowledge, so he was silent about the scriptures. He taught by his life the truth of the Vedas, though he didn't acknowledge their authority. Because his followers didn't honour the Vedas, they lost the support of the Indian people who look on the Vedas as their chief authority. Thus after some time, Buddha's religion declined in India.

Then came Śrī Śaṅkarācārya to re-establish the Vedas. Thought to be an incarnation of Śiva, Śrī Śaṅkarācārya came with the splendour of Knowledge; all Knowledge seemed to be embodied in him.

Jesus Christ came to destroy the sins of all mankind. Christians say that 'original sin' is disobedience to God. The Biblical story of Adam and Eve and 'original sin' has been told previously (Chapter VI). God sent His son, Jesus Christ, to save people from this sin. Christ by his crucifixion accepted the sins of all men and saved them. Next came Mohammed who tried to destroy the darkness of ignorance in which the Arabs were drowned.

Śrī Caitanya and Guru Nānak took birth in India. They tried to remove caste and class distinctions, and were both avatars of love. Through love they destroyed the gulf between the high and low, rich and poor.

Referring to the period after Nānak and Śrī Caitanya, Swamiji says, 'At this time someone was needed in whom could be found the knowledge of Śaṅkara and the love of Caitanya—the mind of Śaṅkara and the heart of Caitanya.' Thus Sri Ramakrishna came; he embodied in himself both Love and Knowledge.

Sri Ramakrishna said about himself, 'He who was Rāma, he who was Kṛṣṇa, is now this Ramakrishna.' He also said, 'This time God has come in disguise, like the king who sometimes wanders about incognito to find out for himself the condition of his people.' Sri Ramakrishna was that king, the King of kings, God Himself. He came in disguise to see for Himself the suffering of the people and to lift them up.

The Master said, **'I saw *Saccidānanda* come of this sheath. It said, "I incarnate Myself in every age". . . . I saw that it is the fullest manifestation of *Saccidānanda*; but this time the Divine Power is manifested, through the glory of *sattva*.'** (p.720) Śrī Rāmacandra and Śrī Kṛṣṇa had the splendour of kings, their royal power and glory; they were characterized by the *raja-guṇa*, the element of dynamic activity. But Sri Ramakrishna did not have the bow and arrow of Rāma or the great missile, *sudarśana*, of Śrī Kṛṣṇa. He did not have the royal splendour of Buddha, or the scholarship of Śaṅkarācārya and Caitanya. In his incarnation there was no splendour at all—only divine purity, adherence to truth and a complete absence of egotism. These are the signs of the *sāttvika guṇa*, the element of purity in human beings.

Still, the special characteristics of other avatars could be found in him. For example Rāma's principal ideal was adherence to truth. His living in the forest, killing Rāvaṇa, banishing Sītā and Lakṣmaṇa were all for establishing truth. In the same way, Śrī Krsna taught selfless action; Buddha, non-violence; Jesus Christ, love; Śrī Caitanya, divine ecstasy; Śrī Śaṅkara, non-dualism. Each of these special characteristic could be found in full in Sri Ramakrishna.

A Bengali song says : 'Rāma, Kṛṣṇa, Buddha, Śaṅkara, Rāmānuja, Caitanya, Kabīr and Guru Nānak—Sri Ramakrishna is the total of all of these. All that they represent can be found in him.' Swamiji said that the Master was 'full of infinite moods. Knowledge of Brahman has limits; but Sri Ramakrishna's moods are limitless. . . . He is the greatest of avatars.'

Swamiji did not look down on other avatars; it is the same God who incarnates Himself in age after age. The avatars who preceded the Master were one and the same God, only there is a difference in the manifestation of power. Every avatar must be judged from the standpoint of his own age. We can't judge the Boar-avatar and Buddha-avatar by the same standards. Each avatar must be evaluated by how he carries out his own particular mission. Viewed in this way, we can't say that one is greater than another. Still, Swamiji said that if we study history, we find that God manifests Himself a little more fully with each avatar. Each avatar comes with more power than the previous one.

Sri Ramakrishna came for the modern age, when the greatest power was needed. The totality of all paths to God can be found in him. Swamiji said he is the *Avatāravariṣṭha*—the greatest of avatars'. (This phrase, *Avatāravariṣṭha*, occurs in the hymn that Swamiji spontaneously composed while performing a puja at the home of a devotee in 1898. The hymn is now sung every evening in most Ramakrishna and Holy Mother temples.)

Men and women proceed through different religions and different ideals, in different times; but all ways are harmonized in Sri Ramakrishna. He is the only person in the history of religion who has demonstrated the harmony of religions through his varied spiritual experiences.

Though Hindus had often heard the verse from the *Rig* Veda, *Ekaṁ sadviprā bahudhā vadanti*—'Truth is one; wise men speak of it in various ways', it was usually viewed as only a theory, a principle. That principle was made living through the experiences of Sri Ramakrishna. He practised all religions, all ways to God, and found that all ways are equally valid. He said, *Yata mat tata path*—'The many religions are so many paths to God.' He not only said these words, he tested their truth and directly experienced it. This all-inclusiveness of the Master makes him 'the greatest of avatars'.

Swami Vivekananda has given his views on Sri Ramakrishna's eminence in letters to various people :

To a devotee in Madras : 'There has been no great soul at any time as lofty as Sri Ramakrishna.'[3]

To Swami Shivananda: 'Brother, if you do not study Sri Ramakrishna, you will not understand the Vedas and Vedānta, the *Purāṇas* and the *Bhāgavatam*. . . . He was the living commentary to the Vedas and to their aim. He had lived in one life the whole cycle of the national religious existence in India.'[4]

To Swami Ramakrishnananda : 'He was the embodiment of all past religious thoughts of India. His life alone made me understand what the Shastras really meant, the whole plan and scope of the old Shastras.'[5]

To Pramadadas Mitra, a scholar and aristocratic landlord of Benares : 'There is no parallel with Ramakrishna—for his unprecedented power, motiveless compassion, intense sympathy for the bound souls.'[6]

To his disciple, Saratchandra Chakravarti : 'Do you know Sri Ramakrishna? We owe all our achievements to him, the whole creation is his—that is Sri Ramakrishna. We worship him because he is of the nature of goodness. He is ever-free, God Himself, who is never bound.'[7]

Again to Swami Ramakrishnananda : 'Sri Ramakrishna was the cup full of nectar—the nectar of the Vedas which was joined with the power of Brahmā, Viṣṇu and Śiva. So many avatars have come to earth; Ramakrishna is the "cup of nectar"—the essence of them all. He is the embodiment of the Vedas, of all gods and goddesses, all avatars. Thus, he is the greatest of avatars.'[8]

In the *Gospel* we find Sri Ramakrishna repeatedly discussing avatars—particularly in his last days. It seemed that he wanted people to understand, to recognize his true nature. Sometimes he would say, 'Before going I will break the pot,' meaning that he would let everyone know who he really was. The educated people at that time did not believe that God takes birth in a human body. One man said in his presence, 'There is no avatar in the *Kali Yuga*.' Sri

Ramakrishna laughed and said, 'How do you know there is no avatar?' He said only these few words.

Swamiji, then Narendra, did not at first believe in avatars. He said, **God is infinite; we cannot even so much as say that the things or persons we perceive are parts of God. How can Infinity have parts? It cannot.** (p.725) How can we limit God who is unlimited? How can you divide the whole? How can the infinite God confine Himself to one body and take part in the divine drama as an avatar? Still, he does just that. Sri Ramakrishna says, **However great and infinite God may be, His Essence can and does manifest itself through man by His mere will.** (p.725)

Śrī Kṛṣṇa says in the *Gītā* :

Ajo'pi sannavyayātmā bhūtānāmīśvaro'pi san
Prakṛtiṁ svāmadhiṣṭhāya sambhavāmyātmamāyayā —

'Though I am unborn, and Myself imperishable, though I am the Lord of all creatures, yet establishing Myself in My own nature, I come into being through My power (*māyā*)'.[9]

Bahūni me vyatītāni janmāni tava cārjuna
Tānyahaṁ veda sarvāṇi na tvaṁ vettha Parantapa—

'Many are My lives that are past, and thine also, O Arjuna; all of them I know but thou knowest not, O Scourge of the foe.'[10]

Sri Ramakrishna echoes these words when he says, **God incarnates Himself on earth in a human body.**(p.883) In the words of the *Bhāgavatam*, *Anugrahāya bhūtānāṁ mānuṣaṁ dehamāsthitaḥ* —'For the blessing of all beings, He assumes a human body.'[11] And the *Kulārṇava Tantra* says, *Sādhakānāṁ hitārthāya brahmaṇo rūpakalpanā*— 'The form of Brahman is assumed for the welfare of the devotees.'[12]

Sri Ramakrishna says that because of the devotees' love, the Indivisible Existence-Consciousness-Bliss Absolute comes to take part in the divine play. The devotees need Him. How can they play alone? Sometimes God appears to the devotee, and sometimes not. This is the game of hide-and-seek between God and the devotee. God hides Himself and the devotee wanders about searching for Him. There is joy in this searching; there are tears, and then there is joy. After weeping comes laughter. If God did not come to earth, there would not be this play.

The Lord loves to play with His devotees, but, such is his all-encompassing love that he comes 'also to draw towards Himself, even persons who are not spiritually inclined, through hearing accounts of these sportive activities.'[13]

'The avatar's descent is for teaching pure Knowledge and Devotion.'[14] We learn from seeing and hearing about the avatar what Knowledge and Devotion are. The avatar points out the ideal for us. Seeing Sri Ramakrishna's life, we understand what intense longing for God is, and how we must cry for Him. We learn the meaning of renunciation, love, endurance, dependence on God, simplicity, and humility. These are the essence of religion. (Formal worship, fasting, vows, etc. are only aids to reach that essence.) When we find these manifest fully in some person, we call him an avatar.

It is the *Sakti*, the Power of God that is born as an Incarnation. (p.726) God is everywhere—everything we see is a manifestation of His power, but the manifestations vary. Sri Ramakrishna says, **Fire, as an element, is present more in wood than in any other object. If you seek God, then seek Him in man; He manifests Himself more in**

man than in any other thing. (p.726) The sun shines on the water, but if the water is still, the sun is seen most clearly, it is most manifest. In the same way, God manifests himself in all, but if we see someone who is free from egotism, full of purity, renunciation, and love, we understand the God is most manifest in him. We call him an avatar. Sri Ramakrishna says, **If you see a man endowed with ecstatic love, overflowing with *prema*, mad after God, intoxicated with His love, then know for certain that God has incarnated Himself through that man.** (p.726)

To explain the concept of the avatar further, Sri Ramakrishna gives an illustration. **By touching the horns, legs, or tail of a cow, we in fact touch the cow herself; but for us the essential thing about a cow is her milk, which comes through the udder. The Divine Incarnation is like the udder.** (p.725) This illustration is in agreement with the scriptures. The *Kulārṇava Tantra* says, 'Milk is distributed all through a cow's body, but it comes from one particular place, from the udder. In the same way, God is everywhere, but He is most manifest in His image.'[15]

The avatar is the best image of God. An ordinary image can be awakened through the force of a devotee's devotion. But the image in the form of the avatar is already awake; out of compassion for the devotees, the avatar becomes a moving image. He goes of His own free-will to the door of the devotee, even after he has finished his Divine Play on earth.

Puruṣaḥ purāṇaḥ[16]—the 'First Man'. He was born as Caitanya, as an ocean of mercy. Why did he come to earth? He came to attract people to himself. People find it easy to love the avatar, thus they grow in spirituality and attain the goal of life—God-realization.

•

Sri Ramakrishna says to everyone, 'Look at me, remember me.' Holy Mother says, 'Always remember you have a mother.' Holy men and women do not advertise themselves. Everything they do is for others. They come to earth out of love; they teach out of love. They know that if people turn to them, they will be blessed. Everything they do and say comes from love.

The *Purāṇa*s say, 'Brahman who is without qualities and actions, becomes Brahman with qualities through the owe of *māyā*'.[17] He assumes a human body and becomes an avatar. We find a similar conception in Christianity. Jesus Christ said, 'I am the Son of God. He who has seen Me has seen God, who is My Father.'

Sri Ramakrishna says, **We see God Himself if we but see His Incarnation.**(p.726) What is meant by 'seeing' or 'knowing' an Incarnation such as Sri Ramakrishna? Does it mean that we must be on earth at the same time he is? Must we see him in person? If that were true, how few could 'see' an Incarnation! Or does it mean to know that he was born in Kamarpukur and his name was Gadadhar Chattopadhyaya? No. To 'know him' or 'see him' means to grasp the meaning of his ideal life, to know that the essence of religion is renunciation, love, purity, knowledge, and devotion. Sri Ramakrishna taught nothing but these. He did not create a new philosophy, a new theory, a new path. The eternal path used by devotees to reach God from time immemorial, Sri Ramakrishna reinstated. And whatever he taught, he practised. This drew many to him when he was on earth, but it is drawing millions more to him now. People pray to him and find he is still living. They love him and try to follow his teachings. They see him in their hearts.

In discussing avatars Sri Ramakrishna uses many illustrations and similes. He says :

Suppose a person goes to the Ganges and touches its water. He will then say, 'Yes, I have seen and touched the Ganges.' To say this it is not necessary for him to touch the whole length of the river from Hardwar to Gaṅgāsāgar. (p.726) My house in on the bank of the Gaṅgā. I can touch the river and use water from it; I don't need the entire Gaṅgā. Brahman is the Gaṅgā in totality; the avatar is the portion of the Gaṅgā near my house that gives me all I need.

The Master continues with his examples :

If I touch your feet, surely that is the same as touching you. If a person goes to the ocean and touches but a little of its water, he has surely touched the ocean itself. (p.726)

Again he says,

'Do you know what an avatar is? Imagine a big field surrounded by a wall. There is a hole in the wall through which you can see that field. The avatar is that hole; through him you can see the Infinite.'

Then he describes the heavy duties of an avatar.

'Let us take for example the caretaker of an estate. After he has returned from one place where he went to settle some dispute, his employer, the landlord, will immediately send him to another place on another assignment. Other employees may take vacations, but the chief caretaker has no rest. In the same way, ordinary people, after many births, at last attain liberation, but the avatar never becomes free. Whenever there is a need, he comes to earth. This play will continue throughout eternity.

Sri Ramakrishna says that this applies to him : 'I will not be liberated but must come again, next time in a northwesterly direction.'

Though Sri Ramakrishna tried to explain the meaning of an avatar, he knew how difficult it was. He said, **God's Incarnation as a man cannot be explained by analogy. One must feel it for oneself and realize it by direct perception. An analogy can give us only a little glimpse.** (p.725)

But a person steeped in ignorance can never recognize an avatar. Śrī Kṛṣṇa says in the *Gītā* :

Avajānanti māṁ mūḍhā mānuṣīṁ tanumāśritam
Paraṁ bhāvamajānanto mama bhūtamaheśvaram—

'The deluded despise Me clad in human body, not knowing my Higher nature as Lord of all existences.'[18]

Still, how can sincere aspirants know him? Sri Ramakrishna says, **I have observed that a man acquires one kind of knowledge about God through reasoning and another kind through meditation.** (p.734) 'Through reasoning' means through the scriptures. In the scriptures signs of an avatar are given. If we find these signs in some person, we call him an avatar. Many renowned scholars, having observed Sri Ramakrishna closely, declared that, according to scriptural definitions, he was an *avatar*. Through meditation our minds become pure and the knowledge that a person is an avatar flashes within us. So meditation is also one way of recognizing a man as God.

The most direct knowledge of God comes through His grace. The Master says: **But he acquires a third kind of Knowledge about God when God reveals Himself to him, His devotee. If God Himself reveals to His devotee the**

nature of Divine Incarnation—how He plays in human form—, then the devotee doesn't have to reason about the problem or need an explanation. . . . Suppose a man is in a dark room. He goes on rubbing a match against a match-box and all of a sudden light comes. Likewise, if God gives us this flash of divine light, all our doubts are destroyed. (p.734)

The Hindu scriptures relate stories about different people doubting the avatar's divinity. Sri Ramakrishna told one story about a Brahmin who became a crow through the curse of a sage. As a crow he could not recognize Rāma as an avatar and tried to escape from him, flying from one celestial place to another. At last he discovered that Rāma was everywhere, there was no escape from him. Though Rāma seemed to be an ordinary human being, the whole universe existed in him.

Another story tells us that there were only twelve sages who could recognize Rāma as an avatar. They said to him, 'You are *Saccidānanda*; you have taken on this form through your inscrutable *māyā*.' Other sages said that Rāma was only the son of Daśaratha, and doubted his divine descent.

Among those who came to Sri Ramakrishna, some thought he was just a priest, but a good man; others thought he was a great devotee. Only a few regarded him as an avatar during his lifetime. The first person to recognize him as an avatar was Chinu Sankhari, a conch-shell seller in Kamarpukur. He was an old man and Sri Ramakrishna was a young boy known as Gadai, but such is the wonder of God's divine play that the two were great friends. Chinu one day worshipped Gadai saying, 'O Lord, I know who you are. I'm an old man and will not live to see your divine play on earth, but please remember that this Chinu Sankhari was the first to recognize you.'

The next person to recognize him was the Bhairavi Brahmani, his Tāntric guru. Later, his devotees Girish Ghosh, the famous actor and playwright, and Ramchandra Datta, a doctor, recognized him as an avatar and tried to convince everyone of this truth. Sri Ramakrishna used to laughingly say that two persons recognized him as an avatar; one was an actor in the theatre, and the other was a doctor dissecting corpses.

Sometimes Sri Ramakrishna would challenge them by asking, 'Can an avatar get cancer?' At other times, he would try to reveal his true nature to his devotees. His days were numbered; and he knew that those who realized who he was would be fortunate.

A Brāhmo newspaper published an article about Sri Ramakrishna written by Keshab Chandra Sen which said, 'We have met a wonderful holy man,' and went on to describe Sri Ramakrishna's renunciation and purity. People were astonished when they read the article and asked : 'Can a person like this live among us in this age when everyone is rushing after wealth, enjoyment, fame and power? How can such a man who throws away all these as nothing live here? Has such a man really come? Where is he?' For the first time the educated and cultured people of Calcutta became interested in Sri Ramakrishna.

Some of them came to see the Master. If he saw they were sincere, he would help them advance on their particular spiritual path. And if he saw some defect or deficiency in anyone, he would try to remove that defect, but he never tried to change anyone's particular spiritual path.

In chapter V, we told the story of four friends, three of whom jumped over a wall because of the beauty they saw on the other side. Sri Ramakrishna is like the fourth man who saw the beauty but stayed behind to tell others about it. He was also like the man who, on getting some delicious food, calls everyone to come and join him in a feast. Other people eat the food and wipe all trace of it from their mouths so no one will know they've been eating. Using still another illustration the Master said, 'Some persons are like small pieces of wood which can somehow stay afloat; but some are like big pieces of wood—like a raft that can carry themselves and many others too.' Sri Ramakrishna is like that big raft; he carries many to bliss and freedom.

Sri Ramakrishna would repeatedly be in a state of *samādhi*, but then he would return to a normal state. He would climb to the top of the Himalayas and then descend. He would not enjoy the blissfulness of *samādhi* alone; he wanted to share it with all. His coming was for this. All avatars come for this. Moved by compassion, they assume a human body. They have no selfish motive whatsoever—only love and compassion.

What amazing superhuman disciplines Sri Ramakrishna practised to realize God! His crying for the vision of the Divine Mother has no comparison. And then he cried for the devotees. He would climb to the roof of the temple and cry out, 'Where are you all? Come!' He could not restrain himself. He was like the sage in the Upaniṣads calling out, 'May the sons of the Immortal, who occupy celestial positions, hear it!'[19] Filled with an intense restlessness, he wanted to share the cup of bliss he had obtained with everyone. He saw that people were ignorant, indifferent to spirituality. They did not want the spiritual treasures he was so eager to give them. In the words of a Bengali song, 'Stretching out both hands, he is calling to everyone to come.'

All avatars are eager to distribute their spiritual gifts. Buddha wandered about on foot setting in motion the wheel of *Dharma*—teaching love, friendliness and compassion. Sri Caitanya and Nityānanda went from door to door giving God's name to all. Caitanya sent his disciples for alms. He said, 'My disciples will go from door to door telling people to worship Kṛṣṇa. They will only beg the people to give their hearts to the Lord. That is the only alms they want.' Caitanya's disciples were insulted and their lives were threatened, but they continued their work. They humbly implored people, 'Say Kṛṣṇa's name just once!' To the ruffian Mādhāi who had attacked them they said, 'You may hurt us with a broken pot, but we will still love you.'

We find the same kind of love in the life of Sri Ramakrishna. There was no rest for him. All day long people would come to him, yet he never became tired or irritable; he only talked with them about God and wakened their spiritual consciousness. He was eager to help everyone, whether they were rich or poor, learned or ignorant, of whatever caste or creed. Because he could not move about without a carriage, he said regretfully, 'Nitāi went from door to door to spread love, I can't do that. I can't move without a carriage.'

Before he became ill, he would visit well-known religious leaders and the elite of society. Who was he? An illiterate Brahmin priest, indifferent to social formalities. He could not even wear his cloth properly. Yet everywhere he went, he was the centre of attraction, the inspired speaker. There are few inspired speakers; God speaks through them. Sri Ramakrishna was one of those rare persons. Highly-educated Westernized people would listen to him spell-bound. Among them was Pratap Chandra Mazumdar who was later to write about the Master : 'What is there in common between him and me? I, a Europeanised, civilised, self-centred, semi-sceptical, so-called educated reasoner, and he, a poor illiterate, shrunken, unpolished, diseased, half-dressed, half-idolatrous, friendless Hindu devotee? Why should I sit spell-bound to hear him?'

Then there was Dr Mahendralal Sarkar who came as a physician to treat Sri Ramakrishna. At first he had little respect for him and his teachings, yet, as the English poet Goldsmith wrote, 'Fools who came to scoff remained to pray.' Not that Dr Sarkar came to scoff, but when he first came to the Master, his only purpose was to treat him. Still, later on we find Dr Sarkar sitting hour after hour by Sri Ramakrishna's side listening to him, completely forgetful of his medical practice. He was not an easy-going man—very firm, adamant, always doing what he thought was right, and extremely outspoken. He believed that certain aspects of Hinduism were nothing but superstition. He was so different from Sri Ramakrishna, still he came to love him. Because Sri Ramakrishna's throat pain would be aggravated when he spoke, the doctor forbade him to speak, but he added, 'When I come, you can speak with me—but only with me.' At dawn Dr Sarkar would wake up wondering about the Master's condition : 'Has his pain become worse? How is he?'

Sri Ramakrishna was always on his mind. When the Master heard about this he said, **You see, he has studied English. I cannot ask him to meditate on me; but he is doing it all the same, of his own accord.** (p.880)

The doctor had received God's grace. God gives his grace in many different ways to different people. A Sanskrit *śloka* says, 'God plays in many ways; but His play as a man is the most charming.' God, who has the power to remove the worldly distress of all, comes to the devotee utterly helpless. In this case, the devotee is the doctor, and God in the form of Sri Ramakrishna depends on Him for his treatment. The doctor believed that the Master could not survive without his treatment. This is the charm of God's divine play.

Sri Ramakrishna seemed to be a very ordinary human being, yet how remarkable his words were! When he went to visit leading members of society, he would sometimes be a little frightened, like a child who is at first afraid when he sees an unknown face. But he would soon regain his composure and start to speak. When he first met the great educationist and philanthropist, Vidyasagar (literally, *Ocean of Wisdom*), he said, 'Today I have come to the ocean. Till now, I have seen only canals, marshes, and rivers, but now I am seeing the ocean.' Vidyasagar smiled and answered, 'Then take some salt-water back with you.' Sri Ramakrishna immediately responded, 'No, why salt-water? You aren't an ocean of Ignorance, but of Knowledge. You are the ocean of condensed milk, not an ocean of salt-water!'

Though he mingled with the highest levels of society, a person's caste or family made no difference to him. To him there was only one caste to be honoured, the caste of lovers of God. If you love God, you are a Brahmin and Sri Ramakrishna is eager to see you. He blessed the low-caste scavenger Rasik and also actors and actresses, who at that time were regarded as immoral and uncultured. He blessed Girish Ghosh, the dissipated playwright and actor, and the actress Binodini, whose reputation was questionable. Sri Ramakrishna had seen her performance in Girish Ghosh's play about Caitanya and had said that she seemed to be the real character, so skilful was her performance.

During Sri Ramakrishna's last illness, Binodini wanted to see him, but it was difficult as the Master's young disciples guarded his door and would never allow such a person to enter. So Binodini disguised herself as a young Englishman and thus entered the Master's room, where he cordially received her. He spoke with her at length, gave her spiritual instruction, and blessed her in many ways.

Holy Mother said, 'Sri Ramakrishna came just for this. Did he come only to eat *rasagollās*?' He came to raise the fallen, the miserable, the weak. Towards the end of his life it was painful for him to speak, still he went on talking about God. He knew that his divine play on earth was coming to an end and there was little time left. He wanted to give all he could in that short time. The avatar is said to be a *Bhūridā*—a giver-of- plenty. He himself was a giver-of-plenty. Did he give material wealth? No, he gave something much more precious — *Yaṁ labdhvā cāparaṁ lābhaṁ manyate nādhikaṁ tataḥ*—'That, on gaining which he thinks that there is no greater gain beyond it.'[20] Sri Ramakrishna gave love bountifully, unstintedly, to the end of his life. He showed us the way out of endless suffering. There was no rest for him, no concern for his own pleasure or health. He blessed even those who had no strong desire for God. He went on his own to them.

In his last days, a crazy woman would come to him to discuss religion. His young disciples protested and did not want to let her enter his room, but the Master said, 'No, let her come.' This is grace, pure, motiveless grace. Swamiji said that he was the 'Eternal ocean of ecstatic love'. He also said that Sri Ramakrishna was 'L-O-V-E personified'.

A Bengali song about Sri Ramakrishna says, 'Come if you want to see a new man!' No one could imagine that there could be such a man in this age when everyone is running after pleasure. The Western education most people were pursuing he dismissed as 'bread-winning education'. From childhood he had no use for book-learning and made a pun on the similarity between the Bengali words for book and knot—*grantha* and *granthi*.

Everyone the world over is eager for money, but what do we find in Sri Ramakrishna? He couldn't touch a coin. He couldn't even bear to have a coin under his mattress, as we find in the incident of Swamiji's testing him that way. He couldn't store up anything, not even a few betel leaves which he tried to carry to his room. We have seen (chapter X) how he wandered about and almost drown in the Gaṅgā till he returned them. His whole nervous system had been disciplined in such a way that he could not take a wrong step even by mistake. We have not found any other person in the history of religion who had this kind of extreme sensitivity.

Sri Ramakrishna bowed down to a fallen woman and said, 'O Mother, in the temple you are in one form and here, in another.' All women were Mother in his eyes. He could see them in no other way.

He is a new man, and those who came with him are also new. He was superhuman, and they were also extraordinary. They can't be compared with other people.

Sri Ramakrishna played a large role in the development of the Bengali theatre through his contact with Girish Ghosh. He would go to the theatre and encourage Girish. At that time cultured people did not go to the theatre and looked with contempt on those who were in any way connected with it. A college principal was walking down the street when a student approached him and asked the way to the theatre. The principal answered, 'I know but I won't tell you.' Swamiji had the same attitude when he was a young man. He said, 'I would not walk on the same side of the street that the theatre was on.'

When people had this attitude, a God-like man like Sri Ramakrishna would go to the theatre. He believed that people would learn through dramas. Because of him, the whole Bengal theatre was changed. Holy Mother said, 'The Master took into account even superstitions.' The avatar does not come to destroy anything, but to fulfil. He works in such a way that whatever is to be discarded, falls off naturally. When I was a young boy, I saw on a theatre billboard the words, Sri Ramakrishna *Śaraṇam*—'Sri Ramakrishna, our refuge'. I could not understand then how Sri Ramakrishna could be connected with the theatre. Now I understand that through Sri Ramakrishna, the Bengal theatre attained prestige and became a force for good.

It was not only the Bengal theatre that was changed; all Bengal, India, the whole world changed with the advent of Sri Ramakrishna. No one has fully understood the historical significance of Sri Ramakrishna's coming. With the passing of time, we will find more and more meaning in his behaviour, his utterances, his spiritual experiences.

Nineteenth-century India was in the midst of a great crisis. The British were firmly in control, and their influence was paramount. We had given up our ancient traditions and were imitating the West. Then came Sri Ramakrishna, the embodiment of eternal India. Living in the outskirts of Calcutta, he at first sight seemed to be only an illiterate village boy. Still, what power of attraction he had! Westernized Indians would come to listen to one who spoke in a rustic Bengali dialect. Slowly, these men and women lost their infatuation with the West. They learned to respect India because they saw in Sri Ramakrishna the real India, the eternal India of renunciation, love, purity, longing for God, selflessness and humility.

Sri Ramakrishna did not publicize himself. Again and again he said, 'I am not a guru; I am nothing,' yet he disseminated knowledge that had accumulated in India from age to age. He taught in a natural way from his own experiences. He was sowing seed for a new civilization, awakening the minds of modern India. In reality he transcended all limits. He and his message are not for any one country or one religion or one age. He belongs to the whole world, to all ages.

Today we can't make the distinction between the East and the West that we formerly did. If we find a new thought in one part of the world, in a moment it has spread to the other part. Knowledge is not confined within any geographical limits.

A society has taken shape through the development of science and technology. It seems that Sri Ramakrishna was able to see today's industrialism which has made the world one, and has also created many problems. The water of the Gaṅgā that Sri Ramakrishna used to call *Brahman-water*, is now polluted by industrial waste. Industries have been built on its holy banks. Sri Ramakrishna seems to have understood that the society that was being formed would change our form of living. We would not return to the age of forest ashramas, but still, the goal of life, God-realization— Self-knowledge—that India has believed in from time immemorial, must not be forgotten. If this goal is kept firmly in mind, then though industrialization, science, and technology all come, they will not be able to harm us. That society will be a model society. Its exterior will be prosperity, activity and happiness, but its centre will be religion.

Knowingly or unknowingly, people today are dreaming of this society. Today's dream will be tomorrow's reality. The future will see this society everywhere on earth. India will show the way, for Sri Ramakrishna has planted the seed of that society.

Swamiji said, 'This time, India is the centre.' Which India? The eternal India that has taken form in Sri Ramakrishna. Religion is the soul of India, and whoever embodies that religion, who is religion itself, is the avatar. Today more and more people everywhere are turning to Sri Ramakrishna, recognizing him as the supreme embodiment of Indian spirituality.

A German writer, Maximillian Von Ragister, wrote an essay in a Bengali weekly (*Indien ist Anders*—'*A Different India*') about his travels and studies in India. After analysing the characters of prominent Indians from Raja Rammohan

Roy to Mahatma Gandhi, he said, 'The man who embodies the essence of India is Sri Ramakrishna.' Von Ragister respected other great Indians, yet in his view they had all been influenced by Western thought; he even included Swamiji in this category. Sri Ramakrishna, he thought, was the only one who completely embodied Indian culture.

The British historian Arnold Toynbee has written : 'At this supremely dangerous moment in human history, the only way of salvation for mankind is an Indian way.' Elsewhere he wrote : 'Sri Ramakrishna's message was unique in being expressed in action. The message itself was the perennial message of Hinduism.' The message of India which Sri Ramakrishna exemplified in his life is the message of renunciation. Modern man is a slave of lust and greed. Sri Ramakrishna points out the error of this way of life. From childhood he rejected both.

Our scriptures say again and again, 'Renunciation is the highest good.' This renunciation is nothing negative. It means giving up the lesser for the greater good, giving up temporary happiness for lasting happiness, renouncing sense pleasure for the bliss of Brahman.

Sri Ramakrishna emphasized this ideal of renunciation. He gave a new definition of man. He called him 'a fully-conscious-being', that is, a person endowed with Self-knowledge, a Knower of Brahman—that was a real man. The Master was a perfect example of that real man, embodying in himself purity, love, unselfishness and all other virtues, at the basis of which was his complete renunciation of lust and greed. His life is a model to us. He is, as if, saying to everyone : 'If you want peace and bliss, if you want to put an end to war and strife, make me your model. Try to build your character from my mould.'

Gradually the teachings of Sri Ramakrishna are spreading everywhere. The world is changing. Swamiji said, 'With the coming of Sri Ramakrishna, the *Satya Yuga*, the age of Truth, has begun.' He said further, 'There will be an awakening of *śūdra*s, the lower classes. Those who are weak and oppressed today will come to power.' He also predicted the rise of women, which we see happening all over the world today.

We don't know the future, but we know that with the coming of Sri Ramakrishna a new age has begun, though it may not be apparent. Any work that is deep, lasting, great, does not advertise itself; so it is often not noticed. We are amazed finding flowers in the morning that were not there before. In the night dew came while we were sleeping and made the flowers bloom. Sri Ramakrishna's influence is like that dew. Unknown to most, he works in silence. His coming has silently ushered in a new age.

We have heard of divine intervention, and how one person who has power from God comes and controls the current of history. Sri Ramakrishna was that kind of person. Whether we understand it or not, whether we resist it or not, Sri Ramakrishna's work will go on; his message will spread all over the world. He came for that.

Different distinguished men have given their opinions of Sri Ramakrishna :

The historian William Digby said, 'During the last century the finest fruit of British intellectual eminence was probably to be found in Robert Browning and John Ruskin. Yet they are mere gropers in the dark compared with the uncultured and illiterate Ramakrishna of Bengal.'[21]

Max Müller did not come to India and never saw Sri Ramakrishna, but he called him 'A Real Mahatman.'[22]

Romain Rolland said that Sri Ramakrishna was 'the consummation of two thousand years of spiritual life of three hundred million people'.[23]

Sri Aurobindo called him 'the epitome of the Whole'.[24]

Christopher Isherwood called him simply 'a Phenomenon'.

How full of variety the Master's life was! How many facets we can see in his personality! All the wisdom of the past has been preserved in one person, Sri Ramakrishna. He is an encyclopedia. Anything that has happened or can happen in the field of religion is collected there. God became small to him, as it were and completely under his control. He conceived of God in all possible ways, according to his whims. People undergo austere disciplines through many lives to get a single experience of God, but Sri Ramakrishna moved easily from one experience to another, just as he pleased. He was like a musician who wanders freely from one song to another. He would rise to the height of the Advaitic experience, seeing only the oneness in everything and everyone; the next moment he would come down to take part in the divine play on earth. He wandered effortlessly between the Absolute and the Relative. Can any words describe him? He was truly incomparable. He is only like himself, utterly unique.

References

1. *Bhāgavatam*, I.3.26
2. *Bhagavad Gītā*, IV.7; IV.8
3. *Patrāvalī*, p.109
4. *Ibid.*, p.255
5. *Ibid.*, p.341

6. *Ibid*., p.36
7. *Ibid*., p.562
8. *Ibid*., p.197
9. *Gītā*, IV.6
10. *Ibid*., IV.5
11. *Bhāgavatam*, X.33.37
12. *Kulārṇava Tantra*, VI.73
13. *Bhāgavatam*, X.33.37
14. *Laghubhagāvatāmṛta* (*Līlāvatāra*), *4*
15. *Kulārṇava Tantra*, VI.76
16. *Caitanya Candrodaya*, V1.74
17. *Brahmavaivarta Purāṇa* (*Kṛṣṇajanmakhaṇḍa*), 43.55
18. *Gītā*, IX.11
19. *Śvetāśvatara Upaniṣad*, II.5
20. *Gītā*, VI.22
21. *World Thinkers on Ramakrishna-Vivekananda*, Edited by Swami Lokeswarananda, 1983, p.29
22. *Ibid*., p.2
23. *Ibid*., p.5
24. *Ibid*., p.18
25. *Ibid*., p.14

XIX

The *Kalmi* Creeper

All of you are coming here again. When you pull one part of the *kalmi creeper*, all the branches come towards you. (p. 359)

When the avatar comes to earth, He does not come alone. Just as a king does not move about without his retinue, so it is with God. When He descends to earth, He brings His companions with Him. We see this in the lives of Śrī Kṛṣṇa, Buddha, Jesus Christ, Śrī Caitanya—in all the avatars. Sri Ramakrishna was no exception. He brought with him a group of men and women. Such persons can't be compared to ordinary people; they were all extraordinary.

Sri Ramakrishna was eager to see them and felt attracted to each one at first sight. That person would think : 'Who have I come to? We seem to have known each other a long time. Why is it that my own parent's love seems trifling compared to Ramakrishna's love?' They did not know then that their lives were inseparably connected with his, but Sri Ramakrishna knew. These men and women had been his companions in birth after birth, his own relatives. And now they were together again.

They seemed to be actors in a drama in which the avatar himself played the leading role. Sri Ramakrishna was the hero in the play and everyone else played the supporting roles of different characters. One was great—that was his role to play. Another was seemingly insignificant—he played that role. But everyone took part in the play. The life, character, and fundamental message of the hero were clearly brought out by the harmonized performance of all.

The Master's followers were divided into two principal groups. One group was composed of his intimate monastic* disciples, such as Naren, Rakhal, and Baburam. They were almost all school or college students. The other group consisted of his householder devotees. Sri Ramakrishna was attracted to them, too, but more to the young students. He said, 'Before the sun rises, butter is churned, because in the heat of the sun butter will not form. The young students have not been subjected to heat—that is, the heat of worldly life has not afflicted them, so renunciation, devotion, discrimination, dispassion, etc., are easily solidified in them.' The Master had special love for them and watched over them carefully. He kept a sharp eye on the

---

*** The monastic names of the Master's intimate disciples who renounced the world soon after his death were as follows :**

Narendra—Swami Vivekananda
Rakhal—Swami Brahmananda
Yogin—Swami Yogananda
Niranjan—Swami Niranjanananda
Latu—Swami Adbhutananda
Baburam—Swami Premananda
Tarak—Swami Shivananda
Sarat—Swami Saradananda
Sashi—Swami Ramakrishnananda
Kali—Swami Abhedananda
Gangadhar—Swami Akhandananda
Gopal (elder)—Swami Advaitananda
Sarada Prasanna—Swami Trigunatitananda
Subodh—Swami Subodhananda
Hari—Swami Turiyananda

Later Hariprasanna joined as Swami Vijnanananda. (p. 976)

development of their spiritual life and protected them from dangers and difficulties.

But his love was not sentimental. If one of the boys ate too many *roṭis* (a kind of bread) at night, he would be displeased; eating would make him sleepy, and night was not for sleep but for spiritual practice. 'Three types of people are awake at night,' he said, '*yogi*s, *bhogī*s and *rogī*s'—spiritual aspirants, pleasure-seekers, and sick people. He would arouse his young disciples in the middle of the night and send them to different places for spiritual practice. One would go to the Panchavati, another to the bank of the Gaṅgā, etc. The special discipline for this age is truthful speech, so it was forbidden to engage in frivolous conversation or gossip. Outside of a few rules like this, he did not give the same teaching to everyone. He taught each person differently and gave each one what was especially suitable for him.

The Master made amazing predictions about these young men, some of which are incomprehensible, but many have been fulfilled to the letter. He called some of his disciples *Īśvarakoṭis**, but not all of them. It is not known why he made this distinction. They were all uncommon, of high calibre, and they were all intimately connected with him. We know this from the remarks Sri Ramakrishna himself made about them.

About Yogindra he said, 'He was Arjuna, Kṛṣṇa's friend.' After Yogin had become Swami Yogananda, he gave devoted service to Holy Mother. He had the shortest life of all the monastic disciples, but it was a wonderful life. He

* Sri Ramakrishna used this term in a special sense to mean a perfected soul born with a special spiritual message for mankind.

was purity itself. Swami Vivekananda used to say, 'Among all of us, Yogin is the one who has most perfectly conquered lust.'

Sri Ramakrishna said about another disciple, 'He is a part of the Divine Mother, pure to the marrow.' That was Baburam Maharaj*, Swami Premananda. When the Master was in ecstasy he could not bear to be touched by everyone, but Baburam, because he was so pure, could touch him. *Naikaṣya Kulīn* 'pure' and *Daradī*—'full of love' (for Sri Ramakrishna), Baburam was able to touch him when he was in that state. Swamiji gave him the monastic name of 'Premananda', meaning the 'Bliss of Pure Love', a name he exemplified in his life. In later days groups of young devotees who came to Belur Math on holidays were attracted by his love. Among them were several learned university students who later on joined the Order. Swamiji had told him, 'East Bengal is yours', and he went there occasionally to preach. In 1917, the last time he went there, so many people came to see and hear him that according to one eye-witness, even Gandhiji's public meeting in that region could not attract so many people. All East Bengal seemed to be floating in Swami Premananda's love. After his passing M. said, 'The love-aspect of the Master is also gone with him.'

Sri Ramakrishna once sat on the lap of another disciple, Sarat Maharaj (Swami Saradananda), to see how much weight he was able to bear. In later years he bore the weight of the Ramakrishna Order as its first General Secretary. He

*Maharaj is used in the Ramakrishna Order with a monk's pre-monastic name as a term of affection and respect—e.g., Rakhal Maharaj, Yogin Maharaj.

was also Holy Mother's protector. She said, 'Sarat is my burden-bearer, my crown jewel.' But he referred to himself as 'Mother's doorkeeper'. Very calm and composed—nothing could disturb him. Swami Vivekananda said that his blood was as cold as that of a fish. There may be other knowers of Brahman, but none of them could be more large-hearted or high-minded than Sarat. And his scholarship and his desire to work for the welfare of all were equally extraordinary. Slow, steady, peaceful, and untiring, he had a remarkable character. Even while carrying out his great responsibilities, he wrote the monumental work, *Śrī Śrī Rāmakṛṣṇa Līlāprasaṅga* (*Sri Ramakrishna, the Great Master*).

Mahapurush Maharaj (Tarak, later Swami Shivananda) said, 'When I first saw Thakur, I felt like calling him "Mother"' Later he would say, 'He is mother, father—everything.' In a letter to Romain Rolland he wrote : 'Exactly who Sri Ramakrishna is, I will never understand—he is so great. But by his grace, I have experienced the joy of *samādhi* three times during his life-time and am still living to demonstrate his greatness.' He was given the name *Mahāpuruṣa* (Great Soul) by Swami Vivekananda who believed that he was a vast receptacle of spiritual power.

The Master said that Swami Niranjanananda was 'ever-pure, there is not the slightest stain in him'. His premonastic name was Nitya Niranjan, meaning 'ever pure'. Sri Ramakrishna also praised his simplicity. Not much is known about Swami Advaitananda, Gopal Ghosh, the only monastic disciple older than the Master. Swami Adbhutananda, Latu Maharaj, was Sri Ramakrishna's miracle. He had come from the state of Bihar to work as a servant in the home of Ramchandra Datta, a householder disciple of Sri Ramakrishna. Coming in close contact with the Master changed the course of his life. Sometimes Latu would carry things to Sri Ramakrishna for Ram Datta. The Master immediately recognized him as a pure receptacle and said to Ram Datta, 'Will you give him to me?' Latu stayed with the Master from then on.

Sri Ramakrishna once said that he had seen a vision of Sashi and Sarat with Jesus Christ. And Swami Vivekananda said that Sashi was the greatest of those devotees who follow the path of service to God. His worship of the Master was awe-inspiring. Whoever saw it felt that Sri Ramakrishna was present—right in front of him. After Sri Ramakrishna's passing the other monastic disciples wandered about on pilgrimage. Only Swami Ramakrishnananda stayed to take care of the Baranagore monastery. Some days he did not even go out of the monastery. Yet, when Swami Vivekananda asked him to go to Madras, he went without a second thought. Sashi Maharaj was very orthodox, as were the people in South India. Swamiji had told them : 'I will send you a person who will surpass all of you in orthodoxy. He is more orthodox than your most orthodox brahmins, yet in worship, knowledge of the scriptures, and meditation, he is beyond compare.'

Sashi Maharaj had to face much hardship when he first went to the South. One day his situation became so unbearable that with a wounded heart he looked at Swami Vivekananda's picture and said, 'Just for you I am suffering so much.' A little later he fell prostrate before the picture and begged Swamiji's forgiveness. (Swamiji had by that time died.) Sashi Maharaj was very scholarly and had a deep understanding of the scriptures, but sometimes no one would attend his lectures. Yet he would stand up in the empty hall and give the lecture anyway. He felt that at least Sri Ramakrishna was listening.

One day he could not get any food to offer Sri Ramakrishna. Entering the shrine he said, 'So you want to test me? That is all right. I will bring sand from the seashore for you and you will have to accept that as offered food. Then I will have to take it as *prasāda*. If I cannot swallow it, I will force it down my throat with my fingers!' He was desperate and meant what he said. Then unexpectedly a devotee arrived with food for offering.

Sashi Maharaj played a great part in publicizing the Ramakrishna Movement in South India. Swami Brahmananda said, 'Like the world-conqueror Śaṅkara, Sashi Maharaj by his power blazed forth in South India.' And after Sashi Maharaj's death he said, 'A great soul has gone away. It is as if the South is in darkness.' He is still remembered there with great reverence.

Swami Akhandananda was the first to put into practice the Master's and Swamiji's *mantra*, *Śivajñāne jīvasevā*—'Service to all creatures knowing them to be God.' His heart went out to the poor and distressed. Once when walking through the district of Murshidabad he came to a little village by the name of Dadpur. There he noticed a little Muslim girl crying. When he asked her why she was crying she explained that on her way to get water at the well she had dropped and broken her earthen pitcher. Now she was afraid to go home because her mother might beat her. Swami Akhandananda also learned that there was a famine in that locality and the little girl had not eaten for several days.

With a few coins he bought her a new pitcher and some flattened rice. Seeing this, other hungry children surrounded him crying for food. With his few remaining coins he bought flattened rice for them. The next morning he left Dadpur, but the further he went, the more he realized that the famine had spread all over the area. He wanted to go away because he could not stand to see such misery, but someone seemed to be pulling him back.

He went to another village and from there sent a letter to the Alambazar Math telling his brother disciples the whole story. Then he began to pray day and night to Sri Ramakrishna to relieve the suffering and hardship of these people.

Some time later, in May 1897, he started relief work in the village of Mahula, near Sargachhi. Swami Vivekananda wrote him a letter encouraging him in his work, and he began to give his whole heart to this service. This was the first work of service by the incorporated Ramakrishna Mission. He eventually built up an ashram for orphans at Sargachhi where he spent the rest of his life. He often recited this Sanskrit verse which he learned from a scholar in Rajasthan named Bhattaji :

Na tvahaṁ kāmaye rājyaṁ na svargaṁ nāpunarbhavam
Kāmaye duḥkhataptānāṁ prāṇināmārtināśanam—

'I do not want a kingdom, I do not want heaven, or liberation,

My only desire is this—to remove the affliction of those who suffer.'

Swami Trigunatitananda was the first editor of the Ramakrishna Order's Bengali magazine, *Udbodhan*. He would work tirelessly to bring it out on time. There was just a small printing press for the magazine. In spite of the great labour required, he would not accept the help of a paid employee but would do all the work of printing himself. At night he worked standing up to keep from falling asleep. He also had great love and reverence for Holy Mother. Once he accompanied her on a journey by bullock cart. It was night and Holy Mother fell asleep. Suddenly he noticed ahead of them a large rut in the road. If the cart went over the rut, he thought, Mother's sleep might be disturbed. So he quickly ran ahead, lay down in the rut and told the driver to drive over his body. Mother woke up just in time and cried out, 'What are you doing? Get up!' After he got up they continued their journey.

Swami Trigunatitananda, at Swamiji's request, went in 1903 to America where he started preaching in San Francisco. After some time he was able to build a Hindu temple there, the first Hindu temple in America. But suddenly calamity struck. One of his students had become deranged and in the middle of a lecture threw a bomb at the Swami. He was mortally wounded, but even as he lay dying he expressed his concern for the young man and would not allow anyone to press charges against him. He said, 'Alas! What a pitiful creature!' He lingered on in pain for fifteen days, then, on Swami Vivekananda's birthday, died.

Both Swami Abhedananda and Swami Turiyananda went to the West at Swami Vivekananda's call. On his first visit to the West, Swamiji sent for Swami Abhedananda to help in his work. He felt that he was the most capable of all the disciples to carry out the work of spreading the message in the West. Sri Ramakrishna had said that next to Naren, Kali was the most intelligent of all his disciples. Swami

Abhedananda spent many years working in the West and did much to spread Vedantic ideas there.

Before Swami Vivekananda went to the West the second time he said to Swami Turiyananda, 'Brother Hari, I am almost dead from carrying on Thakur's work, shedding my blood drop by drop. Will you only stand and watch, and not do anything to help?' Swamiji had previously asked Swami Turiyananda to go to the West and he had refused. Now hearing these words, he could no longer say no. He accompanied Swamiji to America.

Swami Vivekananda had already told his American followers about Swami Turiyananda. He had said, 'I have only talked, but now I am sending you a brother-monk who will show you how to live what I have taught.' He said to Swami Turiyananda, 'Lead the life. Only show them your life. I showed them a Kshatriya hero and confused them with speeches. You show them the brahmin, spiritual ideal.' And that is what Turiyananda did. After Swamiji went back to India, he stayed on in America and established the Shanti Ashrama in a secluded area near San Francisco. He was sometimes completely withdrawn from the world, chanting '*Hari Om Tat Sat*! Śiva, Śiva!' He could often be seen discussing religious topics with a friend as he walked along the street. Passers-by, seeing his strange gestures and hearing his unusual words would laugh, but the Swami would not even glance at them.

He worked very hard for several years in America to firmly establish the work Swamiji had begun. All was going well when a great longing to see Swamiji came over him. He set out for India, but at Rangoon he received word of

Swamiji's death. His heart was broken. He had done his duty; now he would never return to the West. He spent the rest of his life in spiritual practices and in giving out the fruit of his austere disciplines to earnest seekers of God and advising them.

Though often ill, Swami Turiyananda was untroubled—he had very little body-consciousness. As we have noted in chapter IX, when he had to undergo an operation for a carbuncle, he withdrew his mind from his body and the doctor performed the operation without any anesthetic. The operation seemed to be going on in someone else's body.

The lives of all these disciples were indeed extraordinary. Sri Ramakrishna seems to have divided himself into various forms and was manifesting himself through each of them. Their lives were all shaped in his mould. He had once said, 'There are no better monks in the whole world than these.' This proved to be true. In renunciation, in love, in spiritual disciplines, in God-realization—in all these they are beyond compare. Each life could be meditated on deeply, but here only two of them will be discussed at length—Swami Vivekananda, the Master's unique instrument, and Swami Brahmananda, his spiritual son.

Swami Vivekananda and Swami Brahmananda were among the companions of Sri Ramakrishna whom he called *Īśvarakoṭis* or *Nityasiddhas*. There were five others—Swami Yogananda, Swami Premananda, Swami Niranjanananda, Purnachandra Ghosh, and Bhavanath. *Īśvarakoṭi* literally means 'one who is akin to God', while *nityasiddha* means 'the ever-perfect one'. Sri Ramakrishna said many things about these special disciples. Once he said, 'Ordinary people are like flies. They sometimes sit on a flower and sometimes on dung. But the ever-perfect are like bees which sit only on flowers and drink only honey—they won't sit anywhere else.' **The ever-perfect drink only the Nectar of Divine Bliss.**(p.196) An ordinary spiritual aspirant performs disciplines to gain perfection. The flower comes first and then the fruit—that is the usual order. But the ever-perfect are an exception to this rule. They are already perfect, but still they practise spiritual disciplines. **[They] also practise meditation and prayer. But they have realized the *fruit*, God-vision, even before their spiritual practice. They are like gourds and pumpkins, which grow fruit first and then flowers.** (p.249)

The *nityasiddhas* from their very childhood want nothing but God and will have nothing to do with worldly life. Sri Ramakrishna compared them to the *homā* bird, a mythical bird mentioned in the Hindu scriptures and the Persian flok-tales. (The Iranian airline is called 'Homa Airlines'.) The Master said : **The Vedas speak of the *homā* bird. It lives very high in the sky. There the mother bird lays her egg. She lives so high that the egg falls for many days. While falling it is hatched. The chick continues to fall. That also goes on for many days. In the meantime the chick develops eyes. Coming near the earth, it becomes conscious of the world. It realizes it will meet certain death if it hits the ground. Then it gives a shrill cry and shoots up toward its mother. The earth means death, and it frightens the young bird; it then seeks its mother. She dwells high up in the sky, and the young bird shoots straight up in that direction. It doesn't look anywhere else.** (p.563)

The ever-perfect are like that *homā* bird. Their whole lives are directed to God. The Hindu scriptures tell the story of Śukadeva who did not want to come out of his mother's womb for fear of worldly life and remained there for twelve years. When he was finally born, he ran straight to the forest. 'I will not stay in this impermanent world,' he said, 'lest I be bound in *māyā* and take the non-eternal for the eternal. I am running away because of my fear of being bound.' Sri Ramakrishna says, **The ever-perfect form a class by themselves. . . . The ever-perfect are never attached to the world. There is the instance of Prahlāda.** (p.196)

From birth Prahlāda was devoted to Kṛṣṇa (Viṣṇu), but his father Hiraṇyakaśipu, the king of the demons, hated Viṣṇu. He sent Prahlāda to two impious teachers, Śaṇḍa and Amarka, who were to prevent Prahlāda from speaking or hearing about Kṛṣṇa. But Prahlāda was in such a state that every letter of the alphabet reminded him only of Kṛṣṇa.

Akṣare akṣare śiśur kṛṣṇa paḍe mane
Uddīpana hay premadhārā dunayane—

'At every letter the child remembers Kṛṣṇa and becomes ecstatic,
With tears of joy running down his cheeks.'[1]

Hiraṇyakaśipu became very angry and decided to get rid of this boy. He had him thrown from the top of a mountain, trampled under the feet of an elephant, imprisoned with venomous snakes—in all these and other ways he tried to kill Prahlāda, but to no avail. Prahlāda was untouched; he could not be killed. At last Hiraṇyakaśipu asked him, 'Who is protecting you?'

Prahlāda : 'My Hari* protects me.'
Hiraṇyakaśipu : 'Where is your Hari?'
Prahlāda : 'He exists everywhere!'
Hiraṇyakaśipu : 'Is Hari even in this pillar?'
Prahlāda : 'Yes, He is even in that.'

Hearing this, Hiraṇyakaśipu kicked the pillar. Immediately the figure of Nṛsiṁha** sprang out and killed him. Sri Ramakrishna said that Prahlāda was an example of the ever-perfect. No one had to teach him. He was born under adverse circumstances; still, from his very birth his whole mind was on God.

Those who are born as the companions of an Incarnation of God are eternally perfect. For some of them that birth is the last. (p.563) **Narendra, Bhavanath, Rakhal, and devotees like them belong to the group of *nityasiddhas*; they are eternally free. Religious practice on their part is superfluous.**(p.279) **An ordinary man acquires a little devotion after austerities and a hard struggle. But these boys have love of God from the very moment of their birth. They are like the natural image of Śiva, which springs forth from the earth and is not set up by human hands.** (p.196)

In this connection I am reminded of a song that I heard long ago at Belur Math. It was a festival day and as usual, many *Bāuls* came dressed in their colourful apparel. They sang and moved about. On this day, one group sang a remarkable song, the meaning of which was that those who were the companions of Sri Ramakrishna—Narendra,

---

* Hari is a name for Kṛṣṇa.

** Nṛsiṁha was a form of Viṣṇu—half man, half lion.

Rakhal, Baburam and others—each of them was so great if they had come alone, each one would have been worshipped as an avatar. They came together, so we are not able to understand their greatness.

Truly speaking, such men are rarely to be seen. Therefore, if someone calls them avatars, it is no exaggeration. A person like Swami Vivekananda would be the pride of any society, of any country. As Sri Ramakrishna said, the ever-perfect have love of God from the very moment of their birth. His disciples were like that. They were born loving God.

We find this especially noticeable in Swami Vivekananda. As a child, he was very devoted to Śiva, no doubt because Śiva was a sannyasi. Naren (that was his given name) was a strong-willed child, and if for some reason he became angry, it was difficult to pacify him. But if someone would tell him, 'If you behave like this, Śiva will not let you be with him in Kailāsa,' he would immediately become quiet.

But it was not only his love of God that was evident in childhood. Signs of all the other characteristics for which he is now so revered were also observed when he was a child. For example, there was his ability to meditate. He would sometimes play 'meditation' with his friends. It would be play for his friends, but for him it was real meditation. He would become deeply absorbed, losing outer consciousness. One day a venomous snake made its way to the place where the boys were sitting. All of them except Naren ran away in fear. He was in deep meditation, unaware of anything in the outer world. The snake came and went, but he knew nothing about it.

We also find in his childhood evidence of his great heart. When beggars came to his home he wanted to give them everything. To prevent this, one day when they came to beg his family confined him to a room in the upper storey of the house. But he found some clothes in a trunk and threw them out the window to the beggars below.

Although he was very fond of his friends, he was always the leader. The leadership he showed in later life was his birthright. His young friends listened to him and accepted anything he said.

There was also evidence of his future fearlessness. At the risk of his own life, Naren rescued a young companion who was caught in the path of a runaway horse-carriage. His courage as well as his bright mind is revealed in another incident. He and his friends used to climb a tree in the neighbourhood and swing on its branches. An old man living nearby was afraid they might fall and hurt themselves so he tried to frighten them by telling them there was a demon living in the tree who would break their necks. The next day no one played on the tree but Naren, who continued to swing on its branches. One of his friends called up to him, 'Naren, are you still climbing that tree? The demon might break your neck!' Naren replied, 'You fool! We have climbed this tree so many times. If a demon were in the tree, our necks would have been broken long ago.'

The strong practical common-sense shown in this incident was also displayed on another occasion when he and his friends were travelling together in a boat. One of them became sick and vomited on the floor of the boat. The boatmen refused to clean it up. Though the boys offered to pay double the fare, the boatmen told them they would not be able to leave the boat untill they had cleaned the floor.

When the boat reached the shore, Naren leaped out, climbed the river-bank and ran to where some English soldiers were standing. When he explained the situation to them, they came to the boat and frightened the boatmen. The boys were then released.

We find evidence of his bright intellect and sharp reasoning power in his refusal to accept anything on authority without proving it for himself. To cite one instance : Naren's father was a lawyer, and as clients of various castes came to see him, he had a different hookah for each caste. Naren was told that if a person belonging to a particular caste smoked a hookah belonging to a person of a different caste, he might lose caste. Naren wondered what caste was all about. What were all these differences? One day when no one else was present, he smoked each hookah to find out for himself. When his father arrived he asked him what he was doing. Naren answered, 'I was trying to see what would happen if I broke caste.'

By the time Naren had become a young man, Sri Ramakrishna was waiting for him. When the Master first saw Naren, he knew that he was to be his foremost companion. This first meeting was at the home of Suren Mitra where Naren sang several songs. The second meeting was at Dakshineswar. This time when Sri Ramakrishna saw Naren he said : 'Why have you waited so long to come? I have been waiting for a long time.' Then he said, 'I know that you are Nārāyaṇa, born on earth to remove the misery of mankind.' Naren thought : 'He is certainly crazy. I am the son of Viswanath Datta, and he is calling me Nārāyaṇa!' Yet he could not help noticing that Sri Ramakrishna in his conversation with others was perfectly normal.

Then Naren asked him, 'Sir, have you seen God?' And Sri Ramakrishna replied, 'Yes I have. I have seen Him just as I am seeing you, only more intensely.' Naren was astounded. He had asked this question to others before; he had even asked Devendranath Tagore, the esteemed leader of the Brāhmo Samāj, but he had never been able to get such a direct, unambiguous answer. This was quite puzzling. Sri Ramakrishna was obviously an extraordinary person. He could not be called mad, because just seeing him you could understand his wonderful purity, his childlike simplicity. On the other hand, Naren thought, a little while before, he had stood before him with folded hands and uttered words that did not seem normal. Naren then decided that he must be a monomaniac; still, he was a good person and not like others.

After this meeting Sri Ramakrishna became very eager to see Naren again. He would weep and cry, 'Naren, Naren.' Once when Baburam, who did not then know who Naren was, spent the night at Dakṣhineswar he saw that the Master was crying all night long for Naren. Baburam later said, 'The Master felt as if a towel were being squeezed inside his chest, it was so painful. I thought that this Naren must be a very heartless boy to give so much pain to one who loved him so much.' Later, Naren would sometimes reprimand Sri Ramakrishna for this. He would say, 'King Bharata thought so much about his pet deer that he was reborn as a deer. You are the same way. Why do you love me so much?' Hazra also criticized Sri Ramakrishna for his love for the young devotees. Hearing all this, the Master sometimes became worried.

One day, as I was going to Balaram's house in a carriage, I felt greatly troubled about it. I said to the

Divine Mother : 'Mother, Hazra admonishes me for worrying about Narendra and the other young boys. He asks me why I forget God and think about these youngsters.' No sooner did this thought arise in my mind than the Divine Mother revealed to me in a flash that it is She Herself who has become man. But She manifests Herself most clearly through a pure soul. (pp.230-31) Mother made him realize that he was seeing God in these young boys and that is why he loved them so much. God is everywhere, it is true, but He reveals Himself most in pure receptacles. Narendra, Rakhal, Baburam, Tarak—why did Sri Ramakrishna long for these boys? It was because God was clearly manifest in them—they were very pure.

The Master said that Naren was the embodiment of fire—the fire of Knowledge was blazing in him; *māyā* could not come near him. All the rules—about what to eat and what not to eat, what to do and what not to do—were not necessary for Naren. With the other boys, the Master was very particular, but he made few rules for Naren. Naren was a large receptacle. The other boys were good, but they were not like him.

The Master said : **At my first meeting with Narendra I found him completely indifferent to his body. When I touched his chest with my hand, he lost consciousness of the outer world. Regaining consciousness, Narendra said : 'Oh, what have you done to me? I have my father and mother at home!' The same thing happened at Jadu Mallick's house.** (p.231) That day, at a mere touch, Naren lost outer consciousness. At this time Sri Ramakrishna asked him questions about who he was, where he had come from, what his purpose in coming was, etc. The Master had previously seen Naren as one of the seven sages. He had once in an ecstatic state gone to the realm of the unconditioned, nondual, formless Brahman. He said, 'Going there I saw all the ṛṣis sitting there in deep *samādhi*. A divine child approached them and gently threw his arms around the neck of one of them, saying, "I am going. You must go too." The ṛṣi opened his eyes, and though he did not say a word, I understood that he gave his assent.' That ṛṣi was Naren and Sri Ramakrishna himself was the divine child.

In birth after birth they had been together. Time after time they had come to earth. Because of this Sri Ramakrishna was able to recognize Naren and love him at first sight. You always know your own. How could he live without him?

As the days passed I longed more and more to see him. My heart yearned for him. One day at that time I said to Bholanath* : 'Can you tell me why I should feel this way? There is a boy called Narendra, of the *Kāyastha* caste. Why should I feel so restless for him?' Bholanath said : 'You will find the explanation in the *Mahābhārata*. On coming down to the plane of ordinary consciousness, a man established in *samādhi* enjoys himself in the company of *sāttvika* people. He feels peace of mind at the sight of such men.' When I heard this my mind was set at ease. Now and then I would sit alone and weep for the sight of Narendra. (p.231)

Our scriptures say that if a man attains *samādhi*, his body will last only twenty-one days in that state because the body cannot exist without desires. But avatars or those

---

* Bholanath was a clerk at the Dakshineswar Temple.

similar to avatar, after *samādhi*, retain the desire to do good to the world. With that desire they hold on to their bodies. They behave like ordinary men and women, but they are not ordinary. If we try to measure them with our own measuring-rods, we will misjudge them. Are there any rules for them? There are rules for ordinary people, but those who have experienced *samādhi*, Knowers of Brahman, are above all rules.

The *Kulārṇava Tantra* says :

Parabrahmaṇi vijñāte samastairniyamairalam
Tālavṛntena kiṁ kāryaṁ labdhe malayamārute—

'There are no rules for him who has attained Brahman. When the *malay* (vernal) breeze blows, what need is there of a fan?'[2] When a person reaches the Highest Good, he never does anything wrong. Whatever he does, whatever he desires—it is all for the good of the world. He can't harm anyone, even by mistake.

Another verse in the *Kulārṇava Tantra* states,

Yogī lokopakārāya bhogān bhuṅkte na kāṅkṣayā—

'Whatever Realized Souls do is for the good of all. They have no other desire.'[3] This was especially true of Sri Ramakrishna; he never did anything out of selfish desire. Even his love for Naren was selfless. The Master had come to earth for the good of the world, and the Divine Mother had told him, that Naren would be his greatest instrument. Remembering Her words, he was aware that his own play on earth would be fruitful only if Naren played a vital role, so he was very much concerned about him. This is not to deny that Sri Ramakrishna had a great personal love for Naren, but even that personal love was not like what we ordinarily think of as 'love'. There was no selfish element in it. It was intense, pure—not of this world.

The *Kulārṇava Tantra* says further :

Yatra yatra gajo yāti tatra mārgo yathā bhavet
Kulayogī caret yatra sa sanmārgaḥ kuleśvarī—

'In whatever way the elephant goes, a path is made, even though there was no path before. In the same way, whatever way a Realized Soul takes, that way will become a path.'[4] He will not take the ordinary path. Other people will follow his path. Sri Ramakrishna made *his* own path. Though Hazra and others might criticize his love for his young disciples, he continued to go on his own path. Their criticism could not make him swerve an inch from his own way, because behind him was a great ideal. So it is with anyone who does something great. Behind him is a great purpose, a great ideal.

We have seen that from the very first, Sri Ramakrishna was lavish in his praise of Swamiji. He said : 'In my Naren there is nothing counterfeit.' 'Naren is a thousand-petalled lotus.' 'He is an unsheathed sword.' He would silence anyone who criticized Naren. He said : **He doesn't care about anyone. One day he was going with me in Captain's carriage. Captain wanted him to take a good seat, but Narendra didn't even look at him. He is independent even of me.**(p.279) 'Narendra does not listen even to me.' The Master said this with pride. It is the kind of pride an ordinary father feels when he sees his son has great presence of mind and is developing a strong personality.

He doesn't tell me all he knows, lest I should praise his scholarship before others. (p.279) Naren was often embarrassed when the Master praised him so highly, even so, the Master went on telling everyone of Naren's brilliance. One day Sri Ramakrishna said : 'Keshab Sen has become world-famous by the force of one power. In Naren eighteen powers are blazing.' Narendra was annoyed when he heard this and said, 'What are you saying? Hearing all this people will say you are certainly mad—comparing a schoolboy like me with the great Keshab Sen!' But the Master said, 'What can I do? Mother has revealed these things to me, and she does not tell me anything but the truth. What she predicts inevitably happens, so I know she speaks only what is true.'

It is indeed remarkable that Sri Ramakrishna could make such pronouncements at that time. What was Narendra's reputation then? Though everyone knew that he was a very intelligent, self-possessed young man, neighbours and others often misunderstood him. They thought he was conceited and precocious. Having passed his B.A. examinations he has become too boastful. Sarat Maharaj, his future monastic brother, also misjudged him the first time he saw him. He had not at that time started going to the Master at Dakshineswar and so was unacquainted with Naren. One day he went to the house of a friend who did not have a very good reputation. He had heard that his friend was being ruined by bad companions, and so had gone there that day to find out the truth of the matter. Entering his friend's house, he informed the servant that he had arrived. While he was waiting a young man of his own age entered. His hair and clothes were very stylish, and as he reclined on a bolster, he started to hum a Hindi song. Sarat thought, 'Mixing with people like this, my friend has become corrupted.' Just then his friend came in, said a few words to him, and then sat down by the young man and chatted with him. He did not say another word to Sarat. What could Sarat do? He sat for a while listening to their conversation and then left. Some time after this, when Sarat had started visiting

Dakshineswar, he often heard Sri Ramakrishna praising someone called 'Narendra', but he had no idea who this person was. Then one day Sarat went to Naren's house and Sarat was astonished to find that the young man he had seen at his friend's house was no other than Narendra!

Later Sarat was to write in his book, *Sri Ramakrishna The Great Master*, that Narendra was so extraordinary that people misunderstood him.

> Ordinary people, contented with walking along the beaten track, happened very often to regard Narendra as arrogant, and insolent and of improper conduct, when they saw his external behaviour. . . . [but] Narendra's arrogance and insolence arose from his great self-confidence, which was the result of the extraordinary mental power hidden within him, and his indifference to the respect shown by people arose from the self-satisfaction due to his pure character.[5]

But Sri Ramakrishna never misunderstood Narendra. There was a time when everyone misjudged him, even those who loved him. Bhavanath came to the Master one day and said, 'We could not even dream Naren would do such things.' Sri Ramakrishna was irritated and said, 'Be quiet! Mother has told me that Naren would never do such things. I will never believe any of this—even if you say it.' He had that much confidence in Naren.

Afterwards Naren would say, 'From our first meeting, Thakur had such undeviating faith in me such as no one else, not even my own mother and brothers, had. That faith and love have bound me to him forever.'

As we have seen, Sri Ramakrishna often praised Naren. One day he said : **[Narendra] is free from ignorance and delusion. He has no bonds. . . . He has many good**

qualities. He is expert in music, both as a singer and player, and is also a versatile scholar. Again, he keeps his passions under control and says that he will never marry. . . . Narendra doesn't come here very often. That is good, for I am overwhelmed by his presence. (p.279)

When Naren came to Dakshineswar Sri Ramakrishna would look only at him though there might be others sitting in the room. Often just the sight of Naren would cause the Master to fall into *samādhi*—his love for him was that deep.

But this did not mean that he did not test Naren. One time when Naren came to see him, the Master refused to speak to him, though he spoke with others. Every time he came to visit, the Master would ignore him. When he arrived he would be ignored and when he left he would be ignored. For almost a month this went on. At last Sri Ramakrishna asked him, 'Why do you come here when I don't speak to you?' Narendra answered, 'Do you think I come to listen to you? I love you, and that is why I come.' Then Thakur said, 'I was testing you. Only such a great person as you could endure such treatment. Any other person would have gone away.'

Though Sri Ramakrishna loved Naren for this and many other remarkable qualities, he was especially pleased with his rational nature. As we mentioned, he once proudly proclaimed, 'He is independent even of me.' He meant that he did not want Naren to blindly accept whatever he said without understanding it. The Master knew through his divine insight that Naren would be a world-teacher, that he was his chosen instrument. One day the whole world would hear his message, the eternal message of India, through Naren. People in the present age value reason and will not accept anything that does not seem rational. Because of this, Sri Ramakrishna wanted Narendra to be well-grounded in reason so that he could better communicate with them.

There is nothing irrational in religion, though some people think that religion is not for rational thinkers. They believe that reason holds good in the field of science but not in that of religion. But religion is also for those who reason. Holding to reason a person can proceed along the path to God. Sri Ramakrishna guided Narendra along this path. He encouraged him to ask questions; he wanted him to debate with others. The *Gītā* says that you are to learn from the guru by questioning, *Paripraśnena*. Question after question is to be raised and discussed; that way a clear understanding of the truth is arrived at. Narendra followed this method. He argued with Girish Ghosh, Dr Sarkar and others. Sri Ramakrishna was delighted because he could see that Naren knew how to ask intelligent, pertinent questions. A sincere seeker for truth does not ask questions just for asking questions. He wants to get to the heart of the matter. Sometimes the Master himself would argue with Naren, but Naren would also debate with others. Then, when the discussion was over, the Master would in a few words clarify the issue.

Sri Ramakrishna had a very effective method of teaching. Like the best teachers, he did not impose his ideas on his followers, but removed obstacles that came in the way of their free inquiry into the subject. They must only make the effort. We can only fully understand a thought or idea when our unimpeded intelligence is allowed to operate. Sri Ramakrishna taught this way. He did not restrict anyone's freedom of thought.

Narendra at first did not like the philosophy of Advaita Vedānta. Sri Ramakrishna, however, knew that he would eventually accept it, so through various little stratagems he would try to arouse Narendra's interest in it. When Naren came to Dakshineswar, the Master would ask him to read a book which dealt with this philosophy. If Naren didn't want to read it, Sri Ramakrishna would say, 'You don't need to accept it, but read it to me.' Then he would ask Naren to sing one particular song, which was Advaitic in its meaning—'All that exists art Thou'.

At last, when nothing came of his efforts, he gave Narendra an experience of Advaita—of the Oneness at the heart of everyone and everything. It happened one day when Naren and Hazra were sitting together outside the Master's room talking together. They were making fun of the Advaita philosophy. Narendra said : 'What is this—everything is God? The waterpot is God, the cup is God; everything I see is God? And we ourselves are God? How ridiculous!' Sri Ramakrishna overheard these remarks, and coming out of his room with his cloth under his armpit, he stood in front of them, half-conscious of the outer-world. He said, 'what are you saying?' Then smiling, he touched Narendra and went into deep *samādhi*. Narendra at once saw that everything was truly Brahman. He returned to his home where his mother gave him something to eat. But he saw that the person who gave him the food, the food itself, the plate, the cup, even he himself were all one. Eating a few morsels, he sat in silence.

When he walked down the street, he would not move out of the way of the horse-carriage. He felt, 'What does it matter if it runs into me? What it is and what I am—we are both the same.' For three days he was in that state. Through this experience the Master showed him the truth of Advaita. He never again questioned Advaita philosophy. How could he?

We only argue about what we do not know. But if something is directly experienced, all questions come to an end.

Gradually Naren came to accept everything. Formerly, when Sri Ramakrishna would say, 'Kālī spoke with me,' Narendra would tell him, 'All that is a delirium of your mind.' But at last he had to accept Kālī. It came about this way : Narendra's father unexpectedly died and the full responsibility for providing for his mother and brothers and sisters was suddenly placed on his shoulders. He could not find a job and was in extreme financial distress. In this condition he came to Sri Ramakrishna and said, 'The Divine Mother listens to you. Please tell her I must have a job.' The Master answered, 'Why don't you ask her? Today is very auspicious. If you speak, Mother will listen. She will hear whatever you have to say.'

That night Naren went to the Kālī temple. Entering, he saw that the image was not made of clay—it was the embodiment of consciousness. The Divine Mother seemed to him a living presence. Narendra was overwhelmed. He forgot he had come to ask for help and could only pray : 'Mother, give me discrimination! Give me dispassion! Give me Knowledge! Give me devotion!' When he returned to the Master's room, the Master sent him back to the temple. But again he was overcome with emotion and could not ask the Mother for anything. After the third attempt, Naren admitted defeat and asked Sri Ramakrishna himself to relieve his family's distress. The Master assured him saying, 'Very well, your family will never lack simple food and clothing'.

All night long Narendra was in a state of joy and sang the song beginning, 'O Mother, Thou art the Saviour! Beyond the cause of all things, Thou art the substratum of all the three *guṇa*s.' How happy the Master was! The next day he told everyone who came to see him, 'Do you know that Narendra has accepted Kālī!'

But there was something else Narendra doubted. The other disciples of Sri Ramakrishna's inner circle all worshipped him as an avatar, but Narendra was not convinced. Could God be confined within a human body? How was it possible? During Sri Ramakrishna's last days at Cossipore Narendra served him devotedly. There was no limit to his love for him. Still he could not accept him as an avatar, as God incarnate in human form. Then one day, just a few days before the Master's passing, when he could hardly say one word, Narendra, seated at his feet was thinking, 'If even now in this state he declares himself to be an avatar, I will believe it.' At once Sri Ramakrishna said : 'O Naren, even now you doubt! He who was Rāma, he who was Kṛṣṇa, is now in this body, Ramakrishna but not in your Vedāntic sense.'*

Later on we find Swami Vivekananda saying, 'I have offered my head for sale to an illiterate.' In truth he did sell his head, and Ramakrishna after leaving the body protected and guided Naren in the same way he had when he was still living.

Several years later, when Narendra was travelling around India, he met the great holy man Pavhari Baba at Gazipur. Swamiji referred to him many times in his lectures and talks. He devoted one entire lecture to him. People of that locality believed that he ate nothing but air, hence his name, which means 'Air-eating-father'. Swamiji had deep respect for him.

*According to Advaita Vedānta, everyone is essentially divine. The Master was saying that avatars such as Rāma and Kṛṣṇa are God Himself and different from others.

One characteristic of Swamiji was his open-mindedness. He loved Sri Ramakrishna very much, more than any other person. He saw his ideal embodied in him totally. But if he found that ideal embodied in some other person, he would also revere him—that was his feeling. Being so greatly attracted to Pavhari Baba, he decided to take initiation from him and learn Rāja Yoga. But amazingly, on the night before he was to take initiation, Narendra saw Sri Ramakrishna standing before him. Thakur did not say a word—he just looked at him. From the look in his eyes, he appeared to be in pain. This happened again and again. Sri Ramakrishna would appear before him, not saying a word. Swamiji finally came to himself and felt embarrassed. He gave up the idea of being initiated by Pavhari Baba. Writing about this incident in a letter he said, 'I am not going to any other person. No one is equal to Sri Ramakrishna.' He had completely surrendered himself to the Master. Later he wrote a poem describing this incident :

> I am singing a song for you. . . .
> I'm a child playing with you.
> Sometimes I become angry
> And want to go away from you,
> Then at night you stand by my head,
> Silent, your eyes filled with tears
> You look intently at my face.
> I turn and hold your feet,
> But I don't beg your forgiveness!
> You can't be angry with me,

I am your son—who but you will endure my impudence?[6]

In the same poem Swamiji said, 'Thou art within my speech. Within my throat Art Thou, as Vīṇāpāṇi (The Goddess of learning).' In a letter he wrote, 'I am a voice without a form.' That voice, the voice of Sri Ramakrishna, is heard through Swami Vivekananda.

Swami Vivekananda once said, 'If I have told you one word of truth, it was his and his alone, and if I have told you many things which were not true, which were not correct, which were not beneficial to the human race, they were all mine, and on me is the responsibility.'[7] This is not exaggeration nor an outburst of love for his guru. It is the truth. The world got Swami Vivekananda because of Sri Ramakrishna. He gave Swamiji as an offering to the world.

As noted in chapter V, Narendra once expressed the desire to remain in the state of *samādhi*, coming down from that state only to eat enough to preserve his body, and then entering into *samādhi* again. Sri Ramakrishna had scolded him saying, 'Are you really so small? I thought you would be like a big banyan tree in the shade of which everyone could take refuge.'

That Swamiji took that scolding to heart is evident from what he said to Swami Turiyananda before going to the West. He said, 'Haribhai, I am still unable to understand anything of your so-called religion. But my heart has expanded very much, and I have learnt to feel. Believe me, I feel intensely indeed.'[8] Swamiji's love for all beings seems amazing to us, but this love is the great achievement of Sri Ramakrishna.

Not only his love for all, but also his lofty ideals, his exalted emotions—all those wonderful traits which we saw in a budding form in his childhood—grew to fruition under his great Master. Before Sri Ramakrishna passed away, he gave his very self to Naren, and by the force of that Power, Swamiji conquered the world. Sri Ramakrishna was the idea; Swamiji was the expression of that idea. Sri Ramakrishna was the *sūtra*, the aphorism, Swamiji was its *bhāṣya*, its commentary. They were one being, like fire and its power to burn.

Swami Vivekananda first appeared before the public at the Parliament of Religions in Chicago in 1893—an unknown monk. He gave a short speech, but it was an utterly new message. All other speakers had preached their own religion. Swamiji spoke in the language of Sri Ramakrishna, *Yata mat tata path*—'As many religions, so many paths.' There are as many ways to God as there are views of Him. God is One; the ways to Him are many. All religions are true—this is the eternal message of India. Hearing this wonderful conception, the whole audience was enchanted. How beautiful it was, how lofty! Swamiji became famous overnight.

That night he stayed in the home of a wealthy family and was treated like a king, but he could not sleep. Leaving the bed and lying on the floor, he bitterly cried, 'O Mother, what do I care for name and fame when my motherland remains sunk in utmost poverty! To what a sad pass have we poor Indians come when millions of us die for want of a handful of rice, and here they spend millions of rupees upon their personal comforts! Who will raise the masses in India! Who will give them bread? Show me, O Mother, how I can help them.'[9]

How versatile was Swamiji's greatness! He had that large heart; yet, seeing his intellect some of the world's outstanding scholars were dumbfounded. Professor Wright said to him, 'To ask you, Swami, for credentials is like asking the sun to state its right to shine!'[10] To others he said, 'Here is a man more learned than all our learned professors put together.' He had the intellect of Śaṅkara and the heart of Buddha. His love went to all. He was a Vedāntic monk, but to him the world was not unreal.

'The world is pervaded by Brahman; the *jīva* is none other than Brahman.' These Vedāntic truths were very real to him. He said, 'God is in front of you in so many forms. . . . Understand that by loving all creatures, you are serving God.' He further said, 'The only God I believe in—the sum total of all souls—and above all, my God the wicked, my God the miserable, my God the poor of all races, of all species, is the special object of my worship.'[11] And, 'We are the servants of that God who by the ignorant is called MAN.'[12] Not man— God.

Sister Nivedita once asked him, 'What is your life's ideal?' He answered in a letter : 'My ideal indeed can be put into a few words and that is : to preach unto mankind their divinity, and how to make it manifest in every movement of life.'[13] The Indian poet Candīdāsa had said, 'Above everything is man.' Swamiji said the same thing, 'Man is above everything'—because man is God. We do not show compassion to living beings; we serve them knowing them to be God. This conviction Swamiji received from Sri Ramakrishna.

Knowledge, work, devotion—all were harmonized in one incomparable man, Swamiji. Sister Christine said, 'Now and then, at long intervals of time, a being finds his way to this planet who is unquestionably a wanderer from another sphere; who brings with him to this sorrowful world some of the glory, the power, the radiance of the far distant region from which he came. He walks among men, but he is not at home here.'[14] Swamiji was that kind of person. He suddenly appeared, coming from a celestial world, bringing with him the light and power of that world. The Bengali poet Nazrul addressed him in these words :

> You are a sage, the flame of the sacred fire,
> Pure—brightly, vigorously burning.
> India's might warrior—I salute you again and again!

Swami Vivekananda was as pure as the flame of the sacred fire—chaste and holy. In him blazed the light of the fire of Knowledge. No impurity could approach him. He once said, 'If the most beautiful woman in the world were to look at me in an improper way, she would immediately turn into a frog in my eyes.' Such was his character. After his first speech at the Parliament of Religions, everyone surrounded Swamiji. An old woman standing to one side watched all this. Seeing so many women waiting to shake hands with him, she thought, 'Well, my lad, if you can resist that onslaught, you are indeed a God.'[15] Afterwards that lady said, 'If ever there was a God on earth, that is the man.'

When Swamiji was at Thousand Island Park, one rainy night two women climbed the hill to where he was staying. They were Sister Christine and Mrs Funke who had seen him in Detroit. They said to him, 'We have come to you as we would go to Jesus if he were still on earth and ask him to teach us.' Swamiji said, 'Ah, if I only possessed the power of the Christ to set you free!'

There was once an informal meeting in Calcutta on the occasion of Swami Abhedananda's birthday. Many people attended, and I was also there. I remember what Swami

Abhedananda said about Swamiji : 'The first time I saw Swamiji in the West, I was amazed. What a personality he had! How learned he was! I thought, "Can this be the Naren I lived with, discussed the scriptures with, quarrelled with?" His personality was as before, only greater. His intellect, his heart, his power of work—in all ways he was prodigious. Only God's grace could have brought this about.'

Romain Rolland wrote : 'I have not seen nor heard Swami Vivekananda. But today when I read his speeches, I receive a thrill through my body like an electric shock. And what shocks, what transports must have been produced when in burning words they issued from the lips of the hero!'[16] He also said, 'It is impossible to imagine him in second place.' Indeed, he was supreme in all fields of knowledge—philosophy, art, history, literature, the various problems of the country. He was the master of them all. No one could come near him in discussions or arguments on any subject.

But with all this, he was as simple as a child. Always cheerful, he made others cheerful. Even the slightest trouble of someone else would disturb him, but he would be unmoved by a hundred such troubles of his own. When the plague struck Calcutta he was in Darjeeling for his health. He at once hurried back to Calcutta. Finding that there was no money to carry out relief work, he said, 'If necessary, we will sell the Math in order to serve the sick.'

Many people think that Swamiji went to America, gave speeches and became famous. After that what troubles did he have? Only success and more success. But if we look into the facts, we will find that though he had many friends, he had as many enemies. In one letter he wrote : 'I have been ridiculed, distrusted, and have suffered for my sympathy for the very men who scoff and scorn.'

In particular it was Christian missionaries and Brāhmos in India who were attacking him in various ways. There were false accusations and vicious attacks—even to the point of attempts on his life. (Sankariprasad Basu describes all this in detail in his book *Vivekananda O Samakālīn Bhāratvarṣa*.) But Swamiji was unmoved by this. He said, 'May God bless them and give them peace.'

In spite of these difficulties, Swamiji continued to work hard all through his life. There was never any rest for him. He worked so hard that his health was ruined and he passed away when he was only thirty-nine years old. But what must be emphasized is this, that though he grappled with many problems of the world and endured so much suffering, he was always immersed in bliss. He had so much fun! Like his guru, he surpassed everyone in wit and humour. In this also, Swamiji was Sri Ramakrishna's worthy son.

Once a French gentleman came to visit the Advaita Ashrama at Mayavati. I happened to be there then and showed him around the ashram and told him something about Swami Vivekananda. Looking at his picture he remarked, 'But he looks smug.' Swamiji looked so cheerful in the picture that the gentleman did not like it. Many have that conception—that if one takes to religion, one should become emaciated, dry, sad. Because the world is full of misery no one has the right to be happy. But we have a different attitude. We say that a religious person must be joyful, and then he will give that joy to all who come in contact with him.

Swamiji was a perfect illustration of this. He was always cheerful. Someone once asked him, 'Swamiji, can't you ever be serious?' And he answered, 'Yes I can! When I have a stomach-ache I am very serious.' When he was in the West, a man who had once lived on an Indian reservation told him this story : 'An Indian's wife died and he placed her in a coffin, then he came to my house to get nails for the coffin. He saw our cook and was attracted to her and asked her to marry him. When she refused he said, "All right, but wait and see. When I come again, you won't be able to turn me away!" A few days later, he smeared his head with oil, put a feather in his hair and came again to our house. He had smeared his head with so much oil that it ran down his cheeks. He felt that this made him very handsome and that this time the cook would not be able to turn him away.'

Not long after, Swamiji and his friends went to see the portrait of himself which an artist had painted. Noticing that a drop of paint had settled on his cheek in the picture, he exclaimed, 'Getting ready to marry!'

When he was in India he once went to someone's house on a special occasion when many people were present. There were some sweets in a plate. Everyone was supposed to share from it. Swamiji ate one and liked it very much. So what did he do? He took another one, put it in his mouth then put it back on the plate with the others. Then he said, 'Look, all these have become polluted. No one else can eat them.' And he pulled the plate towards himself and started to eat them all.

One incident shows how straightforward and guileless Swamiji was. After he returned from the West he gave many talks on Vedānta in and around Madras. At that time there were fanatical orthodox brahmins there who did not approve of him at all. They said that Swamiji was a *śūdra* and that such a low-caste person did not have the right to teach the Vedas. Swamiji could not endure this kind of talk and one day burst out, 'If I am a *śūdra* you yourselves are the pariah of pariahs!' The next day Swamiji's words were printed in the newspapers, creating a great uproar.

Later, when Swami Vivekananda was visiting Almora, Ashwini Datta, a famous man of the time, was also there. (He had met Sri Ramakrishna and was very devoted to him.) He had seen in the newspapers that Swamiji was in Almora but he had not yet gone to see him. He had also heard from his cook that there was an unusual *sādhu* in town who knew English and was travelling around on horseback. One day Ashwini saw from a distance that a *sādhu* on horseback had stopped in front of a house and that an Englishman was holding his horse as he dismounted. Going nearer, he realized that the unusual *sādhu* his cook had told him about was none other than Swami Vivekananda. He went to the door of the house and asked, 'Is someone named Naren Datta there?' From inside Swamiji heard his voice and called, 'Come in, come right in!' Ashwini Babu went in. The two were delighted to see each other and talked for a long time together. Then Ashwini Babu asked him, 'Is it really true that you said to the Madras brahmins, "If I am a *śūdra*, then you are the pariah of the pariahs?" Swamiji admitted that he had said that. Ashwini said, 'But is it right to talk to people that way?' Swamiji quickly responded, 'Who said it was right? I never say that whatever I do is right. I was in a foul mood, so those words fell from my lips.' At that Ashwini said, 'Today I have understood why you are a world-conqueror and why Sri Ramakrishna loved you so much!' Swamiji had not tried to defend himself, but had candidly admitted his mistake.

It is from such trifling incidents that we are able to judge anyone, though we can never fathom such a person as Swamiji. Shortly before Swamiji died he said, 'If there were another Vivekananda, he would have understood what this Vivekananda has done.' Truly, he was so vast, we can never completely understand him. Only his equal could properly measure his worth—and there was no equal.

Swami Omkarananda used to say, 'When we first started coming to Belur Math, we read Swamiji's books, heard about him, looked at his pictures, and we would think that we ourselves had his energy, his intelligence, his learning. Swamiji had his B.A. degree, but I had my M.A. I would go a step beyond him! But after sometime I began to understand better. Where Swamiji was and where we were! If we spent our whole life trying, we could never understand him. We could never approach his greatness—even in a dream.'

Miss Josephine MacLeod, known to us as 'Tantine'—Aunty, was a wealthy, cultured American woman who was greatly devoted to Swamiji. He also loved her and highly praised her organizing ability. People are not aware of how many of her selfless acts are behind the Ramakrishna Math and Mission. She spent many days at Belur Math, where I had the good fortune to meet her.

She had once asked Swamiji, 'How can I help in your work?' And Swamiji had said, 'Love India!' Some days she would sit on an overturned wicker basket by the Gaṅgā watching the labourers working along the side of the river. If someone asked her what she was doing, she would say, 'Loving India'. We once visited her on her birthday and had some of her birthday cake. We said to her, 'Aunty, how old are you?' We felt she was *really* our aunty, so we could ask this question. She answered, 'I am forty.' She appeared to be much older, so we said, 'Women in your country do not tell their real age, so you are perhaps doing the same.' She answered, 'No, it is not that. The first day I saw Swamiji was the beginning of my real life. I count the years from that day. Was I ever a person before that?'

She had a wide acquaintance among prominent Americans and Europeans. One day we saw her coming to the Math with the British Viceroy. She was friendly with Bernard Shaw. She once said, 'Two persons have captivated me. One is the German Kaiser, the other is Swami Vivekananda.' Something else she said is significant : 'You do not now understand Swamiji. If your country some day becomes free, then you will understand who this man is! If he were born in my country, how we would honour him! We would cherish him as a crown jewel. But your country has forgotten its soul. Not knowing itself, it does not know its own man. You do not honour him who is your true leader.

She said these words long ago, but even now we truly honour him? He tried to awaken the whole Indian nation, and he built a seat of honour for this country in the world's forum. Further, he did this at a time when even we Indians, enchanted with anything from the West, despised India.

Someone once remarked that if such a great genius as Vivekananda had not come in contact with Sri Ramakrishna, the world would have been better off; Swamiji would have been a great revolutionary and the whole world would have honoured him. His brother Bhupendranath talked this way as he was a Marxist. But we find that Swamiji brought about another kind of revolution—a revolution of man-making. He said to everyone : 'You are not low; you are not impure. You are eternal, pure, perfect. You are God; you are

Unlimited. You are Brahman!' *His* revolution was a greater revolution—a revolution of changing man into God.

Swami Vivekananda has been discussed at some length because he was Sri Ramakrishna's principal instrument. But in the Ramakrishna Movement, right after Sri Ramakrishna, Holy Mother, and Swamiji, comes Swami Brahmananda (Rakhal Maharaj). Although almost everyone knows about Swamiji, Swami Brahmananda is not so well-known. Sri Ramakrishna called him his 'mind-born son'. In the West he is referred to as Sri Ramakrishna's 'spiritual son'.

One day Sri Ramakrishna complained to the Divine Mother : 'Mother, my tongue is burning from talking to worldly people, I can't stand it any more.' The Mother said, 'Pure and holy devotees will come.' Some time after that he saw in a vision a beautiful young boy standing at the foot of the banyan tree. Then one day the Divine Mother, in another vision, placed a boy on his lap saying, 'This is your son.' The Master was alarmed and wondered how it could be, since he practised strict continence. But the Divine Mother reassured him by saying, 'He is not a son in the ordinary sense, but an all-renouncing mind-born son.' His mind was set at rest.

Again, just before Rakhal came the first time, Sri Ramakrishna had another vision. He saw on the Gaṅgā, Sri Kṛṣṇa in the form of a young boy dancing on a full-blown lotus with another boy. The next moment Rakhal arrived with one of the Master's devotees, Manomohan Mitra, whose sister he had married. Sri Ramakrishna recognized Rakhal as the boy he had just seen dancing with Kṛṣṇa. He asked him, 'What is your name?' The boy said, 'Rakhal.' The Master was struck with wonder. 'Rakhal!' This was as it should be, for Rakhal is the word for Kṛṣṇa's cowherd companions in Vṛndāvana. And, is it not true that he himself then played with them as Kṛṣṇa? He immediately recognised that this was his 'mind-born son' and welcomed him warmly.

Marriage, in most cases a cause of bondage, was a cause of liberation for Rakhal, because through his marriage he met Sri Ramakrishna. His mother-in-law, Shyama Sundari, was devoted to the Master, and thus her son, Manomohan, brought Rakhal to him. A few days after this event, Manomohan also brought Rakhal's wife to Dakshineswar. Seeing her, the Master said, 'She is a *vidyā śakti*,' meaning a power leading to Knowledge. She would not be an impediment to Rakhal's spiritual progress. He told the Holy Mother to welcome her and accept her as a daughter-in-law.

Rakhal almost immediately began to live with the Master. Although he practised hard ascetic disciplines, he behaved like a little child with Sri Ramakrishna. He was eighteen years old, still he would run about and jump on the Master's lap as a child would with his mother. When the Master asked him to bring him something, he might refuse. This would make the Master laugh; he was pleased that Rakhal was behaving as a real son would. If someone blamed Rakhal for something, Sri Ramakrishna would rise to his defence: 'It is not Rakhal's fault. He is so young that if you press his throat milk will come bubbling out.'

Sometimes, however, the Master would discipline him. One day when butter came from the temple, Rakhal started at once to eat it. Sri Ramakrishna sharply criticized him, 'You are so greedy!' Another day the Master said to him, 'Why is it I can't look at your face? Have you done anything wrong?' At first Rakhal could not think of anything. Then he remembered that he had jokingly told an untruth. The Master said, 'You must never say what is not true, even in fun.' On another day, when he was rubbing Sri Ramakrishna's body with oil, the Master said something that angered him and he decided to leave Dakshineswar. But after going a short distance, he felt his feet becoming very heavy—so heavy that he couldn't go a step further. He had to return. Sri Ramakrishna said to him, 'How could you go? I drew a boundary line which you could not go past.' He loved him and disciplined him—in this way he moulded him.

Rakhal's spiritual life flourished. Once Sri Ramakrishna said to a visitor, 'See what a beautiful state Rakhal is in. He is constantly performing *japa*. He should be serving me, but on the contrary, I now have to serve him.' The Master was happy to see his son advancing along the spiritual path.

Rakhal was born in a village near Basirhat, not far to the east of Calcutta, where his father was the local landlord. (We have now a branch at his birthplace.) Coming to Calcutta to attend school at the Training Academy, he stayed in the Simla area where Swami Vivekananda lived. The two met and eventually became close friends. They used to practise wrestling in a gymnasium, and they also started going to the Brāhmo Samāj together. Rakhal was the first of the two to come to Sri Ramakrishna. Being a member of the Brāhmo Samāj, he believed in the formless deity, but after coming in contact with the Master, he came to have faith in God with form. He would go to the Kālī Temple and bow down to the Divine Mother. When Swamiji started coming to Dakshineswar and noticed this, he scolded Rakhal, 'You belong to the Brāhmo Samāj. Why are you worshipping images?' When Sri Ramakrishna came to know of this he said to Swamiji, 'Why do you criticize him? You should not interfere with someone else's belief.'

The Master once said : 'Rakhal has the intelligence of a *rājā*, he is fit to rule a kingdom.' Swamiji immediately understood and said, 'From today we will call him "Raja".' And that has been his name ever since. In the Ramakrishna Math and Mission, Swami Brahmananda is known as 'Raja Maharaj' or just 'Maharaj'. When Swamiji founded the Ramakrishna Math and Mission he made Raja Maharaj president. And when he returned from the West he placed in his hands all the money that Western devotees had given him, saying, 'This is yours. I have carried it with me so long; now handing it over to you, I am at peace.'

Swamiji said about Swami Brahmananda, 'In spirituality, he is the greatest of all of us.' On first returning from the West, he fell prostrate in making obeisance to Raja Maharaj saying, *Guruvat guruputreṣu*—'The son of the guru is to be honoured like the guru.' Swami Brahmananda then fell prostrate before Swamiji saying, *Jyeṣṭhabhrātā sama pitā*—'The elder brother is to be honoured like the father.' (Swamiji was ten days older than Raja Maharaj.) There are many such wonderful incidents. What love there was between those two! Swamiji said, 'Everyone might leave me, but Raja would never desert me. And if anyone on earth can endure my abuse, it is Raja.' Swamiji once rebuked Raja Maharaj for something he had done. The next moment he was remorseful and said, 'Raja, forgive me; I have abused you wrongly.' Raja Maharaj said, 'What does it matter? You abuse me because you love me.' After Swamiji died, Maharaj said, 'It seems like the Himalayas have disappeared.'

It is true that Rakhal was the mind-born son of God Incarnate, still he performed many spiritual disciplines and austerities, especially after the Master's passing away. Vijay Krishna Goswami once asked him why he was doing so much meditation and *japa* when Sri Ramakrishna had already given him everything. Swami Brahmananda said, 'All that I received by his grace I am now trying to make my own through my own efforts.'

While he was at Vṛndāvana he adopted the *ajagaravṛtti*, the 'python discipline'—asking for nothing, accepting only what came unsought. Some days food would come, some days not. Then he took a vow of silence. Once a rich man laid a blanket beside him. Swami Brahmananda noticed it but did not say anything. After some time another person took the blanket away. Again, Swami Brahmananda said nothing. Depending solely on God, he was utterly unconcerned about his body.

Raja Maharaj, as Sri Ramakrishna's mind-born son, resembled him in many ways. Though there was a strong physical resemblance, they were also similar in their inner nature. Sri Ramakrishna's moods, his demeanour, his religious practices, his character—all these were seen reflected in Swami Brahmananda. These were undoubtedly seen in all of the Master's monastic sons, but they were particularly prominent in Maharaj. When he was at the Math, the young monks would often go to his room to meditate instead of going to Sri Ramakrishna's shrine. Sitting in front of Maharaj was like seeing the object of their meditation, Sri Ramakrishna, alive before their eyes.

Maharaj's mind was almost always indrawn, his eyes half-closed. Sitting in an easy chair, he would hold a hubble-bubble pipe in his hand, but the fire in the tobacco would soon go out. His mind seemed to dwell in another realm. Thinking of his pipe, he would bring his mind down a little—(the way Sri Ramakrishna would say, 'I will drink water,' to bring his mind down from *samādhi).* Then he would see people seated in front of him. They had been sitting there a long time, but he seemed to be seeing them for the first time and was not able to recognize them right away.

This can be understood if we look at his pictures. Seeing his eyes we realize that this is another kind of sight—not like ours. His eyes are open, but he seems to be gazing at something far away. Having given up the world, he could see beyond the world. Sri Ramakrishna used the expression 'aimless look' to describe a yogi's eyes. Swami Brahmananda had that same look in his eyes.

Sometimes famous musicians would go to Belur Math and sing for him. Swami Brahmananda would sit in his easy chair, his eyes closed, absorbed in the music. When the song rose to an exalted level, when the song came from the very depths of the singer's heart, he would open his eyes and nod his head back and forth. Then the singer would be pleased. He would think, 'What I have created, ordinary people cannot understand, but Maharaj at least understands. All my efforts are rewarded.'*

---

* Our Indian songs cannot be learned in books; they are the heart's creation. An English scholar said, 'I am writing down the notation of Indian songs. but no matter how hard I try, the results will not be valid. The songs cannot be captured in notes. The notation for a song is written in one way, but when it is sung it is a different song.' The truth is, our songs are living and constantly changing. The singer's mood and his character are reflected in the way he sings the songs.

Sri Ramakrishna's disciples thought Raja Maharaj was really the Master's son, so they honoured him and lovingly cared for him. Once when Swami Brahmananda was visiting the Madras ashram where Swami Ramakrishnananda was in charge, a devotee brought some fruit as an offering to Sri Ramakrishna. Swami Ramakrishnananda gave it all to Maharaj saying, 'When Maharaj eats, it is the same as the Master eating.' If the son eats, it is the same as the father eating.

Girish Ghosh once became troubled by a terrible doubt : 'Is the Master really an avatar?' For a long time he had gone about loudly proclaiming, 'Sri Ramakrishna was an avatar. Just look at Girish Ghosh and have faith! What I was before and what I am now! Who performed this superhuman feat? Sri Ramakrishna! So you must believe he is an avatar.' He had so much faith. But suddenly his faith left him. The doubt arose : 'Was the Master really an avatar?' He was in great mental agony. Many of his friends tried to help him. Even the Master's disciples tried, but that doubt, that lack of faith, would not go away. At last Raja Maharaj came. He said only a few words and that was enough. All Girish's doubts disappeared and his faith came back. He later said, 'This only Raja could do, and no one else.'

One incident reveals how Holy Mother saw him, and also how he saw her. Swami Vijayananda was present on this occasion. He had heard about Maharaj, but he had never seen him. Someone told him that Raja Maharaj would go on a certain date to Bhubaneswar from Howrah Station; if he went there at that time he would be able to see him. So that day he went to the station. Holy Mother was also at Howrah Station that day, preparing to go to Jayrambati, but Swami Vijayananda did not know that. He was waiting for

Maharaj, who finally arrived in a white Rolls Royce which had been loaned to him by the Maharaja of Cooch Behar. When Maharaj got out of the car, he did not go to his own compartment, but went off in another direction. The Swami followed him. Then he saw that Maharaj had gone to a car where Holy Mother was seated in a compartment. Maharaj stood in front of Mother's compartment, trembling. Then, falling on the floor of the platform, he fully prostrated himself before her on the dirty, dusty platform. When he got up, Holy Mother said to him, 'Child, I hear you are going to Bhubaneswar. Be careful. Drink only boiled water.' Her son might be grown, but the mother always thinks of him as her little child. And Swami Brahmananda? He only said, 'Yes mother, yes mother,' again and again. Then, still facing her, he backed away, saluting her with folded hands.

One time at Vārāṇasī, Holy Mother gave each of her monastic sons there a new piece of *geruā* cloth. But she gave a silk cloth only to Raja Maharaj. Someone asked her why she made this kind of differentiation. She answered, '*Rakhal* is my son.' All were her sons, but Raja Maharaj was the Master's mind-born son.

One day Aunt Bhanu, an old woman who lived near Holy Mother in Jayrambati recited a verse about Kṛṣṇa to Rakhal Maharaj. In no time Maharaj went into a state of deep *samādhi*. Many tried to bring his mind down, but it was a long time till he returned to normal consciousness. Then. Holy Mother said to Aunt Bhanu, 'Aunty, Rakhal is a vast ocean. How did you agitate it so violently just by reciting a trifling verse?' She referred to Raja Maharaj as a 'vast ocean'. That he truly was.

One aspect of Raja Maharaj's character has not been mentioned—his sense of humour. He was by nature deep and grave, but like Swamiji he could have a lot of fun. Once when he was staying at the Math he got indigestion and decided not to eat at night. His attendant, Sujji Maharaj, kept some *sandeś* in a covered dish on a shelf in an adjoining room in case Maharaj would feel better the next day and want something to eat. The next morning Baburam Maharaj came to inquire about Maharaj. Raja Maharaj said to him like a little child, 'Can't you see, I get hungry, but no one ever gives me anything to eat!' Baburam Maharaj called to Sujji Maharaj* who came running. 'What is this?' he said. 'You aren't giving Maharaj anything to eat?' Sujji Maharaj hurried to the next room to get the *sandeś*. He removed the lid from the dish, but the *sandeś* had disappeared! He searched here and there, but it was nowhere to be found, and he had nothing else to give Maharaj. Noticing the delay, Baburam Maharaj called to him. Sujji Maharaj came and told him the whole story. Baburam asked him, 'Are you sure it was covered—the cat couldn't get it?' Raja Maharaj then said, 'Yes brother, a very big cat came, uncovered the dish, ate all the *sandeś* and replaced the cover. Then he came here and sat down.' When he said 'big cat', he pointed to himself. He had become hungry early in the morning and had quietly gone to the next room and eaten all the *sandeś*.

---

* Swami Nirvanananda, Swami Brahmananda's beloved *sevak* and disciple. At the time of Swami Brahmananda's death, he blessed him saying, 'You will attain Knowledge of Brahman.' Later Swami Shivananda also gave him a special blessing. He is regarded as a great spiritual luminary by the monks and devotees of Ramakrishna Math and Ramakrishna Mission. It is a rare privilege to receive the special blessings of two great souls. As long-time Vice President of the Ramakrishna Math and Mission, he was the guru of many men and women. He died in 1984 at the age of ninety-four.

One morning Maharaj was strolling around the grounds of the Math when a boy approached him and said, 'I want to be a sadhu. Where is Swami Brahmananda?' Maharaj realized that the boy did not recognize him, so he decided to have a little fun. He said : 'Go over there and you will find a nice, fat, and happy sadhu sitting at the table. He is Swami Brahmananda.' The boy went to the sadhu, who happened to be Mahapurush Maharaj, and made *praṇām*s. He said, 'I have come to meet you.' Mahapurush Maharaj surmised that something was not quite right, and asked him, 'Who do you want to see?'

'Swami Brahmananda.'

'That is Swami Brahmananda over there, walking around the Math grounds.'

'Sir, he told me that you yourself are Swami Brahmananda.'

'No, that is Swami Brahmananda over there, walking about.'

The boy went again to Maharaj who told him, 'No no, I am not Swami Brahmananda—*he* is. Great souls sometimes play tricks like this. Go again to him. Don't give up!'

Again the boy returned to Mahapurush Maharaj, who sent him back to Raja Maharaj.

But Raja Maharaj said again, 'Great souls are like this—going even so far as to give beatings. Keep going back.' But the boy could take no more and started to weep. Then Maharaj said, 'Very well, you can stay at the Math.'

He loved little children and liked to play with them. One day when he was staying at Balaram Basu's house, he asked to have all the children sent to his room. It was evening. When the children came to his room, they saw in the dim light a strange figure which resembled a bear! All of them ran away in fear except one little boy. Tears fell down his cheeks because he was also frightened, but with both arms extended he went towards the figure and said, 'I know you are Maharaj!' Maharaj then took off the bear-skin he had been wearing and embraced the boy.

On Maharaj's birthday, one food is still given at the Math—*William Bhat*. It is a name invented by Maharaj. What is it? After everyone was fed, there were always left-over fruit, milk, sweets, etc. All these would be mixed together under his supervision and given to all those who were present. He named this mixture *William Bhat*. Another of his inventions was *Moglāi cā*–Mogul tea. Tea leaves were soaked in milk instead of water and various ingredients were added—saffron, cloves, carda mom etc. This was *Moglāi cā*.

Once when Raja Maharaj was staying at Bhubaneswar in Orissa, he sent for Swami Akhandananda, who was working very hard to establish an orphanage in Sargachhi. He wanted the Swami to have a few days rest from his heavy responsibilities. When Swami Akhandananda arrived, there was much happy conversation between the two of them. They were like a pair of school boys. (I have observed this same playfulness when Swami Abhedananda and Swami Akhandananda were together, one poking the other with his finger, laughing. Were they recalling their happy times together with the Master?)

Swami Brahmananda and Swami Akhandananda were enjoying each other's company immensely, but Swami Akhandananda after a few days began to get restless. He must leave! 'The boys at the orphanage need me. I have so much work to do in Sargachhi,' he said to Maharaj. But Maharaj kept putting him off with one pretext after another.

'Today is inauspicious for travelling,' or 'The weather isn't very good,' etc. Then one day Swami Akhandananda made a definite decision: he would have to leave immediately. 'Go if you must,' Swami Brahmananda told him. It was arranged that he would go to the station in a palanquin and take the night train. Raja Maharaj fed him well and placed him in a palanquin. At last Swami Akhandananda took leave of everyone and got into the palanquin. After eating, he became a little drowsy and was not paying much attention to where the bearers were taking him. They wandered here and there. At last Swami Akhandananda noticed a light in the distance. He thought it must be the railway station. Suddenly the palanquin came to a halt and he heard the familiar voice of Raja Maharaj saying, 'Is it you, brother? Have you come back?' Then he saw Swami Brahmananda standing with a light in his hand, welcoming him. He had secretly told the palanquin bearers to carry Swami Akhandananda here and there, and then bring him back again. Swami Akhandananda was angry and said, 'This is very wrong of you. You do not understand anything—I have so much work to do!' Raja Maharaj said, 'What can I do? When you bade farewell to us, you yourself said, "I will come again".' (In Bengal, one customarily says, 'I will come again', —**Ami ābār āsbo**—when saying good-bye.)

It was the nature of Maharaj's mind to remain at a high level—in *bhāva samādhi*. But the body cannot survive if the mind is always in that state, so his brother monks and other persons would try to bring his mind down through jokes and trifling amusements. And he himself would try to keep his mind on a lower level by engaging in these funny escapades.

Swami Brahmananda was president of the Ramakrishna Math and Mission for twenty five years—until his death in

1922. Sri Ramakrishna had said that he had the 'intelligence of a king.' This proved to be true. He ruled the monastery impeccably and greatly expanded its field of work. It was then in its infancy and there were many obstacles to be overcome—financial difficulties, trouble with the government, etc. In the midst of everything he was serene, firm, composed. At the time he was establishing the monastery on a firm foundation, as guru he was also graciously initiating many persons and guiding them along the path to God.

As noted, Sri Ramakrishna also had householder disciples. Two of them, Bhavanath and Purna, he called *Īśvarakoṭis*. Nothing much is known about Bhavanath, who was a hidden yogi. Though living a householder's life, he was like a sannyasin. The Master spoke highly of Purna (Purna Chandra Ghosh), saying that he was in the same spiritual group as Naren, though just next to him.

Sri Ramakrishna said that he had seen M. and Balaram Basu among Śrī Caitanya's followers. He said to M. 'I recognized you when I heard you read the *Caitanya Bhāgavata.*' M. was obviously chosen by the Master to write the *Kathāmṛta*—the *Gospel of Sri Ramakrishna*—though he did not realize this at first. Today this book is read around the world. M. was exceptionally fortunate in being God's chosen instrument for this great work.

Another fortunate person was Balaram Basu because Sri Ramakrishna would often stay at his house, which he called his 'second fort'. He said, 'Balaram's food is pure.' M. wrote in the *Gospel* : **Balaram was indeed blessed among the householder disciples of the Master. Sri Ramakrishna often described him as a *rasaddār*, or supplier of stores, appointed by the Divine Mother to take care of his**

physical needs. Balaram's house in Calcutta had been sanctified many times by the Master's presence. There he frequently lost himself in samadhi, dancing, singing, or talking about God. Those of the Master's disciples and devotees who could not go to Dakshineswar visited him there and received his instruction. . . . Whenever the Master was at Balaram's house the devotees would gather there. It was the Master's chief vineyard in Calcutta. It was here that the devotees came to know each other intimately. (p.724) Balaram's house is now a part of the Ramakrishna Order.

In *Sri Sri Ramakrishna-Punthi*, the author, Akshay Kumar Sen, himself a close devotee of Sri Ramakrishna, says about Balaram :

> His head is always bowed low in humility.
> His smiling face and soft voice
> Betoken his many virtues.
> Balaram's devotion is beyond measure. . . .
> Among those happy souls who played with Thakur,
> Balaram is one of the foremost.
> Among devotees there cannot be high nor low—
> Still, he is greatest who receives God's grace most abundantly.

There are no 'big' or 'little' devotees of Sri Ramakrishna. We are not able to make these distinctions. Can an eggplant-seller judge the value of a diamond? But if we see evidence of God's special grace on someone, we can understand that he or she is a large receptacle of spirituality. Viewed from this perspective, it is obvious that Balaram was such a big receptacle, receiving as he did on many occasions Sri

Ramakrishna's incomparable grace. When Balaram's wife was ill, the Master asked Holy Mother to go to see her. Holy Mother said, 'How can I go? There is no carriage.' The Master exclaimed, 'What is this! My Balaram's wife is suffering and you speak like this? Go by foot if necessary.'

Balaram was extremely devoted to Swamiji and the other monks. When Balaram died, Swamiji shed tears. Someone said to him, 'You are a monk and you cry? What is the death of one person?' Swamiji replied, 'Because I am a monk, am I made of stone? Should I not cry for my beloved brother disciple?'

Another wonderful devotee was Nag Mahashay, a doctor who lived in the village of Deobhog in East Bengal. When he first came to see Sri Ramakrishna, he heard him say, 'With their minds on their little pills in their bags, how can doctors put their minds on God who is vast?' That very day when Nag Mahashay went home he threw his doctor's bag into a pond.

Nag Mahashay was the embodiment of humility. Girish Ghosh truly portrayed both Nag Mahashay and Swamiji when he said, 'Māyā tried to trap Swamiji and Nag Mahashay in her net, but both of them escaped. Swamiji was too big to be caught, and Nag Mahashay was so small he slipped through its holes.'

Nag Mahashay was married, but there was a vast difference between his life and that of an ordinary householder. He had no interest in worldly life and depended solely on God. How devoted he was to Sri Ramakrishna! As noted in chapter XII, he wandered about for three days without food or sleep till he found an *āmalakī* fruit which the Master wanted.

Nag Mahashay was equally devoted to Holy Mother. Once he brought her a basket of mangoes. Mother used them as an offering to the Master and then gave him a few pieces. But how could he eat them? Seeing Holy Mother, he had lost all body-consciousness. He took some of the pieces of mango and rubbed them on his head. Another time he came to see Mother he was able to eat, but he also ate the *śāl*-leaf on which the food was served. It was part of the Mother's *prasāda*, so it was holy to him.

Sometimes when he went to see Holy Mother, he could not control himself. The force of his ecstatic mood would cause him to tremble violently. Once she fed him with her own hand because he could not bring his hand to his mouth. On another occasion she gave him a piece of cloth. He thought it was too sacred to wear on his body, so he wrapped it around his head. He would say, 'Mother is kinder than Father,' meaning that Holy Mother's grace was greater than Sri Ramakrishna's. Holy Mother said that though many devotees came, she had never seen one to equal Nag Mahashay.

There were many remarkable incidents in his life. He was usually self-effacing and humble, but he could become very angry. Once a prominent man of his village came to visit him and started to vilify Sri Ramakrishna on the basis of a rumour he had heard. Nag Mahashay at first tried to reason with the man, but the man would not listen and went on and on criticizing the Master. At last Nag Mahashay could no longer endure this slander and began to beat the man with a shoe, chasing him out of the house. (Amazingly, after a few days, the man understood how wrong he had been and went to Nag Mahashay to apologize.) News of this incident reached Girish Ghosh, and the next time he saw Nag Mahashay he said to him, 'Mahashay, you never wear shoes, so how could you beat that man with a shoe?' Nag Mahashay said, 'How? I beat him with his own shoe!'

Once at the time of an auspicious junction of stars when everyone was going to Calcutta to bathe in the Gaṅgā, he left Calcutta and returned to his village. His father criticized him for leaving the Gaṅgā at this auspicious moment. Nag Mahashay answered, 'If you have faith, Mother Gaṅgā will come to your home.' And when the auspicious moment arrived, suddenly water spouted up from one corner of the courtyard of his house. Nag Mahashay put some on his head, and people of the village came running to take some of it. There were many witnesses to this. When Swamiji heard about this incident he said, 'He is a *siddha-saṅkalpa-mahāpuruṣa*. Nothing is impossible to such a great soul.' Swamiji also said about him, 'All East Bengal is aglow from the fire of Nag Mahashay's spirituality.'

All those who came with Sri Ramakrishna were extraordinary. But some had such special characteristics that they could by no means fit in with others. Swami Vivekananda was one of those. Girish Ghosh was another. He was not a calm, pure devotee—he was just the opposite. Extremely gifted, endowed with a penetrating intelligence and a powerful personality, a famous playwright, an actor—he was also dissipated and lawless. He would do many objectionable things and then abuse those who tried to correct or dictate to him. He himself boasted, 'There are no sins I have not committed!' Still, what amazing devotion and faith he had! Sri Ramakrishna said that he had 110% devotion, as if it were overflowing its bounds. His play

Caitanya Līlā at one time engulfed all Calcutta in a sea of devotion. People were overwhelmed by the beautiful songs in it. If a person does not have deep devotion and faith within, he cannot compose such songs. Still, outwardly Girish was like any other man—or worse.

His biography gives many fascinating details of his life. His first meeting with Sri Ramakrishna was at the home of Dinanath Basu in north Calcutta. He had read in a newspaper that Keshab Sen and other Brāhmos often visited a *paramahaṁsa*, a holy man living at Dakshineswar. Then he heard that this *paramahaṁsa* was going to be at Dinanath Basu's house, so he decided to go to see him. He was simply curious.

When he arrived it was evening and a lamp was burning, but Sri Ramakrishna was in a state of ecstasy and was asking from time to time, 'Is it evening?' It was dark, a lamp was burning right in front of him, and the *paramahaṁsa* did not know whether or not it was evening! Girish was disgusted and could not think of any reason to stay longer, so he left.

The second time Girish saw Sri Ramakrishna was at Balaram Basu's house. Balaram had invited him and others. This time he got a different impression. Girish had always thought that a *paramahaṁsa* did not talk with anyone in an ordinary way, but if someone asked, he might give that person permission to massage his feet. But, Girish could see that the Master was not at all like that. This *paramahaṁsa* talked in a friendly way. He greeted people cordially and bowed touching his head to the floor—the very image of humility and modesty.

The third encounter took place when Sri Ramakrishna came to the Star Theatre to see Girish's play, *Caitanya Līlā*.

When Girish came to receive him, Sri Ramakrishna bowed down to him. Girish then bowed down to the Master, who again bowed down to him. This went on for some time, one bowing to the other and the other returning the bow. At last Girish stopped. He had to acknowledge defeat.

Later Girish was to say, 'Rāma conquered the world with his bow and arrow, Śrī Kṛṣṇa with his flute, but Sri Ramakrishna has conquered the world with his weapon of *praṇāms*.' What did he mean by this? He meant that Sri Ramakrishna did not have any outward riches; he came with only inner wealth. His complete lack of egotism was his particular glory. He used to say, 'I know that I know nothing. I am not a guru. I am the dust of the dust of your feet.' It is this humility that Girish Ghosh called his 'weapon of *praṇāms*'. And this humility has made him honoured all over the world today.

Gradually Girish became drawn to the Master—in reality it was the Master who drew Girish to himself. Girish began to understand that Sri Ramakrishna was an avatar, God incarnate in human form. And when this realization came, he surrendered himself completely. Sri Ramakrishna accepted Girish and took on the 'power of attorney' for him, as we have seen in Chapter 9.

Sri Ramakrishna had told Girish, 'You are a *bhairava* (an attendant of Śiva). You have both yoga and *bhoga*—spiritual discipline and worldly enjoyment.' Once the monks at Belur Math dressed Swamiji like Śiva, with ashes, matted locks, trident, water pot, etc. After he had been dressed like this for some time, he took off everything and put it all on Girish saying, 'Sri Ramakrishna used to say that you are a *bhairava* avatar, an attendant of Śiva. There is no difference between us.'

When *geruā* cloths were given to monastic disciples of Sri Ramakrishna, one cloth was left over. The Master put it aside for Girish, indicating that he regarded him as a monk. Still, he forbade Girish to formally renounce the world, though Girish wanted to. The Master said he wanted Girish to continue his work in the theatre, that he was inspiring many people with his plays. When Sri Ramakrishna saw his play, *Caitanya Līlā*, he felt that Śrī Caitanya was actually present on the stage—so great was Girish's genius.

Girish used to boast, 'I am Girish Ghosh of Baghbazar. There is no sin I am not guilty of. If I had known that Sri Ramakrishna would be so gracious as to forgive them all, I would have committed many more.' There is no doubt that the Master took on all of Girish's sins. He once said, 'Because I accepted Girish's sins, I have this cancer of the throat.'

Girish did much to help the Master and later, the Ramakrishna Order. Towards the end of Sri Ramakrishna's life, the relations among the devotees became strained because of disputes over the financial arrangements for the Master's expenses. Girish put an end to the bickering by offering to sell his house to get the necessary money. Later, after the Master's passing away, Girish helped the young disciples in many ways.

There were many other devoted followers of Sri Ramakrishna who were householders. Among the men devotees were Ram Datta and Surendranath Mitra. And there were women devotees such as Golap Ma and Gopal Ma. These, along with his monastic sons, all became a part of Sri Ramakrishna's troupe. Each had a role to play in his divine drama. Some of the devotees played leading roles, and some were like Rāma's squirrels, who seemed to be insignificant, but by bringing stones, played a vital part in building Rāma's bridge.*

Not much is ever said about Surendra Mitra, for example, but it was he who paid the rent for the first monastery, Baranagore Math. The Ramakrishna Math and Mission was started with his generous gift. Ram Datta did much to publicize the Master's teachings, and in the early days encouraged Narendra to go to Dakshineswar. The woman ascetic, Gauri Ma, also helped to spread the message of Sri Ramakrishna, especially among women. Swamiji highly praised her work.

Not all the Master's devotees could be a Swami Vivekananda or a Nag Mahashay, but they were all extraordinary. It is inspiring to read about them. With Sri Ramakrishna as the centre of their lives, they played their different roles and helped the play of the avatar of the Age to unfold.

In age after age they have come with him, and they will come again and again. In truth, they are like the *kalmi* creeper—if you pull one branch the others come along with it. When God comes to earth, His companions come with Him.

References

1. *Bhakta Mālā*, 7th *Mālā*, Dev Sahitya Kutir, 1384
2. *Kulārṇava Tantra*, IX.28
3. *Ibid.*, IX.75
4. *Ibid.*, IX.81
5. *Sri Ramakrishna the Great Master*, p.753
6. *Bāṇī O Racanā*, Vol. VI, 1383, pp.272-73
7. *C.W.*, Vol.III, p.268
8. *The Life of Swami Vivekananda* by His Eastern and Western Disciples, Vol. I, p.388

9. *Ibid.*, p.439
10. *Ibid.*, p.405
11. *C.W.*, Vol. V, p.137
12. *Ibid.*, Vol. VII, p.349
13. *Ibid.*, p.501
14. *Reminiscences of Swami Vivekananda*, p.152
15. *Ibid.*, p.247
16. *The Life of Vivekananda and the Universal Gospel*, Romain Rolland, p.146

XX

Founding the Order

Sri Ramakrishna passed away on Sunday, August 15, 1886, plunging his devotees and disciples into a sea of grief. They were like men in a shipwreck. But a strong bond of love held them together, and they found assurance and courage in each other's company. They could not enjoy the friendship of worldly people and would talk only of their Master. . . . The young unmarried disciples of the Master, who belonged to his inner circle, had attended on him day and night at the Cossipore garden house. After his passing away most of them returned to their families against their own wills. . . . But Sri Ramakrishna had made them renounce the world mentally. (p.975)

It was Sri Ramakrishna himself who created his own Order. Once when Lady Minto visited Belur Math, she asked Swami Shivananda if Swami Vivekananda had established the Math. Swami Shivananda replied, 'No, it was not Swami Vivekananda but Sri Ramakrishna who created this Order, just before his passing away.'

During Sri Ramakrishna's last illness, when he was staying at a Cossipore garden house near Calcutta, his young disciples became united in an irrevocable bond of love. Before that there had been only a formal relationship between them; they would visit each other's homes, etc., but they were not very intimately related. Holy Mother later recalled : 'They used to call each other "Naren Babu", or

"Rakhal Babu", etc.—it was that kind of relationship. But at the time of the Master's last illness, the disciples would be with him constantly, serving him night and day. Gradually they came to be very intimate with each other. And I saw that even with his body failing, Sri Ramakrishna was planting the seed of renunciation in them and keeping a sharp eye on them.'

Sometimes the Master would teach one separately, and sometimes he taught them all together. They served him devotedly and also practised intense spiritual disciplines. It is hard to say which was more intense, their service to the Master, or their spiritual disciplines.

Narendra was the centre of the circle of disciples. Sri Ramakrishna would often call him aside and give him instruction in private. We do not know what the Master said to Naren, but we can infer that he was teaching him how to guide his brother disciples in the days ahead when he himself would have left the world.

Swami Saradananda once remarked that at this time Thakur's love and the presence of Narendra created a bond between the young men stronger than could be found in any family. Thus, from Sri Ramakrishna's sick bed, the Ramakrishna Order was firmly established by Sri Ramakrishna himself.

One day Burogopal (later Swami Advaitananda) told Sri Ramakrishna that he wanted to serve the holy men at the Gaṅgāsāgar melā. Sri Ramakrishna replied, 'Naren, Rakhal and the others—where will you find holy men equal to them? If you serve them, that will be the best way to serve holy men.' Burogopal, in obedience to the Master, gave one piece of *geruā* cloth each to ten of the young men, and one to himself. This act symbolized the founding of the new Order.

Fifteen days after Sri Ramakrishna's passing, the young monks had to leave the Cossipore garden house. They wanted to keep the house where the drama of their Master's last days had been enacted. However, the rent and other expenses had been paid by Ram Datta along with other householder devotees, and they refused to keep the house longer than the end of August. The young monks would have to leave.

One problem worried them : What should they do with the sacred ashes of Sri Ramakrishna? Ram Datta offered his garden house at Kankurgachi as a fit place for their keeping. But the young disciples were intent on installing the ashes some place on the bank of the Gaṅgā because of their Master's great love for that holy river. Nevertheless, the householder devotees went ahead with plans to carry the ashes to Kankurgachi and selected 23 August, *Janmāṣṭamī*, the birthday of Śrī Kṛṣṇa, as an auspicious day for the event. The young monks vehemently protested. Narendra told the householder devotees, 'Look, having the custody of the Master's ashes is not important. If we are able to build our lives according to his model, that will be the best proof of how much love we have for him.'

In the meantime, Shashi and Niranjan had secretly removed a portion of the ashes and bones from the urn and had taken them to the home of Balaram Bose, a close devotee of the Master who sympathized with the monks. They wanted to keep this portion at his house till a suitable permanent place on the Gaṅgā could be found. When Narendra was informed of this, he was delighted.

So the young monks were able to joyfully take part in the procession which carried the remaining ashes to Kankurgachi on *Janmāṣṭamī*. Shashi carried the urn on his head. In this way a quarrel between the monastic and the householder disciples was averted. Narendra had warned his brother-monks, 'Beware, let no one say in future that the followers of Sri Ramakrishna fought over his ashes.'

After leaving the garden house, some of the young men returned to their homes, but four of them had no place to go, and perhaps their strong determination to renounce the world would not permit them to live with their families. Those four were Tarak, Latu, Kali and Burogopal. Tarak went to Vṛndāvana, and after some time, Kali, Latu and Yogin also went there, accompanying the Holy Mother.

Narendra was then passing through a difficult time. After his father's death, his family was in a desperate financial condition. He had constantly before his eyes the suffering of his mother, to whom he was very devoted, and his little brothers. Some of his relatives had even started a lawsuit against the family to deprive them of their home. In addition to this, Sri Ramakrishna had placed the responsibility for his brother monks on his shoulders. Swami Abhedananda later said, 'We remember Sri Ramakrishna, a few days before his death, saying to Narendra, "Keep these boys together." From that we knew that Narendra was our leader: from then on we followed his orders.'

Years later, Swami Vivekananda said in a letter, 'Sri Ramakrishna ordered me to establish a monastic order. I was bound by my promise to him to serve this band of monks and keep them together.' But it was at first not possible to do this. Half of the disciples returned to their homes. Narendra had no money. What could he do all by himself? Where could he keep these young men?

Then something wonderful happened. A devotee of Sri Ramakrishna, Surendranath Mitra, was meditating in his home after returning from his office, when suddenly he saw Thakur standing in front of him and saying, 'What are you doing? My sons are wandering around here and there. Make some provision for them.' At once Surendranath ran to Narendra's home, which was in his neighbourhood, and said to Narendra, 'Brother, set up a place where you can all be together with the Master. We householder disciples will go there to find peace. I gave money each month at Cossipore; from now on I will give the same amount to you young men.'

Narendra then began to look for a house and wrote a letter to Tarak at Vṛndāvana asking him to return and take the responsibility for the monastery. A house, in very poor condition, was found in Baranagore, a suburb north of Calcutta. It was called the 'Dilapidated House'. The monthly rent for the six rooms was eleven rupees. A few days later Tarak arrived in Calcutta and went directly to Balaram's house where Narendra and Rakhal were staying. All three went to Baranagore by the same horse carriage Tarak had arrived in. It was toward the end of September or the first of October 1886.

This is how the Baranagore Monastery was started. Its first permanent resident was Tarak. After some time, Burogopal and Kali joined him. Some of Sri Ramakrishna's personal belongings, his ashes, etc. were brought there.

Now Narendra had the task of bringing all the young disciples, who had returned to their homes and started their college studies again, to the monastery. Going from house to house, he reminded them of what Sri Ramakrishna had taught them—that they must renounce worldly life and build their lives according to his model. At some of the homes he was not welcomed. The guardians blamed him for encouraging the boys to leave their families. They would say, 'Naren is the one who is at the bottom of all this mischief!'

But nothing could restrain Narendra. He would suddenly appear at a disciple's home, pull him into the street away from his relatives and speak to him of renunciation and dispassion. 'What are you doing?' he would say. 'Will you spend your whole life with school examinations? Is this what your Master wanted? Did he endure so much suffering for this? Are you not a monk? Give up everything at once and hurry to the monastery.' In this way Narendra would arouse in the boys a sense of renunciation.

Narendra himself was unable to stay in the monastery and would come and go between his home and Baranagore. But within a short time all the other monks came and began to stay there permanently. This is how the Order began—through the leadership of Narendra and the generosity of Surendranath. Surendranath, for one or two months, gave thirty rupees a month. After that he would give one hundred rupees a month. Later Swamiji would say, 'Surendra Babu is, on the whole, the founder of the monastery. He bore all the expenses of the Baranagore Math.'

M.wrote in the *Gospel* : **Surendra was indeed a blessed soul. It was he who laid the foundation of the great Order later associated with Sri Ramakrishna's name. His devotion and sacrifice made it possible for those**

earnest souls to renounce the world for the realization of God. Through him Sri Ramakrishna made it possible for them to live in the world as embodiments of his teaching, the renunciation of 'woman and gold' and the realization of God.

The brothers lived at the math like orphan boys. Sometimes they would not have the money to pay their house-rent; sometimes they would have no food in the monastery. Surendra would come and settle all these things. He was the big brother of the monks. Later on, when they thought of his genuine love, the members of this first math shed tears of gratitude. (p.976)

The Baranagore Math had been established for several months when some of the monks went to Antpur, Baburam's home village, over the Christmas holidays. Narendra, Baburam, Sarat, Shashi, Tarak, Kali, Niranjan, Gangadhar and Sarada all went. Rakhal, Hari and Yogin were not in the group. An incident occurred there which has become an important part of the history of the Ramakrishna Order.

One night the young monks were seated together in an open field and decided to light a *dhuni* fire. It was a cold, clear night, and they became immersed in meditation. Then Narendra began to speak about Jesus Christ and his monastic disciples. He spoke fervently about their practice of austerities, and how they spread the religion of Christ all over the world. His words were so glowing that the other monks felt they had been taken to another world.

After he had finished, he said, 'Let us now in the presence of this *dhuni* fire vow that we also, like Jesus Christ's disciples, will renounce the world and like them sacrifice our lives for the welfare of the whole world.' Together they all took that vow. Later, when they discovered that that night was December 24th, Christmas Eve, the evening before Jesus's birth, they were speechless with wonder.

Before that they had not formally taken monastic vows, but now they no longer delayed. When they returned to Baranagore Math after several days, they took the traditional vows of renunciation in front of a *virajā* homa fire, and assumed the names by which they are now known. Narendra took the name *Vividishananda.* Then when he was wandering through India, he sometimes called himself *Swami Sachchidananda.* Just before going to America, he took the name *Vivekananda*, the name he retained the rest of his life, and under which he became world-famous.

How the young monks passed their days at Baranagore Math has been described in a number of books.* From them we have derived facts that will give at least a rough idea of what occurrcd during this time, though it is obvious the story is not fully known.

The young men at Baranagore Math almost all came from good homes, though some families may have been very poor. A few came from aristocratic families. Most of them had studied English. At that time those who learned English had a bright future before them. But these boys were not interested in 'getting ahead'. They were the

---

* Some of the books are : *Āmār Jīvankathā* by Swami Abhedananda. *Śrīmat Vivekānanda Swāmījīr Jivaner Ghaṭanābalī* by Mahendranath Datta, *Swāmī Vivekānanda* by Pramathanath Basu, *Yuganāyaka Vivekānanda* by Swami Gambhirananda, *Atīter Smṛti* compiled by Swami Shraddhananda, *Kathāmṛta*.

playmates of Sri Ramakrishna, a new kind of man. They were also new men—'strange plants', as Sri Ramakrishna used to say of himself. Their rules did not agree with the ordinary rules of society. They were a fire with the ideal of renunciation. They did not want creature comforts or worldly happiness. Although they did not go to the mountains but stayed near Calcutta, they tried to practise the Vedānta of the forest living in a city.

Ordinary people, not understanding them, doubted and mistrusted them and showed their hostility to them in various ways. When they would go to bathe in a pond or river, naughty children in the neighbourhood would shout, 'Look, there go the swans—*pyānk, pyānk*!' The children knew they were disciples of Sri Ramakrishna who was popularly known as *Paramahaṁsa*, which means *swan*. Because of such adverse reactions, the young monks at first did not wear their monastic *geruā* clothes when they went out of the monastery, though inside the monastery they continued to wear them. Bengalis were not used to seeing Bengali monks wearing *geruā*. They would see *nāgā* monks wearing *geruā*, and they would see other *geruā*-wearing monks at holy places such as Gaṅgāsāgar, but the Bengali Vaiṣṇava monks did not wear *geruā*. Also, it seemed strange to the people in the neighbourhood to find educated young Bengali men wearing *geruā* and living in a dilapidated house. Because of this, the young monks asked those writing to them not to use their monastic name on the envelop, but to use their former names.

When they went out for alms women would say, 'You are strong young men, why do you wander about begging? Can't you at least be a conductor on the tram car?' When

Swami Virajananda, Swamiji's disciple, went to live there, he did much of the house work. One day he went to the bank of the Gaṅgā to gather flowers. A gardener seeing him thought he must also be a gardener so he asked him how much money he earned.Swami Virajananda told him that he didn't earn any money at all. The gardener could hardly believe his ears.

One time when Swami Yogananda went to a straw hut to beg for alms, the poor illiterate woman living there began to abuse him in various ways. 'Why do you beg? Can't you work?' she said. Then she continued her tirade, 'You come here for alms in the daytime just to look over my property, then at night you will come back, break into the house and take everything. Don't I know what your intentions are?' With this, she beat a coconut tree with her broom to show her anger. Yogin endured all this in silence. Returning to the monastery, he told his brothers everything, and they all had a good laugh.

How the next-door neighbours used to mistrust them is revealed in another incident. One night they were sitting together singing devotional songs. After a while they stopped singing to listen to Sarat. He sang well but his voice was high-pitched and sounded a little feminine. The neighbours could hear everything and thought some woman was singing. One of them said, 'Are they not monks? How can they sing at night with women? Let's catch them red-handed and expose their hypocrisy.' They then jumped over the wall and came to the place where the boys were seated. When they found there was no woman there, they were ashamed and asked the monks forgiveness. The monks only smiled and bade them farewell.

The young monks took no notice of all these misunderstandings. Their minds were elsewhere. Sri Ramakrishna had taught them many things; all these they must now experience for themselves and make manifest in their lives. So they continued their intense spiritual disciplines and austerities.

Swamiji later said, 'After Sri Ramakrishna died, we used to do a great deal of *japa* and meditation at Baranagore Math. We all got up at three O'clock. Some would bathe and some would not. We would sit in the shrine, immersed in meditation and *japa*. What a feeling of renunciation we had then! We would not be at all conscious of the world.' Their one thought was how to realize God.

M. has described the situation in the *Gospel* :

Narendra and the other brothers of the monastery were full of yearning for God-realization. A fire of intense renunciation raged in their hearts.

Narendra : 'I don't care for anything. You see, I am now talking with you, but I feel like getting up this minute and running away.'

Narendra sat in silence a few minutes. Then he said, 'I shall fast to death for the realization of God.'

M. : 'That is good, One can do anything for God.'

Narendra : 'But suppose I cannot control my hunger.'

M. : 'Then eat something and begin over again.'

Narendra remained silent a few minutes.

Narendra : 'It seems there is no God. I pray so much, but there is no reply—none whatsoever.'

'How many visions I have seen! How many *mantras* shining in letters of gold! How many visions of the

Goddess Kālī! How many other divine forms! But still I have no peace.' (pp.987-88)

All the young monks were full of grief. Days were passing by, and still they had not realized God. The *Vedānta Sāra* describes their condition. *Dīptaśirā jalarāśim iva*—'If a man's head is on fire, he will rush to the water to extinguish the fire.' In the same way, a person in whom the fire of intense renunciation has risen will behave like a madman, running here and there. The young monks were like that.

When M. visited the monastery he would notice all this. Rakhal said to him, **M., let us practise *sādhanā*! We have renounced home for good. . . . Now and then I have a fancy to spend a few days on the bank of the Narmadā. . . . Again, I feel a strong desire to practise the *pañcatapā* for three days.** (pp.994-96) Restlessness for God was constantly goading the monks. The world, the body, did not exist for them.

Swamiji's brother, Mahendranath Datta, has described an incident which occurred in 1888, about two years after the monastery was established. One day Swamiji and Tarak went to Swamiji's family's house, accompanied by Gupta, Swamiji's disciple who later became Swami Sadananda. Though both Swamis were very handsome, they now had a monstrous appearance. They had not bathed or even washed their teeth for many days, so unconcerned had they been about their bodies. Mahendranath and Gupta took them both to the bathroom where they proceeded to scrub them. So much dirt had accumulated, it seemed that an ocean of mud was coming from their bodies.

What did the monks eat? Swamiji later said, 'On many days we had nothing to eat but some rice; we did not even have any salt. Some days we would get a little salt for our rice—but we were completely indifferent to all that. We were immersed in intense meditation and *japa*. Boiled leaves of weeds with rice and maybe salt—that was our diet for months on end. O how those days passed! Even a ghost would have run away from this life—not to speak of men.' Those were happy days. Only the body suffered. The mind was elsewhere—immersed in the joy of God.

Swami Premananda has described their situation. They would not have even one full meal a day. As they had few cooking or eating utensils, they tried to pick banana leaves from a nearby garden to use for plates, but the gardener would not permit this. Then they tried to use arum leaves for plates, but these leaves would irritate their throats. They endured many hardships, but they did not mind. All day and night they were engaged in worship, singing, meditation, etc.

Holy Mother has told of one incident. One day they wanted to test the Master—to see if he were really taking care of them. They decided not to go out for alms, and not even to ask for anything from Surendra. They had left everything for Sri Ramakrishna, now let *him* provide for them. They sat down to meditate. All day long they sat in meditation, but no food came. Then late that night there was a knock at the door. It was someone from a nearby temple bringing a large packet of food. The young monks realized that the Master was really providing for them. They offered the food to him and enjoyed the *prasāda*. This happened on several occasions. Food would come unexpectedly from somewhere.

Sometimes they would say, 'What renunciation and intense yearning the Master had! We can't do even a little of what he did.' They had this divine discontent. We can't even imagine the austerities they undertook at that time. Some would meditate hour after hour, some would be completely lost in singing devotional songs, unaware of the outer world. Some would sit in the cremation ground where they could see in front of their eyes that the body is not lasting. Meditating on death, they would find their minds soaring to regions where there is no death. One would take a vow not to move till he had the vision of the Divine Mother. Another would practise *japa* day and night. Kali, later Swami Abhedananda, practised such intense austerities that he was called *Kali Tapasvī*, Kali the Ascetic. Alone in his room, he was constantly engaged in studying the scriptures and practising meditation. Because he studied Vedānta so much, he was also called *Kali Vedāntī*.

Rakhal's lips would be constantly moving as he incessantly practised *japa*. One day Sarada said, 'I will not stop practising *japa* till I realize God.' Mealtime came, but he did not eat, continuing to practise *japa*. His brother disciples said to him, 'Open the door. Come out and eat a little.' But he paid no attention to them and went on practising *japa*. At last, as they kept begging him to eat he said, 'All right, I will eat something, but brother Tarak must touch me all the time I am eating. If he touches me, that will be the same as my doing *japa*.' Tarak agreed and sat with him, touching him while he ate. Sarada took a few morsels of food then returned to his *japa*.

Latu used to lie down with his brother monks at night and snore as if he were sound asleep. When he thought they were all asleep, he would begin to practise *japa* using his rosary. The rosary gave off a ticking sound which would sometimes awaken the other monks. They thought it was a mouse and would clap their hands to drive it away. Then Latu would stop doing *japa* for a few minutes, till the brothers had gone back to sleep. It went on like this for some days, till at last Sarat discovered what was going on. He said to his brother monks, 'Look, this fellow Latu is going way ahead of us, leaving us far behind. Should we spend all night in sleep while he is having fun doing *japa*? No, let's do *japa* the way he does, all night long.' Intense disciplines were no hardship for the young monks; on the contrary, they were a source of great joy.

They had no money for servants and would do the cooking and all other work for themselves. Later on they may have hired a cook. They all tried to outdo each other in rendering service. But how could the latrine be kept clean. One day Swamiji said, 'Thakur cleaned the latrine of others, can't we follow his example at least this much?' These words touched all hearts. The next day they found that the latrine had been cleaned during the night. One of them had done this work without the knowledge of the others. Then they started competing with each other for this work, trying to get up in the middle of the night before the others were awake.

There was only one latrine and so many monks. If one was using it what could the others do? They would sit together in front of the latrine while they waited, completely nude, discussing the scriptures. They had only one white cloth and one white shawl. These would be kept hanging on a hook. Whoever went out would wear them.

They had no blankets, so in the winter they would lie close together to get little warmth. If it was quite cold they would sometimes get up and wrestle to bring some warmth to their bodies. Their only furniture was one mat covered with a sheet for them to lie on. Their only possessions were some rosaries, a few pictures of gods and goddesses, a *tānpurā*, and about a hundred Sanskrit, Bengali, and English books given them by friends and relatives.

Householder devotees coming to the monastery from time to time would be struck with wonder seeing these young men. Who were these apparitions with eyes aglow? They seemed to be mad! They had really become mad for God. Swamiji used to practise such severe austerities that he seemed to be sacrificing himself in a fire. He would start meditating in the evening and continue the whole night long. At dawn, he would rise. But when he found any of his brother monks injuring their health with their austerities and meditation, he would say to them, 'Do you all think you can become Ramakrishnas? Ramakrishna took one birth on this earth; he came one time. Then sometimes he would say, 'Don't you remember the Master's story of the ant and the mountain of sugar? You are that ant and God is the mountain of sugar. One grain of sugar will fill your stomach, but you want to eat the whole mountain.' In this way Swamiji watched over them and guarded their health.

Swamiji had been chosen to be the leader of the monastic order which Sri Ramakrishna had created. He had promised his Master to nurture it and preserve its ideals. Sri Ramakrishna would live through his Order, and through this Order his message would reach people all over the world.

Rakhal, Baburam, Sarat, Shashi and all the other young monks were apparently nobodies, but they brought about the birth of the Order. In the future Thakur would do great work through them. Their lives were not to be for themselves, but for the good of the whole world. Swamiji was convinced of this, so he kept a sharp eye on them, inspiring them to do spiritual practice and to perform austerities, at the same time warning them against overdoing and injuring their health.

And what love they had for each other! They had one life, one mind. They could not live without each other. Mahendranath Datta said, 'It seemed that they had only one body. If one was pinched, the others would cry in pain. Only those who saw them could understand their love.' But their special love was for Narendra. When he had to go to Calcutta, the others would feel lost and constantly watch for his return. He was their friend, their guardian, their leader—everything. And how much he loved them! How concerned he was about them!

One day on coming back from Calcutta Narendra found that Prasanna had run away from the monastery. He had left a note saying, 'I am going to Vṛndāvana on foot. It is very risky for me to live here. . . . I dream about my parents and relatives.' Narendra heard the whole story and said, **'Just let Raja come back to the monastery! I shall scold him. Why did he allow Prasanna to go away?' (To Harish) 'I am sure you were lecturing him then, standing with your feet apart. Couldn't you prevent his going away?'. . . (To M.) 'You see what a lot of trouble I am in! Here, too, I am involved in a world of *māyā*. Who knows where this boy has gone?'** (p.988)

Prasanna returned after several days. He had been unable to reach Vṛndāvana and had gone only a short way before returning. Rakhal said to him, **'Where do you want**

to go, running away from here? Here you are in the company of holy men. Wouldn't it be foolish to run away from this? Where will you find another like Narendra?' (p.996)

Inevitably they almost all left the monastery. Even Swamiji went away. Probably Swamiji wanted them to stay in the monastery at first so that the Order would be firmly established. After that they could live as wandering monks. Some wandered about for a short time, others for a longer period of time. They travelled all over India. Swami Akhandananda went to Tibet. Sometimes one of the monks would leave the group he was travelling with and after some time, suddenly reappear. Then how happy they would all be!

Monastic organizations are an ancient tradition of India, but the monks usually travel about. They say they are like flowing water, going from place to place. If they stay too long in one place they are afraid they may be bound by the world, by *māyā*. These monks followed that tradition. Swamiji used to say, 'I lit the fire in their minds. I made them leave the monastery and live as wandering monks. Only Shashi did not go.'

From the first Shashi protected the monastery and never left it. While the other monks were engaged in spiritual practice and austerities, unaware of the passing of day and night, Shashi was performing another kind of austerity. He was immersed in the service and worship of Thakur. His service was something to behold. He did not think that Thakur's picture was just a picture; to him it was Thakur in person. The picture was situated on Sri Ramakrishna's bed in the shrine room. In front of it were the container with his ashes, and his shoes.

Swami Virajananda, Swamiji's disciple, who came to the monastery in 1891, has described how Shashi performed the evening worship. 'The smoke from incense filled the shrine room, and while the drum was being played, Shashi would wave the *Cāmara* in front of Sri Ramakrishna's picture, shouting "*Jaya* Gurudev! *Jaya* Gurudev!"—victory to the Guru! Then he would dance so madly that the house would tremble. Though he was very fair, at the time of worship his face would become crimson. He seemed to be the personification of fire. Whoever saw Shashi's worship would be spell-bound.' Shashi was always very careful about the correct performance of worship.

Swamiji said that Shashi's main concern was the service and feeding of the Master and his own brother disciples. He would try to get food for them any way possible—begging or otherwise. 'Some days,' Swamiji said, 'when from morning till late afternoon they had all been practising *japa* and meditation, Shashi would forcefully drag them from their seats and make them eat. Ah, what steadfast devotion we found in Shashi!'

One day it happened that there was no food. The monk who had gone out for alms had returned empty-handed. So the monks decided to pass the whole day without food, doing their meditation, singing, etc. But Shashi could find no peace. If his brother monks wanted to fast, that was all right, but how could Thakur go without food? What was he to do? In desperation he went to a nearby house even though its occupants were very critical of the monastery and its members. Fortunately, a gentleman of that house passed on some rice, a few potatos and little *ghee* through a window without letting anyone know. Shashi returned to the monastery, cooked the food and offered it to Thakur. The other monks were sitting together in one room, meditating, unaware of what Shashi was doing. He went to where they were seated and dropped a little of the offered food into each brother's mouth. They were delighted and said, 'Brother Shashi, where did you get this nectar?' They were so hungry, this simple food seemed like nectar. Swamiji later said, 'Shashi was like the mistress of the house and would take care of everything.' He was the backbone of the monastery.

Pramathanath Basu has written that Swamiji at this time seemed to have inexhaustible energy. Twenty-four hours a day he would be performing spiritual disciplines. He would rise at dawn and rouse every one with his chanting, 'Awake, awake, all ye children of Immortal Bliss!' Then they would all sit in meditation till noon when they would begin to sing hymns, study, discuss the scriptures, etc. After that, they might discuss any subject. It was Swamiji's practice to take up some subject, then spontaneously drift to another subject, as if he were churning the whole ocean of knowledge. When discussing history, he might start in talking about Joan of Arc. From there the talk would drift to the Queen of Jhansi. This might lead to the French Revolution. Swamiji not only talked about the French Revolution, he would quote from memory whole sections of Carlyle's book, *The French Revolution*. And the young monks seated in a circle would sway back and forth crying out, 'Victory to the Republic! Victory to the Republic!'

They had come away from their homes, renouncing everything for God, but their minds were always free. They knew all the latest ideas, and if they found anything good and beneficial, they accepted it. These discussions would sometimes go on for as long as nine hours at a stretch but they didn't notice the time. They did not even think of bathing or eating. At last Shashi would forcibly compel them to bathe and eat. After they had eaten, they would meet and again begin their singing and discussion, continuing throughout the evening. Then they would perform the evening worship for a long time after which they would sit on the roof and chant the Lord's name—*Sītā-Rāma, Sītā-Rāma.*

Swamiji seemed to understand even at this time what form the Ramakrishna Order would take—what its model would be. The basis of the Order was the mantra 'Serve man knowing him to be God'. He inspired his brother monks with the religion of service. They had little to eat themselves, but if they knew of some hungry person, they would go at Swamiji's instigation to feed him. They would nurse the sick—even lepers.

Another aspect which Swamiji stressed was scholarliness. As a young monk, I used to see Swami Akhandananda discussing Buddhism deeply and at length. He had studied only up to class eight or nine, but how much he knew about this subject! And Swami Abhedananda had passed only the final school examination, but in later years, he was noted for his scholarly lectures and writings. Where did all this scholarliness come from? It came from the habit of studying and discussing which began at Baranagore Math. Swamiji was the root of it all. He was the one who inspired them to study.

Later, when new monks joined the Order, Swami Premananda would ask them if they had studied the scriptures. If they had not, he would say, 'Some holy places have become corrupted. This is not that kind of place. Here is a book, finish studying it within such and such a time. If you can't do that, you will have to leave.' Swamiji believed that if studying is not done, the Order would deteriorate. Surely there must be renunciation and spiritual discipline, but there must also be studying. Both must be stressed. This tradition, begun in Baranagore, continues to this day.

How did they study? There was a large room at Baranagore monastery which they called 'the room of the demons'. They would gather there and begin their discussions of religion, music, philosophy, history, physics, sociology, art, etc. They would study the *Gītā*, the Upaniṣads and other scriptures in addition to Western philosophers such as Kant, Mill, Hegel, Spencer, etc. They would even study atheistic and materialistic doctrines.

It was Swamiji's habit to approach a subject at different times from different viewpoints. When he was discussing Advaita, he would reject all other paths. The next day he might speak on dualism and completely reject Advaita. This was his special way of teaching. He was the presiding officer of the meeting as well as the chief speaker. His brother monks would sometimes band together to battle his arguments. But he would bring in a contrary viewpoint and slash their ideas to shreds. Then he would shatter his own arguments.

The question about the existence of God would arise. Narendra would give proof through reasoning that God does not exist, that He is only a mental construct. But they had all left their homes for God! Again, after some time he would prove that God is the only Reality. The discussion would turn to Śaṅkarācārya's philosophy. Narendra would shatter Śaṅkarācārya's reasoning saying, 'There are many holes in his logic.' After some time, he would prove that Śaṅkarācārya's philosophy is the only true philosophy, that his reasoning is irrefutable.

In the same way they would study the six systems of Indian philosophy (*Nyāya*, *Vaiśeṣika*, *Sāṁkhya*, *Yoga*, *Pūrva Mīmāṁsā* and Advaita Vedānta). After discussing these and other profound subjects, they would recite Sanskrit *ślokas*, the *Guru Gītā*, etc. Sometimes they would sing the devotional songs of Rāmaprasāda or songs about Kṛṣṇa. Going back to their studies, they might immerse themselves in the life of Buddha and Buddhism for several days.

Narendra would then feel that they needed to be free from Buddhist influence and would begin to discuss the Hindu *avatars*, great teachers and devotees. For a few days they would discuss Śaṅkarācārya, Rāmānuja, Kabīr, Tulasīdāsa, Caitanya and Rāmaprasāda, and how these great teachers and poets had led the Hindus along the path to God. Then they might spend several days talking about Jesus Christ. At last all discussions would end with Sri Ramakrishna. Whenever Narendra spoke of him, he would become very emotional, his throat would become choked and tears would flow from his eyes.

Then, checking his emotion, he would tell his brother monks how Sri Ramakrishna had laid out a new path, how he had influenced Western-educated Hindus, and how invaluable that influence was. He compared Hinduism to a leaky boat without a helmsman on troubled waters, and pointed out that it had been saved by Sri Ramakrishna and given a new direction. He said, 'The day is fast approaching when you will understand how our Master has brought to life the almost extinct Hindu Religion.'

Historians say that from the earliest times various cultures came to us from outside India, but they did not injure us the way Western culture did. The English cast a spell over us and we began to despise our own culture and religion. Hinduism as a way of life seemed to be dying out. Then Sri Ramakrishna came and brought new life to our withered culture and religion.

The monks at the Baranagore Math also observed the special holy days of all religions. (The Ramakrishna Order continues this practice even now, as it honours and accepts all religions.) One of the first holy days to be celebrated at the Baranagore Math was *Śiva Rātri*, which was observed on the 21st of February, 1887. This has been described in the *Gospel*. All the brothers fasted that day, singing devotional songs from morning till evening. Tarak and Rakhal danced together and sang a song which had been composed by Narendra several days earlier :

> **There Śiva dances, striking both His cheeks; and they resound, Ba-ba-bom!**
> **Dimi-dimi-dimi! sounds His drum; a garland of skulls from His neck is hanging!**
> **In His matted locks the Ganges hisses; fire shoots from His mighty trident!**
> **Round His waist a serpent glitters, and on His brow the moon is shining!** (pp.977-78)

They began the formal worship at nine o'clock in the evening under the *bel* tree in the monastery compound. It was performed four times during the four watches of the night. All the brothers were present. One of them acted as priest while Kali read from the *Gītā*. During the reading, he would now and then argue with Narendra.

After the reading was finished they all began to sing and dance around the *bel* tree. **It was midnight, the fourteenth day of the dark fortnight of the moon. Pitch darkness filled all the quarters. . . . The young sannyasins were clad in *geruā* robes.** (p.979) They interspersed their singing with loud chants of 'Śiva Guru! Śiva Guru!' Just before dawn they ended their worship, bathed in the Ganges and partook of the food which had been offered to Śiva.

They would celebrate Christmas with the lighting of the sacred *dhuni* fire. They also observed Good Friday. On one occasion they spent the whole day of Good Friday in meditation and fasting. They had been able to get a few grapes from which they had made grape juice and they had all had a sip of this. At night as they sat thinking of Jesus Christ, there was a knock at the door and they heard a voice from outside saying, 'Who is there? For Jesus' sake, open the door!' The young monks thought, 'What a strange coincidence. While we are observing Good Friday, someone is coming to us in the name of Christ. It's wonderful that we can hear about Christ from a Christian!' They opened the door, invited the man to come in and tell them something about Good Friday.

But the man said, 'I am a Salvation Army preacher. I know nothing about Good Friday. We observe only two holy days, Christmas and General Booth's birthday.' The monks were very disappointed. They were also angry. They said to the man, 'What? You don't know anything about Good Friday, the day your Christ was crucified? What kind of Christian are you?' One of the monks snatched the man's Bible from his hand and said, 'You don't deserve to hold this

Bible in your hand. Get out of here!' As the man left, the monks gave him back his Bible. The preacher must have been amazed seeing this. He must have been thinking, 'Who are these men? They love Jesus so dearly. It seems that they are his real disciples.'

The monks at that time were opposed to preaching. Narendra used to tell them that they should first form their own characters, then they could preach. How could they teach others what they themselves did not know? After attaining Knowledge, they could preach. Narendra would give the example of Trailanga Swami, a holy man in Benares. He said, 'Trailanga Swami never speaks; he is always immersed in God. But his silence is his preaching. Through the language of silence, he teaches the whole world.'

Then he told them a story about this. 'A king once asked a holy man to tell him what God is like. The holy man did not answer, but remained silent. Time and again the king asked the same question, and each time the holy man would not say a word in reply. At last, when the king became very impatient, the holy man said, "Maharaj, I have been giving the answer repeatedly; you do not understand. My answer is this very silence."' Then Narendra would continue, 'First build your own character. If you do that, that will be the best preaching of all. You may not speak, but people will learn from seeing your life.'

Even though Swamiji said these words about preaching, the young mcnks could not avoid it altogether. Many people were attracted to them and would come to discuss various topics. One time there was such a crowd of people that Swamiji could hardly get a moment's respite but was engaged in constant talk with them through the whole day. They would discuss everything, worldly topics as well as spiritual matters. Sometimes prominent scholars and orthodox pundits would come to discuss philosophy and religion with them. They would challenge the monks, citing passages from the scriptures. Then Narendra would come forth with such powerful reasoning that the pundits' logic would be cut to shreds. They would go away defeated.

Christian ministers would come and start to criticize the Hindu religion. But Narendra would start to reason and they would not be able to withstand his razor-sharp intellect. When they were about to be defeated in the battle, Narendra would begin to talk to them about the love of Jesus Christ. They would be startled; speechless, they must have thought, 'How amazing that these monks have so much love for Jesus Christ!'

Another small incident sheds further light on their life at Baranagore. They were not only poor and harrassed by their neighbours, even the police were after them. A police officer with whom Narendra was acquainted suspected that the monks were involved in revolutionary activities and that the Baranagore Math was the centre for these activities. So one day this officer invited Narendra to his home as part of a plan to deal with these 'revolutionaries'. When Narendra arrived at his home, the officer told him, 'I have irrefutable evidence that you are connected with the revolutionary movement. But if you tell us everything, we will not punish you. We will protect you from prosecution.' Narendra was furious and flared up, 'You invite me here on a false pretext, and then make unfounded charges against me and my companions. This is your habit. But it is my habit to endure insults. Don't you realize that if I were a criminal or conspirator, I could have broken your neck, and no one would have been here to help you? In spite of everything, I am letting you go.' Saying this, Narendra turned and strode out of the house.

Through all kinds of suffering and troubles—through poverty, people's criticism, persecution by the government—the young monks endured. Later Swamiji was to say, 'We had no friends. . . . Nobody. . . . Just think of it—a dozen boys, telling people vast, big ideas, saying they are determined to work these ideas out in life. Why, everybody laughed. From laughter it became serious ; it became persecution. . . . Who would sympathise. . . . None—except one. That one's sympathy brought blessing and hope. She was a woman.' It was Holy Mother. She herself was then lonely and helpless. She was living in extreme poverty, although she did not let anyone know it at that time. But her love, her sympathy, her prayers were always there for the young disciples.

From the beginning she was truly the Mother of the Order. She later said : I prayed so much for this monastery. Crying, I said to Thakur, 'You came and left. Is this the end of everything? Then what was the need of your taking so much trouble to come? It is my desire that all those who follow your ideal will live together and give shelter to people who are scorched by the heat of worldliness.'

It is surprising that many of Sri Ramakrishna's older householder devotees did not understand that the Master wanted to have a monastic order established. They, in fact, strongly disagreed with what the young monks were doing. Nevertheless the monks had the unwavering love and support of Holy Mother. She knew that Sri Ramakrishna wanted to have a monastic order founded; she also knew that through that Order, Sri Ramakrishna's ideals, teachings and power would continue to benefit mankind for generations to come.

The Ramakrishna Order had its beginning at the Baranagore Monastery. The life in the monastery was distinguished by austerity, renunciation and love. These qualities have characterized true religion from time immemorial, and were particularly embodied in Sri Ramakrishna.

We have seen how the Ramakrishna Order slowly took shape at the Baranagore Monastery. We have witnessed the greatness of the young monks' renunciation and austerities, and what immense love they had for one another. Since that time, the Order has grown tremendously; it has branches in many countries, and has within its ranks monks from many different religions. Like Sri Ramakrishna, the Order represents no sectarian religion. It represents religion itself—the truth which is the essence of all religions. Respect for all religions is, therefore, its hallmark.

Sri Ramakrishna saw God in every thing and in every being. Following in his steps the Ramakrishna Order serves man, knowing that in doing so, it serves God Himself.

INDEX

A

Abhedananda, Swami, 475, 482, 483, 507, 508, 524, 539, 543, 549, 556; Ramakrishna about intelligence of, 482
Abhyāsayoga, 204
Abu Sayed, 324
Adam, 111, 112, 115, 448 and Eve, 111, 112, 448 Vivekananda, Swami, recognized original purity of, 115
Adbhutananda, Swami, 475, 478, an illustration of pure love, 298 ; monastic disciple of Ramakrishna, 478-479 ; Ramakrishna's Miracle, 478
Advaita Ashrama, 21, 110, 150, 167, 214, 443, 509
Advaitananda, Swami, 475, 478, 537
Advaita Vedānta, 17-18, 250, 341, 377, 378, 379, 402, 415, 421, 499, 502, 558
Aghormani Devi, see Gopal Ma
Agni, 76
Ahalyā, 294, 295
Aiśvarya (glory) of *anurāga* (longing for God), enumerated by Ramakrishna, 97
Ajagaravṛtti (python discipline), 220, 222, 518
Ajapā, 204,
Ājñā cakra, 404
Akarma, 385
Ākāśa, 250
Akhandananda, Swami; in service of God in man, 227; ideal of '*Śivajñāne Jivasevā*' put into practice by, 480; relief work in Murshidabad by, 480; verse often repeated by, 481
Akshay, 195, 527
Alexander (King), 367, 368, 386, 387, 389, 426
Alexander (King), 367, 368, 395
Anāhata cakra, 404
Ānanda; see also 'Bliss Absolute' 24
Ānanda, Buddha advised, 149
Angulimāla, Buddha showered grace on, 116, 117
Annapūrṇā, Divine Mother, 207
Anurāga, as the *aiśvarya* (glory) antecedent to God-

D

E

highly praised by Huxley, Aldous, 13, 183 ; issue of Bengali version of, 16 ; limitations of, 16 ; main features of, 18 ; nature of Brahman depicted in a song of, 29 ; other books suggested to be read along with, 16 ; the reaction on its publication in English, 11-12 ; reason of popularity of, 17-18 ; Rolland, Romain remarked on the exactitude of, 13 ; Ramakrishna vividly depicted in, 14-15 ; Vijnanananda, Swami, on 16; Vivekananda, Swami praised M. on publication of English version of, 11-15

Goswami, Vijay Krishna, 140 155, 518 ; advised by Ramakrishna, 140

Govinda, 281, 341

Govindadāsa, Śrī Kṛṣṇa described by, 301

Guṇas, 51, 59, 96, 99, 220, 282, 284, 502

Gupta, Mahendra Nath, see M. 1, 9

Gupta, Nagendranath, on *The Gospel of Sri Ramakrishna*, 14, 146

Guru, 52, 80, 91, 92, 101, 103, 121, 122, 131, 138, 161, 173, 174, 200, 214, 217, 239, 240, 263, 272, 299, 329, 359, 363, 373, 415, 421, 449, 450, 460, 468, 499, 504, 509, 517, 522, 526, 532, 554, 558, 560 ; as guide to and giver of spiritual wealth, 91 ; Ramakrishna applauds the grace of, 79

H

Habu, 108

Haldar Pukur, 147, 148

Hamlet, 412

Hanumān, 257, 278, 285, 316, 420, 436

Hari, 3

Haridāsa, 213, 214

Hastāmalakācārya, 100

Hastie, William, Vivekananda learns of Ramakrishna from, 399

Hazra, 29, 41, 62, 130, 491, 492, 495, 500, ; relation between *Śakti and* Brahman according to, 62

Himalayas, 20, 76, 104, 118, 376, 461, 517

Hīnayāna, seeks own liberation, 105

Hinduism, conception of sin in, 7, 54, 111, 173, 218, 240,

I

L

O

P

Pratyāhāra, 401

Prārabdha karma, 196, 355 ; remains even after God-realization, 196, 355

Prema, 284, 285, 290, 291, 292, 340, 345, 455 ; meaning of, according to Ramakrishna, 290 ; signs of, 340

Premā-bhakti 285, Ramakrishna described nature of, 292

Premananda, Swami/Baburam Maharaj, 15, 146, 214, 215, 217, 246, 263, 374, 410, 475, 477, 484, 488, 491, 491, 522, 542, 548, 551, 556 ; Nag Mahashay visited by, 263 ; on Ramakrishna's power, 145 ; remarked on the *Gospel*, 15 ; represented Ramakrishna's love, 477

Premik, about Divine Mother, 42

Preyas, 182

Primal Power (Energy), 37, 38, 54, 60, 95, 96, 430 see also *Śakti*, both as creatress and creatures, 60 ; how to have the vision of, 41

Puri, 31, 239, 262, 274, 275, 414, 430

Puruṣa, 55, 58, 121, 148, 344, 364, 384 ; inseparable from *Prakṛti*, 54

Python discipline, 222, 518 ; observed by Brahmananda, Swami 517

R

Rādhā, 258, 292, 296, 317, 321, 322, 323, 324, 325, 326, 327, 328, 329, 330, 331, 332, 333, 334, 339, 341, 342, 343, 344, 345, 347, 348, 409, 428 ; symbolized as intense love for God by Ramakrishna, 323

Radhu, 184

Ragister, Maximillian, 469

Raja Maharaj, see Brahmananda, Swami

Rāja yoga, 414, 422, 425, 426, 503, Vivekananda wanted to learn, from Pavhari Baba, 503

Rajas, 59, 99 ,220, 282, 283

Rājasika bhakti, signs of, 283

Rakhal, 130, 158, 159, 207, 475, 477, 487, 488, 492, 514 515,b 516, 517, 518, 521, 537, 540, 542, 547, 549, 551, 552, 559 ; see also Brahmananda, Swami

Rākhāl, 337

193, 211, 237, 238, 248, 260, 284, 295, 297, 299, 359, 448, 449, 530, 533 ; *Bṛhadviṣṇu Purāṇa* mentions remedy for, 119 ; Hindu approach to, 113 ; illustration of Christ's attitude to, 122-124 ; in Christianity, 111-112 ; *Les Miserables* nullifies the common meaning of, 123-124 ; Vedānta on, 115 ; Vivekananda, Swami, illustrated how to get rid of, 124 ; Vivekananda, Swami's view on, 115-116

Sītā, 95, 285, 295, 450, 556

Śiva, 4, 31, 35, 42, 55, 58, 81, 93, 104, 207, 229, 266, 267, 285, 301, 302, 344, 356, 365, 406, 419, 430, 431, 448, 452, 483, 487, 488, 532, 559, 560 ; as observer, 58 ; incarnation of, 448 ; inseparable from *Śakti*, 54, 406

Śivamahimnah Stotra, 435

Śiva Rātri, 559

Śmaśāna-Kālī, 59

Socrates, 14

Śraddhā, 210

Śravaṇa, 357

Śreyas, 182

Śrīdāma, 257, 327, 344

Sri Ramakrishna the Great Master/The Great Master, 15, 84, 336, 379, 478, 497 ; see also Saradananda, Swami

Śrī Śrī Rāmakṛṣṇa Kathāmṛta, 1, 2, 13, 16 ; highly valued by Ghosh, Nagendranath, 13 ; ever increasing appeal of, 16-17; Sales Explosion of, 17 ; see also M.

Sudāma, 257

Śukadeva, 3, 104, 177, 187, 486, ; (*Śrīmad*) *Bhāgavatam* recited by, 104

Supreme Soul, individual soul can be united to, 89

Surendra, 321, 324, 329, 330, 331, 337, 533, 534, 540, 541, 542, 548; Ramakrishna became abstracted at the house of, 324, 325

Susumnā, path through spinal cord called, 404-405

Svādhiṣṭhāna cakra, 404

Svāti, 275

Śvetāśvatara Upanisad, declared all as children of im-mortality and bliss 115 ; God as governor of *māyā* conceptualized in, 59 ; nature of Brahman des-

considered goodness as potential characteristic of human being, 116 ; considered human body as temple, 90 ; considered man as God, 394 ; considered Ramakrishna as 'The Emperor of Renunciation', 215 ; creation of Ramakrishna, 488 ; Divine Mother (Kṣīra-Bhavānī) dispelled the egotism of, 289 ; education defined by, 115 ; fatalism castigated by, 240 ; forgiveness illustrated in life of, 224; full of fun, 509; guilelessness of, 512-513 ; his *Karma Yoga*, 184; his deep love for own country, 105 ; his first impression of Ramakrishna, 490 ; his love and reverence for Ramakrishna, 503-504 ; Holy Mother's support in establishing non-dualistic monastery by, 377 ; ideal of Ramakrishna Order formulated by, 229 ; importance of positive thinking emphasized by, 124 ; love and compassion of, 489, 505, 506, 508 ; man as child of immortal bliss emphasized by, 114-115 ; man as manifested divinity in view of, 228 ; 'man is verily Brahman' according to, 61; meaninglessness of astrology illustrated by, 241-242 ; met Ramakrishna, 490 ; mission of life, of, 68 ; negative thoughts held as cause of weakness by, 120 ; never misunderstood by Ramakrishna, 497 ; Nivedita, Sister, on Swamiji's attitude towards work, 396-397 ; often misunderstood by others, 497 ; on contrary characteristics of Divine Mother, 58 ; on detachment in *Karma Yoga*, 184 ; on dignity of labour, 395 ; on future of India, 70 ; on God's taking forms, 34 ; on idol worship, 32 ; on 'I'ness, 77; on real learning, 148 ; on Ramakrishna, 226 ; on the paths of *jñāna* (knowledge) and *Bhakti* (devotion), 90 ; or Swami Vivekananda Purī, 218 ; power of suggestion illustrated by, 125 ; praised M. on publication of *Gospel*, 12-13 ;